Columbia Essays in International Affairs

The Dean's Papers, 1965

Columbia Essays
in International Affairs
The Dean's Papers, 1965

BY STUDENTS OF THE

FACULTY OF INTERNATIONAL AFFAIRS

COLUMBIA UNIVERSITY

EDITED BY ANDREW W. CORDIER

DEAN OF THE FACULTY

Columbia University Press

NEW YORK AND LONDON 1966

Copyright © 1966 Columbia University Press
Library of Congress Catalog Card Number: 66-14078
Printed in the United States of America

Foreword

In the first two years of their graduate training, students of the Faculty of International Affairs or the School of International Affairs are required to prepare a number of substantial research papers and essays in order to develop their ability to conduct original research and present it effectively. This is a central part of their training for careers in scholarship, government or international service, journalism, or business. Not infrequently these studies bring to light new information or fresh interpretations that could profitably be shared with the wider community of scholars and other readers interested in international affairs.

My colleagues at Columbia have often expressed a desire that the best of these studies might be made available in a convenient and accessible form. It is with this thought in mind that the Faculty of International Affairs has recommended the setting up of an annual series, to be known as *Columbia Essays in International Affairs: The Dean's Papers*. *The Dean's Papers, 1965* is the first of this new series.

Even more than other fields of Executive-Legislative competition for influence, foreign aid legislation has been subjected to a wide variety of attempts by Congress to expand its role in the management of foreign relations programs. This competition is given fresh scrutiny by David Allen Kay in his study of " 'Unconstitutional' Restrictions on the President of the United States in Foreign Aid Legislation, 1947–1964."

In "Disengagement in Europe: An Evaluation for United States Foreign Policy," James W. Robinson has presented a rigorous review of the strategic and, in part, the political implications of current proposals for the pulling back and reduction of forces east and west of the postwar demarcation line in Central Europe.

The 1957 Treaty of Rome established a complex combination of national and supranational roles in the further evolution of the Common Market. In her essay Fay R. Papa takes a fresh look at "The Decision-Making Process in the European Economic Community."

In "The British Labour Party and the Council of Europe, 1949–1951," Gordon M. Adams has traced the contradictory pulls exerted by the idea of European integration upon the Labour Party during this early and tentative stage in the movement for the formation of a West European community.

In his examination of "Social Courts and Law Reform in East Germany," Peter Friedman illustrates some of the applications of Soviet-style legal concepts and practices to the judicial system of Communist-ruled East Germany.

"Design or Improvisation? The Origins of the German Protectorate of Bohemia and Moravia in 1939," by Vojtech Mastny, traces the interplay between racist dogma and political improvisation in the system of domination that Hitler imposed on the Czech lands after his seizure of Prague in March 1939.

The creation of Czechoslovakia brought together in one state two related peoples, Czechs and Slovaks, whose outlooks had been shaped differently by history. In "T. G. Masaryk and the Slovaks, 1882–1914," Thomas D. Marzik traces the early interest of Dr. Thomas G. Masaryk in building cultural and political ties between these two peoples.

"China's Relations with Burma, 1949–1964," by B. Lynn Pascoe, traces the changing and massive impact of Communist China on Burma's attempt to maintain both its independence and its neutrality.

In his study of "Development of Modern Science Policy in Japan," Theodore Dixon Long explores the role of science in the modernization of Japan, the central role of government in the acclimatization and development of science, and the significance of the changing balance between applied and basic scientific research.

Nearly all newly independent nations lay claim to a socialist program, but the programs vary greatly from one country to another. In her study of "The Evolution of a Socialist Ideology in Algeria, November 1954–April 1965," Patricia Berko Wild has traced, partly on the basis of first-hand observation, a particularly dramatic phase in the attempt of the Algerian leadership to define the direction and content of its policy.

The turbulent events in the Congo have compelled the newly independent countries of Africa to define their political goals and their styles of action in a situation of great stress. How they coped with this challenge is examined by Peter H. Judd in "The Attitudes of the African States toward the Katanga Secession, July 1960–January 1963."

The emotions that have attended the process of decolonialization cannot be fully appreciated without taking a close look at the varying impact of colonial rule on original inhabitants. "The Causes of the Herero Uprising of 1904–1906 in South-West Africa," by Manfred M. Deckert, presents one very significant case study.

In her study of "The Role of the COPEI Party in Venezuelan Politics," Dona Baron has examined the rise of the program of a new type of reform party, one that has aroused strong interest in other countries of Latin America.

How to provide an adequate and activating system of education for newly independent nations has been and remains a central challenge to each ascendant people. For this reason, the study of "Bolívar's Program for Elementary Education," by John L. Young, has contemporary as well as historical interest today.

Each essay ran the gauntlet of a rigorous selection process. After being recommended initially by a member of the Faculty of International Affairs, each essay submitted was reviewed by one of eight preliminary committees; all essays were then read and commented upon by a selection committee; finally, the recommendations were reviewed by the Dean, as editor of the volume. Needless to say, the choice was not an easy one to make. I am especially grateful to the members of the selection committee, consisting of Professors Philip E. Mosely (chairman), John S. Badeau, Henry L. Roberts, and C. Martin Wilbur, for the extensive time and careful thought which they gave to this responsibility. I should also like to thank Marguerite V. Freund, Administrative Assistant of the European Institute, who managed the process of selection, Robert J. Tilley, Assistant Director of the Columbia University Press, who guided the publication of this volume, and Marian Maury, who edited it with great skill and care.

The Faculty of International Affairs provides advanced training for many able graduate students, drawn from many countries and all parts of the United States. Its faculty includes the staffs of the School of International Affairs and the seven Regional Insititutes. Each faculty member is also a member of the Graduate Faculty of Philosophy or Political Science. Each serves simultaneously in one of several closely related Graduate Departments, such as Public Law and Government, History, Economics, Geography, or Sociology, or in a department of Literature. This "dual citizenship," for both faculty and students, provides a strong basis for developing and measuring excellence. The publication of *The Dean's Papers, 1965* constitutes a recognition of the excellent work accomplished by the authors at an early stage of their advanced training for scholarly or public service.

ANDREW W. CORDIER
DEAN

October, 1965

Contents

Foreword   *Andrew W. Cordier*   v

"Unconstitutional" Restrictions on the President of the United States in Foreign Aid Legislation, 1947–1964
David Allen Kay   1

Disengagement in Europe: An Evaluation for United States Foreign Policy   *James W. Robinson*   31

The Decision-Making Process in the European Economic Community   *Fay R. Papa*   59

The British Labour Party and the Council of Europe, 1949–1951 *Gordon M. Adams*   75

Social Courts and Law Reform in East Germany *Peter Friedman*   107

Design or Improvisation? The Origins of the German Protectorate of Bohemia and Moravia in 1939   *Vojtech Mastny*   127

T. G. Masaryk and the Slovaks, 1882–1914 *Thomas D. Marzik*   155

China's Relations with Burma, 1949–1964   *B. Lynn Pascoe*   175

Development of Modern Science Policy in Japan *Theodore Dixon Long*   205

The Evolution of a Socialist Ideology in Algeria, November 1954–April 1965   *Patricia Berko Wild*   227

The Attitudes of the African States toward the Katanga Secession, July 1960–January 1963   *Peter H. Judd*   239

The Causes of the Herero Uprising of 1904–1906 in South-West Africa   *Manfred M. Deckert*   255

The Role of the COPEI Party in Venezuelan Politics *Dona Baron*   279

Bolívar's Program for Elementary Education
    John L. Young   309

Biographical Sketches   325

Columbia Essays in International Affairs

The Dean's Papers, 1965

"Unconstitutional" Restrictions on the President of the United States in Foreign Aid Legislation 1947-1964

DAVID ALLEN KAY

One of the most striking phenomena associated with the control of American foreign relations in the mid-1960s is the expanded role enjoyed by Congress. While there are several explanations for this, the principal means of Congressional assertion has been the domination of the appropriation process, through which Congress has increasingly placed restrictions in foreign aid legislation which affect the President's control of foreign relations.

The need for an analysis of the extent and constitutional basis of Congressional restrictions on the President's control of foreign relations is underlined by two separate actions of Lyndon B. Johnson. In signing into law the Foreign Aid Assistance Act of 1963 only twenty-five days after his assumption of office, the President specifically declared that he would not under certain circumstances abide by a specific provision of the bill prohibiting aid to Cuba because he regarded its provisions as an infringement of his constitutional powers to conduct foreign relations.[1] And on October 8, 1964, less than a

[1] Lyndon B. Johnson, in "President Johnson Signs into Law Foreign Assistance Act of 1963" (Dec. 16, 1963), *Department of State Bulletin*, L, No. 1280 (Jan. 6, 1964), 26–27: "It [the bill] also reflects, unfortunately, the growing tendency to hamstring Executive flexibility with rigid legislative provisions wholly inappropriate and potentially dangerous in a world of rapid change. I wish to make clear now, for example, that when a free and peaceful government is ever established in Cuba, I intend to exercise my authority to provide essential health, educational, and other assistance to the Cuban people, without waiting for a long and complex adjudication."

year after his first statement on Congressional "hamstringing" of the Executive with respect to foreign relations, the President singled out two provisions of a foreign assistance act as unconstitutional and stated his intention not to be bound by such provisions.[2] Those two statements of Johnson have thrown the spotlight of doubt upon the constitutionality of the growing tendency of Congress to restrict the President's conduct of foreign relations. It is this question of constitutionality that the present study proposes to treat, rather than the political wisdom of such restrictions.

In this study attention will be focused upon foreign aid legislation from 1947 to the present and its relationship to the constitutional powers of the President in respect to foreign affairs. Specifically, what will be sought will be the answers to five questions. First, what restrictions have been placed in foreign aid legislation by Congressional directive with respect to the conduct and control of American

[2] Lyndon B. Johnson (Oct. 8, 1964, on signing of S2687, an act to extend the Agricultural Trade Development and Assistance Act of 1954), *Department of State Bulletin*, LI, No. 1324 (Nov. 9, 1964), 677–78:

"This bill, however, contains several features which concern me. Of these, two provisions are particularly undesirable. One seeks to give either the House Committee on Agriculture or the Senate Committee on Agriculture and Forestry a veto power over certain proposed dispositions of foreign currencies accruing from sales under PL480. The other seeks to prevent the President from making certain loans at interest rates below a specified level unless he has a concurrence of an advisory committee composed in part of Members of Congress and in part of his own executive appointees.

"In recent years, four Attorney Generals of the United States have held that legislative provisions vesting in Congressional committees the power to approve or disapprove actions of the executive branch are unconstitutional. The Acting Attorney General now advises me that a provision vesting such power in a committee made up in part of Members of Congress stands on no better footing. Both such provisions represent a clear violation of the constitutional principle of separation of powers. This is the position taken in similar cases by President Eisenhower, President Kennedy, and by myself.

"However, I appreciate the desire of the Congress to be informed and to be consulted on the operation of all aspects of the PL480 program, and I am directing that executive officials see that this is done.

"Two other provisions of the bill are disturbing. The first, by preventing any foreign currency sales to any Communist countries, inhibits our ability to deal selectively with countries that may demonstrate a tendency toward political and economic independence from communism. I note, however, that the effect of this restriction is somewhat offset by the authorization to make dollar sales on credit to such countries. The second, by requiring that our surplus inventories of extra-long-staple cotton be offered for sale at world prices, could create serious problems in our foreign relations. I am directing that this provision be administered with great care so as to minimize any harmful effects on the economics of the free-world countries which are the principal exporters of this commodity."

foreign policy? Next, what constitutional grounds, if any, have been advanced for those directives? Third, what has been the Executive response to such Congressional directives? Fourth, on what constitutional grounds has the Executive based its response? Finally, what is the constitutional balance in this critical area of Executive-Legislative conflict?

Our attempt to determine the constitutional balance must inevitably reflect the dynamic nature of the American political system and the accompanying lack of a "holy writ" sufficiently clear to provide an infallible guide to the constitutionality of contentious issues. Since issues of Legislative-Executive conflict in the realm of foreign affairs do not generally come before the courts, the lack of any final legal arbiter also hinders the attempt to determine the constitutional balance.

In the belief that the constitutional problems raised by increased Congressional activity in foreign relations can best be understood and evaluated in the historical context of the Executive-Legislative division of the foreign relations field, a skeleton sketch of this relationship before 1947 will be first in the format of this analysis. The analysis will then proceed to an examination of the post-1947 era, first examining the rising Congressional assertions of power and then proceeding to examine the Executive response.

Legislative-Executive Conflict Over the Control of American Foreign Relations Before 1947 [3]

No attempt will be made in the all-too-brief confines of this synopsis to present the full record of the struggle between Congress and the

[3] This synopsis will be confined to attempts by Congress to exert binding direction over the control of American foreign policy, and will not include informal nonmandatory attempts to influence the direction of foreign policy.

For a more complete presentation of the historical background of the control of American foreign relations see:

Dorothy B. Goebel, "Congress and Foreign Relations Before 1900," *Annals of the American Academy of Political and Social Science,* CCLXXXIX (Sept. 1953), 22–39.

Mary E. Bradshaw, "Congress and Foreign Policy Since 1900," *ibid.,* pp. 40–48.

Quincy Wright, *The Control of American Foreign Relations* (New York, Macmillan, 1922).

Edward S. Corwin, *The President's Control of Foreign Relations* (Princeton, Princeton University Press, 1917).

Executive for the control of American foreign relations. Rather, the aim is to provide an overview of the historical setting against which the post-World War II struggle has been played out. In line with the concern of this present study with restrictions in foreign aid legislation, this synopsis will emphasize Congressional attempts to control foreign policy through the appropriation process.

It is a matter of considerable historical controversy whether the Founding Fathers had the original intent of vesting control over foreign relations in the President or in Congress. However, it does seem clear that at a minimum they intended to locate the day-to-day administration of foreign relations in the Executive branch. By an act of Congress of July 27, 1789, a Department of Foreign Affairs was established in the Executive branch.[4] Although renamed the Department of State on September 15, 1789,[5] it maintained its original responsibility for the conduct of the nation's foreign relations subject to the instructions and with respect to the matters assigned to the Department by the President. From the Appropriation Act of July 1790 until 1810, Congress appropriated lump sums for the support of the diplomatic service.[6] The first standing committee of Congress dealing with foreign affairs was not created until 1816.[7]

The first major clash over who was to control the foreign policy of the young nation centered upon Washington's Proclamation of Neutrality in the war between France and Great Britain in 1793. The ramifications of this Presidential action taken without any reference to Congress were fully explored in the famous pamphlet debate between Hamilton as "Pacificus" and Madison as "Helvidius." When the formal approval was given to Washington's action by the next session of Congress, the precedent was set for a commanding role for the President in foreign affairs.[8]

The lump sum appropriation for the diplomatic service ended in 1810, and by 1818 Congress was trying to use enumeration of expenditures to alter the course of American foreign relations. In that year Henry Clay, then Speaker of the House, offered an amendment

[4] *United States Statutes at Large* (hereafter referred to as Stat.) (U.S. Government Printing Office, Washington, D.C.), Chap. 4.
[5] Stat., Chap. 14.
[6] Goebel, "Congress and Foreign Relations Before 1900," p. 27.
[7] The Senate established a standing committee to concern itself with only foreign relations in 1816 and the House followed suit in 1822. *Ibid.*, p. 27.
[8] Wright, p. 270.

to an appropriation bill that would have provided $18,000 for a minister to the South American states whenever the President thought it advisable to send one.[9] President Monroe attacked this proposal as "an act of usurpation and an invasion of executive authority," and it was overwhelmingly defeated 45 to 115.[10]

In 1826 certain members of Congress, in an action that seems very modern in its design, offered an amendment to a bill appropriating funds for the dispatch of a mission to an international conference at Panama. That amendment would have provided the delegates with binding instructions, under the argument that the power to appropriate money for the expense of the mission carried with it the equal right to impose conditions. In a successful attack upon the amendment, Daniel Webster is quoted:

It was, in his [Webster's] opinion, unconstitutional, as it was taking the proper responsibility from the Executive and exercising, ourselves, a power which, from its nature, belongs to the Executive, and not to us. . . . At present it seemed to him that we must make the appropriation without conditions, or refuse it. The President had laid the case before us. . . . If we had not so much confidence in the Executive as to render us willing to trust to the constitutional exercise of the Executive power, we have the power to refuse the money.[11]

The whole field of international conferences was an area of extensive Legislative-Executive conflict during the long period from 1810 on. In 1913, in an attempt to restrict severely the President's freedom to conduct foreign affairs, Congress added the following rider to a deficiency appropriation bill:

Hereafter, the executive shall not extend or accept any invitation to participate in any international congress, conference, or like event without specific authorization to do so.[12]

---

[9] Corwin, p. 74 ff.   [10] *Ibid.*, p. 74.
[11] Quoted in Wright, p. 279.

In the pre-1947 period the Executive power in the area of foreign relations was often defended by members of Congress. Another example is Senator Spooner's statement in 1906 that: "It [Department of State] is a Department which, from the beginning, the Senate has never assumed the right to direct or control, except as to clearly define matters relating to duties imposed by statute and not connected with the conduct of our foreign relations." Quoted in Hackworth, *Digest of International Law*, IV, 645, from the *Congressional Record*, XL, Part 2 (Jan. 23, 1906), 1420.

[12] 37 Stat. 913, 22 USC § 262.

This provision, whose constitutionality has been widely questioned,[13] is still on the books, although specific consent to attend international conferences is apparently no longer sought by the President.[14]

During a period of general Congressional ascendancy in 1921 and 1924, Senator Borah was able, over the opposition of the President, to attach amendments to the naval appropriation bill calling for the convening of an international conference on naval disarmament.[15] The 1921 amendments did lead to, or at least were followed by, the Washington Naval Conference of 1921–22, but the 1924 amendments were apparently completely ignored by the President.

Another attempt was made in 1924 to issue detailed instructions to an American delegation to an international conference. In connection with appropriations for sending an American delegation to the Geneva International Opium Conference of 1924, Congress instructed the delegation to sign no agreement which did not meet certain specified conditions. Those conditions were unacceptable to the other nations represented at the conference, and the United States delegation consequently withdrew.[16] The sequel to this affair was that although the instructions were still in effect at the time of the second Geneva International Opium Conference in 1931, the American delegation ignored them.

Of interest both because of its relevance as an example of the continuing Legislative-Executive struggle over the control of foreign relations, and because of the current importance of one of the principals, is the attempt in 1940 by the House to force the United States to break diplomatic relations with the Soviet Union. Representative John McCormack of Massachusetts, at this writing Speaker of the House of Representatives, sponsored in 1940 an amendment to the

---

[13] Wright, p. 328.

John M. Mathews, *American Foreign Relations—Conduct and Policies* (New York, Appleton-Century, 1938), p. 447.

Edward S. Corwin, *The President—Office and Powers* (New York, New York University Press, 1957), p. 191.

Eli E. Nobleman, "Financial Aspects of Congressional Participation in Foreign Relations," *Annals of the American Academy of Political and Social Science,* CCLXXXIX (Sept. 1953), 155.

[14] Nobleman, *ibid.,* p. 155.   [15] Wright, p. 278.

[16] Elmer Plischke, *Conduct of American Diplomacy* (Princeton, Van Nostrand, 1961), p. 75. The fidelity with which the United States delegation adhered to its instructions may to some extent be accounted for by the fact that Representative Potter, who was then Chairman of the House Foreign Affairs Committee, was not only the author of the instructions in the appropriation bill but also head of the delegation to the conference.

State Department appropriation bill that would have struck out the appropriation for the salary of the United States Ambassador to the Soviet Union. In discussing the constitutionality of his amendment, Representative McCormack forcefully stated a position that has not been out dated by the passing of twenty-five years:

This is the proper place. We have the responsibility of appropriating money. True, the question of diplomatic relationship in itself rests with the Executive branch of the Government, but under the Constitution we have the power of expressing our own views as a body when appropriation bills are under consideration. . . . The argument that this is not the place for this question to be discussed certainly is irrelevant if advanced from a constitutional angle, because the framers of the Constitution left it with Congress to appropriate money. Congress has the power not to appropriate money for any particular purpose.[17]

This amendment was approved on a division vote by 88 to 86, but later on the same day, undoubtedly after much arm twisting, it was defeated on a teller vote by 105 to 108. The narrowness of this margin indicates that as late as 1940 there was a very close division in the House as to the extent of its powers to attempt to sever relations with a foreign state through the device of refusing to make the appropriation for the salary of the United States Ambassador to that state.

The above synopsis of major Legislative-Executive conflicts over the control of American foreign policy prior to 1947 should not obscure the fact that there existed in that period a general consensus about who controlled the direction of American foreign policy. This general consensus was accurately reflected in a report of February 15, 1816 by the Senate Committee on Foreign Relations, which said:

The President is the constitutional representative of the United States with regard to foreign nations. He manages our concerns with foreign nations and must necessarily be most competent to determine when, how and upon what subjects negotiations may be urged with the greatest prospect of success. For his conduct he is responsible to the Constitution. The Committee considers this responsibility the surest pledge for the faithful discharge of duty.[18]

---

[17] Nobleman, "Financial Aspects," p. 157, quoted from 86th *Congressional Record* (76th Cong.), pp. 1172–79.

[18] Quoted in *United States v. Curtiss-Wright Export Corp.*, 299 U.S. 304 (1936), which appears in Walter S. Surrey, "The Legislative Process and International Law," *Proceedings, American Society of International Law,* LII (1958), 11.

The extent and means by which Congress has since 1947 deviated from this view of the primacy—not always unchallenged—of the Executive over foreign policy, is the subject of the next two sections.

Congressional Assertions of Restrictions

Although foreign aid first became a standard term in the American political lexicon in the post-World War II period, the first instance of such aid being extended by the Government of the United States dates from 1794. Relief for victims of the Haitian Massacre was approved by Congress in 1794, and this was followed in 1812 with the appropriation of aid for victims of a Venezuelan earthquake.[19] In spite of the fact that the United States did not recognize the Soviet government at the time, Congress voted relief for Russian famine victims from 1923 to 1924.[20] The destruction wrought by the severe Japanese earthquake of 1923 was also met by a Congressional authorization of relief.[21] However, in spite of these scattered historical precedents, foreign aid did not become a regular recurring item of Congressional concern involving large sums of money until the post-World War II period.[22] Therefore, it is upon this period of intense Congressional action, commencing in 1947, that this analysis will concentrate.

TYPES OF ASSERTIONS

The years since President Truman—in enunciating the Truman Doctrine—committed the United States to a major and continuing program of foreign aid, have been marked by both large appropriations and increasing Congressional restrictions upon the conduct of foreign aid activities. This trend to greater legislative detailing of the methods of providing aid is quite noticeable in the long and complex Foreign Assistance Act of 1948, the real start of the postwar foreign aid program.[23] From this act in 1948 until the present, Congress has

[19] "The Evolution of United States Foreign Assistance," *Congressional Digest,* XLII (June–July 1963), 164.

[20] *Ibid.*   [21] *Ibid.*

[22] From the beginning of Fiscal Year 1946 through the close of Fiscal Year 1962, the United States extended $97.112 billion in direct foreign aid to over one hundred nations, colonies, and territories. About two-thirds of this amount, i.e., $66.45 billion, was in economic assistance while the remaining one-third, i.e., $30.67 billion was in military assistance. *Ibid.,* p. 166.

[23] 62 Stat. 137 (1948). When one contrasts the complex provisions of this act with the broad grants of executive discretion in the various Lend-Lease Acts, 55 Stat. 31 (1941), it becomes apparent that the complexity and detailed enumeration are not inherent characteristics of foreign aid legislation. Surrey, in "The Legislative Process," p. 12, also discusses this contrast.

exerted very tight control over the question of which countries have received United States aid.[24] The Mutual Defense Assistance Act of 1949 (63 Stat. 714) was so restrictive in this respect as to prevent any aid from being given to any country outside Western Europe unless it was named in the act or was located in the general area of China.

The Yugoslav break with Moscow required the State Department to go to Congress to request specific permission to aid Yugoslavia, and this was finally granted in the Yugoslav Emergency Relief Assistance Act of 1950.[25] Also in 1950, Congress in appropriating funds for the Economic Cooperation Administration (ECA) "directed" the President to extend aid to Spain, in spite of President Truman's repeated insistence that this action not be taken.[26] In the ensuing fourteen years, Congress repeatedly altered the status of the eligibility of Yugoslavia for foreign aid. The 1956 Mutual Security Act prohibited the extension of any aid to Yugoslavia unless the President found and reported to Congress:

(1) that there has been no change in the Yugoslav policies on the basis of which assistance under this act has been furnished to Yugoslavia in the past, and that Yugoslavia is independent of control by the Soviet Union, (2) that Yugoslavia is not participating in any policy or program for the Communist conquest of the world, and (3) that it is in the interest of the national security of the United States to continue the furnishing of assistance to Yugoslavia under this Act.[27]

By the time the Mutual Security Appropriation Act of 1957 was passed, an absolute ban on all new military assistance to Yugoslavia had been written into the Act.[28] The fate of foreign assistance from the United States to Yugoslavia has continued to be subject to the whim of Congress, with an escape clause usually being provided the President allowing him to approve the extension of economic aid.[29] Cuba and Indonesia have also been honored by Congress with specific references in foreign aid legislation.[30] The ban on aid to the latter two countries has also contained the Presidential escape clause.

Congress has by no means limited itself merely to naming those

---

[24] This again is a departure from lend-lease practice, which placed few restrictions upon countries to which aid could be extended.

[25] 64 Stat. 1122.

[26] For a study of the entire aid-to-Spain controversy see Theodore J. Lowi, "Bases in Spain," in Harold Stein, ed., *American Civil-Military Decisions* (Birmingham, University of Alabama Press, 1963), pp. 667–705. The Congressional directive is 64 Stat. 758.

[27] 70 Stat. 555, § 5.   [28] 70 Stat. 733.   [29] 76 Stat. 255, § 301 (f).

[30] 74 Stat. 134, § 401 (m). 75 Stat. 424, § 620 (a). 77 Stat. 379, § 301 (e)(z).

countries to which aid could or could not be extended. Starting with the Foreign Assistance Act of 1948, Congress has devoted considerable effort to ensuring that any foreign country receiving aid give an adequate *quid pro quo* in return. Being unwilling to trust the Executive to extract an adequate *quid pro quo,* Congress has channeled its effort into the task of spelling out in fine print what is adequate. The 1948 Act laid down ten specific items that had to be included in a bilateral agreement between the United States and each country desiring aid before even one dollar of assistance could be extended.[31] The required terms involved items of such intimate domestic concern as currency stability, tariff levels, and a commitment by each country to use its own resources efficiently.

In the continuing search for a *quid pro quo,* the Mutual Defense Assistance Act of 1949 prohibited the transfer even on cash-and-carry terms of certain military items unless a country had entered into a collective defense and security arrangement with the United States. To the embarrassment of the United States and the chagrin of Canada, this provision, until its amendment in 1950, prevented Canada from obtaining in the American market some critically needed aviation equipment.[32]

The Mutual Security Act of 1951 set forth eleven items to which a country must agree before receiving any United States foreign aid.[33] The recipient country among other things had to agree to "join in promoting international understanding and good will, and maintaining world peace" and to "fulfill the military obligations, if any, which it has assumed under multilateral or bilateral agreements or treaties to which the United States is a party." Because of these requirements the President had to conduct extensive and often delicate negotiations with foreign countries along a format laid down by Congress before any foreign aid could be extended.

Early in the history of foreign aid legislation, Congress on its own initiative began to attempt to modify the existing or prospective behavior of states, by threatening to cut off aid as a punishment for certain behavior. At the time of debate on the Foreign Aid Appropriation Act of 1949, it was suggested in Congress that all aid should be cut off to countries continuing to nationalize basic industries and that no assistance should be given to any country with a socialist govern-

[31] 62 Stat. 137, § 115 (b).
[32] Michael H. Cordozo, "Foreign Aid Legislation: Time for a New Look," *Cornell Law Quarterly,* XXXVIII (Winter 1953), 167.
[33] 68 Stat. 832, § 142.

ment.[34] Those two amendments, so obviously aimed at Great Britain and the ruling Labour Party for approving the nationalization of the steel industry in November 1949, failed to win the approval of Congress. In the following year the House initially approved and then rejected an amendment to an ECA authorization that would have barred all aid to Britain so long as Ireland continued to be partitioned.[35]

In approving the Mutual Security Act of 1951, Representative Kem successfully attached an amendment providing that no economic aid could be given to any country which exported to the Soviet Union or its satellites any military equipment or anything used in the manufacture of military equipment.[36] It also required a complex certification and reporting system. Perhaps the only saving grace of the Kem Amendment was the provision allowing the Director of Mutual Security to grant exceptions to its provisions. The Kem Amendment was indicative of the changing mood of Congress resulting from the Korean War.

Also indicative of this changing attitude was the provision of the Foreign Aid Appropriation Act of 1951 directing the President to cut off aid to any country that in his opinion "had failed, refused or neglected to support the United Nations in resisting aggression." [37] Since 1951 all foreign aid legislation has included a standard provision registering the opposition of Congress to the seating of Communist China in the United Nations and requesting the President to inform Congress of the implications of the seating of Communist China, if it should occur.[38]

An even more direct attempt to influence the actions of aid recipients was the 1954 directive in the Foreign Aid Law that delivery of all military goods provided with that year's aid funds be halted until all six signatories had ratified the European Defense Community (EDC) Treaty.[39]

With the rise of Castro in Cuba, increasing Congressional attention has been directed at isolating that island from the network of world trade. The intensification of this attention can be traced in the attempts to force other countries to follow the United States policy of trade

[34] Willard L. Thorp, "Strings on Economic Aid," *Yale Review*, XLIV (Dec. 1954), 207.
[35] *Ibid.*, p. 209.
[36] *Department of State Bulletin*, XXIV (June 25, 1951), 1027–29.
64 Stat. 1044 (Supplemental Appropriation Act, 1951, Section 1304).
[37] 64 Stat. 758.   [38] 76 Stat. 1163.   [39] Plischke, p. 73.

embargo through the sanction of withholding foreign aid. While the foreign aid legislation of 1960, 1961, and 1962 allowed aid to be cut off if a recipient was found to be assisting Cuba, all those acts had a Presidential escape clause. However, the Foreign Assistance Act of 1963 contained an absolute prohibition on any aid to a country assisting Cuba.[40] Under its provisions small amounts of aid to Britain, Yugoslavia, and France were cut off.[41]

Congress in the mid-1960s also attempted to influence the conduct of foreign countries by imposing penalties, through its control of foreign aid, on the nationalization of property of United States nationals owned abroad. Following the trend of denying the President an escape clause to mitigate the operation of a Congressional restriction, the Foreign Assistance Act of 1962 contained a detailed amendment that provided for the cutting off of all aid to any country that expropriated United States-owned property without taking appropriate steps within six months to discharge its obligation under international law as Congress sees it, and which must include compensation.[42] In connection with the Congressional attempt to impede foreign nationalization of United States-owned property, section 311 (3)(1) of the Foreign Assistance Act of 1963 prohibited all assistance to countries who had not entered into an agreement with the President by December 31, 1965 to establish an investment guaranty program.[43]

The attempts by Congress to modify the conduct of foreign countries by controlling the sluice gate of foreign aid has, thus, been a continuing part of foreign aid legislation since 1948. However, one change in this attempt has been the frequency with which Congress since 1962 has denied the President an escape clause to override a restriction when he found it necessary to do so in the national interest.

A final type of restriction placed by Congress in foreign aid legislation has been that directed at maintaining some degree of active control over the actual administration of the program. While detailed provisions regarding the manner of carrying out aid have been common since 1948, relatively few attempts were made in the early years to insert Congress, or members of Congress, into the day-to-day operation of the agencies administering foreign aid. One exception was Section 529 of the Mutual Security Act, which provided for the immediate termination of aid on passage by the two Houses of Con-

---

[40] 77 Stat. 379, § 620 (a)(3).
[41] *Department of State Bulletin,* L (April 13, 1964), 598.
[42] 76 Stat. 255, § 301 (d)(3)(e) (Foreign Assistance Act of 1962).
[43] 77 Stat. 379, § 301 (3)(1).

gress of a concurrent resolution not needing Presidential approval.[44] The essentially negative nature of this provision was duplicated in the 1964 extension of the Agricultural Trade Development and Assistance Act of 1954. Within this act was a provision that either the House Committee on Agriculture or the Senate Committee on Agriculture and Forestry have a veto over certain proposed dispositions of foreign currencies accruing from sales under PL480.[45] However, another provision of the same Act had a more positive orientation in that, rather than giving Congress a veto over existing programs, it required the approval of certain members of Congress before an action could be taken. This provision endeavored to prevent the Executive from extending loans at less than a specified interest rate without the concurrence of an advisory committee composed jointly of members of Congress and Executive appointees.[46] These two provisions added by Congress in 1964 may well portend a move to interject certain elements of Congress into the current operational segment of foreign aid.

The foregoing review of the seventeen years of foreign aid legislation since 1947 indicates repeated and frequent attempts by Congress to use its fiscal powers to control and direct foreign policy in pursuit of various goals. From the primitive punishing or rewarding of a country by specifically naming it in the bill, Congress early in the aid-giving process progressed to detailing in numerous terms the specific *quid pro quo* to be sought from each country receiving aid. To this Congress added the variant of cutting off aid unless a specific action, such as ending the partition of Ireland or ratifying EDC, was taken by the aid recipients. In 1964, and as a logical complement to its setting forth of detailed provisions for extending aid, Congress indicated a desire to become involved on a more current basis with the administration of foreign aid.

CONSTITUTIONAL BASIS FOR ASSERTIONS

Foreign aid, as one of the central elements of American foreign policy since 1947, has been the subject of an immense amount of scholarly analysis. Although a large part of that analysis has been directed in a critical vein at the hamstringing by Congress of the Executive's freedom of action in administering aid, almost no attention

[44] 65 Stat. 373, § 529.
[45] Senate Bill 2687, 88th Cong., 2d Sess. (An Act to Extend the Agricultural Trade Development and Assistance Act of 1954).
[46] *Ibid.*

has been paid to the constitutional basis of the restrictions. In analyzing the few comments that are made about the constitutional foundations, one is faced with a solid wall of unanimous opinion which holds that the power to make appropriations is a more than adequate foundation for the constitutional power to attach conditions to those appropriations. This unquestioned acceptance—and so little attention has been devoted to it that "unquestioned" is probably closer to the truth than "unanalyzed"—of the *constitutional right* of Congress to impose restrictions on foreign aid exists side by side with condemnations by political scientists of the *practice* of extended Congressional control. For example Corwin, after discussing the hindrance presented by detailed restrictions and suggesting the "leaving to Congress of its proper function of consent and grant," hastens to add:

Of course, I am not suggesting that Congress may not stipulate any terms it chooses as the condition of making an appropriation and thereby limit the effective scope of the inherently executive prerogative of planning and directing expenditures.[47]

In another case, a thorough study devoted exclusively to the exercise of control over foreign relations by Congress through its control of the appropriation process, the author, a lawyer, devoted only the following passing attention to the constitutional basis of the phenomenon which he was setting out to analyze:

Whatever their intention may have been, when they wrote into the Constitution the clause, "No money shall be drawn from the Treasury, but in consequence of appropriations made by law," they gave to Congress a means of exercising control concerning which there can be no doubt.[48]

A reading of the Congressional debates on the various amendments follows a strikingly similar pattern to that of the scholarly literature. Little, if any, attention is paid to the constitutional basis for action, and discussion in passing a restriction is focused upon the wisdom or lack of it from a policy point of view.[49]

[47] Corwin, *The President*, 1957 ed., p. 129.

[48] Nobleman, "Financial Aspects," p. 145.

[49] One exception to this pattern is found in the Congressional debate over specifically directing the President to extend aid to Spain. (*Congressional Record*, XCIV, Part 3 [80th Cong., 2d Sess., 1948], p. 3719.) In this debate Representative Douglas of California raised the broad constitutional issue as follows: "The Founding Fathers, when they wrote the Constitution, never intended that the foreign policy of this nation was to be formulated in heated, ill-considered, and hasty debate by the Lower House. Foreign policy that affects our national security into the far future demands mature consideration. It cannot be arrived at in the manner in which we adopted the amendment on Spain."

The constitutional basis, as seen by Congressman and scholar, for the multitude of restrictions placed in the foreign aid bills seems to rest on the following logic: Congress has the undisputed right to appropriate any sum, large or small, for foreign aid. It may certainly refuse to make any appropriation at all for foreign aid for whatever reason it chooses. Therefore, it is argued, the greater power to refuse all appropriations absolutely necessarily includes the lesser power to appropriate with conditions.[50] The essence of this logical construct will be analyzed in the concluding chapter, after an examination of the Executive response to the Congressional restrictions.

Executive Responses to Congressional Restrictions

Americans have long been accustomed to a pattern of interaction between the Executive and Legislative branches of their Government that can be characterized as "assertion and challenge."[51] Therefore it seems quite natural, after having examined the rising trend of Congressional assertions, to turn to an examination of the Executive responses and their constitutional bases.

FORMS OF EXECUTIVE RESPONSES

The challenge of responding to the increasing stream of Congressional directives attached to foreign aid bills in the conduct of foreign policy first fell to Harry S. Truman, as the President under whom the postwar foreign aid program was initiated and expanded. That the response was not long in coming, even at a time of greatly diminished political power, is a tribute to the respect and historical responsibility with which he viewed the office of President. In the last days of March 1948 the House had added Spain to the European Recovery Program, the Marshall Plan, in spite of the vehement objections of all the Western European countries. On April 1 President Truman released a statement through a press secretary in which he registered his oppo-

[50] Plischke adds the corollary argument that this power of Congress deprives the President of none of his powers over foreign policy "because an appropriations act requires executive approval." Hence he can avoid the restrictions by vetoing the restrictive foreign aid bill. Plischke, pp. 75–76.

[51] Corwin in this often-quoted passage takes note of the constitutional basis for this struggle with respect to matters of foreign affairs when he says, ". . . the Constitution considered only for its affirmative grants of power capable of affecting the issue, is an invitation to struggle for the privilege of directing American foreign policy." Corwin, *The President*, p. 171.

sition to this move and demanded that it be "stricken out."[52] The joint conference committee yielded to the President's demand, and the requirement that Spain participate in the program was removed from the bill. However, this was not to be the end of the aid-to-Spain controversy. In 1950 Congress attached an amendment to the ECA bill that "authorized and directed" that $62,500,000 be extended in loans to Spain.[53] The President had opposed this provision, and in signing the bill stated that he believed the provision to be unconstitutional and hence would not regard it as a mandatory directive.

I also feel obliged to comment upon the provision of the bill which authorizes loans for the purpose of assistance to Spain. I do not regard this provision as a directive, which would be unconstitutional, but instead as an authorization in addition to the authority already in existence under which loans to Spain may be made.[54]

In the preceding chapter the rise of restrictions in foreign aid legislation resulting from the outbreak of the Korean War was traced. President Truman faced the choice in 1951 of either signing an appropriations bill containing one of the more objectionable of the restrictive amendments, or vetoing a bill containing the appropriations for a major segment of the foreign aid program. This restriction was the Kem Amendment, which endeavored to halt trade between aid recipients and the Soviet bloc by cutting off all United States foreign aid to countries engaged in such trade. In signing the appropriation bill containing the Kem Amendment, President Truman clearly recognized his dilemma.

This rider is seriously defective. I have signed this act because the appropriations it carries are so urgently needed, and because Section 1302 [the Kem Amendment] does authorize exceptions from its provisions in the interest of national security. Unless the power to make exceptions is broadly used, this rider will result in weakening, rather than strengthening, the security of the United States and the collective security of the free world. I strongly urge the Congress to replace this hasty rider with more workable legislation at the earliest possible moment.[55]

Within Truman's statement on the Kem Amendment are the hints of an explanation for his failure (and later that of Eisenhower and Kennedy) to protest all Congressional restrictions on the President's control of foreign policy contained in foreign aid bills. First, Truman

[52] Felix Belair, Jr., "Conferees Bar Spain in ERP," *New York Times,* April 2, 1948, p. 1.
[53] 64 Stat. 758.
[54] *Department of State Bulletin,* XXIII (Sept. 6, 1950), 517.
[55] *Department of State Bulletin,* XXIV (June 25, 1951), 1027.

recognized the urgent need that existed at the time for foreign aid funds, even if encumbered with restrictions. Implicit in this recognition is the realization that because of the incessant attack upon foreign aid since its inception, a demand for unrestricted aid or none would probably result in none. Second, Truman recognized the saving grace of a Presidential escape clause that allowed Congress to stand before the people as the protector of the nation's true security against sinister interests (i.e., the State Department), while allowing the President to actually operate the program more or less as he sees the national interest.[56] Increasingly in the Eisenhower administration, the *modus operandi* became to accept most restrictions with little opposition as long as they contained a Presidential escape clause, and to concentrate one's effort upon minimizing the slashes in the total amount of aid. Often facing cuts in the range of one billion dollars from a program of only about $5 billion, the Eisenhower administration clearly faced the choice that Truman had of accepting restrictions or losing vitally needed aid funds. Hence, it is not too surprising that the choice was usually made in favor of taking even restricted funds.[57] Eisenhower did have one advantage that Truman lacked, and that was an unassailable personal political position. This he often used in his annual battles with Congress, but again usually for the purpose of extracting more aid rather than reducing restrictions. A typical example of trading on the personal popularity of the President was the statement by Secretary of State Dulles before the Senate Foreign Relations Committee on April 30, 1956:

The President has, under the Constitution, the responsibility to formulate the foreign policy of the United States. . . . To have this program appreciably reduced, interfered with, or put in jeopardy would gravely endanger the security of the United States. That is the considered judgment of the President and all his advisors who are charged with safeguarding our national security. I urge, therefore, that the requested authorization be granted.[58]

The fact that Congress continued to reduce the President's foreign aid requests, even in the face of a long string of statements similar to the one above, probably indicates that the Administration was not

[56] Of course, in an era of public diplomacy the initial Congressional action often wreaks more havoc than a subsequent Presidential exception under an escape clause can repair.

[57] The choices as Eisenhower recalls them are revealed in an insightful three pages of Dwight D. Eisenhower, *The White House Years: Mandate for Change 1953–1956* (New York, Doubleday, 1963), pp. 214–16.

[58] *Department of State Bulletin*, XXXIV (May 14, 1956), 791.

wrong in calculating that if it forced Congress to choose between aid without restrictions and no aid the results might have been no aid.

In spite of the great differences in style between Presidents Eisenhower and Kennedy on most issues with respect to foreign aid, their performances were remarkably similar. President Kennedy had written before he was elected President that:

It has become a fashionable cliché—especially in the State Department—to suggest that Congress constitutes the major block against the development of an imaginative foreign policy. But the events of the last session of Congress suggest rather that it is the intractable and unresolved differences within the Executive branch—and *its* failure of nerve—that inhibit decisive action.[59]

One can but wonder whether President Kennedy after assuming office in 1961 ever directed his own remarkable wit at these words he had written four years earlier. During his three years in office, he had to struggle continually against the wave of Congressional resentment against foreign aid appropriations that by 1963 had reached monumental proportions. In his State of the Union address in 1961 the President had called for the granting of greater discretion to the President in giving aid to Eastern Europe, and had followed this up with duplicate letters to the leaders of the House and Senate requesting the same authority.[60] However, the Congressional revolt over foreign aid soon reached such proportions that most of the Administration's effort, as during the Eisenhower Administration, became concentrated on seeing that an adequate amount of aid would be appropriated regardless of restrictions.

By May 1961 the Under Secretary of State, George Ball, was telling the Senate Foreign Relations Committee that "it is anticipated that this authority [to extend at the President's discretion aid to Eastern Europe] would not need to be used frequently." [61] And indeed it was not, since Congress did not give the Administration the greater discretion which it had requested. In 1962 the Kennedy Administration did not even have the opportunity to ask for more discretion; instead, the Administration had to fight simultaneously against

[59] John F. Kennedy, "When the Executive Fails to Lead," *The Reporter*, XIX (Sept. 18, 1958), 14.

[60] *Department of State Bulletin*, XLIV (Feb. 13, 1961), 212 (State of the Union Address).

Department of State Bulletin, XLIV (March 22, 1961), 444 (Duplicate letters to Vice President Johnson and Speaker Rayburn).

[61] *Department of State Bulletin*, XLIV (May 22, 1961).

cuts on the order of one billion dollars and a crippling amendment that would have denied aid to Poland and Yugoslavia with no provision for Presidential waiver. When this amendment of Senator Lausche's was approved by the Senate on June 6, 1962, the President delegated the duty of responding to the State Department. The comment of Secretary of State Rusk called the amendment "unfortunate," and noted that it "would deprive the President of the discretion which he needs in an explosive world." [62]

The only mention of the constitutional issues involved was contained in a high school commencement address given by Carl T. Rowan, the Deputy Assistant Secretary of State for Public Affairs. In this speech he said of the Senate's action the day before:

Let me make it clear that under our form of government the Congress holds the purse strings and has every right to influence policy by tightening or loosening those strings. That is what the Senate seeks to do with regard to our foreign policy where Yugoslavia and Poland are concerned.[63]

After denying that any constitutional principal was involved, Mr. Rowan then proceeded to attack the wisdom of the move on its merits.

The final result was a slightly watered-down amendment coupled with an even more damaging denial of "most-favored-nation" treatment to Poland and Yugoslavia. There were few public comments by the Kennedy Administration on either past restrictions retained in the foreign aid law or on new ones that were proposed in Congress, but in those comments that were made no instance was found in which the Executive challenged the constitutional right of Congress to impose the restrictions. Instead of discussing the Constitution, the Administration preferred to discuss the merits of the restriction or the merits of using inflexible laws to achieve policy goals in a dynamic world. And even in preference to discussing restrictions on the President's discretion, the Kennedy Administration—out of a sense of necessity—chose to discuss the meat-ax mood of Congress when authorizing foreign aid funds.

President Johnson assumed office after Congress had just cut President Kennedy's foreign aid bill for 1963 by a greater amount—34 percent—than any other foreign aid bill in history.[64] However, when

---

[62] *Department of State Bulletin*, XLVII (July 2, 1962), 25.
[63] *Department of State Bulletin*, XLVII (July 9, 1962), 71.
[64] Elizabeth Brenner Drew, "Mr. Passman Meets his Match," *The Reporter*, Nov. 19, 1964, p. 40.

President Johnson, less than a month after assuming office, signed into law this emasculated foreign aid bill that had been cut by $1.9 billion from the level of the initial request, he, unlike his two immediate predecessors, did not fail to notice and comment upon the restrictions contained within the bill.

It [the bill] also reflects, unfortunately, the growing tendency to hamstring Executive flexibility with rigid legislative provisions wholly inappropriate and potentially dangerous in a world of rapid change. I wish to make clear now, for example, that, when a free and peaceful government is ever established in Cuba, I intend to exercise my authority to provide essential health, educational, and other assistance to the Cuban people, without waiting for a long and complex adjudication.[65]

This is the strongest statement by any President with regard to restrictions on his control of foreign policy since Truman declared in 1950 that he regarded a provision of a foreign aid appropriation act as unconstitutional.[66] However, this statement by President Johnson is more than strong, it is disturbingly perplexing. The only example the President chose to give of the hamstringing of the Executive dealt with a possible need to give aid to Cuba if Castro should be overthrown. Yet, the only provision relating to Cuba in the Foreign Assistance Act of 1963, the bill the President was signing, states:

Except as may be deemed necessary by the President in the interest of the United States, no assistance shall be furnished under this Act to any government of Cuba . . .[67]

Either the President and/or his advisors misread the provision and hence mistakenly chose Cuba as an example of Congressional restrictions that would necessitate the President's acting in the national interest in violation of the law, or else Cuba was chosen as the best example for argumentative purposes with full knowledge that the Pres-

---

[65] *Department of State Bulletin,* L (Jan. 6, 1964), 26–27. "President Johnson Signs into Law Foreign Assistance Act of 1963" (Dec. 16, 1963).

[66] *Supra,* note 54.

[67] 77 Stat. 379, § 301 (e)(2): "Except as may be deemed necessary by the President in the interest of the United States, no assistance shall be furnished under this Act to any government of Cuba, nor shall Cuba be entitled to receive any quota authorizing the importation of Cuban sugar into the United States or to receive any other benefit under any law of the United States, until the President determines that such government has taken appropriate steps according to international law standards to return to United States citizens . . . or to provide equitable compensation to such citizens and entities for property taken from such citizens and entities on or after January 1, 1959, by the Government of Cuba."

ident's hypothetical example would be clearly legal under the Act.[68]

Less than one year after the above incident the President again commented upon the provisions of a foreign aid act. In signing an extension of the Agricultural Trade Development and Assistance Act of 1954 on October 8, 1964, the President noted that two provisions were unconstitutional and would not be applied, and that two others were disturbing.[69] Of these two disturbing provisions, one was to be "administered with great care" so as to minimize its harmful effects, and the other, the President believed, was "somewhat offset" by another provision of the Act.

With President Johnson's assertion of opposition to restrictions on the President in foreign aid laws, even in the face of signs of immense Congressional opposition to the very principal of foreign aid, a completely new concept of Executive response to the previous seventeen years of growing Congressional assertions of control over foreign policy seemed to be emerging.

CONSTITUTIONAL BASES OF RESPONSES

In examining the record of the responses of the Executive to Congressional restrictions in foreign aid legislation, one is struck by the sparsity of Executive responses that question the adequacy of the constitutional power of Congress to impose such restrictions. The standard pattern of Executive response has been to admit explicitly the adequacy of Congressional power, and then to proceed either to attack the proposed restriction on its merits or to question more generally the wisdom of providing restrictions in static legislation for dealing with a dynamic world.

President Truman's action with respect to aid to Spain is an exception to this general pattern. Although he did not enumerate his reasons for believing that an attempt by Congress to issue a mandatory directive to the President to grant aid to a specified country would be unconstitutional, the constitutional grounds for this belief can be reconstructed. From the President's statements during the 1948 flare-up over aid to Spain and the debate that took place over the

[68] The task remains for the future historian to decipher the tangled web of facts around the President's apparent misreading of this provision of the law. However, it seems altogether plausible to argue that the President chose an issue with wide emotive appeal—a free Cuba—in disregard of the actual provisions of the law, to argue the case for fewer restrictions on the President's power to conduct foreign relations.

[69] This statement is reproduced *supra,* note 2.

1950 Congressional decision to aid Spain, it is apparent that the President's action was partly based on his interpretation of the Constitution as making the President the sole organ of communication with foreign countries.[70] However, another constitutional element of President Truman's opposition to the mandatory nature of this appropriation was quite possibly his entanglement in the then raging controversy over whether Congress could force the President to spend funds appropriated for defense items.[71]

Truman was quite probably concerned not to give the Congress a precedent for the view that expenditures could be made mandatory upon the President by Congressional action. Truman's attack upon the Kem Amendment in 1951 as "seriously defective" was in the vein of what was to become the traditional mode of Executive response to such restrictions. In attacking the Kem Amendment after signing into law the bill containing it, Truman raised no constitutional issues and stated his intention to abide by the amendment. In fact his attack upon the amendment did not question the constitutionality of the amendment but only the wisdom of such a restriction upon the Executive.

The Eisenhower and Kennedy responses were in the mold of this latter Truman response and raised no questions of constitutional authority. However, with the assumption of office by President Johnson the extent of the constitutional power of Congress to restrict the actions of the President in foreign affairs was once again raised. What are the constitutional bases for President Johnson's assertions that those restrictions are unconstitutional? Unfortunately, he failed to answer this question in his first assault upon such restrictions.[72]

As to where this authority resided to act in specific contravention of an act of Congress "without waiting for a long and complex adjudication," [73] and which funds were to be used, the President gave no clue.[74] Indeed, the statement on its face sounds remarkably simi-

---

[70] The statements of 1948 indicate that this was probably the sole ground for the Presidential objection to the contemplated Congressional action. *New York Times,* April 2, 1948, p. 1.

[71] This controversy and its constitutional ramifications are thoroughly discussed in Elias Huzar, *The Purse and the Sword* (Ithaca, Cornell University Press, 1950), pp. 62–96, pp. 320–56.

[72] *Supra.,* pp. 1–2.

[73] *Department of State Bulletin,* L (Jan. 6, 1964), 26.

[74] In this part of the discussion the writer has assumed, as the President appeared to, that the Foreign Assistance Act of 1963 did indeed forbid all aid to Cuba. *Supra.,* note 67.

lar to those of the President's acknowledged mentor, Franklin Delano Roosevelt, who also asserted that there existed a broad Presidential power to act contrary to the law.[75] However, the striking difference is that Roosevelt specifically limited his asserted power to wartime, while Johnson's statement included no such restriction. That he may indeed have had in mind a constitutional concept very closely akin to Roosevelt's is indicated by Johnson's assertions that the restrictive legislative provisions in question were "wholly inappropriate and potentially dangerous in a world of rapid change." [76] Perhaps the existence of a dangerous world of rapid change serves as both the justification and restriction on this broad assertion of Presidential power, just as the existence of war served such a dual function for Roosevelt. The evidence is simply not available to determine whether President Johnson was asserting the first elements of an inchoate theory of Presidential stewardship of the national interest, or merely making a tactical attack against Congressional restrictions that are becoming increasingly difficult for the President to live with.

The constitutional grounds underlying President Johnson's declaration that two provisions of an act to extend the Agricultural Trade Development Assistance Act of 1954 were unconstitutional are much clearer. In this declaration of October 8, 1964, he was quite definite in enumerating the precedents for his action. One of the provisions vested in two Congressional committees the power to veto certain dispositions of foreign currencies, while the other provision required the President to obtain the approval of an advisory committee composed in part of Congressmen and in part of Executive appointees before making loans at interest rates below a specified level. In declaring both provisions to be unconstitutional because they "represent a clear violation of the constitutional principle of separation of powers," [77] the President rested his determination not only upon the opinion of his own Acting Attorney General but also on similar opinions by four previous Attorneys General.[78] Although the earlier opinions during the Eisenhower and Kennedy Administrations concerned provisions in legislation other than foreign aid bills, the Congressional provisions were essentially similar and Johnson's stand was completely consistent with that of his predecessors.[79]

[75] *Congressional Record,* LXXXVI, 7042–48, "Presidential Message of Sept. 7, 1942."

[76] *Department of State Bulletin,* L (Jan. 6, 1964), 26.

[77] *Department of State Bulletin,* LI (Nov. 9, 1965), 677.   [78] *Ibid.*

[79] In *Opinions of the Attorneys General,* XLI, 230–35, the then Attorney

The narrowness of the President's October 1964 assertion that a provision of a foreign aid bill is unconstitutional stands in stark contrast with the tone of his assertion a year before. The later action was carefully rooted in well-established constitutional precedents and certainly made no reference to a new theory of Presidential stewardship of the national interest. If one searches for the key difference in the two actions, it appears to be that in the later case a clear line of constitutional precedent allowed the President to disregard the two Congressional restrictions, while in the earlier case the President was unable to find any such precedent to allow him to disregard provisions of the law that he believed to be potentially dangerous to the nation. Lacking such a precedent, the President was forced to articulate an inchoate theory of presidential stewardship of the national interest.

The Constitutional Balance [80]

In this, the concluding section of this study, attention will be focused first on the current state of the constitutional balance between the President and Congress with respect to restrictions in foreign aid legislation. Inasmuch as our governmental system is a dynamic one, with shifts in the constitutional balance reflecting among other things the interests and skill of the actors in addition to the constantly changing world environment, an effort will also be made to discern the direction of movement of this constitutional balance. Finally, attention will be focused on an analysis of the constitutional balance and a skeleton proposal of guidelines for future action.

CURRENT POSITION AND DIRECTION OF MOVEMENT

Though a quality as imprecise as constitutional balance defies quantitative measurement, an accurate statement of the current posi-

---

General, Herbert Brownell, Jr., examined the history of similar attempts of Congress to intrude on the Executive branch by insisting on the veto right of committees of Congress over Executive actions. On the basis of this history and the clear line of precedent of disregarding such action, he advised President Eisenhower that a provision of an act of Congress attempting to do this was unconstitutional and could be disregarded. This is exactly what President Eisenhower did.

[80] Balance is used in the sense of a factual description of the existing distribution of constitutional power. It means no more than any distribution of power does and does not connote any balancing of forces. The various uses of the word balance are discussed in Ernst B. Haas, "The Balance of Power: Prescription, Concert, or Propaganda," *World Politics,* V (1953), 442–77.

tion of the clashing forces does seem possible. On the basis of the foregoing examination of the seventeen-year history of Congressional assertions of restrictions in foreign aid acts and the Presidential responses to those restrictions, the constitutional balance seems heavily weighted in favor of Congress.[81] In the overwhelming majority of cases, no question of the constitutional authority of Congress to enact such restrictions has ever been raised. On the contrary, the procedure of the Executive has been to confirm the power of Congress and then to proceed to debate the restrictions on their merit. In the two cases where Presidents have flatly declared provisions to be unconstitutional and announced their intention not to abide by such restrictions, a strong body of historical precedent existed for such action, and the very nature of the provisions tended to proscribe a wider application of those precedents.

The Congressional assertion that the constitutional grant of the exclusive power to appropriate funds and the accompanying grant of the power to refuse appropriations must include necessarily the lesser power to appropriate with conditions, has been accepted by the Executive. That the Congress has made increasing use of this power to restrict the President's discretion in foreign affairs is widely recognized even by members of Congress.[82] Thus the constitutional balance with respect to Congressional restrictions in foreign aid legislation upon the President's power to control foreign policy is heavily weighted in favor of Congress, as a result of wide acceptance of its constitutional power and seventeen years of precedent.

There are, however, two conflicting trends that developed between 1961 and 1964 that have the potential for causing a change in this dynamic balance. The first trend, which came to attention in 1961, has the potential of restricting the President to an even smaller position in the control of foreign relations. From 1961 onward not only has the number of Congressional restrictions increased but that venerable institution, the Presidential escape clause, has been removed from more and more of the restrictions. It is within the first trend, the removal of the Presidential escape clause, that the potential exists

[81] This conclusion is supported by an eminent member of Congress in J. William Fulbright, "American Foreign Policy in the 20th Century Under an 18th Century Constitution," *Cornell Law Quarterly,* XLVII (Fall 1961), 1–13.

[82] *Ibid.*

Felix Belair, Jr., "Fulbright's Plan Stirs a Wrangle over Foreign Aid," *New York Times,* Dec. 25, 1964, p. 1.

for restricting the role of the President in foreign affairs even more.

However, since 1963 evidence has arisen of a second factor which has even greater potential for rearranging the constitutional balance, not only in this one issue but over a wide spectrum of American political life. That second factor is the embryonic suggestion by President Johnson of a theory of Presidential stewardship of the national interest, which would allow the President in times of grave danger—i.e., the world as constituted today—to act in contravention of the law. That the President is not consciously striving for such a new result is indicated by his willingness to resort to accepted historical precedent, when it exists, for declaring unconstitutional those provisions of the foreign aid laws that he so finds. However, the President's own acceptance of the logic of the Congressional argument asserting its power [83]—when combined with the increased drive of Congress to impose more restrictions with fewer escape clauses—seems inevitably to be working toward a collision with the national safety as the President sees it in a world of rapid change.

There can be only two outcomes to such a clash. Either the President resigns himself to immediate inaction until the law is changed, and hence sees the nation endangered, or else the President must search for a basis for acting in disregard of the law. It is to be doubted, with the stakes of national safety so high in the last half of the twentieth century, that Presidents will long ponder this choice. In fact, the danger is that the increasing restrictiveness of Congress will interact with an active President to lower the threshold of recognition of the degree of national safety which must be involved before the President will violate the law. When the President himself has accepted the logic of the Congressional argument of power, his only escape is to formulate some sort of theory of Presidential stewardship. It should be immediately apparent that a theory of Presidential stewardship cannot be easily limited to foreign aid laws, and has inherent within itself a great potential for rearranging the constitutional balance over a broad spectrum. The discernible trends of the future indeed seem to indicate that increased Congressional restrictions may well lead the Executive to further articulate the embryonic suggestion of President Johnson of a theory of Presidential stewardship of the national interest.

[83] It is interesting to note that even Members of Congress who are critical of the extension of the restrictions nevertheless fully accept the constitutional right of Congress to enact them. *Ibid.*

GUIDELINES FOR FUTURE ACTION

Although the trends seem to indicate a movement toward the assertion of a theory of Presidential stewardship, such an assertion not only would be dangerous for the American form of government but would be unnecessary for the objective it attempts to achieve. The dilemma that faces the President is the result not of the Constitution's being surpassed by the onrush of history, but rather of a too facile acceptance of the logic of Congress' argument of its constitutional power to impose any restriction it desires in foreign aid legislation. Congress has advanced, against little opposition, the following argument: Congress has the undisputed right to appropriate any sum, large or small, for foreign aid. It may certainly refuse to make any appropriation at all for foreign aid for whatever reason it chooses. Therefore, it is asserted that the greater power to refuse all appropriations absolutely necessarily includes the lesser power to appropriate with conditions. The fallacy in this seemingly impregnable logic lies in the assertion that the power to impose conditions is a lesser part of the greater power to withhold absolutely. This is far from the case, as anyone who has examined the restrictions must conclude.

Can it be seriously maintained that Congress is exercising its constitutional power to appropriate monies when it conditions such appropriation upon the ending of the partition between Northern and Southern Ireland? The power to impose conditions upon foreign aid appropriations is not a lesser part of the greater power to withhold all foreign aid appropriations; rather, it is a distinct exercise of power which must find its own constitutional justification.[84] Each and every

[84] Research for this paper has turned up several discussions of limitations upon Congress' power to impose conditions in appropriations bills (but this research has failed to reveal any attempt to analyze the logic that underlies the permitted and the prohibited Congressional restrictions and the criteria that distinguish between them). For example, Attorney General Cushing in 1855, in discussing an attempt by Congress to limit the President's range of selection in appointing diplomatic officers, wrote, "He [the President], with the advice of the Senate, enters into treaties; he, with the advice of the Senate, appoints Ambassadors and other public ministers. It is a constitutional power to appoint to a constitutional office, not a statute power nor a statute office. Like the power to pardon, it is not limitable by Congress; . . ." in *Opinions of the Attorneys General*, VII, 217. The nearest approximation that was found to a clear analysis of the limits of Congressional power to impose conditions was in the writings of William Howard Taft, certainly no particular partisan of a powerful Executive: "Two principles, limiting Congressional interference with the Ex-

restriction that Congress would attempt to impose on foreign aid legislation should be examined to see if it is the exercise of a specific constitutional power given to Congress; the old argument, that Congress may impose any restriction it likes on appropriations, should not be accepted.

The reason that the old argument has gone so long unchallenged on constitutional grounds, is that in all areas other than foreign affairs substantive policy for which money is appropriated is also made by Congress. The difficulty has arisen in that foreign affairs is the one area where general policy is made by the President but money is appropriated by Congress. If the argument which is suggested here is admitted, the uniqueness of foreign affairs in the United States constitutional system would be accepted, by that admission, as the justification for restriction on the latitude of Congress to attach certain conditions to monies appropriated.

While it is impossible in the space available to examine every restriction by Congress from the viewpoint suggested above, a few typical restrictions can be so examined. The Foreign Assistance Act of 1948 contained a section declaring that no aid could be extended to any country until such country had entered into an agreement with the President, and that this agreement should include ten enumerated provisions.[85] If one is to examine this section (which has been repeated in one form or another in all the foreign aid acts since 1948) from the viewpoint suggested, the first task is to find its constitutional justification. One will indeed search the Constitution in vain for any provision giving Congress power to intrude into the field of international negotiation, for, as Justice Sutherland said in the Curtiss-Wright case,

In this vast external realm, with its important, complicated, delicate and many fold problems, the President alone has the power to speak or listen as a representative of the nation. . . . Into the field of negotiation the Senate cannot intrude; and Congress itself is powerless to invade it.[86]

It also seems doubtful that a constitutional basis exists for the provisions of the foreign aid law requiring the President to make

---

ecutive powers are clear. First, Congress may not exercise any of the powers vested in the President, and second, it may not prevent or obstruct the use of means given him by the Constitution for the exercise of those powers." William Howard Taft, *Our Chief Magistrate and His Powers,* p. 126.

[85] 62 Stat. 137, § 115 (b).

[86] *United States v. Curtiss-Wright Export Corp.,* 299 U.S. 304 (1936).

specific representations to foreign governments and ultimately to cut off aid if a foreign government should nationalize property owned by United States nationals.[87] The Supreme Court has spoken of "the very delicate, plenary and exclusive power of the President as the sole organ of the federal government in the field of international relations," [88] and it seems questionable, if these powers are indeed "exclusive," how much specific, mandatory direction Congress can include in a foreign aid bill without requiring "operation of the Government in a way forbidden by the Constitution." [89]

To those who will object that the framework suggested here for analyzing conditional appropriations would result in as much harm to our constitutional system as a doctrine of Presidential stewardship, an answer exists.

In the first place, this framework, which views each condition as a distinct exercise of power that must find its own constitutional basis, is limited by its very nature to the appropriation process. Secondly, the suggested framework of analysis leaves Congress free to subject to detailed scrutiny every aspect of the foreign aid program when funds are requested each year. If the aid has not been administered in a manner consistent with the wishes of Congress, the proper and clearly constitutional action is to reduce or terminate the funds.

Admittedly, once the genie of Presidential stewardship is out of the bottle there is no easy way to limit it to the appropriation process. The pressures for generalizing such a theory would be so great that it seems very doubtful that it could long be restricted to overturning Congressional restrictions in foreign aid legislation. And a theory of Presidential stewardship would by its very nature be arbitrary and destructive of the very spirit of the law.

But the argument advanced here does not assume the necessary concomitance of Presidential stewardship. Rather, what is suggested is that the myth of Congressional omnipotence in respect to the conditions Congress attempts to impose be examined for its constitutional justification, and that those conditions that do not have adequate constitutional justification be discarded.

[87] 76 Stat. 255, § 301 (d)(3)(3).   [88] *United States v. Curtiss-Wright.*

[89] *Opinions of the Attorneys General,* XLI, 233: "It [Congress] may also impose conditions with respect to the use of the appropriation, provided always that the conditions do not require operation of the Government in a way forbidden by the Constitution. If the practice of attaching invalid conditions to legislative enactments were permissible it is evident that the constitutional system of the separability of the branches of Government would be placed in gravest jeopardy."

Disengagement in Europe:
An Evaluation for
United States Foreign Policy

JAMES W. ROBINSON

Since mid-1955 the idea of military disengagement in Europe has stimulated a remarkable flow of military and political discussion. A proliferation of more or less thoughtful proposals has been generated. Many of the ideas aired are in the nature of competitive propaganda thrusts designed only to force the onus of refusal upon the opposition; others represent creditable and imaginative pitches at the narrow and shifting strike zone of mutually acceptable compromise between the Warsaw Pact and North Atlantic Treaty Organization (NATO) blocs.

Leading Disengagement Proposals

Disengagement within the cold war syndrome is not a new idea. At the Foreign Ministers Conference at Paris in April 1946, Secretary of State James F. Byrnes proposed a complete troop withdrawal from Germany backed by a forty-year, four-power treaty as a guarantee against any new German aggression. At a later conference at Moscow in April 1947, Foreign Minister Molotov proposed a complete troop withdrawal after the introduction of measures to assure the complete demilitarization of Germany. In 1949, James P. Warburg proposed, as a first step toward a disarmament agreement and a test of good faith, a phased withdrawal of foreign troops from Germany, and eventually from Europe, combined with United Nations supervision of a neutralized Germany.[1] In hindsight these early

[1] The Committee for World Development and World Disarmament, *Disengagement* (218 East 18th St., New York, N.Y.), July 1959, p. 1.

plans seem rather modest attempts to prevent further solidification of the cold war blocs, and to retain an area of political fluidity within which diplomatic maneuver would remain possible.

With Stalin's death and the gradual, uneven slackening of the cold war atmosphere, a variety of proposals for disengagement has been advanced from both camps. A number of the schemes bear distinguished signatures. Sir Anthony Eden, Sir John Slessor, Hugh Gaitskell, Dennis Healy, Pierre Mendès-France, Jules Moch, Selwyn Lloyd, Hubert Humphrey, Nikolai Bulganin, Andrei Gromyko, and Nikita Khrushchev are among them.

WESTERN PROPOSALS

At the Berlin Conference of Foreign Ministers in January and February 1954, Sir Anthony Eden advanced a proposal for 1) free elections to be held throughout East and West Germany, supervised by the Big Four or neutrals or both; 2) a national assembly chosen in the election to adopt a constitution and choose a provisional government; 3) a unified Germany free to assume or reject any international agreements of the present East or West regimes; and 4) the West to withdraw its military forces if the new German Government requested such action. The future German Government, neutralized or aligned with either the East or the West, would be freed of any international obligations of the Federal Republic or East Germany. The disputed Oder-Neisse Line between East Germany and Poland was to remain until reunification took place.[2] The Soviet delegation rejected Eden's proposal.

Eden's modified proposal at the 1955 Summit Conference included: 1) an agreement to keep the Eastern half of Germany demilitarized; 2) guarantees by the Western Big Three of the Soviet Union's western frontiers; 3) general and simultaneous limitations on armaments for both Eastern and Western blocs; and 4) negotiation of a general security arrangement for Europe embracing all or any part of the above. At the conclusion of the 1955 Summit Conference the foreign ministers were directed by their respective heads of state to examine the possibility of establishing a zone between East and West, in which the number of military forces were to be subject to a future general agreement. This provision was also discussed in the Foreign Ministers' Conference in 1959.

[2] The Eden Plan is fully printed in the British Information Services' text of the Summit Conference, Geneva, July 18 and 22, 1955.

In December 1956, Senators Sparkman and Flanders, and James P. Warburg, Norman Thomas, and other prominent United States citizens met at Arden House in New York to discuss the problem of disengagement. They proposed that the United States advocate the principle of mutual withdrawal under a carefully phased step-by-step plan. As a first step, the Russians should redeploy their forces behind the Oder-Neisse Line in exchange for NATO withdrawal to the western bank of the Rhine, with East Germany to be released from Soviet control and West Germany to be released from NATO. It was proposed that both German states be militarily neutralized under United Nations supervision, and that the four-power status in Berlin be preserved until German reunification. The Arden House conferees pointed out that their proposal, if accepted, would 1) constitute a first step in removing Soviet coercive power from Eastern Europe, 2) prevent the nuclear armament of Germany, 3) liberate 17 million East Germans and create the conditions in which German reunification could come about, and that 4) the neutralized area would serve as a testing ground for the techniques of inspection and enforcement.[3]

The Arden House proposal enjoyed wide discussion in 1956, but its persuasive edge was seriously dulled by the crushing Red Army thrust in Hungary. Its critics argued that, in the absence of clear and massive military deterrence, the Soviet Union would resort to coercive power in Eastern Europe whenever it deemed necessary; liberalization in the satellite nations was not to be hoped for by means of negotiation and compromise. The Arden House proposal was also attacked by arguments to the effect that our 1950 Korean "disengagement" had invited Communist attack.

In December 1957, in his fourth Reith Lecture on the B.B.C. network, George F. Kennan proposed the creation of a zone free of all atomic weapons in Germany, Poland, and Czechoslovakia; and the withdrawal of the Red Army from East Germany and other Warsaw Pact satellites together with the withdrawal of the armed forces of the United States, Great Britain, and France from the territory of the Federal Republic. He reasoned as follows: "If the armed forces of the United States, and Britain were not present on the Continent, the problem of defense for the Continental nations would be primarily one of the internal health and discipline of the respec-

[3] The Committee for World Development and World Disarmament, *Fact Sheet Series: A Discussion of the Problem: Disengagement,* July 1958, p. 2.

tive national societies. . . . We must get over this obsession that the Russians are yearning to attack and occupy Western Europe and that this is the principal danger. The Soviet threat . . . is a combined military-political threat, with the accent on the political." [4]

The late Hugh Gaitskell, the opposition leader in the House of Commons, offered a plan for disengagement in February 1958; it was designed, he said, to reduce the danger of a nuclear clash, achieve German reunification, offer the prospect of greater freedom for the satellite countries, and introduce an experiment in Central Europe. The Gaitskell plan for disengagement called for 1) a gradual withdrawal of foreign forces from both halves of Germany, and from Poland, Czechoslovakia, and Hungary (if necessary, before reunification of Germany); 2) agreement to limit and control conventional forces permitted to the nations concerned, and to deny nuclear weapons acquisition by the nations covered by the agreement; 3) German reunification; 4) a security pact underwritten by the great powers and guaranteeing the frontiers of the countries in the neutral zone; and 5) withdrawal of Germany from NATO, and of the three Eastern nations from the Warsaw Pact.[5]

In April 1959, Pierre Mendès-France, the former French Premier, proposed a system of graduated zones of controlled disarmament on both sides of the Iron Curtain as a step toward solving the German problem.[6] It was based on the establishment of three parallel north-to-south strips, situated symmetrically along the present demarcation line, with gradually decreasing arms restrictions. Zone Zero, perhaps thirty miles wide, to be completely demilitarized, would be policed by United Nations forces and/or local police. Zone One, consisting of two strips on each side of Zone Zero, would have only the conventionally armed national forces of the countries through which it passed and would be subject to an international control. Zone Two,

[4] "Kennan Ideas That Are Stirring Up Europe: Excerpts from B.B.C. Broadcasts," *United States News,* Jan. 10, 1958, pp. 45, 46. Kennan further argues for the concept of disengagement in his "A Chance to Withdraw Our Forces in Europe," *Harper's Magazine,* Feb. 1958, and in "Disengagement Revisited," *Foreign Affairs,* Jan. 1959.

[5] Hugh Gaitskell, "Disengagement: Why? How?" *Foreign Affairs,* XXXVI, No. 4 (July 1958). Gaitskell's plan and those of other members of Parliament led to a full discussion of disengagement in the House of Commons throughout 1958.

[6] The Mendès-France disengagement proposal is summarized in the *Handbook on Arms Control and Related Problems in Europe,* prepared by the Subcommittee on Disarmament of the Senate Committee on Foreign Relations, issued May 1959 (Washington, D.C., U.S. Government Printing Office).

east and west of the Zone One areas respectively, would be armed with the most modern weapons and allied to NATO in the West and to the Warsaw Pact in the East. The mutual withdrawal of Soviet and Western forces from Zones Zero and One would, according to Mr. Mendès-France, make possible "a new life" for the people of East Germany and represent the first step toward German reunification.

In May of 1959, President de Gaulle, in rejecting the Mendès-France proposal and that of Jules Moch (involving concentric circles centered on Berlin in 125 mile outward radial increments with gradually decreasing arms and forces restrictions), stated that "'disengagement' in itself says nothing to us which is of value. For if disarmament does not cover a zone which is as near to the Urals as it is to the Atlantic, how will France be protected? How then, in case of conflict can we prevent an aggressor from crossing by a leap or a flight the undefended German no-man's land?" [7] This is reasonable military thought so long as the General's concern is primarily with defense as opposed to deterrence, a focus of concern ill attested to by his present *Force de Frappe* doctrine.

In a thoughtful study entitled *Disengagement,*[8] Eugene Hinterhoff synthesized over 170 disengagement and disarmament proposals made since 1946, and then developed his own blueprint.[9] The zone of redeployment would include both halves of Germany, all of Poland, Czechoslovakia, Hungary, and possibly Rumania. In the first of two linked phases, demilitarization would be carried out by 1) a gradual reduction in foreign troop strength leading to general withdrawal; 2) the establishment of a ceiling for the national armed forces; and 3) denuclearization in Poland, Czechoslovakia, Hungary, and all the other nations of Eastern Europe. All existing alliances would remain in force until the second phase, when, with all foreign forces withdrawn, the nations in point would withdraw from their respective alliances and assume a status of military nonalignment. The guarantees and controls of the comprehensive plan would involve 1) an International Security Treaty which would guarantee territorial security in the great buffer zone through a strong non-

---

[7] Subcommittee on Disarmament of the Senate Committee on Foreign Relations, "Policy Statement of President de Gaulle," *Handbook on Arms Control and Related Problems in Europe.*

[8] Eugene Hinterhoff, *Disengagement* (London, Stevens, 1959).

[9] Occasional reference will be made to various plans outlined in Hinterhoff's appendix.

aggression pact enforced by flexible United Nations sanctions, and 2) international inspection and control of adherence to national troop strength ceilings and denuclearization agreements. The result would then be simply a zone of controlled conventional armaments. Hinterhoff's second phase also includes reunification of Germany either through free elections or any other mutually acceptable method.

EASTERN PROPOSALS

Foreign Minister Molotov, in the January–February 1954 Foreign Ministers' Conference in Berlin, proposed a mutual withdrawal of troops from Germany to take place within six months after the conclusion of a peace treaty with that nation.[10] The mutual withdrawal was not to be complete; small contingents were to remain in a unified Germany. The second part of Molotov's proposal illustrated a Soviet penchant which opponents of the concept of disengagement point out as a major justification for their position. His plan called for the right to reoccupy the disengaged zone (Germany) in the event of a threat to Soviet national security. Molotov also showed interest in the Eden proposal; at the Geneva Foreign Ministers' Conference of 1955, he is reported to have expressed a wish to approach the British disengagement plan by way of "a zone of limitations and inspection of armaments in both parts of Germany and neighboring states." [11]

Polish Foreign Minister, Adam Rapacki, advanced his initial denuclearization proposal in a speech before the United Nations General Assembly on October 2, 1957. Due to strong objections to it by the Western Powers, Rapacki revised it in November of 1958, expressing the hope that his revised plan would meet with the approval of the West.[12] This thoughtful proposal stimulated wide discussion and found considerable support in the West. The scheme was one envisaging an atom-free zone in Europe, diligently inspected, to be accompanied by appropriate reduction in conventional armaments. The states within this zone, consisting of Poland, Czechoslovakia, and East and West Germany, would be: 1) Committed not to produce, stockpile, import for their own use, or allow the deployment on their territories of, any type of nuclear weapons. They would not

---

[10] "Soviet Proposal of European Security," *Pravda*, Feb. 10, 1954, p. 1. (Translated in the *Current Digest of the Soviet Press*.)

[11] Hinterhoff, p. 436.

[12] "New Version of the Rapacki Plan," *The Bulletin*, Bonn, Germany, Nov. 11, 1958, pp. 2, 3.

install or allow to be installed on their territories equipment for delivering nuclear weapons. 2) The Big Four (France, Britain, the United States, and the Soviet Union) would assume the following commitments: a) to withhold nuclear weapons from their forces on the territory of the states comprising the zone, and to remove and/or refrain from installation on the territory of these states equipment for the delivery of nuclear weapons; b) in all ways and under any circumstance to refrain from providing governments, or any other agencies in the zone, with nuclear weapons equipment or plant for their manufacture. 3) The powers possessing nuclear weapons should undertake not to use them against the territory of the zone or any targets within it. 4) The other nations whose troops are stationed on the territory of any of the states of the zone would also commit themselves not to have nuclear weapons among the armaments of those troops, and not to supply any such weapons to governments or agencies within the zone.

The implementation of the above commitments would require the countries concerned to establish and submit to an extensive system of effective controls in the proposed zone. Mr. Rapacki suggests that this system might include both land and air controls. Cognizant of the difficulties inherent in effectively inspecting so large an area, he proposed that the appropriate control machinery might include representatives appointed by bodies of the Warsaw Pact and NATO as well as representatives of states belonging to none of the European military groupings.

Implementation of the Rapacki Plan would proceed in two stages. The first stage called for the banning of the production of nuclear weapons in Poland, Czechoslovakia, and East and West Germany. Parties to the agreement would be obligated to refrain from building installations or giving nuclear weapons to armies that did not possess them. The second stage called for the nuclear installations of the Soviet Union and the West in the zone to be banned, but only after agreement was reached on conventional forces and arms reduction in the zone.

In addition to supporting the Rapacki Plan, and initiating a suggestion for total disarmament, Khrushchev proposed a disengagement plan for consideration "if for any reason the Western Powers do not show a readiness to embark on general and complete disarmament." [13] This "partial measure for disarmament" called for 1) the creation of

[13] "Khrushchev Proposals," *New York Times,* Sept. 18, 1959, p. 3.

a control and inspection zone with a reduction of foreign troops on the territory of Western Europe; 2) the creation of an atom-free zone in Central Europe; 3) the withdrawal of all foreign troops from the territory of Eastern Europe and the dismantling of foreign military bases on European territory; 4) the conclusion of a nonaggression pact between the member states of NATO and the Warsaw Pact; and 5) an agreement on the prevention of surprise attack by one state on another.

Overview of Disengagement Proposals

Although the disengagement proposals vary considerably in their intent and provisions, they offer some common points. First, the serious, politically realistic proposals all provide for a mutual redeployment, gradually or at a stroke, of troops and/or weapons. Second, the least ambitious of these are the ones proposing small zones or strips of demilitarized terrain between the armed blocs for the purpose of reducing friction and reducing the likelihood of war by accident or by an emotional overreaction to a border incident by a local officer. This would be done without altering the military balance. Third, the more far-reaching plans envision a buffer zone of nations in Central Europe, denuclearized, without—or with drastically reduced numbers of—nonnational troops, with border guarantees by alliance or greatpower pact. These plans have as their purpose the creation of a more stable, less strained military balance in Europe, a reduction of East-West tensions, a reduction of the likelihood of nuclear war, and (in some) a gradual reunification of Europe. The Western proposals on this scale ordinarily provide for German reunification; the Eastern plans, after 1956, ordinarily do not. The schemes of this scale which are meant for serious consideration purport to leave the East-West military balance reduced but equal. Finally, the plans involving the greatest changes envisage, either eventually or quickly, the withdrawal of all foreign troops from the nations of Europe along with armaments limitations. This type of plan aims at a major reduction in armaments, a first step in a general arms agreement, a reduction of East-West tensions and, perhaps, a healing of the great economic and political split in Europe. The military balance would, it is said, remain equal, but at a low level.

Not a few of the proponents of disengagement have seen the device as a first step, a desirable causal factor, in a general European or international political settlement. Others consider disengagement only as one of the benefits to be derived from, and possible only in, a general East-West settlement of major political differences. Still a third conception of disengagement places the geographical solution only within the general framework of a comprehensive agreement on functional arms limitation. There is much to be said in favor of the latter two formulations of disengagement; both however, rest heavily upon political and technological developments not within the scope of this study.

The discussions of European disengagement in the last decade have taken place within the context of a rapidly shifting military and political situation. Tension takes different forms today than it did in the early postwar years. In the earlier period the hostility which arose between the United States and the Soviet Union was due to the Soviet subjection of Eastern Europe and Stalin's manifest designs upon Germany. Europe was the focus of contention between the two powers that had emerged supreme from World War II. Today, however, the United States and Russia are locked in a conflict of interest and ideologies which covers the globe and extends to outer space. Spatial separation of Soviet and NATO forces in Europe would obviously not constitute a disengagement of Soviet and Western (U.S.) power. With the advent of intercontinental bombers and missiles, the two great adversaries cannot "disengage" militarily. Nevertheless, Europe remains the most vital area of conflict; hence, it is in Europe that the wish of both powers to avoid general nuclear war is most threatened.

The strategic confrontation of the great powers has changed geographically since the mid-1950s. At that time the Soviet lacked the capability to inflict extensive damage on the territory of the United States; the Soviet leadership relied on the threat to seize or destroy Western Europe in order to deter United States attack. The American Strategic Air Command still needed European bases for a great proportion of its bomber force. Today, the two powers face each other across the Arctic wastes and are mutually vulnerable to massive destruction by missiles and bombers. Europe need have no direct part in a strategic confrontation between the two great antagonists. At the same time, a major military loss in Europe remains clearly unacceptable to both powers.

Nor, of course, has the economic and political position of Europe remained static through the years of disengagement discussion. The various members of NATO have committed themselves to different and, to some extent, competitive economic groupings. Several of the nations of Western Europe have prospered dramatically. A marked increase in the independence of the individual states of NATO has occurred. The Warsaw Pact nations have made economic progress and have formed their own economic organization, but very embarrassing economic problems continue to harass the Communist nations of Europe, and in the past decade they have been outstripped by their Western counterparts. There is a strong trend toward increasing trade between the two blocs. Clear indications of a modest but growing independence in foreign and economic policy have appeared among the satellite states in the wake of the Sino-Soviet dispute. Nevertheless, the Soviet Union continues to stand at the head of a more centralized alliance than does its American adversary, and will ordinarily be able to act more quickly and with less attention to the wishes of its allies. However, even this last assumption, appears less certain with each passing year.

Armed Forces of NATO and the Warsaw Pact

Knowledge of the present deployment and quantity of military forces of the opposing blocs is necessary for a competent evaluation of the disengagement proposals outlined above. Where comparisons involve ground force divisions it is well to bear in mind that the size and capabilities of "divisions" vary considerably from nation to nation. For example, the present American divisions, commonly termed ROAD as opposed to the previously employed "pentomic" structure, are designed for maximum self-sufficiency and versatility, and have roughly twice the size, weapons strength, and internal support capability of a Soviet division. The Soviet division, however, employs the higher ratio of tanks to infantrymen. On both sides units designated as divisions are not infrequently skeletal or understrength units, consisting of a cadre and an equipment inventory sufficient for a full strength division, but requiring extensive troop allocations to bring them to the combat capability expected of a division. Thus, Secretary of Defense Robert S. McNamara has estimated that the Soviet Union's 175-division army has a combat-ready strength of 80 to 88 Soviet divisions, equivalent to perhaps 50 United States combat-ready divisions (of which there are now 16).[14]

The nations of NATO have an aggregate population of 450 million, a total annual product nearing one trillion dollars, a vast modern technological base, active armed forces totaling 5,900,000 men, and a total annual defense outlay of 70 billion dollars. The signatory nations of the Warsaw Pact (not counting Albania) have the lesser population by 100 million, one-half the aggregate output, 4,750,000 in the active armed forces, and a total yearly defense outlay in the area of 35 billion dollars.[15]

In terms of strategic war-making capability the NATO forces stand as follows: 630 B-52s (315 of which are on 15-minute alert), 600 Minuteman missiles, 5 Regulus firing submarines with 17 missiles, 9 Polaris submarines with 144 missiles, 180 British V Bombers, 50 French Mirage IV bombers with strategic capability in an aerial refueling system, and a diminishing number of obsolescent B-47s in Spain and Britain. The United States Sixth Fleet in the Mediterranean is capable of conducting heavy nuclear strikes on the Balkans and Southern Russia. A crucial inequality appears upon examining the Soviet strategic arsenal. On the strength of its ability to hit United States population centers, the Soviet Union can presently do little more than deter a nuclear first-strike by the United States; however, Soviet nuclear destructive power deliverable by medium-range missiles and bombers is sufficient to crush the European NATO establishment. It is estimated that the Soviet Union now possesses 200 long-range bombers, a few more than 100 ICBMs and, at most, two dozen rocket-firing submarines roughly comparable to the United States Regulus firing force (surface-launched, short-range missiles), which are capable of striking the United States. (The Soviet strategic missile force may employ much larger nuclear warheads than the United States missiles.)

But, although American long-range destructive power may be larger than the equivalent Soviet Union Strategic Air Command power by a factor of four or five, the Soviet Union has built up a force of 600 MRBMs in western Russia which can cover every form of target—cities, air bases, installations—in NATO Europe. This force is being

[14] Robert S. McNamara, address to the Economic Club of New York, Nov. 18, 1963, reproduced in "Major National Security Problems Confronting the United States," *Department of State Bulletin*, XLIV, No. 1277, pp. 914–21.
[15] *Ibid.*, pp. 916, 917.

expanded. To reinforce it the Soviet has 1000 TU-16 medium bomb-ers.[16] European NATO has no comparable strategic force; the 60 Thor missiles in Britain and the 45 American Jupiter missiles in Italy were dismantled in 1963, leaving in Europe only the Mirage IV, V Bomber, B-47, and the naval nuclear forces.

(The United States proposed a multilateral fleet of Polaris missile-equipped merchant vessels designed, among other things, to provide Europe with a nuclear deterrent which could not be knocked out by a Soviet first-strike.) The Soviet Union possesses something approach-ing a first-strike capability in Europe, and at present the "balance of terror" is held even only by the United States commitment to use its superior strategic strike forces in defense of Western Europe. It is nowhere doubted that the cost of honoring this commitment in the event of an attack on European NATO would be, for the United States, a nuclear exchange with the Soviet Union. The cost of not honoring the commitment would be the abandonment of the productive plant, and the human and natural resources of Western Europe, devastated but replenishable, to Soviet hegemony.

If, in the balance of strategic war power, the security of NATO Europe is based on the American guarantee, the same is true to a lesser degree in the balance of ground and tactical forces. Secretary of Defense McNamara has recently stressed the fallacy of the military concept which pits Communist conventional might and relative nu-clear weakness against the awesome megatonage and smaller conven-tional capabilities of the West.[17] It is true that there are about as many men under arms in NATO Europe as in the Warsaw Pact and western Russia—about 3,300,000 on either side. The 2,200,000 NATO ground forces in Europe equal the total Soviet Red Army manpower, and with the increasing hostility from China, the propor-tion of total Red Army strength that could safely be deployed west of the Urals may decline. Although NATO military analysts feel that the satellite forces, numbering 941,000 in 60 divisions (12 armored) with 11,700 tanks, would not be reliable in offensive actions, those forces cannot be disregarded in the military balance.[18] Indeed, the

[16] See Richard F. Starr, "How Strong is the Soviet Bloc?" in *Current History*, Oct. 1963, p. 213.

See also Buchan and Windsor, *Arms and Stability in Europe* (London, Chatto and Windus for the Institute for Strategic Studies, 1963), p. 21.

[17] Committee on Armed Services, House of Representatives, *Hearings on Military Posture and National Security* (88th Cong., 2d Sess.), HR 9637, p. 6978.

[18] Buchan and Windsor, p. 22; Starr, p. 215.

chief problem with which NATO military planning has been confronted for years is that the Soviet Union could expect, by concentrating its forces against one sector of the NATO perimeter, while using East European troops to hold the long flanks in a defensive posture, to achieve a decisive local superiority.

The balance in Central Europe seems both the most equivocal and the most crucial. Here the local balance of ground power is not unfavorable to NATO; 24 NATO divisions in Germany and the Low Countries with 5,500 tanks face 25 Soviet divisions with 7,500 tanks (20 in East Germany, 3 in Hungary, 2 in Poland). But the Soviet Union possesses sufficient tactical air strength here to achieve local superiority.[19] McNamara notes, without stressing it, the Communist advantage in fast mobilization of the rear and in reinforcement.[20] A study by Britain's Institute for Strategic Studies lends disquieting quantification in concluding that the Soviet Army could, in war, reinforce its 25 forward divisions with 75 to 80 at the rate of about 40 per month. By contrast, the NATO powers could reinforce the central front with only about 12 divisions in the first month.[21] It is well to note also the difference in quality and flexibility between the homogeneous forces of one nation in attack and that of a force drawn from eight nations, two of which must reinforce their troops across the Atlantic, in the defense.

From 1957 to the present, NATO has tried to remedy this imbalance by introducing short-range tactical nuclear weapons into its forces. Presently 600 fighter-bombers, capable of conducting nuclear interdiction strikes, are dispersed across NATO Europe. The air arm of the United States Sixth Fleet can perform tasks of nuclear interdiction. In the ground forces, most NATO divisions have Honest John missiles (range 15 miles) as an integral part of their structure, with the warheads in the custody of an American team. The United States Seventh Army possesses a nuclear arsenal consisting of Davy Crockett atomic mortars (range 4,300 yards, with ¼-kt warhead), Sergeant missiles (range 85 miles, 20-kt warhead), and Pershing missiles (range 350 miles). In Germany there are three squadrons of MACE missiles which approach IRBM range, effective up to 1,380 miles. The Honest John missiles and the United States 175-mm rifle and 8-inch howitzer are

[19] Starr, p. 214.
[20] House of Representatives, *Hearings on Military Posture and National Security*, p. 6943.
[21] Buchan and Windsor, p. 21.

all capable of using either conventional or nuclear warheads.[22] McNamara asserts: ". . . the nuclear firepower available to a single U.S. infantry division in Europe is sufficient to destroy the combined populations of the 50 largest cities in the U.S." [23]

I have found no assessment purporting to provide an accurate account of Soviet short-range nuclear firepower. It is known however, that ground launchers, short-range missiles and artillery exist in abundance. As many as 2,000 fighter-bombers may be available for nuclear interdiction in support of the Red Army in Europe. McNamara asserts that in the field of tactical nuclear weaponry the United States is presently superior in design, diversity, and numbers.[24] Some credence may be lent this statement by the fact that Soviet military doctrine presently stresses a series of massive, rapid attacks mounted by mobile forces; this strategy means that the divisions of the opposing armies would be so closely intermingled that no short-range nuclear weapons would be used.[25] The Soviets appear to feel it to their interest to forego the use of battlefield nuclear weapons if the NATO powers can be deprived of the use of theirs.

NATO enjoys a very considerable superiority in naval forces. The tally sheet is as follows: Aircraft Carriers, NATO—37, WP—0; Cruisers, NATO—27, WP—20; Destroyers and Escorts, NATO—700, WP—100. The Soviet hopes to balance this with a two-to-one superiority in submarines; she has 460, 280 of which are long-range types.[26]

FORESEEABLE TYPES OF WAR IN EUROPE

The armaments and forces of both sides are designed to fight a wide range of conflicts; an appraisal of comparative strength, to be meaningful, should measure the respective abilities of each side to conduct each of several types of war.

European Unlimited War. In a purely European confrontation the Soviet Union enjoys a strategic nuclear advantage of such magnitude that it might hope in a first-strike to deprive the Continental NATO forces and Britain of capability for strategic retaliation. At present, the overwhelming Soviet advantage in MRBMs and long-range jet bombers is balanced only by the American ICBM, SAC, and Polaris forces stationed in the United States and at sea. In essence, NATO

[22] U.S. Army, *ROTC Manual 145–45*, p. 98.
[23] *Christian Science Monitor*, Sept. 21, 1964, p. 3.
[24] Robert S. McNamara, address of Nov. 18, 1963, in *Department of State Bulletin*, XLIV, No. 1277, p. 917.
[25] Buchan and Windsor, p. 97.   [26] *Ibid.*, p. 20.

cannot hope for anything more than swift, total defeat in a war unlimited in weaponry but restricted to the European continent. In the face of such a war, NATO would be forced to expand the war to intercontinental proportions or face certain defeat. The United States Government has been at pains to assure all powers concerned that its strategic forces would be thrown into the fray in the event of a Soviet nuclear strike against its NATO allies. At present there seems little reason to doubt that this firm commitment would be kept if the promise itself failed to deter. However, as Soviet ICBM forces grow in numbers and efficiency and United States damage-limiting capability decreases, American resolve to enter a European war may well weaken.

Under conditions of rational choice, the balance of terror should function to make this type of war less likely than those discussed below.

European Limited War—Conventional. In this type of war, both geographical depth for maneuver and mobilization and reinforcement capability are important factors; in these the Warsaw Pact nations have a probably decisive advantage. Battle-ready troop strength along the Iron Curtain is nearly equal; conventional infantry and artillery firepower is comparable; the Soviet bloc maintains a small advantage in tank strength and a considerable superiority in tactical air power. NATO has not found any way to offset the Soviet ability to concentrate overwhelming strength drawn from its reserves in order to break through small sectors of the NATO perimeter while neutralizing any threat from the flanks by the use of satellite forces. In the future, NATO might hope to counter this Soviet conventional warfare advantage by developing highly effective, nonnuclear antitank and antiaircraft weapons for infantry use (such as the Red Eye, Mauler, and Hawk) while building a large and well-trained militia system. At this time, however, the NATO forces must resort to tactical nuclear weapons in order to interdict Soviet lines of reinforcement and render large troop concentrations imprudent.

NATO is a dispersed, maritime coalition with its strongest member separated by an ocean from its weaker allies and the most likely area of conflict. The Warsaw Pact is a centralized land power with all its members contiguous to the most likely area of conflict. In the present state of technology and military organization, this geopolitical circumstance provides the European Communist forces with an over-all advantage over its NATO opponents in a continental, conventional war.

European Limited War—Tactical Nuclear Weapons. In this type of European war the forces of the opposing sides seem better balanced, and the outcome of such a war is not at all predictable. The NATO planners appear to feel that Soviet bloc advantages in reinforcement strength could be neutralized by nuclear interdiction, and that the Soviet ability to concentrate overwhelming forces against perimeter defense sectors would be rendered useless. Soviet tactical air supremacy, it is felt, could be countered by NATO's presumably superior array of battlefield nuclear weapons. But the limited nuclear war threatens the greatest probability of escalation to an intercontinental missile exchange. The American MACE missiles stationed in Germany with a range in excess of 1,300 miles are considered by NATO to be "tactical" weapons. Would the Soviet Union consider them tactical weapons, or MRBM strategic weapons? If the MACE were used in anger, would the Soviet leaders not feel justified in unleashing their MRBMS on "tactical" targets? The proper classification of a nuclear interdiction strike against rail marshaling yards in a major industrial city 600 miles from the front would evoke disagreement between men of good will in a time of calm debate. Yet this is the type of usage envisioned for "tactical" missiles such as the MACE and, to a lesser degree, the Pershing. NATO military analysts are aware of this dangerous ambiguity involved in the war of limited nuclear weapons. But they feel that NATO would be forced to escalate a conventional, general war to the "nonstrategic nuclear level" in order to escape eventual defeat. Although tactical nuclear weapons may be viewed as the most effective way to fight a nuclear war, they can be the surest agents of escalation.

Local War of Intervention. The form of conflict here considered typically arises when one nation sends its armed forces across the border of another on the pretext of supporting one disputant in a local, civil disorder. As the political and economic division of Europe has hardened into opposing alliances and economic communities, the likelihood of such armed adventures has decreased. So long as it appears probable to the nations in each bloc that any armed intervention by one bloc into the affairs of a nation in the other will be met by alliance action, such local wars of intervention will remain unlikely. Europe, divided by a clearly marked and mutually guarded line, may be criticized for its economic and political absurdity, but the line and the relationship between the two power blocs are not ambiguous. A stability exists, however unpleasant. As alliances weaken, as blocs break up, the presently clear consequences of a wide range of foreign policy alternatives among the European nations will become unclear. War by miscalculation will become a greater likelihood. So long as the alliances of East and West Europe remain reasonably solid, nations are unlikely to attempt armed intervention into the civil disputes of states across the Iron Curtain, unless the intent is a prelude to general, continental war. The comparative strengths of NATO and the Warsaw Pact forces in such a war are outlined above. It would be foolhardy to now attempt a comparison of the combatant forces if the two great blocs were to dissolve into a more fluid network of smaller alliances and nonaggression pacts in the fashion of Europe's past.

The various proposals for arms reduction and troop redeployment in Europe have as a chief concern the assurance that the balance of power in Europe will not be disturbed, but will be maintained at a reduced level. From the above summary, it seems clear that power in Europe is in a state of balance only with reference to the "European limited war with tactical nuclear weapons" model depicted previously. Power is not balanced with respect to a European conventional war or for a European unlimited war; in both cases a preponderance of military strength lies with the Warsaw Pact nations. Insofar as the peace is sustained in Europe by a rough parity of forces, it is because NATO would not presently accept a conventional war and would unilaterally escalate it to a limited war of tactical nuclear weapons, wherein power is roughly balanced.

The question, in that case, is clear: Why would not the Soviet Union then escalate the struggle to the European unlimited nuclear model, where it holds a massive preponderance of strength? The obvious answer is that the war would then cease to be a European war and become a global missile exchange, in which NATO holds the massive edge. Hence, initiation of (or escalation to) a European unlimited war is inhibited, not by a balance of power in Europe, but by the global balance of terror. Only European limited war then can be said to be inhibited by the European balance of power (a parity of military forces presently in Europe); European unlimited war is theoretically invited by the continental unbalance of power, but is deterred by the prospect of a war broadened to include the continental United States with its strategic nuclear arsenal.

Three Models of Disengagement and
Three Types of War: Evaluation

The discussion of disengagement must start from the assumption that neither the United States nor the Soviet Union would willingly accept a military pullback, in the absence of a general political settlement of differences, which would seriously injure its relative power position in Europe. Hence, the proponents of disengagement (with the possible exception of Kennan) are at pains to assure the unconvinced that their proposals, if accepted, would result in reduced but balanced opposing military forces in Europe. This study will now examine the consequences of three general plans of disengagement for the relative defensive strength of NATO in Europe.

To the European it may well seem a matter of slight consequence whether any future continental war is conventional, tactically nuclear, or unlimited and nuclear. In each case Europe's cities and lands would be devastated. The West European might reasonably argue that it is better to build a war-deterring nuclear force, which could not defend Western Europe in a limited war if the deterrent failed, than to spend the money and effort necessary to create a land army capable of conducting a prolonged conventional or "tactically nuclear" war.

To the American analyst, however, the difference is of very great consequence. So long as in any future war Western Europe could be successfully defended without resort to an intercontinental missile and bomber exchange, the United States would not need to sacrifice its cities, civilian population, and productive plant for the defense of Europe. It is eminently reasonable to assume that the Soviet Union also would seek to avoid a transpolar ICBM exchange. Thus, the United States presently has, and should seek to maintain, more than a single alternative in the event of a limited attack by the Warsaw Pact nations upon European NATO. It is very much to the interest of the United States to maintain, with or without disengagement and/or disarmament agreements, a balance of European ground power as well as the nuclear deterrent. The stark alternative of defeat in Europe or nuclear holocaust is one that must be avoided.

GENERAL DISENGAGEMENT IN EUROPE

The most ambitious of European disengagement schemes advocate a Europe free of American and Soviet arms and troops, a disengagement to the Soviet border and the United States east coast respectively. Such plans have been presented by James Warburg (1949), Kuznetsov (1957), and Khrushchev (1959),[27] but have not received the serious consideration accorded the schemes of less ambitious scope. These plans are replete with pacts of nonaggression and agreements on the prevention of surprise attacks, agreements that in fact could not and would not be relied upon by either side in the absence of clear military dissuaders to pact violation.

Let us imagine, for the moment, the Europe Khrushchev proposed: there are token United States forces in Western Europe; no Soviet troops in non-Russian Europe; no tactical or strategic nuclear weapons in the Central European zone or any foreign military (air or missile) bases in all of Europe. There is a zone of inspection and arms control in Germany. The conventional forces of European NATO and non-Russian Eastern Europe remain in rough parity, with any advantage lying with the NATO forces offset by the Soviet presence 500 miles east. Britain's V Bomber force and the 50 French Mirage IV nuclear bombers remain; American Polaris submarines roam the seas near Russia; the Soviet MRBM and United States ICBM forces, together with the long-range bombers of both, are unaffected by disengagement. The very considerable striking power of the United States Sixth Fleet remains mobile in the Mediterranean.

Thus the mutual nuclear deterrent remains unaffected. The advocates of this formula of disengagement contend that the peace in Europe is ultimately kept by the balance of terror which would remain unaffected by this mutual withdrawal. It may be argued that the new West German Army (353,000)[28] would be quite able to hold the line of defense against thrusts from East Germany (80,000-man army) and Czechoslovakia (185,000-man army), and capable of withstanding a Warsaw Pact attack comprised of troops from East Germany, Czechoslovakia, and Poland (257,000)[29] until reinforced

[27] These proposals are summarized in Hinterhoff's *Disengagement*. In fairness to Mr. Warburg, it should be noted that he formulated his plan in reference to the strategic confrontation of the late 1940s, when Western conventional strength in Europe was at its lowest ebb.

[28] *New York Times*, "NATO Survey," Nov. 8, 1964, p. E–3.

[29] Figures for the Warsaw Pact forces are taken from Richard F. Starr, "How Strong is the Soviet Bloc?," p. 213.

from France and England. Greek forces (145,000) would be able to cope with any Bulgarian attack (210,000-man army) so long as it was not supported by other powers. The tactical conventional and nuclear support of the United States Sixth Fleet would be immediately available in the defense of Greece. Norway and Turkey would have no less in the way of NATO defense than they have presently.

All of the above is well noted, but consideration of the consequences of a Soviet Army reentry in force reveals a ruinous inequality in logistic ability. A force such as the 25 mobilized divisions now present in Central Europe could be returned to the West German border across 500 miles of flatland, traversed by many roads and railroads. European NATO, though it would doubtless be aware of such a great troop movement, would not be in a position to interdict it. The Soviet Union could muster a high quality fighter umbrella sufficient to maintain air superiority over the troop movement; the British and French nuclear weapons (bombs) are designed for strategic, deterrent, "countercity" use rather than troop and supply interdiction; European NATO without the United States has no tactical nuclear artillery or missiles for massive interdiction. There seems little firm reason to doubt that the Polish, Czechoslovak, and East German governments would be anything but cooperative if the Soviet was determined to cross their territories.

Thus with the disengagement of United States forces to the North American continent and Soviet withdrawal to its European borders, the Soviet Union would have the option of returning its forces to the West German-Austrian borders within two weeks, with minor losses. Before them would lie a denuclearized zone defended by 12 German divisions, perhaps reinforced by a French contingent. The situation would be as it is presently, minus the United States Seventh Army (300,000+ men) with its tactical nuclear weapons and air support. With a reinforcement capability of 40 divisions per month, the Soviet Union would be capable of quickly mounting a conventional force of breakthrough strength. The United States, facing a return across the Atlantic (where Soviet submarine strength would be felt), would in essence, be denied its alternative to the choice of a limited armaments defeat in Europe or nuclear holocaust. Even if the United States were able to airlift special combat teams equipped with Davy Crockett mortars and Sergeant missiles, late-arriving forces of this type would be confounded by the Soviet attack strategy of keeping NATO and Soviet frontal forces so intermingled as to preclude the use of tactical nuclear weapons.

Though it is an error to assume malevolent intent on the part of the Soviet Union in all disengagement and disarmament negotiations, it is equally ill-advised to rely in matters of great consequence upon Soviet compliance with the terms of international agreements. I have not discussed the political consequences, beneficial and otherwise, of this form of disengagement. The fact that the scheme, if accepted, would destroy the present European power parity for limited warfare and make possible a situation wherein the defense of Western Europe would become completely dependent upon United States willingness to initiate an intercontinental missile exchange, is sufficient ground for its rejection by the West.

STRIP DISENGAGEMENT AND ITS CONSEQUENCES

Some statesmen, who, like Spaak of Belgium (in 1952) and Mendès-France (in 1959), would proceed toward a militarily stable relaxation of tensions in Europe by modest steps, have proposed demilitarized strips between the great forces. The Mendès-France plan, though rejected by De Gaulle, has much to recommend it and is sufficiently representative for use in analysis here.

Mendès-France would have a Germany traversed north to south by a demilitarized zone 30 miles wide along the line where NATO and Warsaw Pact forces now confront each other across barbed wire and mine fields. This zone, inspected and policed by United Nations Security troops, would follow the Czechoslovakian-German border to Austria. On both sides of the demilitarized strip, only the conventionally armed force of the nations whose territory was affected would remain. Those areas, called Zone One, would be of a specified depth, perhaps 50 to 100 miles, and would also be inspected for the presence of foreign troops, massing of troop formations, and missile-launching vehicles with a range greater than 15 miles. The final zone, behind Zone One on either side, would be unrestricted in depth, arms, and forces.

Through this redeployment nothing is gained or lost either by an aggressor or a defender in an unlimited European war; the population centers and military complexes of either side remain helplessly vulnerable to the missiles of the other. The long-range missile forces cannot be "disengaged," and the balance of terror must be relied upon to provide stability. In the cases of attack with limited weaponry, a small advantage over the present situation accrues to the defender, hence, in all likelihood, to the West. A conventional attack by the concerted forces of the Warsaw Pact, led by the forward 25 Soviet mechanized divisions, would have to cover from 80 to 130 miles before reaching NATO lines. NATO would be far less subject to surprise attack and could hope to inflict severe losses upon spearhead forces as they crossed the 30 miles of Zone Zero. If the NATO Commander elected to fight a conventional defense, he would be in no worse position than he is at present; if the Soviet forces violated Eastern Zone One, he would be free to bring non-German forces into positions in Western Zone One. If the NATO Commander elected to initiate the use of tactical nuclear weapons in defense, he would have time to withdraw the West German forces rapidly across Zone One, thus extending the area within which the Soviet forces would be subject to tactical nuclear bombardment.

In the event that the forces of the East initiated an attack with tactical nuclear weapons, the NATO defense position would not be inferior to its present one. In either case, a surprise missile attack could not be prevented, and losses could be crippling, depending upon the nature of defensive deployment. The attacker would be denied his present forward launch sites in the first hours; his ability to take advantage of the shock suffered by the defense by pressing the attack with armor and mechanized infantry would be reduced by the greater distance to be crossed in reaching the defending forces.

The United States would retain its forces, combat-ready, in Europe; the United States' option of meeting an attack of limited arms from the East without commiting itself to a transpolar missile exchange would be maintained. A small but possibly important improvement in the Western position in defense against surprise attack would be accomplished with no appreciable sacrifice in the effectiveness of NATO's "forward strategy."

Figures for the simple financial cost of the redeployment are both unavailable and difficult to reckon, but such an undertaking would necessarily be very costly. The present fixed installations, not only for tactical defense, but for maintenance, housing, communications, and forward central supply for a huge army would have to be moved 65 to 115 miles and reestablished. It is doubtful that over-all gains from the strip disengagement over the present situation would justify the expense.

In today's confrontation a "disengagement" already exists, though the zone of noncontact between forces is only a few hundred yards wide. Inflammatory military incidents have been few; when they have occurred, the disciplined reaction of forward troops and officers has been prudent. Indeed, the actions of aroused civilian groups have been more dangerous than those of the armed forces. The two great armies have stood face-to-face for more than a decade, and appear to have developed a great tolerance for minor irritations and high tensions. The decade has witnessed the growth of a stability along the Iron Curtain, which has resulted from habitual discipline and prudent patterns of behavior rather than from spatial separation. Stability in today's Europe is not threatened so much by the proximity of opposing armies as by the escalation of intentional though miscalculated probes and by the technological syndrome which gives so great an advantage to the side delivering a nuclear first-strike. Neither of these principal threats to the military stability of Europe is reduced by the "strip disengagement."

Mendès-France has argued that the adoption of his proposal would be a first step in solving the "German problem." The solution to the German problem is no more or less than reunification; without reunification the problem will just have to be lived with. There is nothing in the strip disengagement formula that in itself advances the process of reunification. This will occur only in a general settlement between the Soviet Union and West Germany.

The populations within the 30-mile Zone Zero would doubtless intermingle freely, though compatibility is not to be assumed. The East German forces occupying Eastern Zone One would necessarily seal the border with Zone Zero in order to prevent the outflow of skilled workers. There is no evidence that a trend toward government more responsive to the wishes of the governed would result from the removal of Soviet troops from Zone One. The prospects of rebellion by East Europeans in their Zone One are slight; even if the national armies could be brought to oppose the national governments involved, there is nothing but a loss of prestige to prevent Soviet forces from reentering Zone One to "restore the peace."

I have found no advocacy of the strip disengagement idea by Warsaw Pact leaders, nor have West German leaders shown any enthusiasm for the idea. In overview, then, the Mendès-France type of disengagement is unlikely to meet with acceptance by the Soviet Union, its proposal by the United States would annoy its NATO ally, Germany, while its adoption would entail expenses beyond its value as a stabilizing device. The plan offers no progress toward a general settlement of differences between East and West, and no clear prospect of encouraging liberalization within Eastern Zones One and Two, but does promise a slight improvement in the NATO military position. Hence, an evaluation of the strip disengagement idea for American foreign policy must be a negative one.

THE BUFFER ZONE DISENGAGEMENT

There have been many Western proposals for the creation of a buffer zone of states in Central Europe, partly as a result of Khrushchev's endorsement of the Rapacki Plan. It should be noted in the beginning that Eastern proposals of buffer state disengagement have been few, vague, and tentative; none of these since 1956 has included a provision for German reunification. Further, the Rapacki Plan, even in its revised version, is a plan not for the disengagement of armed forces but for the creation of a nonnuclear zone, for the disengagement of tactical nuclear weaponry. It should not be assumed that Soviet endorsement of this plan implies a willingness to negotiate the disengagement of nonnational forces in Central Europe and German reunification.

From the various Western proposals, I have selected a composite model closely resembling the Gaitskell Plan of February 1958, and the Social Democratic Party "Deutchland" Plan of March 1959. The following is a reasonably representative Western idea of disengagement in Central Europe, and may profitably be used for analysis.

A) Foreign armed forces would be withdrawn gradually from both parts of Germany, and from Poland and Czechoslovakia. B) The national armed forces remaining in the zone would be limited in size so that a rough balance of power would exist between Germany and its Eastern neighbors. The introduction of manufacture of nuclear weapons would be forbidden, and the area would be inspected for compliance with this prohibition and with the troop ceilings. C) Germany would be reunified in general elections. D) States in the disengaged zone would withdraw from NATO and the Warsaw Pact. E) A security treaty would be signed by the major powers, as well as by the states in the disengaged zone, guaranteeing the territorial borders within the zone.

The military case for this type of disengagement appears to be stronger than the political one. The present NATO defense of Europe is dependent primarily upon the United States strategic nuclear deterrent, the United States Seventh Army with its arsenal of tactical weapons, and the ground strength of the West German Army. Conversely, the primary threats to NATO are the Soviet MRBM nuclear force with a first-strike capability, the proximity of large, fast-moving Soviet forces capable of mounting a powerful attack with little or no warning, and the advantage of the Soviet Union in reinforcement ability—the capability of concentrating numerically superior forces in breakthrough strength.

What then would be the effect of the "buffer state" disengagement? First, neither the Soviet MRBMs nor the United States ICBMs would be affected; both sides would retain their deterrents. (Germany would be, at least temporarily, denied the option of joining the nuclear club.) Second, United States forces with full nuclear arsenal would remain in Europe, probably deployed along the Franco-German border. These forces would not be stationed as far forward as they are now, but they would remain capable of engaging with aircraft and tactical rockets Soviet forces moving to the attack across the central plain. Once Soviet violation of Polish and Czech borders became known, mobile United States short-range missile, mortar, and artillery teams could be moved to forward positions with the West German Army. In essence, the Soviet (and NATO) opportunity of surprise ground attack in force would be lost. The Red Army would be forced to launch a ground attack from points 500 miles east of its present position. NATO officers would be given a valuable interval in which to choose their response and launch air and missile strikes against the approaching forces. This clearly represents a net loss in the Soviet military position and a gain for NATO. Third, the withdrawal of the West German Army from NATO would not greatly change its function or its ability in an East-West war in Europe. In either case it would be defending its homeland. In reunification it could absorb the present East German Army, which is less than one quarter its size, scattering its men through all divisions so that no individual units would be of questionable loyalty in battle. Such an army, consisting of 12 excellent divisions or more, would be sufficiently formidable in defense that any Soviet attack with a chance of success would necessarily involve very large forces, forces of a dimension to make general war inevitable; thus, the German Army could perform the "tripwire" task as well as the United States Seventh Army. In case of attack, or imminent attack, NATO could reinforce the forward German forces, even to the extent of sending Honest John and Davy Crockett teams to positions near the front.

The Soviet reinforcement advantage would not be appreciably affected by the redeployment. The Soviet Union would retain the ability to mass and move enough conventional ground power to win a nonnuclear European war without the advantage of surprise. The Gaitskell—SDP model of disengagement in Central Europe would considerably improve NATO's military position for a war of limited nuclear weapons. It would result in a slight improvement in NATO's position for a conventional war, and it would make little change in its unenviable situation in a European unlimited war. Judged by the military merits alone, the United States would do well to press negotiations for Soviet acceptance of the plan.

A number of political problems of some magnitude are presented by this model of Central Europe, however. Not the least of these is the unlikelihood of cooperation by Gaullist France in the redeployment of the non-German NATO forces now in Germany. The stationing of a quarter million or more American, British, and Canadian troops in France would seem to accord ill with De Gaulle's image of France as the hub of an independent European third force in World politics. His present refusal to allow the reserve positioning of United States nuclear warheads in France indicates a view of French interests hardly compatible with the permanent redeployment of NATO main battle strength to France. As noted previously, De Gaulle has stated a disinclination to support any known disengagement scheme for military reasons. French refusal on this score would preclude NATO negotiations with the Soviet Union for the disengagement in question. A further problem is encountered when one imagines the difficulties attending the peacetime stationing of another quarter million foreign troops in the already overcrowded Low Countries.

The long-range position of a unified Germany not aligned with NATO is a subject due careful thought by Western leaders considering a Central European disengagement. A well-armed, independent, united Germany certainly would hold the central and crucial position in the European power balance. Once in this position, it is hard to imagine how either NATO or the Warsaw Pact could prevent the acquisition of the nuclear armaments by West Germany. The prospect of Germany as a completely independent nuclear power, able to tip the European power balance, holds little charm for the Soviet Union, Britain, France, East Europe, or the United States. A divided Germany is certainly a destabilizing factor in the present configuration, but a unified, independent, nuclear-armed Germany would be a factor of serious instability in Europe and one of no presently clear benefit to United States interests in Europe.

Would the departure of Soviet troops in disengagement enable Poland and Czechoslovakia to pursue independent foreign policies? The present Soviet coercive power regarding the foreign (and domestic) policies of those two nations is not embodied in the few Red Army divisions stationed on their soil. Rather, this power lies in the existence of the massive Red Army within the Soviet borders and the lack of Western ability to intervene in force in their defense. Disengagement would not affect this situation. Some degree of independence has been demonstrated by Poland and other satellite states, even with Soviet troops present in their territories. It is doubtful that the removal of Red Army troops in a disengagement would markedly increase this independence in foreign relations.

The plan for the creation of a buffer zone of states with controlled armaments in Central Europe may be evaluated for United States foreign policy as follows. The withdrawal of foreign troops from both parts of Germany and from Poland and Czechoslovakia would improve the NATO military position, but necessary redeployment of NATO forces to positions in France would almost surely be disallowed by De Gaulle. Accomplishment of this disengagement would create a unified Germany in circumstance of very questionable benefit to United States interests. The buffer zone plan provides little to effect a liberation of the foreign policies of Eastern European nations from Soviet domination. Finally, there is no reason to believe that the Soviet Union would accept such a disengagement, and several good reasons to expect that it would summarily refuse the venture. Hence, disengagement in Central Europe by the establishment of a buffer zone of nations cannot be recommended as a feasible and beneficial element of United States foreign policy.

Does the rejection of all three models of disengagement imply long-term acceptance of the *status quo* in Europe? Three power vacuums are proposed; one simply invites the resurgence of force, one is too small to be of value, and the last, if it were acceptable to the nations involved, would appear to encourage the development within of a force undesirable to all concerned nations outside. The rejection of all three proposals implies that the evolution of a stable, undivided Europe must take place, not within or across power vacuums, but in the presence and with the influence of military strength, including that of the two superpowers. All of Europe, East and West, is coming to view the division as unnatural, uneconomic, and undesirable; yet severe political differences remain and distrust abounds within and between the blocs. The next decade should witness incremental, creative economic and political experimentation between East and West Europe, and we should be aware from the beginning that this process will create tensions, dislocations, and conflicts that will tempt both sides to precipitous actions. If in this period of experimentation the West makes clear the peaceful intent of its policy, the presence of strong military power on both sides can be a stabilizing influence both to discourage rash exploitation of tensions and to give both sides the confidence necessary to proceed with experimentation for common gain. As political trust and economic interdependence grows between Eastern and Western Europe in such a way as to threaten neither the United States nor the Soviet Union, gradual military disengagement may occur—but as a result, not as a cause, of political settlement.

The Decision-Making Process in the European Economic Community

FAY R. PAPA

The signing of the Rome Treaty in March 1957 has been followed by a broad spectrum of predictions regarding the viability of the European Economic Community. Some have argued that the successes of the organization in harmonizing external tariffs and working out an agreed program for agriculture point to the inevitability of a politically united Western Europe. Others, less optimistic in outlook and orientation, view the Community as a temporary and inherently unstable "alliance" between visionary federalists and shrewd *laissez-faire* economists and businessmen, whose goals are mutually incompatible and whose interests are ultimately bound to diverge. Still others, critical of the secrecy and exclusiveness of decision-making within a bureaucracy, deplore the Community's casual legitimization of bureaucratic methods and procedures.

What is, in fact, the decision-making process in the European Economic Community? What are the actual working relationships among the three institutions of the Community: the Commission, the Council, and the Parliament? Is the positive momentum of integration irreversible? To what extent is policy initiated and executed by groups of individuals with only a vague and informal responsibility and accountability?

The Dialogue between Council and Commission

At the center of the decision-making process within the European Economic Community is the Commission, a novel type of international machinery. Adhering to the classic characteristics of a traditional international secretariat, the Commission is composed of nine members who, although appointed by the Community's member states, are, according to Article 157 of the "Treaty Establishing The European Economic Community," to be independent and impartial international civil servants acting ". . . in the general interest of the Community." [1] Endowed with autonomous dynamism, the Commission, according to Article 155 of the Treaty of Rome, is to ". . . assure that the provisions of [the] Treaty . . . are carried out . . . ," to ". . . formulate recommendations . . . if it [the Treaty] expressly so provides or if the Commission considers this necessary . . . ," and to ". . . have power itself to take decisions . . ."

Although armed with impartiality and independence, initiative and supervisory powers, and a highly flexible but definitive timetable, the Commission has not presumed to dictate policies to the constituent states of the Community. The tactics of the Commission have been to employ and engage the member governments in the entire process of policy formulation and execution. While the Commission has been sharply criticized by its inventor for its "deference" to member states, [2] it has by this method avoided the creation of competing and parochial national and international bureaucracies, by harmonizing and interlocking those structures at all levels. In fact, Walter Hallstein, President of the Commission since 1958, views the states and their institutions as organs of the Community. [3] When the Commission hesitates to exert extreme pressure on governments, the Commission may be simply exercising its statutory position of defining and applying the timetable laid down in the Treaty.

Before drawing up its proposals, the Commission consults with the Council and its Permanent Representatives and with groups of experts called upon from each of the six national administrations. Hallstein has estimated that within a single year over 910 meetings were held with more than 16,000 governmental and nongovernmental experts. [4] In all such confrontations the Commission, acting as an organ of mediation whose impartiality is unquestioned, seeks to accommodate the national points of view. The Commission, however, goes

[1] *Treaty Establishing the European Economic Community: Rome, 25th March, 1957* (London, Her Majesty's Stationery Office, 1962). (Referred to herein as the Treaty of Rome.)

[2] Paul-Henri Spaak, "Europe 1964," *The Atlantic Community Quarterly,* II, No. 2 (Summer 1964), p. 169.

[3] *Débats, Assemblée Parlementaire Européenne,* Séances du 15 au 19 octobre 1962, p. 108.

[4] *Ibid.,* p. 109.

beyond this role. As Hallstein has commented, the agreements which a flexible and agile Commission extracts from these meetings are not the lowest common denominator but represent a "community interest" which entails temporary sacrifices of "purely national interests." [5] Decisions thus are not the result of traditional compromises but rest rather on an objective appraisal of the requirements of the Community as a whole.

Both the institutions and the decision-making process in the European Economic Community are a combination of traditional intergovernmental practices and innovative supranational techniques. Thus, although the Council of Ministers, EEC's intergovernmental institution, would seem to correspond to the familiar loose association among states based upon national separateness, it also presents some significant differences from that kind of association. While it is true that virtually all new decisions that might expand the functions of the Community must be approved unanimously by the Council, Article 148 of the Rome Treaty also stipulates that all other resolutions may be reached by a majority or a qualified majority. A government is thereby committed to decisions to which it itself may be opposed. This provision alone is a remarkable variation in the basic operating principles of international organizations, most of which have been initially paralyzed or subsequently obstructed by a rigid decision-making process based on the requirement of unanimity.

It has been argued that the integrative effects of a Council of Ministers are naturally limited.[6] Ministers are burdened by overcrowded schedules and must represent and defend divisive national interest. Moreover, individual ministers may be reluctant to propose new steps toward integration for fear of being accused of thereby promoting some specific national interest. Although the Council of Ministers usually meets once each month for about three days, decision-making and consensus-gathering are continuous processes, and in this the Council is an active participant. To facilitate constant and current consultations and communication between the Commission and governmental representatives, the Council established, as was authorized by Article 151 of the Treaty, a Committee of Perma-

[5] Walter Hallstein, *United Europe: Challenge and Opportunity* (The William L. Clayton Lecture Series, 1961–1962. Washington, D.C., The European Community Information Service, 1962), p. 17.
[6] Ernst B. Haas and Peter H. Merkl, "Parliamentarians Against Ministers: The Case of Western European Union," *International Organization*, XIV, No. 1 (Winter 1960), p. 50.

nent Representatives in Brussels. The Permanent Representatives prepare the decisions of the Council. They provide the continuity, stability, familiarity, and informal atmosphere which ministerial councils ordinarily lack. Its procedures are comparable to those within the Commission.

Like the Commission, the Committee of Permanent Representatives has been responsible for expanding considerably the circle of involvement in Community decision-making and consensus-gathering. The Committee is authorized to convoke working groups of experts and to assign them special tasks; for example, with respect to agriculture and technical assistance to underdeveloped areas. Furthermore, each of these *ad hoc* committees can request additional groups of experts to aid in the gathering of data and the preparation of reports.

Although some observers have feared that initiation in policy may pass from the Commission to the Permanent Representatives and ultimately to the individual states, it has been noted that the Committee considers itself a Community institution.[7] While the Permanent Representatives defend their national points of view, they are also influenced by participation in Community affairs and have become advocates of Community solutions within their own governments.[8] Hallstein, certainly one of the originators of the Commission's conscious policy of encouraging wide participation in the preparation of decisions, has noted that the talent and additional *expertise* provided by the Committee and its myriad working groups are invaluable to the Commission in carrying out its statutory obligations.[9]

It is important, moreover, to note that in meetings of the Committee of Permanent Representatives and the Council, which usually consider only these problems that have defied solution at the level of the experts, the Commission is present as the seventh member. As the representative of the Community, the Commission can exercise its positive power to steer, push, mediate, and maneuver

. . . often in ways that will make anything but exceptional use of the veto extremely difficult. . . .[10]

[7] Leon N. Lindberg, *The Political Dynamics of European Economic Integration* (Stanford, Stanford University Press, 1963), p. 79.

[8] Roy Pryce, *The Political Future of the European Community* (London, John Marshbank Limited, 1962), p. 33.

[9] *Débats, Assemblée Parlementaire Européenne*, Séances de juin–juillet 1960, p. 69.

[10] William Pickles, "Political Power in the European Economic Community," *Journal of Common Market Studies*, II, No. 1, p. 83.

Whatever the specific origin of a policy proposal, the Commission is always responsible, in one way or another, for its maturation.

The relationship between the Council and the Commission can best be described as a dialogue. Accordingly, it is neither possible nor profitable to define explicitly what is meant by the "balance of power" in policy-initiation and policy-making between those two unique organizations. The dialogue is continuous, flexible, cooperative, and minimally institutionalized. To achieve this process of continuous interaction, the Council and the Commission have purposely engaged national officials at all levels in the decision-making and consensus-gathering processes. In fact, it is the aim of the French Government to have its administrative elite "pass through" the Commission.[11] National civil servants are therefore "detached" for four or five years to serve in the Commission and then are reassigned to important posts in Paris. The methods of copenetration and participation commit the six member states and their administrations to the procedures, decisions, and goals of the Community. Certain further questions remain. How far is this delicate equilibrium precariously predicated upon the active cooperation of the six member governments? Moreover, can a third party, the Parliament, assert its role in the decision-making process without disrupting its flexibility?

The Powers and Function of the European Parliamentary Assembly

It has been aptly observed that most assemblies established within contemporary European organizations tend to dissipate their effectiveness by performing disparate and diffuse educational, supervisory, and conversational functions.[12] The European Parliamentary Assembly, which has called itself the European Parliament, seeks "deliberately" and "self-consciously" to create a federal Europe.[13] Although its statutory authority is limited, the Parliament has stressed its latent

---

[11] Leon Lindberg, p. 85.

[12] Kenneth Lindsay, *European Assemblies: The Experimental Period 1949–1959* (London, Stevens and Sons, 1960).

[13] Ernst B. Haas concludes that the Assembly has played a crucial role within the European Coal and Steel Community by its efforts to stimulate the conclusion of new treaties and to facilitate the growth of practices typical of federal arrangements. *The Uniting of Europe* (Stanford, Stanford University Press, 1958), p. 390.

legislative powers and has attempted to prescribe policies for the Council and the Commission.

One of the most essential prerogatives of a national parliament is its control of the executive. While the European Parliament has no statutory control over the Council of Ministers, it can force the Commission to resign. Article 144 of the Treaty of Rome reads as follows:

If the vote of censure is carried by a two-thirds majority of the votes cast, and representing a majority of the members of the Assembly, the members of the Commission shall collectively resign their office.

A new Commission, however, is appointed by the Community's six constituent states, not by the Assembly.

The motion of censure, although a formidable weapon, is largely irrelevant.[14] The European Parliament and the Commission are both institutions of the Community. More often than not, those two organizations opt for a "community" solution to a given problem. The Commission also looks to the Parliament for a vigorous endorsement of its proposals. The Parliament seems to have been consistently in favor of the centralization of powers within the Commission. On numerous occasions the Commission has deliberately abstained from including in its initial proposals to the Council certain provisions which it was confident the Parliament would later introduce.[15]

Since the Commission relies upon the European Parliament for support of "community" policies, it has become customary for the President of the Commission to report regularly to the Assembly. According to Article 143 of the Treaty of Rome, the Assembly is required to discuss the Commission's annual report "in open session." In presenting the Commission's report to the Assembly, Hallstein has initiated lengthy and lively debates by his appraisal of the Community's economic policies and political objectives.

Although those reports are debated intensively, economic policies contested, and political objectives asserted, the European Parliament's primary intention is to intervene in the decision-making dialogue between the Council and the Commission. In attempting to influence the Council, the Parliament finds some support in the provisions of the Treaty. Before making decisions, the Council is obligated by the Treaty to seek the advisory opinion of the Parliament in twenty-three

[14] See statements by Frederick van Dijk to the European Parliament. *Débats, Assemblée Parlementaire Européenne,* Séances du 15 au 19 octobre 1962, p. 123.

[15] "The Parliament of the European Communities," *Political and Economic Planning,* XXX, No. 478 (March 9, 1964), 83.

different cases.[16] For example, Article 14, which deals with the time-table for the reduction of tariffs, reads as follows:

The provisions of this article may be amended by the Council, acting by unanimous vote on a proposal of the Commission after the Assembly has been consulted.

Generally, consultation is required for important decisions, but some critics have suggested that the selection of topics for obligatory consultation was made in a haphazard fashion, without general and uniform criteria.[17] By May 1963 the Parliament had been consulted 71 times: 26 times concerning agricultural matters; 16 on social matters; 16 concerning freedom of establishment and free supply of services; 5 times on administrative matters; 3 times concerning rules of competition; 3 times concerning external relations; and twice concerning transport.

The European Parliament, however, is not satisfied with the operation of the consultative process. Whenever decision-making between the Council and the Commission gains final momentum, the Parliament's opinions tend to have less weight as the pressures to reach an agreement are intensified. To guarantee that its proposals are given serious attention, the Parliament has strongly urged major revisions of the current techniques and practices of consultation.

Instead of the existing haphazard listing of issues requiring consultation with the Assembly, the latter has proposed that the Council should seek its advice on all important issues. A general requirement of this nature would eliminate instances in which the Parliament has been informed of a Council decision by reading it in the Community's *Journal Officiel*. Hallstein, usually a supporter of a stronger role for the Parliament, has commented to the Assembly that, while he would favor additional parliamentary participation, he would not support a rigid or general rule. This kind of regulation would, according to Hallstein, inhibit the Council's flexibility and its ability to cooperate, would endanger delicate and confidential negotiations, and might give rise to unacceptable delays.[18]

[16] See the following Articles of the Rome Treaty: 7, 14, 43, 54, 56, 57, 63, 75, 87, 100, 126, 127, 201, 212, 228, 235, 236, and 238.

[17] Raymond Lane-Legrand and Bubba Elena, "Le pouvoir de consultation de l'Assemblée Parlementaire Européenne," *Revue du Marché Commun*, No. 39 (September 1961), p. 315.

[18] Walter Hallstein, "Intervention lors du débat consacré par le parlement européen au rapport de M. Furler relatif aux compétences et aux pouvoirs du parlement européen, le 27 juin 1963," *Commission* [Communauté économique européenne], p. 15.

In addition to seeking to participate in all major decisions by the Council and the Commission, the Parliament has demanded that each of those organizations account for its policy positions during the final dialogue. A parliamentary committee observed in 1963 that, in reaching a final agreement, the Council and the Commission revise and alter proposals so that they bear little resemblance to the proposal which the Parliament was asked to evaluate.[19] It has even been suggested that the Commission submit its own proposals to the Council with little prior consultation or guarantee of agreement. This procedure would tend to locate responsibility for policy more sharply as between the Commission and the Council; it would also result in more frequent rejections of the Commission's proposals by the Council.[20]

In responding to these suggestions, Hallstein has recognized that the Commission is responsible in part to the Parliament. Thus, he suggested in 1963 that the Commission's proposals to the Council, as well as the final proposals as amended by the Council, should be published. Moreover, he promised that the members of the Commission would state their views on parliamentary reports during committee meetings and during the public debates in the Assembly. More than once, however, Hallstein has reaffirmed his conviction that reaching an agreement is more essential to the viability of the Community than attempting to involve the European Parliament effectively in the final stages of the decision-making process. Thus, the Parliament could not expect the Commission to refrain from defending its own proposals in meetings with the Council when those proposals differ from the recommendations of the Parliament. Moreover, information would be withheld from the Parliament when it is confidential or essentially technical in character.[21]

Most of the suggestions of the European Parliament, if accepted by the Commission, could readily be introduced into the working procedures of the Community. One proposal, however, would involve an amendment to the Treaty of Rome. The Deringer Committee recommended in 1962 that the Council be obligated to request a

[19] Hans Furler, "Rapport fait au nom de la commission politique sur les compétences et les pouvoirs du Parlement européen," *Assemblée Parlementaire Européenne, Documents de Séance 1963–1964,* Doc. 31, June 14, 1963, para. 67.

[20] Deringer Comité des Présidents, "Rapport sur le cinquième rapport général sur l'activité de la Communauté économique européenne," *Assemblée Parlementaire Européenne, Documents de Séance 1962–1963,* Doc. 74, October 5, 1962, para. 123.

[21] Walter Hallstein, "Intervention lors du débat . . . ," pp. 7–10.

second report from the Parliament if extensive changes in the original proposal were being contemplated. If Parliament then adopted its second report by a two-thirds majority, the Council could not reject the report except by a unanimous vote.[22] Hallstein unequivocally repudiated this proposal, for its acceptance would destroy the "equilibrium" between the Council and the Commission. This alteration would, moreover, increase unanimity voting when the ultimate objective of the Treaty is to introduce majority voting, slowly but inevitably.[23]

The European Parliament, frustrated in its attempts to become an equal party in the decision-making dialogue between the Council and the Commission, has advocated a variety of remedies, all of which could conceivably subvert the flexibility of the system as it presently operates, and decrease the probability of reaching agreement. The structure, procedures, and organization of the European Parliament, however, readily lend themselves to certain types of participation in the Community's decision-making process.

The European Parliament is organized not on the basis of nationality but according to political affiliation. The 142 members of this Assembly, nominated by the respective Parliaments from among their members, are encouraged to formulate and debate "community" policies instead of reiterating and reinforcing national antagonisms.[24] Within each of three major political groups, the Christian Democrats, the Socialists, and the Liberals, parliamentarians of six different countries acquire the techniques and methods of reaching agreements, just as the six ministers have learned to accommodate their differences in the Council.

According to Article 142 of the Treaty of Rome, the Assembly is alone responsible for its internal organization and procedures. The formation and support of political groups is, consequently, given strong impetus in the Parliament's rules of procedure.[25] Each politi-

[22] Deringer Comité des Présidents, para. 76.
[23] Walter Hallstein, "Intervention du débat . . . ," p. 14.
[24] According to Article 138 of the Treaty of Rome, representation is as follows: France, Germany, and Italy, 36 delegates each; the Netherlands, 14 delegates; and Luxembourg, 6 delegates.
[25] "Rules of Procedure of the European Parliament," *Political and Economic Planning*, XXX, No. 478 (March 9, 1964), 98–118. See esp. Arts. 36–40. The European Parliament, at its first meeting on March 19, 1958, adopted *mutatis mutandis* the rules of procedure of its predecessor, the Common Assembly of the Coal and Steel Community. See Pierre Wigny's evaluation of the experience of the Common Assembly, "L'Assemblée Parlementaire dans l'Europe des Six," *Communauté Européenne du Charbon et de l'Acier 1957–1958*, Doc. 14.

cal group, consisting of a minimum of seventeen persons, receives financial support from the Parliament's funds; additional support is provided for the expansion of each group in proportion to the number of its members beyond seventeen. This support enables each group to maintain a small secretariat and a permanent office, and to publish a monthly newsletter. Meetings are frequent and are often attended by members of the Commission. For example, Walter Hallstein and M. Lambert Schaus attend the meetings of the Christian Democrats, while M. Robert Marjolin and Dr. Sicco Mansholt attend the meetings of the Socialists. During the Assembly's debates, each political group, represented by its President or some other member with particularly pertinent technical expertise, presents and contests proposals.

While the Assembly's political groups dilute the prejudices and intensity of nationality and foster a "community" orientation and out-look, its committee system concurrently supplies the Assembly with its most effective means of supervising the work of the Council and the Commission and participating in the decision-making process. The European Parliament has thirteen permanent committees whose sub-ject matter roughly corresponds to the division among the nine General Directorates of the Commission. The largest of these com-mittees consists of thirty-three members; the usual number is twenty-nine. Committee meetings are far more frequent than the plenary sessions of the Assembly, and are held *in camera*.[26]

Since committee meetings are frequent and secret, and since com-mittee members are or become competent technical experts, Par-liament can exercise continuous supervision over the work of the Council and the Commission. Committees can invite members of the Council and the Commission to closed hearings to explain decisions already taken, to probe current business, and to ascertain positions taken by the Commission on parliamentary reports to the Council. Since this testimony is received in confidence, influential parliamentary leaders are kept well informed without a broadcasting of the disagree-ments that inevitably arise within the Commission and the Council of Ministers. Moreover, since the Commission is interested in securing wide participation in its consensus-gathering, it can certainly benefit from the expertise and interest of parliamentary leaders and com-mittees.

[26] During the years 1959–63, the average number of Assembly plenary ses-sions per year was 7. In this same period, the average number of committee meetings per year was 219.

In spite of the supervisory and educational function of the parliamentary committees, the Assembly has not become an equal third-party in the decision-making process of the European Economic Community. The European Parliament "engages" many national parliamentarians in the procedures and problems of the Community. Yet, it has none of the traditional powers of a legislative body. At a time when there is great concern about the effective role of national parliaments, the European Parliament has even fewer powers than national legislators enjoy. Does the absence of an effective parliamentary control at the Community level indicate that the Community is "undemocratic"?

Some Questions for the Future

A democratic system of government can be broadly defined as one in which the citizens possess legitimate instruments for impressing their views and preferences on those who make political decisions. The organizational structure of the European Economic Community appears to many Europeans to be a vast and complex bureaucracy which operates with little or no accountability to elected representatives. All major initiatives are taken by small groups of men whose decisions are far removed from public control. Moreover, the Council and the Commission are empowered to make rules which are directly applicable within each of the six states and which supersede their own legislation and judicial acts.

A vigorous, expanding, and uncontrolled executive bureaucracy and a lethargic and relatively powerless legislature are problems which are not confined to the European Economic Community. In no large contemporary democracy is the legislative branch the supreme power in fact. In many European countries, the initiative in legislation has passed into the hands of the executive.[27] This pronounced trend has many sources. One of the principal causes lies in the responsibilities that governments have assumed for managing a complex industrial society. Governments are now responsible for seeking comprehensive and perhaps irreconcilable social and economic goals, such as full

[27] For comprehensive analyses on the current condition of legislative bodies, see: Karl Dietrich Bracher, "Problems of Parliamentary Democracy in Europe," and Alfred Grosser, "The Evolution of European Parliaments," *Daedalus*, XCIII, No. 1 (Winter 1964), pp. 179–99 and 153–79, respectively; and Gerhard Loewenberg, "Parliamentarism in Western Germany," *The American Political Science Review*, XL (March 1961), 87–102.

employment, high rates of investment, equitable income distribution, and price stability.[28] In this new political environment, leadership and *expertise* are indispensable. If a government is to satisfy the economic and social aspirations of its people, its responsibility cannot be too far in excess of its power.

If the European Economic Community has succeeded in matching responsibility and power, it, like its national counterparts, has not seriously tackled the problems of how to control bureaucracies and how to supervise the process of decision-making. Those who insist that the position of the European Parliament will be the touchstone for judging whether or not the Community is "democratic" may be confusing a traditional and familiar device for achieving democracy with the ideal itself. In the nineteenth century, universal manhood suffrage was a device by which the people came to participate in and to control their governments. The twentieth century has yet to find and use effective and inclusive devices for bringing bureaucratic decision-making into the open where it can be surveyed and controlled; and for placing leaders, commissions, and councils under direct and effective supervision by elected representatives.[29]

To meet the problems of making the European Economic Community both efficient and responsive to the desires of the people whose affairs it runs, numerous proposals have been made for changing its structure and competence and its decision-making processes. Those proposals have been put forward primarily by "European federalists" and "European democrats." The "federalists" are concerned above all in sustaining the momentum of supranational cooperation and institution-making. The European "democrats," on the other hand, seek to moderate the tendency to expand supranational jurisdictions by strengthening the elements of election, control, and accountability.

These questions come to a focus in the decision to fuse the European Economic Community, the European Coal and Steel Community, and the European Atomic Energy Community into a single European Community. This treaty, under preparation by the Com-

[28] For an analysis of the Community's economic goals, see George Lichtheim, *Europe and America: The Future of the Atlantic Community* (London, Thames and Hudson, 1963).

[29] One device already in use but of inherently limited importance is the Scandinavian *Ombudsman*. An officer of parliament, it is his job to investigate complaints from citizens about governmental officials. See Donald C. Rowat, "The Parliamentary Ombudsman," in Roy C. Macridis and Bernard E. Brown, eds., *Comparative Politics,* Rev. ed. (Homewood, Dorsey Press, 1964), pp. 470–81.

mittee of Permanent Representatives, should become effective by January 1, 1969. Meanwhile, at the beginning of 1966 a single Council of Ministers and a single "European Community Commission" (tentative name) will be created. The single Commission will consist of fourteen members between the merger of the executive institutions and the later fusion of the three communities, when it will be reduced to nine. The model for the final treaty and single executive institution is the European Economic Community. It has obviously been concluded by the member states that the methods and structure included therein have been the most successful, or the least objectionable.

The effects of this merger and fusion will be diffuse, contradictory, and controversial. Perhaps it is the intention of the constituent states to intensify their control over the Commission. Then again, a single Commission will have a vastly augmented jurisdiction, which is more likely to accelerate the centralization of power within the Community executive. Consequently, there will be more pressure to give the European Parliament real competence and authority to control the Council and the Commission. Lastly, the conclusion of a new treaty will be interpreted as a sign of the inevitability of full economic—and finally political—integration in Western Europe.

While an assortment of plausible motivations makes prediction very hazardous, it is reasonable to assume that the merger and fusion of the institutions and three communities will provoke the European "democrats" into pressing more vigorously for direct elections to the European Parliament. Thus, with the "moral and psychological power" of a mandate from over 175 million people, the European Parliament would be in a sufficiently strong position to demand significantly augmented authority; for example, that its opinion on proposed legislation become final and that it should play a major role in the appointment of the nine members of the Commission.[30]

It becomes obvious at this point that the steady progression of economic and political integration and the evolutionary advancement of parliamentary authority cannot be simultaneous. It is clear from an analysis of the decision-making process in the European Economic

[30] The European Parliament adopted a Convention on elections by direct universal suffrage on May 17, 1960. (Article 138(3) of the Treaty of Rome directed the Assembly to draw up such a proposal.) The directly elected parliament would consist of 426 members (each representing about 396,000 people). Initially, two-thirds of the Assembly would be directly elected; the remaining third to be temporarily designated by national parliaments. For a full discussion of this Convention see "Direct Elections and the European Parliament," *Political and Economic Planning*, Occasional Paper No. 10, Oct. 24, 1960.

Community that agreement among the six states is critically dependent upon highly pragmatic, delicate, flexible, and informal arrangements. Decision-making is currently a process of seeking technical
solutions to given economic problems. A directly elected parliament
would disrupt this existing equilibrium by introducing conflicting and
competing personalities, parties, promises, and platforms. Moreover,
a directly elected parliament would undermine the present cooperative
orientation of the Community's six member states by challenging and
competing with their authority and performance in the field of economic and political integration.

There are, however, less dramatic, more immediate and practical
methods by which members of the European Parliament can influence
the decisions of the Council and Commission. Given the way in which
power is divided between the Council and the Commission and the
fact that the Council is not responsible to the Assembly, the most
effective means of influencing the action of the ministers is to challenge
them in the national parliaments. In the Netherlands, for example,
membership in the European Parliament is considered a representative's specialty; his *expertise* then enables him to question the ministers
who have served on the Council.[31] Moreover, each national parliament could establish some sort of formal mechanism—for example, a
committee—for dealing with European Community affairs. This committee would then be responsible for supervising the Government's
"European activities."

While these few possibilities, which involve new procedures rather
than extensive alteration of existing equilibria and treaties, are inherent
in the institutions as they exist today, there are dangers in maintaining
the *status quo* of assigning absolute priority to the objectives of economic and political integration. Most observers agree that the
European Economic Community has been fully accepted only by
the most directly interested political elites.[32] It has been further bol-
stered by widespread apathy rather than by the active and determined
loyalty of the broad mass of voters. Once the effects of Community
functions and policies are felt more widely and more directly, they
may be resisted or rejected by previously unconcerned groups and by
wider segments of the population. The political integration of Western

[31] For a description of the six different selection procedures for membership
in the European Parliament, see Kenneth Lindsay, *European Assemblies.*
[32] See, for example: Karl W. Deutsch, "Supranational Organization in the
1960's," *Journal of Common Market Studies,* I, No. 3, pp. 212–19; and Roy
Pryce, *Political Future of the European Community,* p. 68.

Europe therefore requires that, at some point, the public be interested and mobilized in its favor. Of course, the critical problem is to determine at what point widespread participation becomes a necessity as well as a positive contribution to the process of integration.

It is the conscious policy of the Commission to encourage an ever-widening circle of participation in its consensus-gathering and policy-preparation. Positively, this procedure is gradual and orderly and commits individuals to the objectives and codes of action of the Community as their interests are affected. On the other side, however, this practice involves a large number of government officials; it could result in an "engaged" bureaucracy and an "alienated" public.

Acceptance of the European Economic Community, whether by participation or apathy, is directly related to an unequaled period of prosperity throughout most of Western Europe. The Commision has been given a group of difficult and perhaps incompatible economic targets. The goals of full employment, high investment, equitable income distribution, and price stability require difficult compromising between liberals and socialists, and between those favoring the operation of market forces and those who prefer central planning. What would happen to the Community during a minor or severe general economic crisis?

Finally, the conclusion seems inescapable that the entire pragmatic, informal, and flexible decision-making process of the European Economic Community is precariously predicated upon the continuation of governmental cooperation. Agreements have been reached simply because the six governments wanted to reach an agreement. If one of these six or several of the six were to become recalcitrant, the processes of economic and political integration could very easily be obstructed. A government could refuse to attend the sessions of the Council of Ministers. Anti-Community people could be appointed to the Commission. The Commission itself could be subjected to severe pressures. The size of the Commission could be increased, thereby jeopardizing its customary working procedures. Moreover, while the Treaty of Rome contains provisions for unanimity and qualified-majority voting, there is no formula or method by which a deadlock could be broken.

The European Economic Community cannot be confidently viewed as indestructible and as having initiated an irreversible process of economic and political integration. Public participation may be postponed too long. An economic crisis might frighten governments into promulgating separate and parochial remedies. Lastly, the Community, in spite of its novel institutions and imaginative and politically astute procedures, is still only a voluntary association of "independent" national states.

The British Labour Party
and the Council of Europe
1949-1951

GORDON M. ADAMS

There has been no military conflict between the nations of Western Europe since 1945. Not only has war been avoided in that region, but its prospects seem increasingly unlikely. It would appear that Western Europe has become, to a degree, a security community, which Deutsch has defined as a group of people in a territory which has attained agreement that common social problems must and can be resolved by institutionalized procedures, without resort to war, and which has proceeded to create institutions and practices strong enough and wide-spread enough to assure for a long time dependable expectations of peaceful change among its population.[1]

Deutsch also indicates that there are two distinct types of security communities: amalgamated, in which there occurs a formal merger of previously independent units into a larger unit with a common government; and pluralistic, in which the separate governments retain their legal independence. Both types require some organization for peaceful change.[2]

The amalgamated type cannot be said to exist in present day Western Europe. Some states have agreed to submit the decision-making responsibility for certain areas of common interest to common institutions, involving coal and steel, trade (and eventually economic and social policy), and nuclear energy. However, the governments participating in these communities have retained their legal independence to a large degree. The remaining nations of Western

[1] Karl Deutsch, *Political Community and the North Atlantic Area* (Princeton, Princeton University Press, 1957), p. 5.
[2] *Ibid.*, p. 6.

Europe have not been willing to go even this far. Thus, the expectation of some political leaders at the end of the war that, because of common desire and necessity, European federation would be quickly achieved, has not been fulfilled.

Although there are several reasons for this failure, this paper is concerned with one in particular, the refusal of the British Labour Party to commit the United Kingdom to participation in supranational Western European institutions. As Paul Henri Spaak has said:

Britain represented something pure and untarnished and we looked to her—all of us—for moral leadership . . . but, alas, we looked in vain.[3]

This paper will attempt to analyze some of the reasons for this reluctance of the British Labour Party while a Government, and its manifestations in the creation and activity of one Western European institution, the Council of Europe, during the first three years of that organization. It will attempt to show that Britain, under the Labour Party, lacked the necessary background conditions for participation in an amalgamated security community, and that consequently the Labour Government was interested only in the creation of a pluralistic security community.

Labour's Attitude Toward Europe

The British Labour Party's attitude toward and participation in the Council of Europe was strongly influenced by the absence, as Britain under the Labour Government saw it, of the basic conditions necessary for successful integration. Karl Deutsch has given a useful definition of those conditions which appear to be present in the successful creation of security communities in history and absent in abortive attempts to achieve security communities.[4]

Of the ten basic conditions considered essential for the formation of security communities, four can be said to have been absent, to some degree, in the relation between Labour Government's Britain and the Council of Europe countries. The first of these is the compatibility of major values among the politically relevant strata, of which Deutsch finds constitutional democracy, economic structure, and religion to be the most important for the North Atlantic area.

The Labour leaders had struggled long and hard to purge Com-

[3] Anthony Nutting, *Europe Will Not Wait* (London, Hollis and Carter, 1960), p. 3.
[4] Deutsch, pp. 43–58.

munist influence from their party structure and the trade union movement. In this, Ernest Bevin, as head of the Transport and General Workers Union, the largest of the unions, had been particularly successful, and Bevin was foreign secretary in the Labour Government. Believing strongly that Communism was incompatible with and a threat to constitutional democracy, the leaders of Labour distrusted the leadership of several Continental governments, which had formed coalitions with the Communist Party after the war.

The Labour Party emphasized the importance of centralized national planning. While they were instituting such planning in Britain, simultaneously the Communists and Socialists were disappearing from the Continental governments, and were being replaced by non-Socialist governments of the center-right.

Britain, under Labour, became very concerned about a loss of economic sovereignty and the right to plan its economy in a Europe which might be predominantly non-Socialist.[5]

The value they placed on national planning was incompatible with what they perceived to be the Continental emphasis on liberal economics.

Finally, though it is often trite to refer to British empirical, anticonstitutional pragmatism, still the Labour leaders perceived this tradition as quite incompatible with the Continental political attitude. They were skeptical of the revolutionary ideas and proposals emanating from the Continent, and preferred to act with caution, by means of diplomatic feelers and functional approaches, by seeking areas of common interest without attempting to define any specific end goal of "federation" or "total unity."

A second basic condition, absent as far as Labour Britain was concerned, was the existence of a core area with enlarging political and administrative capabilities and superior economic growth. After the war neither Britain nor any other major Western European country could be considered such a core area, since many of them were in ruins and, particularly in Britain's case, were deeply in debt to the United States. Although Deutsch postulates the United States as a potential core area for the North Atlantic area, the Labour leaders, as will be shown, considered their dependence on America as excluding participation in a West European amalgamated security community.

The third basic condition, absent in the British case, was implied

[5] U. W. Kitzinger, *The Challenge of the Common Market* (Oxford, Blackwell, 1961), p. 9.

in the previous paragraph: superior economic growth. Economic recovery rather than economic growth was the immediate concern of
the Labour Government, and this recovery depended heavily on the
assistance of the United States.

The fourth basic condition needs little explanation. Although data
are difficult to obtain, it seems clear that there was a relatively low
mobility of persons between Britain and Western Europe during the
Labour Government period. Indeed, there was little desire on the
part of the British to travel to the war-torn Continent. There was in
Britain a greater desire for mobility in the Commonwealth, a fact
which has particular importance for the six remaining essential conditions of community-building. Although these conditions were present in the relations between Britain and the rest of Western Europe,
they also existed between Britain and the other Commonwealth countries, sometimes to a greater degree than with the Continent, and also
between Britain and the United States. This fact tended to exclude
British participation in an amalgamated Western European security
community as far as the Labour Government was concerned.

In the remaining six conditions enumerated by Deutsch, compatibility existed to a greater degree.

As the first such condition, Deutsch says that the countries participating in the security community should have a way of life different
from that of external areas, and he cites, particularly for the North
Atlantic area, high incomes, the welfare state, and civil liberties. In
spite of the war destruction, the British and Continental peoples still
had a high level of income; their governments guaranteed a good
amount of public welfare; and civil liberties were particularly important in the aftermath of Europe's experience of Nazi Germany and
Fascist Italy. However, the Labour leaders felt strongly that the same
way of life was shared, perhaps to an even higher degree, among the
nations of the Commonwealth. Labour, which was rather uncertain
about the Continental countries' desire to guarantee this way of life,
felt that certainty about the Commonwealth countries, particularly
Canada, Australia, and New Zealand.

Second, Deutsch maintains that there must be a wide range of
mutual transactions among countries that are seeking to form a security community. Although Britain under the Labour Government
had many mutual transactions with the Continent, including trade
and mail flow, an even wider and more voluminous range of transactions was simultaneously being carried out with the Commonwealth.

In addition, Britain was particularly dependent at this time on trade with the United States. The Labour leaders felt that Britain's responsibilities to the sterling area and the maintenance of imperial preference were more important to Britain than amalgamation with Continental Europe.

A third background condition, closely related to the previous two, is the necessity for a sense of community, with horizontal and vertical links of social communication between the countries to be included within the security community. The sense of community between Britain and the Continent was weak; national boundaries had not lost the significance for Britain that they had on the Continent as a result of the World War II. Still, as Deutsch points out, political parties can play an important cross-boundary role, by providing new channels of communication. Although the Labour Party was active in recreating the Socialist International after the war, still the International reflected only a general consensus, had no European program, and had an unimpressive degree of organization.[6]

On the whole, the Labour Government felt a greater sense of community with the Commonwealth than with Continental Europe. The former provided what Deutsch has called in another context an "alternative channel of communication," [7] and the continual exchange of goods, labor, and elite groups among the Commonwealth countries reinforced this channel. The worldwide network of the Commonwealth also helped Britain maintain its role as a world power, a role to which its leaders were deeply committed. Lord Gladwyn has pointed out that Britain did not feel itself part of the Continent, but rather a great power separate from it.[8] Another English commentator has observed that

. . . the Commonwealth is both in its scope and in its nature a more precious association than any European Union could ever be.[9]

As a fourth condition, Deutsch states that there must be an expectation of joint economic rewards as a result of the increased integra-

[6] Ernst Haas, *Consensus Formation in the Council of Europe* (Berkeley, University of California Press, 1959), pp. 9, 39.

[7] Karl Deutsch, from *Nationalism and Social Communication*, excerpts in W. A. Douglas Jackson, *Politics and Geographic Relationships* (Englewood, N.J., Prentice-Hall, 1964), p. 117.

[8] Interview with Lord Gladwyn, British Representative to the Brussels Treaty Permanent Commission, March 13, 1964.

[9] George Watson, *The British Constitution and Europe,* in collection, *European Aspects* (Leyden, Sythoff, 1959), p. 16.

tion of a security community. Yet the Labour Government was more concerned with economic recovery than with growth, and this implied the active participation of the United States, with which the Labour Government was attempting to maintain special ties, which would be incompatible with a commitment to an amalgamated security community. The Labour Government also expected economic rewards from the Commonwealth through the system of Imperial Preferences.

Fifth, Deutsch points to the essential need for a reluctance on the part of all countries in the community to wage fratricidal war. After two devastating wars, this reluctance was clearly as characteristic of the Labour Government as it was of the Continental governments. Again, however, this same reluctance was felt among the states of the Commonwealth, and particularly between Britain and the United States, whose shoulders, as the Labour Government saw, would have to bear the responsibility for the security of Europe.

Sixth and last of the essential basic conditions is the need for mutual responsiveness among politically relevant strata in the participating countries, meaning attention to, and communication and perception of, each other's needs. The Labour Government was, indeed, particularly responsive to two West European needs, recovery and defense. Both involved the active participation of America, with whom the Government was trying to maintain a special relationship. Moreover, the Government was also very responsive to the needs and demands of the members of the Commonwealth.

Deutsch posits three nonessential background factors, two of which were key to the Labour Government's policy in Western Europe. The third, ethnic-linguistic assimilation of the peoples involved in the security community, was not present in Britain's relations with the Continent, though it was very present in her relations with the Commonwealth, increasing the attraction of that community.

Much has been said indirectly of the two remaining nonessential background conditions. The first is the presence of an outside military threat. One key to British Labour's European policy was its perception of this threat and its attempt to meet it, first through the Treaty of Brussels and the decision to maintain British troops in Europe, and second through NATO, in which the United States assumed the ultimate responsibility for the military security of Europe. The Labour Government's realization of the military helplessness of Western Europe and the need for an American guarantee resulted in perhaps their most extensive commitment to the Western European security community. A key element was Labour's desire to promote Europe's economic recovery, which was crucial to its security from the Soviet threat. Consequently, the second Labour commitment to the Western European security community was in the economic field, in the form of the Organization for European Economic Cooperation (OEEC). Again, the assistance of the United States was necessary to guarantee economic recovery.

In summary, four of the ten essential background conditions for the formation of an amalgamated security community were absent so far as Britain under the Labour Government was concerned. The remaining six were present, to varying degrees, but were equally strong, if not stronger, in her relations to the Commonwealth than to Western Europe. Of the three nonessential background conditions, two seem to have been key to the Labour Government's European commitments: an outside military threat, and strong economic ties. Consequently, Britain under the Labour Government was not likely to be interested in entering an amalgamated security community with Continental Western Europe, and was likely, because of her defense and economic interests, to seek a pluralistic security community in that region.

The Role of Institutions

Regional integration, as a process interacting with the background conditions, is thoroughly discussed by Deutsch.[10] However, this paper is not concerned with the process of integration in Western Europe as a whole, but rather with the actions of the British Labour Party with regard to one institution, the Council of Europe.

Ernst Haas has gone a step beyond Deutsch's analysis of regional integration, asserting that

. . . institutions are crucial causative links in the chain of integration.[11]

Previous to the creation of regional institutions, Haas argues, aspirations for regional integration unite only certain individuals and groups peripheral to the national decision-making process. Contacts across national boundaries lack intensity, programs, consensus, and results.

[10] Deutsch, Chap. 3, pp. 70–116.
[11] Ernst Haas, "The Challenge of Regionalism," *International Organization*, XII (1958), 450; see also Ernst Haas, "International Integration: The European and the Universal Process," *International Organization*, XV (1961), 366–92.

Converging expectancies of elites, plus the influence of certain key figures (such as Adenauer, Schuman, De Gasperi, Monnet) may result in the creation of common institutions, as in the case of the European Coal and Steel Community (ECSC). That new institution can then play a key role in accelerating integration, by causing a transnational communication. Conceivably, the decision-making elites in the various states, realizing that the benefits outweigh the sacrifices of unity, will seek to influence the central institutions by forming a regional lobby. This will result in what Haas calls "spill-over," meaning that the actions taken by the central institution in fulfilling a demand will create a situation in which the goal can only be assured by further central action, drawing wider powers to the institution. Governments will thus be forced to delegate more powers to the institution in order that it may take the actions they desire.

Certain institutional characteristics may create better possibilities for spill-over than others. Supranationality, meaning a central decision-making body responsible only to the institution, which can make decisions in the interests of the community, decisions which are binding on its member states, is the most integrative characteristic. Decisions in a supranational framework tend to upgrade the common interest; in other words, they involve the participation of autonomous groups, besides the governments, which in turn help set the terms of further actions.

Intergovernmental institutions, in which the central decision-making body is generally composed of representatives of the member governments, tend to be less integrative; decisions are made either by defining the minimum common denominator (going only as far as the least willing member is willing to go), or by splitting the difference (arriving at an agreement somewhere between the proposals of the members). Such institutions can, however, create decision-making precedents and foster transnational elites. At any rate, whether the institution is supranational or intergovernmental, it is integrative to the degree that it is strong enough to overcome the functional autonomy of its members and survive changes in their policies.

Economic institutions tend to be quite integrative, since they involve mass interests and maximize spill-over by rallying the economic interest groups of the members. They must, however, be functionally specific to have such an effect. Noneconomic institutions advance integration only to the degree that they call for a supranational decision-making process.

Regional parliamentary assemblies, as a special type of institution, utilize a fourth type of decision-making process, parliamentary diplomacy. This means that by the

> . . . existence of a continuing organization with a broad frame of reference, public debate, rules of procedure governing the debate and the statement of conclusions arrived at by some kind of majority vote . . .[12]

such assemblies may set the limits within which the eventual settlement comes about. They are most integrative when they are functionally and responsibly related to specific organs or areas of policy. This is particularly true when they are related to economic policies or organs, or can give birth to supranational decision-making processes.

The Institutional Policy of British Labour

Since the Labour leaders felt that proposals for European federation would inevitably involve supranational decision-making processes, they rejected federalism in their first major policy statement on institutions, *Feet on the Ground* (1948):

> Federation would not solve the immediate problems of Western Europe, while the attempt to achieve it would exaggerate the differences between the West European states instead of exploiting their common interests. . . . An attempt to consolidate Europe now by federation, even if it progressed favorably, might find these countries in a crisis having lost their capacity to react effectively as individuals without having developed the ability to meet the situation as a collective unit.[13]

The Labour leaders endorsed the intergovernmental method:

> Governments are much more likely to carry out decisions already agreed on by their own expert representatives than decisions recommended by a group of international civil servants without executive responsibility.[14]

The two major institutional commitments of the Labour Government to regional integration were the OEEC and the Brussels Pact. They represented Labour's predominant interest in recovery and defense, and reflected the Government's reluctance to go beyond the intergovernmental approach into institutions with large capacity for spill-over. The OEEC was a functionally specific economic organiza-

[12] Ernst Haas, "International Integration: The European and the Universal Process," pp. 367–68.
[13] British Labour Party, *Feet on the Ground, A Study of Western Union* (London, Sept. 1948), p. 20.
[14] *Ibid.*, p. 13.

tion, designed to meet the need for a study of the European requirements for American aid and the allocation of that aid to the participating countries.

> The essential power of the organization rests with the national representatives, and not with a supra-national collective authority. . . . None of the organs of the OEEC can compel its members to carry out its decisions; moreover, decisions are reached by mutual agreement, and not by majority vote. But a country may abstain from committing itself to an agreement without preventing the others from going ahead. . . .[15]

The Brussels Pact represented the Labour response to the Soviet military threat. While committing the Government to stationing British troops on the Continent, it was so organized as to prevent an encroachment on Britain's worldwide responsibilities.

> As in the OEEC, decisions are reached by mutual agreement and not by majority vote . . . the members are not obliged to aim at similar policies outside Europe. . . . Thus Britain may accept commitments in European co-operation which leave her freedom of action in other areas which more directly concern the dominions.[16]

Thus, the first two Labour Government proposals for Western European institutions mirrored their regional motives of military security and economic recovery. Moreover, the characteristics of those institutions reflected the strong desire of the Labour Government to preserve their freedom of action with regard to the countries of the Commonwealth, and the United States, with which they felt a strong sense of community. On the other hand, the creation of the Council of Europe was not due to a British initiative, and it was seen as a threat to Labour's strict devotion to the intergovernmental method.

The Congress of the European Movement, meeting at The Hague in May 1948, which had launched the proposals for a European parliamentary assembly, was heavily influenced by the federalist point of view of the European Movement. Moreover, it brought together nongovernmental political elites, both peripheral and influential, whose participation in a regional institution could have potential spill-over results. The Labour Party had deliberately refused to take an active part in the European Movement, and was reluctant to participate in the nongovernmental Congress at The Hague. Both the Government and the head of the National Executive Council of the Labour Party, Emmanuel Shinwell, refused to send official participants; they con-

[15] *Ibid.,* p. 22.   [16] *Ibid.,* pp. 16–17.

sidered European unity too important to be left to unrepresentative interests.[17]

The approval by the Congress of the projected European Assembly forced the Labour Government to take a stand. Its first objection was to the proposed format.

If an Assembly is to be convened this must, in view of the vital importance of the matter, be done by governments. On the other hand I think that this is not the right time for governments to take this major initiative, when their hands are so full already with urgent and difficult problems . . . it would be best that it should not be brought forward at this stage.[18]

The second Labour objection, as Foreign Secretary Bevin remarked, was that the proposed Assembly was not, from its point of view, the proper response to the needs of Western Europe.

Only when governments have settled the issues of defence, economic co-operation and the political developments which must follow, might it be possible to establish some kind of European Assembly . . . otherwise, it is like putting on the roof before building the house.[19]

Nevertheless, when Foreign Minister Georges Bidault of France put the proposal for the Assembly before the Council of the Brussels Treaty Organization, the Labour Government found itself under heavy pressure from Continental governments and from a British lobby, led by Winston Churchill, to agree to its creation.

The Belgian-French proposals laid before the Council of the Brussels Treaty Organization sought a prestigious Assembly, one which would be able to speak firmly, if not authoritatively, to the European governments. It would have vast legislative and constituent powers, would meet twice a year, and would make decisions by majority vote.

The Labour Government's counterproposals sought to bring the institution under the control of the national governments. It proposed the simultaneous creation of a council of ministers composed of the foreign ministers of the member governments, which would review all Assembly recommendations and, by unanimity only, pass them on as recommendations to the governments. The Assembly was to have a wide, but vague, mandate as a purely consultative organization; it

[17] Godfrey Blakely, *The Attitudes of Major Political Parties in Great Britain. Germany, Italy, Towards the Successive Stages of European Integration* (Unpublished paper done at the College of Europe, Bruges, 1960), p. 12.
[18] Letter from Attlee to Churchill, in European Movement, *The European Movement and the Council of Europe* (London, Hutchinson, 1949), p. 53.
[19] Speech by Bevin to the House of Commons, September 15, 1948, in *ibid.*, p. 53.

was to have no competence in matters of defense and was not to take over the economic work already underway in the OEEC; and governments were to be responsible for the selection of delegates to it.[20]

The Labour delegation's reluctant attitude during the negotiations of the five-power commission set up by the Council of the Brussels Treaty Organization was expressed by its head, Hugh Dalton.

The new organ should not interfere with the OEEC, the most significant example of economic co-operation yet forthcoming where agreement is reached through government representatives meeting in private. It would never have been reached in a European Assembly, attended by no ministers and meeting and voting in public. . . . We are not prepared to merge our identity with that of Europe, if this means cutting ourselves off from our kinsmen in Australia, New Zealand, etc. . . . There are many points where we shall be determined not to give up existing controls which, under our present government, have gained us full employment, social security, fair shares, price control and checks on inflation. . . . The Labour Party has declared itself for a "functional" rather than a "federal" approach to these questions.[21]

Although the Labour delegation finally agreed to the creation of the Council, it was reluctant to allow any bodies other than governments to participate in the negotiations. It was, for example, the only delegation to reserve its position on the European Movement proposals put before the five-power negotiating commission in January 1949.[22]

The organization which emerged conformed to most of Labour's demands. Its structural framework made it unlikely that it could go beyond the desires of the least willing of its members. Of its two organs, the Committee of Ministers and the Consultative Assembly, the former has more power and embodies the intergovernmental point of view. It is composed of the foreign ministers of the member states, and has the power to decide, by unanimity, to forward Assembly resolutions to the governments as recommendations. Its membership and powers are in no way dependent on the will of the Assembly.

The Assembly was to have a purely consultative character, over a

[20] Negotiation proposals are thoroughly studied in Pierre Duclos, *La Réforme du Conseil de l'Europe* (Paris, Librarie Générale de droit et de jurisprudence, 1958), pp. 7–8.

[21] Hugh Dalton, *Memoirs: High Tide and After* (Excerpts from diary and speeches during the negotiations) (London, Frederick Muller, 1962), pp. 317–18.

[22] European Movement, p. 56.

potentially wide range of subjects, specifically excluding defense. It had no formal ties with any other European organization. Its members, their number weighted by population in favor of the larger states, were to be appointed, each delegation according to the method its own government should choose. On these conditions the Labour Government was willing to accept individual voting. This meant that the Assembly members would have no constituency to report to, and no common public opinion to appeal to, and would thus be isolated from the potential demands of nongovernmental interest groups and individuals.

The Labour Party was thus instrumental in bringing into existence a regional parliamentary assembly whose integrative impact would be very weak. First, the Council of Europe lacked functional specificity; in particular, it had no functional ties with the OEEC and the Brussels Treaty Organization. As Haas points out, the European Parliamentary Assembly and its predecessor, the Common Assembly of the ECSC, were able to develop an integration consensus

. . . largely as a result of the increased opportunities to criticize meaningfully and continuously the activities of a true administrative agency.[23]

The Council of Europe was consultative only in relation to the member governments, and the statute gave only vague indications of the types of problems it could take up in the economic, social, cultural, and legal fields. Thus, it was bound to be difficult to create, administer, or take on regional tasks, and equally difficult to mobilize nongovernmental interest elites around the Consultative Assembly. As Duclos points out, the diplomatic character of the Council gave it no authority. It was central and well-informed, but in no way directing.[24]

Second, the Council had practically no authority in relation to the member states. It could only transmit its recommendations to the member states by way of the Committee of Ministers. The states were free to implement them or not as they wished. This meant, in addition to the fact that the rule of unanimity prevailed in the Committee of Ministers, that the Council was

. . . given to the rule of the equality of states, and to the diplomatic procedure of unanimity, all with their classical meaning.[25]

[23] Haas, "The Challenge of Regionalism," p. 453.
[24] Duclos, *La Réforme,* p. 75.
[25] Pierre Duclos, *Le Conseil de l'Europe* (Paris, Presses Universitaires de France, 1960), p. 10.

It meant as well that it would be difficult for the Council to overcome the functional autonomy of its members and survive the changes in their policies. Moreover, the Council was born with little potential for the creation of organs of a supranational character unless the governments were willing to agree to them.

Consensus in the Council of Europe

The Labour Party's participation in the Council of Europe during its first three years of existence indicated its desire to restrict the integrative impact of the institution and to seek a pluralistic, rather than an amalgamated, security community in Western Europe.

Once in operation, the Council might have been able to break out of the restrictions imposed upon it by the Statute. As Haas points out, regional parliamentary assemblies that do not have a legislative mandate can advance regional integration to the degree that the opinions expressed result from a clear and consistent meeting of minds of all or certain groups of its members who are influential in the national decision-making bodies that, in turn, determine the course of integration. This consensus implies an agreement on a clearly stated program of action endorsed by a clear majority of the members.

Two kinds of consensus must be examined: procedural and substantive. The parties in the assembly must become procedurally responsive to each other, affirming the legitimate right of the organ to discuss regional issues. They must also become parties of integration, seeking to change the social order, rather than just parties of representation. The key to both these concepts is the evolution of international parties and their relation to the national delegations.[26] On the basis of the lack of conditions in Britain and the Labour Government's role in the creation of the Council of Europe, it could be anticipated that the Labour Party, during the first three years of the Consultative Assembly, would not participate in the formation of a consensus in favor of integration.

Haas tends to underrate, at least in the case of the Council of Europe, the importance of procedural consensus or the lack of it for the integrative capabilities of parliamentary assemblies. There seem to be three elements in this consensus: first, the acceptance of the legitimacy of the assembly for the discussion of certain questions;

[26] Haas, *Consensus Formation*, pp. 1–14.

second, the acceptance of the legitimacy of the assembly in relation to certain organs, including its own creations, other intergovernmental organs, and national organs; and third, the acceptance of the legitimacy of the organization to reform and enlarge its own powers.

The Labour Party had been willing to endow the Council of Europe with a rather broad mandate for discussion; thus, it was logical for the Labour delegation to be willing and even interested in allowing the discussion of a wide range of problems. During the Council's first three years the Labour delegations made no objection to the large number of social, cultural, and legal questions taken up by the Assembly. The only exception was a side comment by Labour delegate Mitchison during the third session, questioning whether the Council was the appropriate body to concern itself with the question of refugees, as this was a worldwide rather than an exclusively regional problem. It is generally agreed, moreover, that the Council has been most successful in the social, cultural, and legal fields, though none of this success is thought to have promoted greater political unity.[27]

Labour participation was more active in the realm of economics, but the Labour delegation was quite hostile to the consideration of defense questions by the Assembly, in keeping with the letter of the Statute. Because of the outbreak of the Korean War and the fears for the defense of Europe, the Assembly at its second session, in August 1950, entertained a motion by Winston Churchill calling for the creation of a European Army. The Labour delegation was united in objecting to the consideration of this motion; delegates Mitchison, Callaghan (Minister of Defence), and Dalton (delegation leader) all referred to the terms of the Statute. At the third session, in November 1951, Labour delegate Hall also spoke against its consideration.

The right of the Assembly to create new regional organs in the social, cultural, and legal fields was generally not disputed by the Labour Party. True, delegates Nally and Ungoed-Thomas had both opposed the creation of the European Court of Human Rights; yet the Labour Government was the first to ratify the Convention establishing the Commission and the Court. The Labour delegation also accepted the creation by the Assembly of the Council on Municipalities and the appointment of a High Commissioner for Refugees.

From the beginning, the Labour Government had opposed the

---

[27] Duclos, *Le Conseil de l'Europe,* p. 127.

A. H. Robertson, *The Council of Europe,* 2d ed. (New York, Praeger, 1961), p. 255.

creation of functional ties between the Council and other European intergovernmental bodies, and its opposition persisted throughout most of the first session. Nevertheless, it soon became clear that, unless the Council could obtain a steady flow of information from other bodies, a great deal of duplication of effort was bound to occur. Closer relations with the OEEC were particularly necessary, and the Labour delegation actively supported such ties during the second and third sessions. They were, however, to be of a purely informational character, giving the Council an opportunity to keep in touch with the OEEC, but leaving the OEEC completely free from Council participation in its decision-making process. The Labour delegation also accepted the creation of similar ties with other organs, including the International Labor Organization (ILO), the social and cultural activities of the Brussels Treaty Organization, and the ECSC. The latter was an example of the Labour decision to accept the creation of ties between the Council and the so-called "Specialized Authorities," which Labour expected would include only those countries that wished to go farther in the development of supranational institutions. On the other hand, Labour objected strongly to any attempts by the Assembly to establish ties with or to dictate to national parliaments. At the second session, delegation leader Hugh Dalton stated that the Labour Party could not accept a mandate from a body outside parliament as to how it should vote in Westminster.

Perhaps the most crucial part of the procedural consensus in regional parliamentary assemblies is the common acceptance of the right of the organization to reform and enlarge its own powers. The British Labour delegation abstained most conspicuously from this consensus. The large federalist group present during the first session of the Assembly sought immediately to capitalize on its strength by passing proposals for federation and reform within the structure of the Council. In contrast, during the fifth sitting of the first session, in August 1949, Labour delegate Ungoed-Thomas sought to convince the Assembly that it should not function as an instrument of opposition to the governments and that the Committee of Ministers was not composed of "irresponsible autocrats."

However, a number of federalist motions were introduced seeking, among other things, the creation of a central European bank under the Council, the transfer of the OEEC to the Council, the creation of a European economic department, responsible to the Council, which would make proposals for economic integration, and the transfer to the Council of responsibility for deciding the nature and extent of cooperation among its members. All met with the hostility of the Labour delegation, but the last one was the only one rejected outright. The most notable success of the federalist group was the motion sent to the Committee of Ministers that

The Assembly considers the aim and goal of the Council of Europe is the creation of a European political authority with limited functions but real powers.[28]

Although Labour delegates Dalton and Morrison had succeeded in preventing this proposal from being included in the report of the Committee on General Affairs, it was adopted on the floor of the Assembly as an amendment to that report.

Although the major reforms proposed by the federalist group were turned down by the Committee of Ministers, a number of less important procedural changes were accepted. The Assembly gained control of its own agenda, and affirmed the right of its members to submit written questions to the members of the Committee of Ministers and the right to receive progress reports from the Committee. The Assembly committees gained the right to meet between sessions of the full Assembly. All these changes had the tacit consent of the Labour delegation, but they were not of a nature to increase the integrative capabilities of the Council.

The second session of the Assembly saw a more concerted effort by the federalist group to reform the Statute. The basic federalist proposal was submitted by Labour delegate R. W. G. Mackay, a thoroughgoing federalist, who, as will be shown later, could not in any way be considered representative of opinion in the Labour delegation as a whole. The Mackay Protocol asked that the OEEC be merged with the Council of Europe in a new, single authority; that the Council be given executive and legislative authority; and that the Assembly and Committee of Ministers be given mandates as an upper and lower house of parliament to make binding decisions. This protocol was passed by the Assembly over the implacable opposition of the Labour delegation. Delegate Bacon asked that the Council remain "consultative, with the Governments ratifying by consent its suggestions." Delegate Hall spoke of the Assembly as a "sounding board" which could be responsible for a large amount of "propaganda for good." Delegate Callaghan said that the Labour Government felt the Assembly should be purely consultative: "That is the purpose for

[28] Council of Europe, *Official Documents of the First Session*, Doc. 57 (D).

which it was set up; that is what it is; and subject to the amendments in respect of specialized authorities, that is what it should remain." Finally, delegate Dalton argued that the Mackay Protocol led the Assembly once again on a "false scent" down the federal path.

The federalist group also presented a motion attacking the report to the session by the Committee of Ministers as a "confession of bankruptcy." Although Labour representative Edelman referred to the report as "a toot on a penny whistle," the Labour delegation opposed the motion (with the exception of Mackay, one of its twenty-three sponsors) when it was put to a vote.

A third federalist proposal was that the members of the Assembly be elected by the national parliaments rather than being appointed by the governments. The Labour delegation accepted this Statute amendment, as it also allowed the national parliaments to fix procedures other than parliamentary election for the selection of delegates. The Labour delegation did participate in the procedural consensus calling for closer informational ties with the OEEC, and for the creation of Specialized Authorities, such as the ECSC, for those countries that were willing to take part in them.

The federalist group which attended the third session was considerably weaker than those attending the first two. It was clear, moreover, that Labour's resistance to increasing the powers of the Council was likely to block any major changes. The only truly federalist proposal called for a European conference to discuss the reform of the Statute of the Council. This was opposed by the Labour delegation; its spokesman, delegate Hall, objected to letting Statute reform leave the hands of the Assembly or be discussed by unrepresentative figures who were not parliamentarians. The motion died in committee.

Moreover, Labour delegate Crosland's proposal that the Mackay Protocol be removed from the agenda, though it failed of adoption, persuaded the Assembly to weaken the federalist implications of that document.

The Labour delegation repeated its support for Council proposals on Specialized Authorities and tacitly accepted the Assembly's decision to allow member Ministers other than those on the Committee of Ministers to speak before the Assembly, and to empower the Assembly to appoint its own clerk, who would have the rank of Deputy Secretary General. In general, the Labour Party's opposition was instrumental in preventing any major changes in a federalist direction. Its resistance made it difficult for the Council to serve as a rallying point for nongovernmental interest groups and individuals.

Substantive Consensus Formation
and the Labour Party

The British Labour Party's contribution to the growth of a substantive consensus in the Council of Europe can be analyzed in the framework of the nine-point model suggested by Haas.[29] As was seen above, consensus grows as parties of integration replace parties of representation; in this, the key indicator is the evolution of international parties and their changing relations to national delegations.

According to Haas, as the value-sharing of various nationalities grows in a regional parliamentary assembly, unity declines within each national delegation. During the first three years of the Assembly the Labour Party within the British delegation seemed at first glance to be in the curious position of having a low level of value-sharing with other nationalities (except the Scandinavians) and a high level of disunity with the other members of the British national delegation. However, a deeper analysis of this period shows a higher level of unity within the British delegation than appeared on the surface.

It has been pointed out previously that the major value incompatibilities between the Labour Party and the Continent were, first, in the area of socialist planning versus liberal economics, and second, in the area of pragmatism and anticonstitutionalism versus revolutionary supranationalism and federalism. A third value incompatibility played a strong role during this period as well: Atlantic and Commonwealth ties versus a European orientation.

The absence of national planning on the Continent was invoked frequently by the Labour delegates to justify their reluctance to participate in any supranational or federal agencies. Twelve of the twenty-eight Labour members who sat in the Assembly spoke, at one time or another, of the necessity for Continental countries to institute national planning in employment, social security, health, agriculture, and other areas before any European authority could take on regional planning responsibilities. Sufficient authority for a European planning body could only derive from sufficient national authority to handle the same problems. The Labour Government, in particular, could not surrender its power to maintain full employment into the hands of a European body dominated by governments which pursued no such policy. Moreover, new European bodies such as the Human Rights

---

[29] Haas, *Consensus Formation*, p. 14.

agencies and ECSC should pay more attention to the nature and guarantee of the economic and social well-being of the European peoples.

Two of the major motions submitted by the Labour delegation confirmed this attitude. One called for the Council to urge its members to seek full employment in their countries, and the other proposed the creation of an intergovernmental Atlantic Joint Resources and Planning Board.

The incompatibility of federal and supranational thinking with the British attitude of pragmatism and anticonstitutionalism also entered frequently into Labour delegates' remarks and proposals. Fifteen of the Labour delegates made reference to this problem. During the first session it was argued that, although European unity was the goal of many Assembly members, it was most likely to be achieved through efforts to adjust national differences and merge national practices without disturbing national feelings. The main responsibility should lie with the national parliaments and governments, not with a centrally designed straitjacket. Uniformity should not be sought for its own sake, for there was nothing sacrosanct in federation.

The second session saw the proposal of the Schuman plan and attempts to create both a federal European political authority and a European army. The refusal of the Labour Government to participate in the negotiations on the Schuman plan was explained by Labour delegate Edelman as a difference in method, not in purpose. Delegate Blyton added later that the Labour Government felt that the intergovernmental method allowed greater tolerance and flexibility in the attempt to achieve European unity. In fact, the Labour delegates approved of the Schuman plan to the degree that it represented a functional approach, in contrast to the latter two proposals, which smacked of federalism. Functional intergovernmental agencies, argued delegate Callaghan, were perhaps preferable, as sovereignty could be merged without federalism. Delegate Edelman felt that the political and defense proposals were causing the Assembly to wrangle over "pure paper constitutions." Hugh Dalton agreed, and added that the time-tested methods of conciliation, concession, and agreement in an intergovernmental framework were bound to produce more durable unity. Delegate Crosland pointed out that successful integration in NATO showed that a political authority was not needed to achieve unity.

The third session saw a general repetition of the above arguments, plus the more specific counsel that, if the Continental countries desired British participation in the integration process, as George Brown pointed out, they should seek "a road along which we can travel together. . . . We will not be bludgeoned along a road which we honestly think is the wrong alley."

The Labour-sponsored motions reflected their overriding concern with the pragmatic, intergovernmental method. One first-session motion called for organs of consultation in iron and steel, coal, chemicals, agriculture, and other industries. The proposal for an Atlantic Joint Resources and Purchasing Board motion also called for an intergovernmental arrangement.

Ten of the Labour delegates to the Assembly referred to the importance of the Atlantic Community and the Commonwealth, both to Britain and to Europe as a whole. It was often implied that the British ties to those two communities made it less feasible for the Labour Party to commit itself to far-reaching proposals for European integration. The first session references were almost exclusively to the Commonwealth. The Labour delegates asked the Council not to try to force Britain to choose between Europe and the Commonwealth, as most Britons were tied more closely to the Commonwealth and those ties were basically unbreakable.

During the second session, as a result of the Korean War and the proposal for a European army, the Labour speakers placed more emphasis on the Atlantic tie. It was pointed out that the Labour Party leaned toward its Atlantic and Commonwealth ties, and that they were thus an integral part of its European policy. The Atlantic nuclear umbrella, moreover, made an independent, supranational European army unnecessary.

As the Labour Government had chosen not to participate in the Schuman plan and the European army negotiations, it was forced to make the importance of its external ties even more clear during the third session. Although one delegate called for Council ties with Atlantic and Commonwealth countries, delegate Hall made it clear that Britain was not a purely European power and that the chances for unity within the two external groups was perhaps more attractive for it than unity within Europe. Mr. Gordon-Walker added that those ties made it necessary for Britain to retain her independence for extra-European action.

The Labour motions, too, reflected those external ties, in calling for the extension of guaranteed markets to overseas territories and for the creation of an Atlantic Joint Resources and Purchasing Board.

There was one notable exception to the incompatibility of Labour values with those of many Continental delegates in the Assembly. Labour delegate R. W. G. Mackay was considered

. . . the champion of a democratic, European federation, of a union endowed with a constitution in the form of a treaty.[30]

Delegation leader Hugh Dalton spoke of Mackay as

the only Federalist in the Labour delegation at Strasbourg and, indeed almost the only thoroughgoing Federalist in the whole Labour Party.[31]

Mackay was the most active member of the Labour delegation during the first three years of the Council of Europe, but his proposals often brought vociferous opposition from his fellow party members. In statistical terms, Mackay delivered thirteen of the sixty-two major speeches made by Labour delegates during his stay in the Assembly (from 1949 through the first half of the third session in 1950), many more than any other Labour member. Of approximately two hundred and fifty minor remarks by Labour delegates, Mackay made seventy, again the highest number. Of thirty-five motions in which the Labour Party participated during this time, Mackay alone was responsible for sixteen. Of the twenty-five amendments in which the Labour delegates participated, Mackay alone was responsible for nine. Both of these totals were higher than those of any other Labour delegate.

The motions sponsored by delegate Mackay during the first two sessions were generally cosponsored by Continental federalists such as André Philip, Guy Mollet, or Mr. Cassimatis of Greece. They included proposals for central economic institutions such as a European loan council and a European bank, legislative and executive authority on the Council of Europe, and a proposal to set the Council's goal as the creation of a European political authority with limited functions but real powers. Those proposals were quite federal in nature, and frequently unacceptable to a majority of the Assembly. However, several of them, particularly Statute amendments seeking to enlarge the power of the Council and the proposal for a political authority, were approved by the Assembly, only to be rejected by the Committee of Ministers.

Mackay recognized the incompatibility of the Labour Party stands with those of the federalists in the Assembly. As early as the second session he warned the Assembly that it would have to choose the

---

[30] Duclos, *La Réforme*, p. 97.　　　　[31] Dalton, pp. 326–27.

intergovernmental approach if it wished to include Britain in European organizations. If Continental delegates wished to move on to supranationality or federation, they would have to do so without Britain. Mackay's stand did not bring about a fragmentation of the Labour Party delegation. Indeed, the far-reaching nature of his proposals often increased the hostility of other Labour delegates to the cause of European integration. With the exception of Mackay, the unity of the Labour members of the British delegation was quite high, particularly on issues concerning the methods of European integration. They frequently supported each other's remarks and referred to the fact that they were speaking for the Labour delegation as a whole.

There remains the question of the lack of unity between the Labour group and the British Conservatives. It has been argued that one of the weaknesses of the British delegation was its tendency to export its domestic quarrels.[32] Certainly, there were more than a dozen instances in each session of one party chiding the other. The Conservatives generally tried to encourage the Assembly's desire for increased authority in order to arouse Labour's opposition and put it in a bad light. The Labour members, on the other hand, chided the Conservatives for the inconsistency between the policies they supported in the Assembly and those they voiced in Westminster.

This inconsistency seems to be the key to the realization that the disunity of the British delegation in the Assembly was merely a surface phenomenon. It reflected the domestic political situation in Britain, and was not related to an increased value-sharing between the Conservatives and the Continental delegates. Once the Conservatives came into power, before the second half of the third session of the Assembly, they based their European policy statements in the Council on the same incompatibility of values, with the exception of planning, as had the Labour Party. They shared with Labour the view that the pragmatic British method was incompatible with supranationalism and federalism, and that Britain's Atlantic and Commonwealth ties precluded any closer integration with the Continent.

The second point in the Haas model of consensus is that, as the unity of the national delegation declines, international parties will increase in unity. The unity of the British delegation, which was high to begin with, was reinforced by the Government's control over the

[32] Kenneth Lindsay, *Towards a European Parliament* (Strasbourg, Council of Europe, 1958), p. 35.

composition of the delegation. The fact that the British representatives were appointed by the Government after consultation with the Party whips tended to insure their adherence to orthodox views. Moreover, the frequent turnover within the British delegation helped prevent fragmentation of the delegation in the Assembly. For example, the total of thirty-seven seats held by the Labour Party during the first three sessions was filled by twenty-eight Labour MPs.

Haas has pointed out the difficulty of measuring the extent of international party formation, because so many of the votes in the Consultative Assembly are unanimous; usually motions reflect the minimum common denominator obtainable between the members. The extent to which the Labour group was isolated can be partially indicated by the proportion of the total number of motions and amendments in which they participated and of which they alone were the sponsors. These data suggest the degree to which the Labour Party was part of a larger group sponsoring proposals in the Assembly. The motions in which Mr. Mackay participated alone or with Continental representatives are subtracted, since, as has been pointed out, he represented a minority of one within the Labour delegation. Of the remaining six motions in which Labour Party representatives participated during the first session, they were the sole sponsors of three. They were sole sponsors of seven of the remaining twelve in the second session, and were joined by others in the only motion in which they participated during the third session.

The willingness to join as an incipient international party in amending motions before the Assembly would indicate an even higher degree of transnational party unity. Of eleven non-Mackay Labour amendments presented in the first session, the Labour members were alone in proposing eight. Of two in the second session they were alone in one, and they were isolated in all three amendments they proposed during the third session.

These figures allow three tentative observations. First, the Labour delegation grew more reluctant to seek out allies actively for the parliamentary game of amendment. Second, although they presented more motions in the second than in the first session, they had become somewhat more isolated from other groups in the Assembly. Third, with the realization that any policy moves during the third Assembly session were likely to remain unimplemented because of the impending change of government in Britain, the Labour delegates became reluctant to make any proposals at all.

Who were the cosponsors of the remaining motions and amendments in which the Labour Party was not alone? Examination of those motions and amendments does not support any hypothesis of greater Socialist unity. During the first session, Labour's allies were generally found among the British Conservatives, the Scandinavian group (strongly antifederation), and the Dutch, the latter two including both Socialists and non-Socialists. Conservative members continued to ally themselves with Labour on certain motions during the second session. In addition, Continental Socialist support was given to the two motions on full employment and the Atlantic Joint Resources and Purchasing Board; those motions also received Conservative and Christian Democratic support. The Labour motion at the third session was again for the creation of an Atlantic Board, and it was again supported by the same members.

Haas points out that the Socialist International, reestablished after the war on the initiative of the Labour Party, represented only a vague consensus on principles and had no European program. The Socialist caucus in the Assembly, again the result of a Labour Party initiative, was rather weakly organized and had very poor discipline.[33] Lindsay has written of the Continental Socialists'

. . . despair at the sheer inability of British comrades to understand their point of view.[34]

There were rare signs of Socialist unity in the debates of the first three years of the Assembly; in only one case could those signs of unity be considered a positive gain for European integration. Socialist support for Labour delegate Edelman's resolution backing the United Nations in Korea during the second session was relatively insignificant, as the motion passed by a vote of 82–3. German Social Democrat support for Mackay's observation that Britain would only evolve slowly toward the acceptance of supranationality was not directly relevant to any proposal before the second session. Integration was not advanced by the Social Democrats' agreeing with Labour that the Council could not legitimately discuss defense. Finally, unanimous Socialist support for the Labour resolution on the Atlantic Joint Resources and Purchasing Board was useful in securing its approval, but the proposal itself was not of great importance to European integration.

In sum, the British delegation retained a high degree of unity during the first three years, and Labour members found themselves increas-

[33] Haas, *Consensus Formation,* pp. 9, 39.   [34] Lindsay, p. 35.

ingly isolated from other groups in the Assembly. There is no indication that any substantial degree of unity prevailed between the Labour group and the Continental Socialists.

The third postulate in the Haas model is that, as a country is outvoted, either the national delegation or the national party increases in unity. The previous discussion has indicated the extent to which the British delegation, and particularly its Labour members, were united. One reason for this probably lies in the fact that the Labour group came to the Assembly expecting to be outvoted by the prevailing federalist coalition. Robertson has called the first three years of the Council a period of searching for a political authority with limited functions but real powers. The Labour opposition to this goal has already been shown. That they recognized their minority position was indicated by Mr. Callaghan in the second session:

The Assembly would not run true to form if, within a quarter of an hour of starting on its voyage, it had not delivered a broadside at the Committee of Ministers and fired off all its light armament against the British Government.[35]

It was clearly around the party that the Labour members rallied, rather than around the British delegation, since proposals they opposed, such as the European army, were often put forward by the British Conservatives. As has been pointed out, the Labour representatives referred to themselves as a group quite frequently.[36]

When a national party is outvoted, it not only increases in unity but, at least in the Labour case, its interest in the work of the Assembly seems to decline. The decreasing number of Labour Party motions and amendments, mentioned above, is reinforced by the decline in its participation in the debates. Subtracting Mackay's interventions, the figures are approximately as follows:

	Major Speeches	*Minor Remarks*	*No. of Sittings*
Session I	16	90	18
Session II	24	68	28
Session III	19	45	40

[35] Council of Europe, *Official Report of Debates of Second Session,* Sitting 22, p. 1318.

[36] Both Løchen and Robertson point out that the national party was the usual locus of group activity in the Council of Europe. See: Einar Løchen, "A Comparative Study of Certain European Parliamentary Assemblies," *European Yearbook, IV, 1958* (The Hague, Nijhoff, 1958), pp. 150–67; and A. H. Robertson, "The Council of Europe, 1949–1953, Part I," *International and Comparative Law Quarterly,* April 1954, pp. 235–55.

Thus, as the Labour delegates became aware of their minority position, they also began to realize that they could not act effectively in the Assembly to change that position and tended to reduce their participation from year to year.

The fourth postulate of the Haas model is that the national delegations will unanimously support initiatives marginal to their national policies and attitudes, but will split along party lines on votes relating to issues vital to the program of each party. Haas holds that this is particularly true for the British delegation, which, while generally united on cultural, social, relief, and human rights issues, was divided along party lines on foreign policy, economics, integration, and reform of the Council structure.

The experience of the first three years in the Assembly does not support this conclusion. The Labour Party had Conservative support on two motions which bore the closest relation to its domestic economic program: the call for Council support for a policy of full employment in all the European countries, and the creation of a European manpower board. Moreover, the Conservatives' foreign policy, their views on integration, and on the reform of the Council did not, in fact, differ substantially from those of the Labour Party. In addition, policy on those particular external questions was not particularly crucial to the national program of either party, since both tended, during election campaigns, to focus primarily on domestic issues. Much of the dissension between the two parties seems to have been exported from the rather structured Government-Opposition framework of the British Parliament; it reflected a Conservative desire to put the Labour Government in a bad light, rather than profound disagreement with its policies.

The fifth point in the Haas model holds that, as value-sharing among ideologically similar parties grows, national parties will modify their national aims to make them compatible with internationally defined objectives. The four examples of Socialist unity in the debates, mentioned above, do not show any indication of a change in the Labour Party program as a result of greater Socialist unity. Moreover, of the modifications that did occur in the Labour Party position in the Assembly—namely, favoring ties between the Council and the OEEC, supporting the creation of Specialized Authorities for those countries which sought closer integration, and giving increased emphasis to the Atlantic Community—only that on Specialized Authorities could be said to have any relation to Socialist unity, particularly unity with the

Socialist parties of the Six. However, there is no evidence that such unity actually existed. Moreover, none of those modifications was closely related to changes in the Labour Party's national aims.

The sixth postulate is that, as value-sharing among ideologically related parties grows, the number of unaffiliated groups and members declines. The increased value-sharing among the federalists and among the Christian Democrats of the Six in the Assembly does not appear to have pressured the Labour Party into closer affiliation with the Continental Socialists. However, it did to a certain degree bring about an antifederal, antisupranational coalition between the Labour group and the delegates of all parties from Scandinavia during the three years under study. This affiliation did not, however, take the form of an organized caucus, nor did it result in increased Labour participation in the work of the Assembly.

Haas's seventh postulate holds that a national delegation whose members participate in subregional European organizations tends to achieve agreement within itself more readily than with other national delegations. Since nearly all nations represented in the Council were also members of the OEEC, that regional tie clearly had little influence on agreement among delegations in the Assembly. Moreover, the members of the Brussels Pact were quite split on methods of further integration—particularly with reference to the ECSC and the European army—between the British (particularly Labour) and the Continental delegations. Finally, the British found their allies more commonly among the Scandinavian delegates, with whom they maintained no regional organization.

Eighth, Haas argues that national parties whose countries participate in subregional organizations tend to achieve agreement with kindred subregional parties more readily than with similar parties from outside countries. In the Labour Party case, during the period under study, agreement was more frequently arrived at with Scandinavian Socialists and occasionally the German Social Democrats than with the Socialist parties in the Brussels Pact nations.

Ninth, Haas argues that a catalyst party comes to dominate early in such an assembly; by its cohesion, it advances consensus through compelling antifederal and uncommitted parties to regroup and adjust themselves to federal institutions and the federal context. The cohesion of the Christian Democrats, as has been pointed out, forced the growth of a negative coalition of antisupranationalists made up primarily of the British and Scandinavian delegates. This did not, however, lead to greater consensus, as the Council was not a federal context to which the antifederal group had to adjust. The Christian Democrats' determination to create the ECSC and the European army, however, probably influenced the antifederal coalition, and particularly Labour, to support closer ties between the Council and the OEEC and the creation of Specialized Authorities for those who wished to participate in them. Those positions were probably adopted in order to preserve the spirit of cooperation in Europe necessary to the solution of the problems of recovery and defense. They were a means to deflect the damaging impact on relations that could have occurred as a result of the federal-antifederal split.

It is clear, in the light of the foregoing analysis, that the British Labour Party did not participate in the development of a substantive consensus in the Consultative Assembly of the Council of Europe during the first three years of its existence. Key to this failure seems to have been the absence of substantive unity between the Labour delegation and the Continental Socialists. Although the Labour Party had taken the initiative in the creation both of the Socialist International and of the Socialist Caucus in the Assembly, the two groups did not share a common consensus on the methods and goals of European integration. That such a consensus did not develop significantly during the period under investigation was due to the lack of shared values; to the weakness of the Labour Government, which would have made implementation of a common policy difficult; to the general absence of the Socialists from the Continental governments; and to the absolute decrease of Labour Party activity in the work of the Assembly as a result of its continued isolation from the majority.

Conclusion

Western Europe in 1945 faced serious economic and military problems as a result of the devastation of the war and the presence of large Soviet forces in Eastern Europe. It is to the credit of the Labour Government that it responded to the common need for rapid economic recovery and military security by sponsoring the OEEC and the Brussels Pact. Many Continental Europeans saw those two organizations as the takeoff toward European federation: the creation of a federal state that would guarantee peace and prosperity to the entire Western European area. Britain, which had survived the war with relatively little internal destruction, and with its army intact, was expected to serve as the focal point for this federation.

The Labour Government, too, sought peace and prosperity in Western Europe, but it felt unable to respond to the Continental demands for leadership. Britain lacked the necessary basic conditions that would have enabled the Labour Government to commit itself to federation. The Labour leaders placed great value on internal planning and pragmatic evolution toward European unity, but felt that the Continental emphasis on liberal economics and constitutional federalism was incompatible with those values. Even more important, the Labour Government felt it essential to retain Britain's freedom of action in relation to other parts of the world with which it felt a greater sense of community and responsibility than with Europe. The Atlantic Community was crucial to the Labour view; it saw the security and recovery of Europe as depending on the United States, where a return to isolationism had to be prevented. The Commonwealth was also important; Britain was responsible for its defense and from it drew much of its raw materials and trade.

The Labour Government did not wish to make any commitments to the Continent that would weaken Britain's ties with or destroy its freedom of action in the Atlantic area and the Commonwealth. When pushed to a decision with the proposal of a European Assembly, the Government sought to retain Europe's good will and simultaneously prevent federation, by approving the project and then in negotiations attempting to insure that the profederation Assembly would be thoroughly subordinate to the will of the participating governments. It sought and achieved such control through the creation of the intergovernmental Committee of Ministers, and through the assurance that the members of the Assembly would depend on the governments for their selection. The Labour Government sought especially to keep the new organization from having any functional ties with the OEEC or the Brussels Pact, in order to prevent federalist interference with the intergovernmental work of those bodies. In sum, the Council of Europe was to operate in a void, allowing the governments to retain their autonomy and freedom of action in all areas of common European interest.

A pluralistic security community, through which the member governments agreed that war was impossible among themselves and within which they cooperated unanimously in the solution of problems which they felt were common among them while all retained their legal independence, was clearly the goal of the Labour Government of postwar Britain.

The consensus of the majority of the members of the Consultative Assembly during the first three years of the Council of Europe, however, was that the end goal of the European security community was amalgamation. The Labour delegates thus found themselves in a minority in the Assembly during this period. Their lack of a sense of community with the Assembly majority, with whom they shared few compatible values, meant their absence from consensus formation in the Assembly. Realizing that their point of view was not likely to dominate the proceedings, the Labour group with the exception of one member tended to deny the right of the Council to create functional ties with other European organs or to reform and expand its own powers in relation to the national governments.

The extent of the Labour group's participation in the work of the Council tended to decline in reaction to its minority position. It found itself increasingly isolated from the support of other delegations and unable to cultivate a Socialist bloc in the Assembly. Perhaps more to preserve good will for its pluralist point of view than for any other reason, the Labour delegation conceded the necessity of ties of an informational nature with the OEEC and the possible creation of Specialized Authorities of a supranational character by those nations who wished to move toward federalism.

The pluralist community goal, which the Labour Party pursued in its policy toward Western Europe, dominated its activity in the Assembly so long as it was a governing party; it tended to freeze, in spite of changing conditions in Europe, after the Labour Party had entered the Opposition. Its persistence to the present has continued to have important implications for Britain's attitude toward contemporary and future supranational communities within Europe.[37]

[37] Readers interested in a further investigation of the subject of this paper may wish to consult the following works:

Florinsky, Michael. *Integrated Europe?* New York, Macmillan, 1955.
Socine, Roberto. *Rapports et Conflits entre Organisations Européennes,* in collection *Aspects Européens.* Leyden, A. W. Sythoff, 1960.
Haas, Ernst B. "Regionalism, Functionalism, and Universal International Organization," *World Politics,* VIII (1956), 238–63.
Mackay, R. W. G. "Strasbourg in Perspective," in *European Yearbook.* The Hague, Nijhoff, 1958. Vol. IV, pp. 174–88.
Mower, A. Glenn, Jr. "The Official Pressure Group of the Council of Europe's Consultative Assembly," *International Organization,* XVIII, No. 2 (1964), p. 292.
Council of Europe, *Official Documents,* Sess. 1, 2, and 3.
Council of Europe, *Official Reports of Proceedings,* Sess. 1, 2, and 3.

Social Courts and Law Reform
in East Germany

PETER FRIEDMAN

In 1959 the East German parliament (Volkskammer) enacted a law amending the basic statute on the organization of the courts.[1] This new law marked the beginning of a period of legal reform involving important changes in both the theory of law and its practical application. Since 1959 the pages of East Germany's official law journal, *Neue Justiz,* have been filled with articles debating the meaning of law for a socialist country. The debate has focused primarily on the criminal law and on the relationship between punishment and education. Many of the reforms enacted between 1960 and 1963 have as their avowed purpose the strengthening of law as a means of education. Changes in sentencing policy, repeated demands for the strict observance of legality, and, especially, provisions for increasing mass participation in the administration of justice, have been introduced with the statement that they will aid in realizing the educative function of law. The social courts, or conflict commissions, as they are called in East Germany, represent the direct incorporation of the working masses into the judicial process. A series of decrees and proclamations by the Council of State [2] have expanded the jurisdiction of the conflict commissions since 1961 to include a variety of subjects previously handled only by the regular courts.

East Germany's conflict commissions draw upon two Soviet institu-

[1] Gesetzblatt der Deutschen Demokratischen Republik (*GB1*) 1, S.753 (1959).

[2] Resolutions of the Council of State of January 30, 1961 and May 24, 1962, "on the further development of the administration of justice." *GB1*. 1, S.3 (1961) and *GB1*. 1, S.53 (1962); Decree of the Council of State (confirmed by the Volkskammer on April 17, 1963) "on the basic tasks and methods of the organs of the administration of justice." *Recht In Ost Und West* (Berlin, Verlag A. W. Hayn's Erben, May 1963), VII, 112 ff.

tions: the labor dispute commissions and the comrades' courts. The
Soviet Union views its reemphasis on its social courts as part of the
process of transferring state functions to social organizations in aid of,
and in preparation for, the eventual withering away of the state with
the achievement of Communism. East Germany also presents its
social courts as part of the transfer of state functions to social organizations. However, as East Germany is not yet allowed to claim that it
has fully achieved socialism, the transfer of functions to social organizations is spoken of as a step on the way to the complete construction
of socialism. Thus, the same institutions, the social courts, are given a
different theoretical foundation in East Germany than in the Soviet
Union. This paper will seek to analyze the conflict commissions, first
in terms of the Soviet models upon which they are based,[3] and
second through a consideration of the recent history of legal reform
within East Germany.

East German Conflict Commissions
and Their Soviet Models

Soviet comrades' courts and East German conflict commissions
both consist of a variable number of members elected by the workers
within each factory from among their colleagues. They meet after
working hours,[4] on the factory premises, and have jurisdiction over a
wide range of relatively minor violations of law and morality. East
Germany and the Soviet Union both mention prevention and reeducation as the goals of their social courts.[5]

The chief duty of the comrades' courts is to prevent violation of the law
and misdemeanors detrimental to society, to educate people by persuasion
and public influence, and to create an intolerant attitude toward any anti-
social acts.[6]

The social courts prevent violations in two ways. In the first place,
potential offenders are deterred by the knowledge that they will be
called to account in a public hearing before their fellow workers.

[3] For a comprehensive review of the comrades' courts in the Soviet Union,
see Harold J. Berman and James W. Spindler, "Soviet Comrades' Courts," 38
Washington Law Review (1963), 842.

[4] In the Soviet Union, comrades' courts also function in collective farms,
apartment buildings, educational institutions, and other organizations.

[5] Harry Cruezburg and Wolfgang Schmidt, "Die Aufgaben der Konflikt-
commissionen nach dem Staatsratserlass," 17 *Neue Justiz* (East Berlin,
1963), 328.

[6] Statute on Comrades' Courts, July 3, 1961.

Secondly, the social courts have the authority to investigate factory conditions facilitating violations and to recommend corrective steps to the factory leadership. Education of offenders is accomplished by the "measures of influence" which the social courts may order as well as by the public hearing and deliberation in which such measures are decided upon. Relieving the regular courts of the burden of a number of petty cases may be another function performed by the social courts, although East German and Soviet officials vehemently deny this.[7, 8]

Instead of simply taking over the Soviet models intact, East Germany modified them to take account of its own legal traditions and also, perhaps, of its differing social conditions. These modifications show up in the theoretical foundations for the social courts, and in their spheres of competence and places in the two judicial systems.

The conflict commissions in East Germany have developed in two distinct stages. From 1952 until 1959 they were patterned on the Soviet labor dispute commissions. The period 1959 to 1960 marked an essential change in the make-up of the conflict commissions and in the tasks assigned to them;[9] since 1959 they have been based upon the Soviet comrades' courts as well as upon the labor dispute commissions.

In the Soviet Union,

The labor dispute commissions are the compulsory first organ to examine labor disputes arising in enterprises and offices between workers and office workers on the one hand and the administration on the other, except for disputes on matters of dismissal and for other matters stated in law.[10]

The labor dispute commissions fall under the control of the trade unions. They are composed of one or more representatives of labor and an equal number of representatives of management.[11] Until recently, a decision of the commission generally could only be reviewed by higher union authorities.[12] An appeal to the regular courts was allowed only if the members of the commission either failed to agree or

---

[7] Leon Lipson, "The Role of the Public in the Processes of Soviet Justice: Non-Courts and Im-Police" (Paper delivered at the 1963 Annual Meeting of the American Political Science Association), p. 7.

[8] Michael Benjamin, "The Work of the Disputes Commissions in the Settling of Minor Breaches of Criminal Law," *Law and Legislation in the German Democratic Republic,* Issue No. 2 (1962), p. 9.

[9] Rudolf Walter, "Hüter der Sozialistischen Moral," *SBZ—Archiv,* 1 Februarheft 1963, p. 34.

[10] Article 62 of the October 1959 draft of the *Basic Principles of Labor Law of the U.S.S.R. and of the Union Republics.*

[11] Harold J. Berman, *Justice in the USSR* (Cambridge, 1963), p. 360.

[12] The 1959 draft of the *Basic Principles of Labor Law* provides for an appeal to the people's courts in certain cases.

if their decision had been disapproved by the labor inspector, a central union official.[13] Official Soviet sources maintained that the labor dispute commissions decided most cases in favor of the worker.

In 1952, conflict commissions were set up in East German state-owned and comparable enterprises with 200 or more members. Their formation was discretionary for enterprises having between 20 and 200 members. Conflict commissions were restricted to "socialist" enterprises because,

They have abolished the private ownership of the means of production and thus blocked the source of exploitation of man by man. Consequently, labor conflicts in such enterprises no longer have their roots in the antagonistic class relations whose basis is the contradiction between capital and labor.[14]

East Germany faced certain problems in taking over the Soviet model. The regime wanted essentially to preserve the existing court structure. While the East German constitution derives primarily from that of the Soviet Union, the court structure is based on that existing under the Weimar Republic. An established system of labor courts already existed by 1952, when conflict commissions were first introduced. To respect the preexisting jurisdiction of the labor courts, the conflict commissions could only be fitted in as a court of first instance in labor disputes. A failure by the members of a conflict commission to agree upon a unanimous decision opened the door to immediate removal of the case to the labor courts. Furthermore, decisions of the conflict commissions could be appealed to the labor courts. The Soviet Union, by contrast, had no labor judiciary; therefore, Soviet labor dispute commissions would not run into conflict with the regular courts.

The leadership of the Socialist Unity Party (SED) in East Germany distrusted the middle and lower echelons of the trade union organization (FDGB).[15] This provided a second reason for keeping the conflict commissions independent of the trade unions. Freedom from trade union control was achieved by incorporating the conflict commissions into the structure of the labor judiciary and providing for a

---

[13] Berman, p. 360.

[14] Rude Kranke, "The Disputes Commission—Manifestation of Advancing Democracy in the Legislative Field in the German Democratic Republic," *Law and Legislation in the German Democratic Republic*, Issue No. 2 (1962), p. 12.

[15] Rudolf Walter, "Hüter der Sozialistischen Moral," p. 36.

direct appeal to the labor courts, instead of to a higher instance of the union as in the Soviet Union.

Both West [16] and East German [17] commentators agree that the conflict commissions scored an early success. They provided quick, on-the-spot decisions by men familiar with the particular problems of the firms in which they worked. Conflict commission members seem to have made a real effort to acquire the necessary knowledge of the law and to do a competent job. The restricted jurisdiction of the conflict commissions (limited to labor disputes not infringing upon the disciplinary prerogatives of the manager) helped to keep their members from going beyond their depth in matters for which they lacked competence. A case could be brought before a conflict commission only by a party directly involved in a labor dispute, not by a third party, an organization, or even the trade union. Decisions of the conflict commissions directed against employees were subject to execution upon application to the competent district labor court. Since claims against state enterprises in East Germany are not subject to execution, decisions against an enterprise could only be carried out through administrative channels.[18]

The popularity of the conflict commissions during this first stage resulted in part from their willingness to uphold the law even against the wishes of the Party. Leaders of the Party and high officials in the FDGB increasingly criticized the commissions for deciding cases on the basis of "formal legality." The Party wanted political decisions.[19] Western sources praised the occasional courage of commission members who decided cases against management, but criticized the system for demanding too high a level of knowledge and skill from the factory workers who sat on the commissions.[20]

One of the original reasons for creating the conflict commissions was a desire on the part of the SED to diminish the importance of the labor courts. Most labor judges were professionally trained men, who had incurred the Party's wrath by deciding cases against state-owned firms. The civil and criminal courts, on the other hand, were often presided over by "people's judges," who had no academic background, but had merely received a training course of 6 to 24 weeks, consisting largely of political indoctrination. Party officials praised the people's

---

[16] *Ibid.*   [17] Kranke, "The Disputes Commission," pp. 17–18.
[18] Rudolf Walter, "Hüter der Sozialistischen Moral," p. 36.   [19] *Ibid.*
[20] Gerhard Haas und Alfred Leutwein, *Die Rechtliche und Sozial Lage der Arbeitnehmer in der Sowjetischen Besatzungszone* (Bonn/Berlin, Bonner Berichte aus Mittel-und Ostdeutschland, 1959), p. 206.

judges as politically reliable while condemning the labor judiciary as "a brake on the socialist economy." [21] A 1953 "reform" of the labor judiciary did away with employer and employee representation on the labor courts, and provided that only trade union organizations would have the right to nominate lay assessors.

That meant that the policies of the dictatorship of the proletariat would also be successfully carried out by the labor courts, and that representatives of private-capitalist undertakings would be excluded from participation in the judicial process of the labor courts.[22]

The heart of the 1953 reform, however, was the legislative establishment of the conflict commissions, which had already been introduced in 1952 on a voluntary basis. It was hoped that the conflict commissions would prove politically more reliable than the labor courts and would be more subservient to the wishes of the Party. As we have seen, the conflict commissions thwarted this expectation by their surprising independence. Thus, the regime had to criticize the conflict commissions for falling into the same "error" which they had been introduced to correct.

A secret conference of trade union leaders from all the Eastern Bloc countries took place in the Soviet Union toward the end of 1957. The conference put forward the Soviet labor dispute commissions as prototypes for the countries of Eastern Europe.[23] Following the 1957 conference, a series of discussions took place within the SED and the FDGB on how best to insure that the conflict commissions achieve those goals for which they were originally created. The SED wanted the conflict commissions to make political, rather than purely legal, decisions. The Fourth Plenary Meeting of the Central Committee of the SED, in 1959, decided to widen the jurisdiction of the conflict commissions and accord them the functions of both the Soviet labor dispute commissions and the Soviet comrades' courts. In addition, the conflict commissions when deciding labor disputes were to concentrate on judging breaches of socialist morality.[24]

The Soviet model to be used now became primarily the comrades' courts. In the Russian Republic the comrades' courts handle minor offenses, including violations of labor discipline; failure to observe industrial safety regulations; drunken or unworthy conduct in public

---

[21] *Ibid.*, p. 195. [22] *Ibid.*, p. 196 (quoting *Neue Justiz*).
[23] Rudolf Walter, "Hüter der Sozialistischen Moral," p. 36.
[24] *Ibid.*, p. 37.

places or at work; unworthy behavior toward women and parents and the failure to rear children properly; insults, beatings, and offensive language; slight damage to communal equipment, dwelling places, and other premises; violations of apartment or dormitory regulations, and disputes between tenants over the use of common facilities and payment for communal services; property disputes, up to 50 rubles, between members of the same collective, when the parties to the dispute agree to its being heard in a comrades' court; injury to trees and other greenery; and "other anti-social offenses, not entailing criminal liability." [25] In October 1963 the Supreme Soviet of the Russian Soviet Federated Socialist Republic (RSFSR) issued a decree broadening the jurisdiction of the comrades' courts to take in various criminal offenses, including petty hooliganism, petty speculation, petty theft of state and social property, unauthorized individual use of state collective vehicles and other property, and making of home-brewed liquor. The "measures of influence" or punishment which could be applied by the comrades' courts were also extended to include recommendations of dismissal, or assignment for up to 15 days to a lower paying job.[26] In January 1965 the jurisdiction of the comrades' courts was further enlarged to include petty economic crimes.

The conflict commissions in East Germany, like the Russian comrades' courts, hear a wide range of offenses against criminal law and socialist morality, but there is a difference in emphasis. Whereas the Russian comrades' courts have only recently acquired an extensive criminal jurisdiction, in East Germany criminal cases have formed the heart of the conflict commissions' work since 1960. In this area, especially, the conflict commissions are expected to achieve their goals of prevention and education.[27] The broadened jurisdiction of the conflict commissions over criminal violations is an important example of how East Germany transformed the Soviet (or Russian) model in the course of adopting it.

The criminal jurisdiction of the conflict commission is spelled out in detail. It includes—in addition to those offenses that the Russian comrades' courts are empowered to hear—injury to personal property and traffic offenses. Even if an offense falls within the class over which the conflict commissions have jurisdiction, it may only be heard if certain conditions are met. The offense must be a petty crime, committed

[25] Lipson, "The Role of the Public," p. 4.
[26] 8 *Recht in Ost und West* (1964), 18.
[27] Creuzburg and Schmidt, "Die Aufgaben der Konflikt-commissionen nach dem Staatsratserlass," p. 289.

(generally) by a first offender, and which has caused only slight damage. The guilt of the offender must also be slight and he must acknowledge his violation. In addition, the offense itself and the relevant circumstances surrounding it must be uncomplicated and not in need of further clarification.[28]

East Germany's requirement that the defendant must have confessed before he can be tried by a conflict commission stands in contradiction to the practice in the Soviet Union. One of the main purposes of a hearing before a Soviet comrades' court is to get the defendant to confess to his violation, if he has not done so already. The hearing will be considered a success only if during the course of it the defendant confesses and shows repentance. In East Germany, on the other hand, the hearing can never even take place unless the defendant has previously confessed. Evidently, East Germany considers that the conflict commissions can more effectively educate if they do not have to spend most of the hearing in trying to get the defendant to admit his guilt.

Only petty crimes belong before the conflict commissions. In determining which violations are petty, the courts are instructed to consider both the subjective and objective sides of the act. In other words, the degree of guilt ("the guilty mind") of the defendant as well as the damage caused by him must both be minor. Either one alone is insufficient to make the case suitable for the conflict commissions. A test approximating the American tort law rule of proximate cause applies to the question of the extent of damage attributable to the defendant. He is not responsible for damage resulting from an unforeseeable intervening cause.

The rule that only first offenders belong before the conflict commissions should not be applied "schematically." [29] In each individual case the decision should depend upon the educational potential of a hearing before a conflict commission. Repeated violators, already proven immune to "measures of public influence," generally belong before the regular courts.

The requirement that the offense and its surrounding circumstances be uncomplicated is held to apply primarily to the issue of causality in criminal negligence cases. The conflict commissions may only hear cases in which causality is clear. Responsibility for clarifying the facts and issues in each case rests essentially with the investigating organs. "The educational effectiveness of the conflict commission hearing de-

[28] *Ibid.*, p. 290.   [29] *Ibid.*, p. 291.

pends to a high degree upon the results of the inquiry conducted by the investigating organ." [30]

Civil jurisdiction of the conflict commissions extends to simple conflicts involving actions for money up to 500 marks (*DM-Ost,* or East Marks) as well as other cases involving a simple set of facts and law. They may also handle disputes over the carrying out of legally binding support obligations.[31] The decree of the Council of State does not give an illustrative list of the types of civil cases included, as it does for criminal cases. Only individuals may ask the conflict commission to sit on a civil dispute; state or social organizations may not initiate proceedings, whereas they may in a criminal case. The parties are not legally obligated to bring civil disputes before the conflict commission; they may choose to turn directly to the courts instead. Cases brought before a conflict commission may only be brought against citizens working in a factory over which the particular commission has jurisdiction. In the Soviet Union both the plaintiff and the defendant must work in the same factory. Most important of all, the conflict commissions, unlike the Soviet comrades' courts, have no authority to hand down binding decisions in civil cases. They may confirm a compromise or other solution agreed to by the parties, thereby making it legally enforceable. But if the parties refuse to agree, the case must be dismissed. In civil disputes their role is limited to that of a conciliation organ seeking to bring about an amicable agreement, with no power to take a decision on their own.

Aside from their criminal, civil, and labor jurisdiction, the conflict commissions also decide certain disputes with the social insurance system. In the Soviet Union the social courts hear a greater proportion of tenant disputes (over rental contracts and apartment house regulations) because of the existence of residential as well as factory social courts. East Germany experimented with a few social courts on a residential basis, but then reversed its plans and decided not to establish more until the factory conflict commissions had proven themselves.

East German conflict commissions, in contrast to their Soviet counterparts, do not have the power to levy fines. The conflict commissions also have no power to recommend dismissal or demotion to a lower paying job. Apart from those major differences, the social courts in both countries have about the same assortment of "measures of influence" at their disposal, running the gamut of warnings, repri-

[30] *Ibid.*   [31] *Ibid.,* p. 326.

mands, and required apologies, and including at least a limited authority to order the defendant to make good any damage he has caused. The law in East Germany enumerates measures merely by way of example. The conflict commissions may resort to other measures, and they make use of this possibility. For example, "a motorist who had violated the traffic rules was bound by the conflict commission to organize and attend a driving course, together with his colleagues, in collaboration with the traffic police." [32] This is similar to the leeway sometimes taken by American magistrates in tailoring measures to fit individual situations. It is further left to the discretion of the conflict commissions to confine themselves to the hearing and examining of the case,[33] which may itself have the desired educational effect on the defendant without requiring any additional measures.

A conflict commission may not, under any conditions, hold a hearing in the absence of the accused; his presence is essential. In the Soviet Union, if the accused does not appear after two invitations, the comrades' court may proceed to trial in his absence. This difference would seem to follow naturally from the East German requirements that the accused admit his guilt as a necessary prerequisite to the conflict commission's competence to hear the case.

Neither the Soviet nor the East German social courts follow any prescribed formal procedure. In East Germany special emphasis is placed on the right and obligation of the defendant's colleagues to participate in the hearings, and on the public nature of the proceedings.

Not only the hearing, but also the adoption of the resolution takes place in public. . . . [T]he different members of the conflict commission must express their opinions and discuss separate aspects of the case publicly. That, too, contributes to making the resolution more widely comprehensible to the parties, due to the fact that they follow personally the course of reasoning, the arguments and counter-arguments put forward by the members of the conflict commission endeavoring to arrive at a correct resolution in accordance with the law.[34]

East Germany has recently provided for the functioning of "social prosecutors" and "social defenders" in cases before the conflict commissions. They are appointed on the spot by the conflict commission from among the accused's fellow workers who are well acquainted with him. Approval of the accused is required for the appointment of

---

[32] Benjamin, "The Work of the Disputes Commissions," p. 7.   [33] *Ibid.*
[34] Kranke, "The Disputes Commission," p. 19.

the social defender. These temporary officials aid the conflict commission by presenting their own views on the accused's wrongdoing, on his personality and social consciousness, and on the objective factory conditions which facilitated the violation. Any colleague of the accused present at the hearing is encouraged to contribute whatever relevant knowledge or opinion he feels may be of assistance. The conflict commission, like the Soviet comrades' court, may decide by vote of a simple majority, "but it is expected that in the future decisions will continue to be essentially unanimous." [35]

One of the basic changes enacted in 1963 was to give the accused the right to appeal to the district court against any measures decided upon by the conflict commission. In the Soviet Union an appeal from a decision of the comrades' court may be taken only to the appropriate trade union committee or local Soviet executive committee (except for appeals against the imposition of a fine or a requirement to make compensation for damage, which may be taken to the regular courts). Therefore, the Soviet comrades' courts form a separate organization, not part of the regular court structure. By allowing the accused to appeal against any decision of a conflict commission, East Germany has incorporated its social courts into the over-all judicial hierarchy.

The task of the conflict commission does not end with handing down a decision. It has the duty to control the carrying out of the measures it has ordered and the suggestions that it has made for prevention of future violations.

The conflict commission, together with the factory trade union leadership, must see to it that the educational process, beginning with the preparation of the hearing and continued through the hearing, is further continued in the collective. [36]

One method for accomplishing this purpose is by the conflict commission's asking the accused worker's collective to undertake to "stand surety" for him or act as his custodian. The collective thereby obligates itself to take the responsibility of "educating the accused," usually for a period of one year. [37] If the accused changes his place of work within six months after the hearing, the conflict commission may send a copy of its decision to the trade union leadership in the enterprise where he is now working. The union leadership in the new factory

---

[35] *7 Recht in Ost und West* (1963), 170.
[36] Creuzburg and Schmidt, "Die Aufgaben der Konflikt-commissionen nach dem Staatsratserlass," p. 330.
[37] *7 Recht in Ost und West* (1963), 117.

has the power to assure the carrying out of any portion of the educational measures which the accused had left unfulfilled.

Prevention of future violations is considered at least as important for the conflict commission as dealing with present offenders. In Russia, "the comrades' court shall inform public organizations and officials of the reasons and conditions uncovered by it which contributed to a violation of the law or other offense." [38] East Germany goes much further by giving the conflict commission the authority to make recommendations to the factory management and to social organizations and state organs, and providing that those bodies must take a position in writing on the suggestions within two weeks. Therefore, at least some attention must be paid to the conflict commissions' suggestions. In labor disputes, the conflict commissions have the same right as the regular labor courts to issue "court criticism" (*Gerichtskritik*), taking to task individuals or organizations which have been lax. The conflict commissions should be reminded

. . . that it is not sufficient simply to decide a dispute, but above all they must discover the causes leading to the dispute and deal with these, in order thereby to prevent future disputes from arising. [39]

The conflict commissions have the duty to criticize colleagues of the accused worker who may have sympathized with him and helped to make it easy for him to commit his violation. Even where no case is brought before them, conflict commissions have the right to take action on their own initiative to combat breaches of socialist morality. If members of the conflict commission see a worker drinking too much in a public place or loitering too long after the lunch hour, they should lecture the errant offender and bring him up short before he commits a serious violation. In this area, of violation of socialist morality rather than law, the conflict commissions' function is almost solely preventative.

To summarize briefly some of the differences between the two systems: The Soviet comrades' courts may levy fines (up to 10 rubles); they may sit even in the absence of the defendant, and there are no appeals to the regular courts except on executions of money judgments. They now have a fairly broad criminal and civil jurisdiction over petty matters. The East German conflict commissions have no power to levy fines, but otherwise have a broader criminal jurisdiction

[38] Article 16 of the RSFSR Statute on Comrades' Courts.
[39] Heinz Paul, "Die Gerichtskritik im arbeitsgerichtlichen Verfahren," 17 *Neue Justiz*, 197, 199.

than the Soviet comrades' courts. The conflict commissions also have fairly broad civil jurisdiction, yet without the power to lay down a binding decision that is not agreed to by the parties to the dispute. The presence and confession of the accused are both necessary prerequisites to the conflict commission's taking jurisdiction over a criminal case. Appeals lie in all cases to the regular courts. The preventive role of the conflict commissions is especially emphasized by their power to make recommendations on which a position must be taken by the competent authorities.

The Conflict Commissions as Part of a New Emphasis on the Educative Function of Law in East Germany

East Germany's conflict commissions may be considered as an institution taken over from the Soviet Union, but they may also profitably be viewed as an outgrowth of internal developments in East German legal thinking. The aim here will be to analyze the conflict commissions as part of a broad program for legal reform in East Germany. This reform movement began in 1958 and 1959 and seems to have continued right up to the present day.

Until 1958, the East German Government saw every criminal offense as an expression of animosity toward the state or an attempt to undermine the social revolution. Even nonpolitical offenses were considered to involve a threat to state security. Judicial policy fluctuated between periods of leniency and severity, with no clear pattern emerging. The undue severity with which punishment had been meted out was at times criticized by the Government, which temporarily ordered the courts to ease up on sentencing. On June 11, 1953, just a few days before the widespread uprising against the SED, the Government issued a communique stating that, ". . . the Ministry of Justice and the Attorney General must immediately review all arrests, prosecutions and sentences to eliminate any possible harshness." [40] A short period of leniency followed, during which the "new course" in the Soviet Union (after Stalin's death) made itself felt in East Germany. By 1955 the East German new course had come to a complete end, and the judicial system had swung once more to extreme harshness. The Twentieth Congress of the Communist Party of the Soviet Union (CPSU) brought a return once more to mildness. The Central Com-

[40] *Democratic German Report*, June 19, 1953 (East Berlin), p. 3.

mittee of the SED admonished Minister of Justice Hilde Benjamin and Attorney General Ernst Melsheimer for unjustified arrests and ruthless administration of justice.[41] A general amnesty led to the release of over 19,000 persons from prison. Otto Grotewohl (Chairman of the Council of Ministers) told the Third Party Conference of the SED that,

The slightest deviation from the rule of law is exploited by the enemies of the State. The Attorney General must insist, more than he has done hitherto, that the laws are strictly complied with, particularly with regard to the rights of citizens.[42]

Yet only seven months later, in January 1957, the same Central Committee of the SED

. . . deplored the fact that less harsh judicial and penal practice had resulted in a flagging vigilance for reactionary and imperialist subversion; the judiciary was sternly admonished to heed warning signals from the working class, reportedly indignant over the recent leniency in sentencing policy.[43]

The liberalism of 1956 was soon repudiated. The examples of the Hungarian and Polish revolutions led to a new swing back to severity. During the early 1958 movement against revisionism, the state leaned toward finding calculated hostility and probably sedition in critical behavior which merely expressed personal displeasure. "More recently, the counsel of moderation has prevailed." [44]

The manner in which the law was administered fluctuated back and forth, but there were never the wide doctrinal swings that occurred in the Soviet Union as to the place and function of law. There never came a time when it was seriously thought in East Germany that law would become entirely obsolete. In fact, the Thirtieth Plenary Session of the SED Central Committee, in January 1957, condemned "the doctrine that had viewed spontaneity and economic self-government as stages in the 'withering away of the state.' " The shifts in East German ideas on legality have been within a much narrower range.

In East Germany a great deal of publicity has been given to the principle of punishment for the purpose of reeducation. Article 137 of the East German Constitution states that the "imposition of penalties shall be based on the concept of reformation of persons capable of

[41] Joachim Joesten. *New Germany Reports,* No. 38 (New York, 1954–58), p. 19.
[42] *Democratic German Report,* April 13, 1956.
[43] Otto Kirchheimer, "The Administration of Justice and the Concept of Legality in East Germany," 68 *Yale Law Journal* (1959), 742.
[44] *Ibid.,* p. 746.

rehabilitation through collective productive work." For the most part, however, only lip service was paid to the educative role of penal law in the pre-1959 period. Prison conditions were bad. The courts handed down inordinately long sentences for the types of offense committed, with imprisonment for 25 years common even for juvenile offenders. The only hint of the importance attached to punishment as education was the frequency with which sentences were handed down accompanied by such statements as, "the length of the punishment is sufficient for the education of the accused." [45]

Before 1958 the educational role of law did not find expression in sentencing policy or in the trial itself. East German judges, on the other hand, were expected to devote their time liberally to educating the citizenry on problems in the administration of justice and to take part in various election campaigns. In 1957 judges conducted 11,280 meetings on the administration of justice, drawing 530,000 visitors. The prosecutors topped this by holding 15,130 meetings with 830,000 visitors.[46] Show trials held in factories and other places where a large audience could attend were pointed to as educational in proportion to the number of people present.

An amendment to the criminal code, which took effect on February 1, 1958, provided for two new forms of punishment, the suspended sentence and the public reprimand, and for broadening the work of lay judges in preparing as well as trying cases.[47] This marked the first concrete manifestation of the notion that punishment should be educational. The idea that all criminal acts are rooted in a hostile attitude toward the working class has gradually yielded to the view that most crimes merely reflect a lack of socialist consciousness, which can be corrected by proper reeducation. As Walter Ulbricht said in October 1960:

What we mean by justice is that we should patiently convince and educate such persons as have not fully recognized their responsibility to our society; but that those who threaten the life of our people and the existence of our nation will be sternly punished.[48]

A sharp line would be drawn between those who had merely gotten off on the wrong foot and those who were true enemies of the state. Educational measures would be applied to the former, while the latter

[45] *Injustice the Regime* (Bonn, West German Ministry for All-German Affairs, 1959), p. 183.
[46] Kirchheimer, "The Administration of Justice," p. 724.
[47] Strafrechtsergänzungsgesetz vom 11. Dezember 1957 (*GBl*) S.643.
[48] Heinrich Toeplitz, "Zwei deutsche Staaten—zwei Konzeptionen im Strafrecht," *Deutsche Aussenpolitik* (East Berlin), Februar 1963, p. 94.

could continue to expect harsh punishment. A resolution of the Council of State, of January 30, 1961, "On the Further Development of the Administration of Justice," [49] (1) called for the organs of criminal justice to develop closer ties with the people; (2) ordered that for every criminal act a far-reaching investigation be made of all the objective circumstances and consequences of the act and of the personality of the actor, his development, level of class consciousness, and social behavior; and (3) demanded that the organs of criminal justice conscientiously stay within the legal limitations placed upon their activities. A second resolution, passed on May 24, 1962,[50] criticized the legal organs for not sufficiently "utilizing the growing power of the socialist order of society to educate lawbreakers"; and re-emphasized the fact that the majority of violations did not stem from "antagonism towards the Workers'-and-Peasants' State and that, therefore, the use of punishment not involving deprivation of freedom and the handling of minor offenses by the conflict commissions becomes even more important."

A resolution in April 1960, incorporating an agreement between the Trade Union Organization and the State Planning Commission, provided the basis for widening the jurisdiction of the conflict commissions and thereby transforming them from labor dispute organs into true social courts. This resolution was confirmed a year later by the new East German Labor Code of April 4, 1961.[51] In June 1961, the resolution of April 1960 was revoked and replaced by a new one, not essentially different. The new type of conflict commission was pointed to as evidence of a change in the character of law itself:

> The conflict commission comes into existence as a logical consequence in the course of developing socialist law, insofar as the law loses increasingly its compulsive character and becomes instead a factor extending its influence into the economic, administrative, cultural and educational fields.[52]

The reform movement culminated in the confirmation by the Volkskammer, on April 17, 1963, of the Decree of the Council of State "On the Basic Tasks and Methods of the Organs of the Administration of Justice." Previously, law in East Germany had been defined simply as "the statutory expression of the will of the laboring class, which exercises authority in alliance with the working farmers and other working sections of the population." [53] The decree redefined

---

[49] *Ibid.*, p. 95.　　　　[50] *Ibid.*, pp. 96–97.　　　　[51] *SBZ von A bis Z*, p. 249.
[52] Kranke, "The Disputes Commission," p. 21.
[53] *SBZ von A bis Z*, p. 388.

law as "an important instrument of our State for organizing social development and for regulating socialist cooperative life and the relationships of citizens to each other and to their State." [54]

Whether the new definition represents a basic change in legal theory, or simply a change in emphasis as Western commentators imply,[55] it does pave the way for assigning an increasingly large role to the educational approach to law.

Besides broadening still further the jurisdiction of the conflict commissions to include competence in civil as well as criminal cases, the decree also downgraded the Ministry of Justice by depriving it of control over the lower courts, which are now responsible solely to the Supreme Court, which in turn must account only to the Volkskammer and the Council of State. Control over the whole hierarchy of prosecuting attorneys was, similarly, taken away from the Council of Ministers and given solely to the Volkskammer and the Council of State. The decree marks the widest extension of the jurisdiction of the conflict commissions up to the present date.

East German and Western Evaluations of the Conflict Commissions and the Recent Legal Reforms in East Germany

East German official sources have been critical of the way the new directives are being applied. The courts and other legal organs are criticized for not making sufficient use of the new types of punishment —for too often meting out short jail sentences in cases where a suspended sentence or other form of punishment not involving deprivation of freedom would be suitable. Warnings have been issued to the courts for interpreting the new decrees and directives as a sign of general leniency. Specifically, the courts have come under fire for dealing too mildly with crimes of violence and for placing too much emphasis on the individual cases before them [56] instead of on the educational effect which the trial might have. Another complaint against the way in which the courts have been interpreting the developing course of the law is the charge that they have been dealing too mildly with cases of criminally negligent damage to or theft of state and social property, and with cases of all kinds involving defendants who have proven not subject to the good influence of educational measures. In all such cases the courts are said to have shown an

[54] *7 Recht in Ost und West*, p. 112. [55] *Ibid.* [56] *Ibid.*, p. 204.

erroneous tendency to overestimate the importance of positive aspects of the defendant's character, such as his good work record. In this connection, the courts have been rebuked for forgetting that only circumstances directly connected with a crime may be considered as mitigating circumstances.[57]

East German sources have had only praise for the conflict commissions. Criticism has been directed instead at the failure of the regular courts to fully recognize the importance of the conflict commissions or to adequately carry out their responsibilities with respect to them. For example, the regular courts have continued to try a number of criminal cases which should have been handed over to the conflict commissions. This shows a persistent tendency to "underestimate the effectiveness of social education." [58] Regret has also been expressed at the "mistaken view" that the conflict commissions exist primarily in order to relieve the work load of the police and the regular courts.[59] Not only are the courts and the investigating organs criticized for not handing over suitable cases to the conflict commissions, but also for not doing a thorough preliminary job of clarification on those cases which they do turn over.[60] The directive to the conflict commission in each case must clarify the fact situation and suggest to the conflict commission those areas on which it might most profitably concentrate its energies. Perhaps the one criticism directed at the conflict commissions themselves is their failure to make sufficient use of their right to make suggestions and recommendations for the clearing up of conditions which facilitate violations.

Praise of the conflict commissions has come from various East German sources. According to one authority, "the conflict commissions are gradually developing into one of the most effective instruments for the combatting of criminal offenses and criminality." [61] They already handle one-third of all criminal violations, and the quality and volume of their work is steadily increasing.[62] Complaints against conflict commission decisions on minor criminal offenses are exceedingly rare, as are the cases of recidivism.[63]

It happens not infrequently that offenders, on learning that their case is to be handed over to the conflict commission for a hearing, approach the criminal prosecuting authorities with the request to have the case tried

[57] *Ibid.*　　　　　[58] Toeplitz, "Zwei deutsche Staaten," pp. 97–98.
[59] Benjamin, "The Work of the Disputes Commissions," p. 9.
[60] 7 *Recht in Ost und West* (1963), 292–93.
[61] Benjamin, "The Work of the Disputes Commissions," p. 10.
[62] *Ibid.*　　　[63] *Ibid.*, p. 3.

in a court of law instead. They would prefer to stand trial rather than account for their offenses to their workmates.[64]

West German authorities, who have commented on the conflict commissions, have expressed the view that the price which the defendants must pay, in loss of human dignity and exposure to petty jealousies and animosities, outweighs whatever educational or deterrent benefits the system may have.

The accused are exposed by their fellow workers or neighbors in such a way as recalls the medieval pillory. Self-criticism to the point of self-humiliation is demanded in order to achieve the certainty that the defendant will strive in the future to become a useful member of his collective. Such a process often leads to the complete nervous collapse of the accused. . . . In such manner, the system of social courts brings about the conscious humiliation of a person before his fellow workers.[65]

As another souce put it:

Since everyone, including organizations, may bring a complaint, the door is open wide to denunciation from personal motives. Private, or after-work affairs are indiscriminately brought before the conflict commissions.[66]

The factors which the West German observers criticize most about the conflict commissions are the very ones to which the East German authorities point with pride as the key to the successful use of law as a means of education. West German writers denounce the conflict commissions as leading to the humiliation of the people they are intended to educate. East German sources say that it is just this fear of humiliation which makes the conflict commissions so successful in preventing violations. They would maintain that if the fear of humiliation deters potential offenders, then the social courts must be counted as a success. As for those who are not deterred, the East German view of law as education would hold that it is better for them and for society that they be humiliated and then released, rather than sent away for a short prison term.

---

[64] *Ibid.,* pp. 2–3.

[65] Walther Rosenthal. *Die Justiz In Der Sowjetzone* (Bonn, Bundesministerium Für Gesamtdeutsche Fragen, 1962), p. 26.

[66] *SBZ von A bis Z,* p. 17.

Design or Improvisation? The Origins of the German Protectorate of Bohemia and Moravia in 1939

VOJTECH MASTNY

At the Munich conference of September 1938, Hitler achieved his announced objective of annexing the frontier areas of Czechoslovakia to Germany. In November 1938, German and Italian pressure in the Vienna Award forced Czechoslovakia to cede further territories to Hungary. In March 1939, the rest of the country was dismembered: its eastern part, Carpathian Ukraine, annexed to Hungary, Slovakia proclaimed independent, and the western provinces of Bohemia and Moravia occupied by the German Army. On March 16, 1939, the latter became part of Germany as the Protectorate of Bohemia and Moravia.

The dismemberment of Czechoslovakia became an object of investigation at the Nuremberg trial of the major war criminals. The International Military Tribunal, passing judgment on September 30, 1946, attributed the end of Czechoslovakia to a design on the part of German Nazi leaders.[1]

This opinion of the Nuremberg tribunal has become the dominant interpretation ever since. Most liberal Western historians, as well as influential journalists (Mendelssohn, Namier, Wheeler-Bennett, Shirer) have been satisfied with the published documentary evidence and did not challenge the standard interpretation in any important way.[2]

[1] International Military Tribunal, *Trial of the Major War Criminals* (Nuremberg, International Military Tribunal, 1947–49), Vol. XXII, pp. 436–39.
[2] Peter de Mendelssohn, *Design for Aggression: The Inside Story of Hitler's War Plans* (New York and London, Harper, 1946).
Lewis B. Namier, *Diplomatic Prelude: 1938–1939* (London, Macmillan, 1948). [Footnote continued.]

Czechoslovak Marxist historians (Král, Hájek, Křen, Graca) did not question the validity of the design thesis either, although they used additional, previously unknown, documents from Czechoslovak archives.[3] Their contribution has been the thesis that the Czechoslovak leadership in 1938–39 shared responsibility for the Nazi aggression by facilitating the implementation of Hitler's plan.[4] This thesis, however, all too often did not rest upon fair analysis, free of simplifications.[5]

On the extreme right wing, attempts have been made, most recently by David L. Hoggan, to disprove the thesis of intentional Nazi destruction of Czechoslovakia.[6] In Hoggan's writing, Nazi actions were presented as improvisations, provoked by outside events and the policies of foreign statesmen. The supporting historical evidence, however, was founded either on misrepresentations of the previously known historical sources, or on unreliable information from persons reasonably suspect of whitewashing tendencies (Weizsäcker, Hesse).[7]

John W. Wheeler-Bennett, *Munich: Prologue to Tragedy* (London, Macmillan, 1948).

William L. Shirer, *The Rise and Fall of the Third Reich: A History of Nazi Germany* (New York, Simon and Schuster, 1960).

[3] Václav Král, *Pravda o okupaci* (The Truth about the Occupation) (Prague, Naše vojsko, 1962).

Miloš Hájek, *Od Mnichova k 15. březnu* (From Munich to March 15) (Prague, Státní nakladatelství politické literatúry, 1959).

Jan Křen, *Do emigrace: Buržoazní zahraniční odboj, 1938–1939* (Into Exile: The Bourgeois Exile Resistance, 1938–1939) (Prague, Naše vojsko, 1963).

Bohuslav Gracia, *14. marec 1939* (March 14, 1939) (Bratislava, Slovenské vydavateľstvo politickej literatúry, 1959).

[4] A variant of this thesis was presented in an excellent Ph.D. dissertation by Ivo K. Feierabend, "The Pattern of a Satellite State: Czechoslovakia 1938–1939" (Unpublished, Department of Political Science, Yale University, 1960), p. 380: "The Czechs and Slovaks pursued certain policies and adopted changes in the direction of the Nazi totalitarian example, not only because Germany wished them to or because they were bowing in face of irresistible pressures. They themselves wished to see certain changes made."

[5] Miloš Hájek, for example, grossly misrepresented the nature of fascism by applying the epithet "fascist" to most right-wing politicians in post-Munich Czechoslovakia.

[6] David L. Hoggan. *Der erzwungene Krieg: Die Ursachen und Urheber des Zweiten Weltkrieges* (Tübingen, Verlag der Deutschen Hochschullehrer-Zeitung, 1961). For criticism of Hoggan see: Gotthard Jasper, "Ueber die Ursachen des Zweiten Weltkrieges: Zu den Büchern von A. J. P. Taylor und David L. Hoggan," *Vierteljahrshefte für Zeitgeschichte*, X (1962), 311–40.

[7] Ernst von Weizsäcker, *Memoirs* (Chicago, Regnery, 1951).

Joachim von Ribbentrop, *The Ribbentrop Memoirs* (London, Weidenfeld and Nicolson, 1954).

Fritz Hesse, *Das Spiel um Deutschland* (Munich, List, 1953).

In 1961 A. J. P. Taylor's *The Origins of the Second World War* was published.[8] Taylor's provocative questions succeeded in undermining many an established interpretation, including the assumption of the German design for the occupation of Czechoslovakia. Although the answers provided by Taylor himself were frequently inconclusive (for example, his interpretation of the occupation as an "unforeseen by-product" of Slovak independence),[9] they made further research into the problem "design or improvisation" imperative. The inadequacy of older interpretations became obvious. On the other hand, the hitherto known documentary evidence was not sufficient to support valid new conclusions.

A great amount of material concerning the Nazi policies toward Czechoslovakia has been published in the West. Additional important sources have become accessible through Czechoslovak publications, which, however, are little known abroad. Yet even greater quantities of documentary material have remained unexplored. Some of them are in the hopelessly disorganized and fragmentary files of the German Foreign Office, of the High Command of the Armed Forces, and of some other military authorities. Only the Foreign Office files were used, to a limited extent, by German authors writing about the Czechoslovak crisis. Other documents were taken out from the original folders and assembled as evidence for various war crime trials. Most of them were never used and are still buried among the trial materials. In addition, there exist the records of countless interrogations of German officials, conducted by the Allies soon after the end of the war, which have received no attention by historians. The present study is an attempt to use these unknown or neglected primary sources with the aim of achieving a better understanding of Nazi political behavior in 1938–39.[10]

[8] A. J. P. Taylor, *The Origins of the Second World War* (New York, Atheneum, 1962).

[9] *Ibid.,* p. 202.

[10] The following collections of unpublished documents, preserved in the National Archives in Washington, D.C., were used in the preparation of this study:

In the Diplomatic, Legal, and Fiscal Branch: Microfilmed records of the German Foreign Office (T–120), Headquarters of the German Armed Forces High Command (T–77), Headquarters of the German Army High Command (T–78), and German Army Areas (T–79). DeWitt C. Poole Collection (RG–59).

In the Military Branch: Interrogations, proceedings, defense and prosecution briefs, defense and prosecution documents of the cases *United States v. Weizsäcker et al.* and *United States v. Leeb et al.*

The peaceful annexation of Czechoslovakia's Sudetenland as a result of the Munich agreement is usually considered one of Hitler's greatest diplomatic triumphs. Great Britain and France yielded to his threats of a military invasion of Czechoslovakia and joined Germany and Italy in forcing the Czechs into territorial cessions. Hitler's objective to incorporate the border areas of Bohemia and Moravia, mostly inhabited by Germans, into the Reich was thus achieved without a single shot.

Yet in view of the annexation of the whole of Bohemia and Moravia less than six months later, we may ask whether such a partial annexation was not actually less than what Hitler had desired. In fact, the opinion has been expressed that Hitler was furious because the Munich agreement had postponed the execution of his ultimate plan. Referring to British Prime Minister Chamberlain, one of the Munich signatories, Hitler was reported as saying: "That fellow has spoiled my entry into Prague." [11]

On November 23, 1939, Hitler boasted in a speech to his highest military officers:

From the very first moment it was clear to me that I could not be contented with the Sudeten German area. It was only a partial solution. The decision to invade Bohemia was made.[12]

Less than two weeks after Munich, Hitler asked General Keitel, Chief of the Armed Forces High Command, about the readiness of the German Army to crush "all Czech resistance in Bohemia and Moravia." [13] On October 21, 1938, Hitler issued a directive to the armed forces:

It must be possible to smash at any time the remainder of the Czech state, should it pursue an anti-German policy.[14]

None of the above evidence, impressive as it may seem, is a conclusive proof that the annexation of Bohemia and Moravia was planned immediately after Munich. The information about Hitler's dissatisfaction with Munich comes from a biased defendant in the Nuremberg

[11] International Military Tribunal, *Trial.* Vol. XII, p. 531.

[12] *Ibid.,* XXVI, 329.

[13] Office of the Chief Counsel for the Prosecution of Axis Criminality, *Nazi Conspiracy and Aggression* (Washington, D.C., U.S. Government Printing Office, 1947), Vol. III, pp. 372–73.

[14] *Documents on German Foreign Policy,* Series D (Washington, D.C., U.S. Government Printing Office, 1951), Vol. IV, p. 99.

trial, Hjalmar Schacht. Hitler's speech of November 1939 was delivered *ex post facto* and intended to demonstrate in highly emotional terms his own clairvoyance and the working of Providence. The military directive made the destruction of the remainder of Czechoslovakia explicitly conditional upon pursuance of an anti-German policy. Other military documents, all originating from the time before the Sudeten crisis, mentioned occupation and even annexation as possibilities in the course of the military action aimed at the incorporation of the Sudetenland, but not as the objective of that action.[15]

An analysis of German behavior toward Czechoslovakia in the fall of 1938 will provide an answer to the question of whether the Nazi policy was directed toward the ultimate annexation of that country. The German attitude toward the Slovak separatists, whose objective was to break up the unity of Czechoslovakia, therefore deserves special consideration.

In October 1938, high officials of the Berlin Foreign Office and the armed forces weighed possible alternatives concerning Slovakia's future position: independence, autonomy within Czechoslovakia, autonomy within Hungary, autonomy within Poland.[16] The Zilina agreement of October 6, which gave the Slovaks an autonomous status within the Czechoslovak state, was welcomed by the Foreign Office and the Armed Forces High Command. Slovakia's continued union with Prague was seen as the best guarantee against Polish and Hungarian efforts to establish a common frontier by annexations in Slovakia.[17] "It is in our *military interest* that Slovakia should not be separated from the Czechoslovak union but should remain with Czechoslovakia under strong German influence." [18]

On the other hand, the Slovak separatist leaders, Tiso, Ďurčanský, Sidor, and others, made repeated attempts to enlist German support for their independence plans.[19] On October 12 Ďurčanský visited

[15] In that respect, Hitler's famous statement "We want no Czechs" in his speech of September 26, 1938, was probably true at that time. Norman H. Baynes, ed., *The Speeches of Adolf Hitler, April 1922–August 1939.* (London, Oxford University Press, 1942), Vol. II, p. 1526.
[16] Woermann's memorandum, Oct. 5, 1938 (NG–3056), *U.S. v. Weizsäcker et al.*, Prosecution Document Book No. 3B (in English), pp. 244–47.
[17] Woermann's memorandum, Oct. 7, 1938, *Documents on German Foreign Policy*, IV, 46–47.
[18] Keitel to Foreign Office, Oct. 6, 1938, *ibid.*, p. 40.
[19] Outline of Göring-Ďurčanský conversation, Oct. 12, 1938, *ibid.*, pp. 82–83. Its date corrected according to Ferdinand Ďurčanský, "Mit Tiso bei Hitler," *Politische Studien*, VII, No. 80 (Dec. 1956), 9. Minutes of Ribbentrop-Tiso conversation, Oct. 19, 1938, *Documents on German Foreign Policy*,

Göring; on October 19 Tiso was received by Ribbentrop. The Slovaks' objective was independence under German guarantee, which would enable them not only to break away from the Czechs but also to fortify their position against Hungarian and Polish territorial demands.

Nevertheless, in the fall of 1938 Germany did not effectively support Slovak efforts for independence which would have led to the dissolution of Czechoslovakia.[20] On the contrary, Germany pursued a policy which was to give some permanence and stability to Czechoslovakia's position, after satisfying Hungary's territorial claims at the Slovaks' expense. Germany and Italy attempted to settle the Hungarian demands by arranging for the Vienna Award of November 2. By that act Hungary received an extensive territory in southern and eastern Slovakia. Henceforth Germany did not favor any further acquisitions of Czechoslovak territory by the neighboring states.[21]

For other reasons as well, Germany was interested in the stabilization of Czechoslovakia. After Munich the rump state was politically, militarily, economically, and morally weakened to such an extent that it was in no position to resist whatever demands Germany might decide to make.

Czechoslovakia's Foreign Minister Chvalkovský indicated that in exchange for a guarantee of her territory Czechoslovakia was willing "to comply with Germany's wishes in every respect" and in foreign policy "to rely on Germany if Germany would allow this." [22] On the domestic scene, there was a clear turnaway from democracy: dis-

---

IV, 86–92. Report of an SS agent on conversation with Sidor, Nov. 1, 1938 (NG–3099), *U.S. v. Weizsäcker*, p. 259.

[20] Several Foreign Office documents quote Göring as favoring Slovak independence. Since no actions along the line of Göring's idea can be documented from German records of the fall of 1938, it is probable that at that time Göring's opinion was only personal and did not represent an official policy directive. Cf. the outline of Göring-Ďurčanský conversation, Oct. 12, 1938, *Documents on German Foreign Policy*, Vol. IV, p. 83.

[21] Concerning Carpathian Ukraine, the easternmost province of Czechoslovakia, Hitler in the fall of 1938 cherished dreams about that country's becoming the nucleus of a future independent Ukraine under German influence. For the time being, however, Germany supported the province's autonomy within Czechoslovakia as preferable to independence or annexation to Hungary. *Ibid.*, IV, 49.

Cf. also R. G. D. Laffan and Veronica M. Toynbee, "The Crisis over Czechoslovakia, Oct. 1938 to 15 March 1939," *Survey of International Affairs 1938* (London, Oxford University Press, 1953), Vol. IV, pp. 105–12.

[22] Minutes of Ribbentrop-Chvalkovský conversation, Oct. 13, 1938, *Documents on German Foreign Policy*, IV, 61.

solution of most political parties, transfer of power from the National Assembly to the President by an Enabling Act, increased censorship of the press, official endorsement of anti-Jewish policy. The Government was dominated by right-wing politicians who blamed parliamentary democracy for the decline of the state and advocated close cooperation with Germany.

Czechoslovakia was on her way to becoming a German satellite: a country formally independent but in fact controlled by Germany, upon whom she also modeled her internal setup. Such a development, rather than outright annexation, coincided with the pronounced aim of Berlin's policy.[23]

As a guideline for the forthcoming talks with Chvalkovský, Woermann, Under Secretary of State in the Wilhelmstrasse, noted on October 12:

If it is the intention to establish really close relations with Czechoslovakia, we must not impose a Versailles on the country.[24]

It was assumed, however, "that in the future the 'Czech and Slovak' Rump State will of necessity depend to a considerable extent on Germany." [25]

Germany deliberately encouraged Czechoslovakia's development into a satellite. In the conversation with Chvalkovský on October 14, Hitler made it clear that the country must submit to German leadership in foreign policy, reduce her army, introduce anti-Jewish measures, further limit freedom of the press, and adjust her economy to the needs of the Reich. "[Czechoslovakia] must realize that she was in the German sphere, and it was in her own interest to adapt herself to the conditions of that sphere." [26]

The satellite relationship of Prague to Berlin was to be safeguarded and made permanent by bilateral treaties. On November 19, 1938,

[23] It is interesting that three memoranda, which originated in Oct. 1938 with the Sudeten German leaders, noted for their chauvinism, preferred independent Czechoslovakia under strong German influence to annexation: Proposal of the Konrad Henlein Staff concerning the solution of the Czech problem, in Václav Král, ed., *Lesson from History: Documents Concerning Nazi Policies for Germanization and Extermination in Czechoslovakia* (Prague, Orbis, 1961), pp. 35–38. Memoranda by deputies Hans Neuwirth and Ernst Kundt to the Foreign Office, in Václav Král, ed., *Die Deutschen in der Tschecho-slowakei, 1933–1947: Dokumentensammlung* (Prague, Nakladatelstvi Československé akademie věd, 1964), pp. 349–53, 357–62.

[24] Woermann's memorandum, Oct. 12, 1938, *Documents on German Foreign Policy,* IV, 58.

[25] Keitel to Foreign Office, Oct. 6, 1938, *ibid.,* p. 40.

[26] Minutes of Hitler-Chvalkovský conversation, Oct. 14, 1938, *ibid.,* p. 70.

a treaty was signed providing for the construction of a highway between Breslau and Vienna, giving Germany extraterritorial rights in
the section across Czechoslovakia. On the same day a similar treaty
foresaw the construction of an Oder-Danube canal. On November 20
treaties regarding citizenship, option, and protection of minorities
were concluded, giving a privileged position to the Germans who
remained in Czechoslovakia.[27]

A far-reaching "friendship" treaty, consisting of three parts, was
prepared by the Wilhelmstrasse during November 1938.

In the political part, prepared by Ministerial Director Friedrich
Gaus, Germany guaranteed the territorial integrity of Czechoslovakia.
It was assumed that Prague would renounce her desire for a British
and French guarantee. Czechoslovak foreign policy was to be con-
ducted in conformity with German desires. It meant in particular that
Czechoslovakia should withdraw from the League of Nations, accede
to the Anti-Comintern Pact, and extend recognition to the Franco
Government of Spain.[28]

The military part was prepared by General Keitel in three subsequent drafts. According to the final draft of December 9, Czechoslovakia was required to renounce her foreign alliances and not to
enter into any new ones. Her armed forces were to be reduced and
surplus armaments offered to Germany. Germany was to receive
military privileges, such as the rights of passage for military trans-
ports.[29]

The economic part of the treaty was prepared by Ambassador
Karl Ritter. Czechoslovak trade negotiations with foreign countries
were to be conducted only by Berlin. Germany and Czechoslovakia
were to form a monetary and customs union. Ritter himself considered the economic union project so far-reaching that he recommended its temporary postponement. He pointed out potential bur-
dens the economic union would bring upon Germany: obligation
to provide raw materials for Czechoslovak industry and to supply the
needs of additional consumers. He therefore suggested that for the

[27] *Ibid.,* pp. 153–54.
Records of the German Foreign Office, microcopy T–120, film 1094, frames
450629–630, and film 1004, frames 391220–227.
[28] Woermann's memoranda, Nov. 23 and 25, 1938 (NG–3613 and NG–2993),
U.S. v. Weizsäcker, pp. 269, 273–77.
The text of the treaty in Heinrich Bodensieck, "Der Plan eines 'Freund-
schaftsvertrages' zwischen dem Reich und der Tschecho-Slowakei im Jahre
1938," *Zeitschrift für Ostforschung,* X (1961), 464–65.
[29] *Ibid.,* pp. 470–73.

time being German goals would be better served by specialized agreements which would guarantee that Germany could utilize Czechoslovakia's armament industry and exploit her natural resources.[30]

The German Foreign Office planned that Minister Chvalkovský would come to Berlin before Christmas, to be presented with the draft treaty. In addition, he was to be told that besides the provisions of the treaty Czechoslovakia would be expected to put into effect certain internal measures: control over press and propaganda according to German needs, and anti-Jewish legislation. In a commentary to the draft treaty, Under Secretary of State Woermann stated: "An extensive assimilation to the internal German structure will have to be consummated by Czechoslovakia itself." [31]

Chvalkovský's visit, as planned by the Wilhelmstrasse, never took place. He did not have an opportunity to come to Berlin until January 21, 1939. At that time the treaty was no longer mentioned. It is probable that Prague was not even informed about its preparation. The draft disappeared into the Wilhelmstrasse files and was never revived.

A German historian, Hans Schiefer, and an American political scientist, Ivo Feierabend, were among the few authors who believed that Hitler's decision to occupy Bohemia and Moravia had reversed his earlier policy of preserving Czechoslovakia's formal independence after Munich. Yet neither of the two scholars was able to offer more than hypotheses as to the time the decision had been taken and military preparations begun. Schiefer speculated about the time "before Christmas," Feierabend—working only with published documents —about February 1939.[32]

In fact, the indications about the change in Hitler's policy objectives dated from mid-December 1938. A supplementary order to the armed forces, issued by Keitel upon Hitler's instructions on December 17, 1938, stated in regard to Czechoslovakia:

The case is to be prepared on the assumption that no appreciable resistance is to be expected.

[30] *Ibid.*, pp. 466–70.
The proposed *terminus a quo* of the currency and customs union was to be April 1, 1939. *Records of the German Foreign Office,* microcopy T–120, film 1159, frames 468040–048.

[31] Woermann's memorandum, Nov. 25, 1938, *U.S. v. Weizsäcker,* p. 277.

[32] Hans Schiefer, "Deutschland und die Tschechoslowakei von September 1938 bis März 1939," *Zeitschrift für Ostforschung,* IV (1955), 55. Feierabend, "The Pattern of a Satellite State," p. 84.

Outwardly it must be quite clear that it is only a peaceful action and not a warlike undertaking.

The action must therefore be carried out *only* with the peacetime Wehrmacht, without reinforcement by mobilization . . .

. . . the army units detailed to march in must not as a general rule leave their stations until the night before the crossing of the frontier, and must not, as previously planned, deploy on the frontier.[33]

General Warlimont, Chief of the National Defense Department in the Armed Forces High Command, told the following story to the American military interrogators on September 22, 1945:

About the middle of December, Warlimont accompanied Hitler and a suite of officers on a trip into Sudeten areas for the purpose of inspecting Czech fortifications. . . . During lunch at the inn of a small Sudeten town, on the first day of the trip, Hitler dominated the table conversation and startled his audience by declaring that he continued firm in his original plan for the incorporation of Bohemia and Moravia within the Reich. He was confident that he would accomplish this by political means. The Wehrmacht need therefore concern itself solely with the problem of the most rapid possible occupation of Bohemia and Moravia . . .

As a result of this pronouncement, which apparently had the force of an order, Warlimont received from Keitel the instruction to prepare the proper directives for the Wehrkreise in the areas bordering on Bohemia and Moravia. These entailed the creation of a system of "accelerated readiness to march" (*beschleunigte Marschbereitschaft*) in which it was emphasized that the bulk of the troops of these Wehrkreise, particularly motorized formations, should be ready to march on 12-hour notice.[34]

There are moreover indications that Hitler considered the possibility of using the Slovak independence movement for his own purposes. Keppler, the State Secretary for Special Tasks in the Foreign Office, testified at his trial in Nuremberg as follows:

Toward the end of 1938 . . .—I think it was about November or December—the Führer invited me to a social function in Munich. On this occasion the Führer took me aside and gave me instructions to inform myself about Slovak matters and to keep informed so that I might be ready at any time to be used in this matter.[35]

With all due mistrust of the testimonies of war criminals, it can nevertheless be stated that in December 1938 Hitler seriously con-

[33] *Documents on German Foreign Policy,* IV, 186.

[34] Interrogation of Walter Warlimont, Sept. 22, 1945, pp. 3–4, *DeWitt C. Poole Collection,* RG–59.

[35] Examination of Wilhelm Keppler, *U.S. v. Weizsäcker,* Proceedings (in English), microfilm frame 12896.

templated the occupation of Bohemia and Moravia in the near future. The above-quoted instruction of December 17 to the armed forces may not have been accompanied by actual military preparations in the same month. But the preparations were to follow soon. The fact that the December directive was used in the orders issued to the troops when they were actually carrying out the invasion in March 1939 also suggests that the directive was a guideline to be taken seriously.[36]

What was the cause of the change in Hitler's policy and of his decision in favor of occupation? It should be noted that the execution of the prepared "friendship" treaty would have given Germany practically the same measure of control as she eventually acquired as a result of the military occupation.

Wilhelmstrasse interpreter Paul Schmidt, a competent and intelligent observer with first-hand knowledge of the Nazi leaders, suggested —not seriously—a rather amusing explanation which nevertheless duly called attention to the role of the purely emotional factor in Hitler's policy decisions:

The Czechs were now for Hitler against the red cloth. At that time I attributed it to his Austrian background, whereas today I am putting Hitler's insane fury against the Czechs in some relation to the theory that he himself had Czech blood in his veins.[37]

The explanation of Hitler's decision may not lie in the realm of the rational. It can only be suggested as a possibility that Hitler was not satisfied with the Czech leaders, no matter how servile and compliant their attitude, and decided therefore to substitute a more direct German control. It was apparent that the Czech leaders' behavior was dictated by fear or opportunism. Yet they were the only men available for the role of German puppets. Among the Czech people no group with a genuine authoritarian program, sympathies for Nazism, and a sizable mass following, could be found to be put in charge of the state. In this respect the Czech situation was different from that of the Nazi wartime satellite states elsewhere in Europe. In post-Munich Czechoslovakia the Nazis could rely only on colorless civil servants and second-class politicians who commanded little respect. The absence of real personalities was a notable and ominous phenomenon in Czech political life.

[36] Order to the 10th Division, Army Area XIII, March 11, 1939, *Records of German Army Areas,* microcopy T–79, film 131, frame 301.
[37] Paul Schmidt, *Statist auf diplomatischer Bühne, 1923–1945.* (Bonn, Athäneum, 1958), p. 428.

Unpublished German Army materials make it clear that military preparations for the invasion began in mid-January 1939. From that time on there frequently appeared in the papers of the Armed Forces High Command the word "special timetable" (*Sonderkalender*) in relation to the action against Czechoslovakia. A basic document, often referred to, bore the date January 16, 1939.[38]

Military records from February 1939 used the terms "Y day" for the day of the invasion and "Y minus" days for the period immediately preceding. On February 15 the 10th Division, with headquarters in Regensburg, received orders concerning its alarm readiness for the night of Y–1 day to Y day. The division was to be ready between Furth im Walde and Kaplice for an assault against Milevsko in southern Bohemia in early morning.[39]

The High Command assumed that no serious military resistance of the Czechoslovak Army would be encountered. Nevertheless isolated acts of sabotage, causing destruction of industrial and military establishments, might take place. Power stations in particular were therefore to be swiftly occupied. In order to assure their uninterrupted operation, Technical Emergency Squads (*Technische Nothilfe*) would be at the disposal of the army. Similarly, the telephone and telegraph network was to be taken under control with utmost speed.[40]

It is possible that in January the Nazi leaders were not yet sure as to what political means should be used to bring about Y day. In a conversation with Chvalkovský on January 21, Hitler overwhelmed the Czechoslovak Minister with complaints about the conditions in Czechoslovakia and the disloyal behavior of the Czechs toward the Germans.[41] Nevertheless he did not hint at any action which would be likely to precipitate a crisis. In particular, he did not present any specific conditions or demands which Prague would be unable to fulfil and thus give Germany an excuse for military intervention.

Understandably enough, the result of the Hitler-Chvalkovský conversation did not dispel Czech nervousness about German intentions.

[38] Correspondence of the "OKW-Wehrwirtschaftsstaab" with subordinate organs, Jan. to March 1939, *Records of Headquarters, German Armed Forces High Command,* microcopy T–77, film 170, frames 904448–463.

[39] Order to the 10th Division, Feb. 15, 1939, *Records of the German Army Areas,* microcopy T–79, film 174, frames 664–67 and 671–74.

[40] Order of March 2, 1938, *ibid.,* film 131, frames 261–63. Orders of the Army High Command to Army Groups, Feb. 10 and 24, 1939, *Records of Headquarters, German Armed Forces High Command,* microcopy T–77, film 732, frames 1958368–371.

[41] Minutes of Hitler-Chvalkovský conversation, Jan. 21, 1939, *Documents on German Foreign Policy,* IV, 190–95.

There were speculations, according to Hencke, the German chargé d'affaires in Prague, about whether Germany wanted to "introduce a second period of probation" or whether Hitler's attitude signalized a prelude to "further decisive actions." [42]

Nine days later, Hitler hinted at the possible course of action in a major speech in the Sport Palace. He mentioned, in a relatively moderate yet ominous tone,[43] the urgency "to reestablish order in Czechoslovakia."

The next step was a reversal of Berlin's noncommittal attitude toward the Slovak separatist movement. In a conversation on February 12 with Vojtech Tuka, the emissary of the Slovak separatists, Hitler began by regretting that he had not formerly understood Slovak aspirations.

Had he known then [by the time of the Vienna Award] how things really stood in Slovakia, he would have had the Slovak leaders come and would have guaranteed them the integrity of their country—and this still held good today.[44]

A "far-reaching solution" was very likely to be expected against the Czechs, since the spirit of enmity against Germany had not disappeared among them and their mentality would probably not change. In that case, Slovakia would be threatened as well, because she would be *"mitgefangen, mitgehangen."* Hitler made his desire completely clear by declaring that he "could not guarantee Czechoslovakia today. . . . He could guarantee an independent Slovakia at any time, even today." [45]

On March 1 another Slovak leader, Ďurčanský, was received by Ribbentrop. Ribbentrop reportedly stated that

. . . in case of the proclamation of independence the Reich government would be ready to guarantee Slovakia's frontiers against any aggression from the outside, provided this step would be taken in a favorable moment.[46]

On March 7, a delegation consisting of Tuka, Ďurčanský, and others was received by Göring.

---

[42] Hencke to Foreign Office, Jan. 27, 1939, *ibid.,* p. 204.
[43] Baynes, p. 1578.
[44] Minutes of Hitler-Tuka conversation, Feb. 12, 1939, *Documents on German Foreign Policy,* IV, 212.
[45] *Ibid.,* pp. 211–12.
[46] Ďurčanský, "Mit Tiso bei Hitler," p. 5.
Cf. also excerpts from Keppler's file dated Aug. 9, 1939 (NG–3956), *U.S. v. Weizsäcker,* Prosecution Document Book No. 3B, p. 312.

Since the news about German military preparations and about increasing German-Slovak contacts leaked out, the Czechoslovak Government made an attempt to clarify the situation. On February 22, in notes to the signatories of the Munich agreement, Czechoslovakia inquired about the promised guarantees. The action, without bringing any positive response, was considered by Berlin an unfriendly act and resulted in an increase of political tension. Equally disappointing was the mission of the Prague Foreign Minister's chef de cabinet, Hubert Masařík. Masařík arrived in Berlin with an offer of virtually unlimited concessions to Germany, in exchange for a German guarantee of Czechoslovakia's territorial integrity. He did not get any farther than to the head of the Czechoslovak desk in the Berlin Foreign Office, Günther Altenburg, and his proposals were not even considered.[47]

At the beginning of March the political atmosphere was full of rumors about Germany's imminent action. After the war, former State Secretary Keppler was interrogated about a large meeting of some forty to fifty persons on March 8, at which Hitler supposedly had announced his decision to invade Czechoslovakia at a definite date. Keppler's testimony was inconclusive. There is no other evidence of the meeting's being held, and it is probable that this rumor was false.[48]

As late as March 9 the date of the invasion was probably not set. The crisis, however, was expected to break out at any time. The Nazis only awaited an opportune moment.

During the night of March 9 to March 10, Czechoslovak President Hácha dismissed the autonomous Slovak Government headed by the separatist leader Jozef Tiso. Thus were culminated the repeated attempts of the Prague Government to find a solution to the Slovak question. At first the central and the autonomous governments tried to negotiate. When the negotiations did not bring any satisfactory

[47] Altenburg's memorandum, March 1, 1939, *Documents on German Foreign Policy*, IV, 221–24.

[48] Interrogation of Wilhelm Keppler, Nov. 6, 1945 (Unpublished documents, *U.S. v. Weizsäcker et al.*, Nuremberg War Criminals Trials, 1945–1949. Washington, D.C., National Archives, No. 3876), p. 3.

Examination of Keppler, *U.S. v. Weizsäcker*, Proceedings (in English), microfilm frame 19723.

The rumor originated with U.S. Ambassador to Berlin Bullitt. Bullitt reported it to Washington on Sept. 19, 1939; attached to the prosecution documents of the above case as L–133.

result, the central government preferred to bring about an internal crisis, rather than to face a possible international one which might result in German interference in Slovak affairs.[49]

The internal crisis alone, however, was enough to give the Nazis sufficient pretext for intervention. In a few hours after the announcement of the dismissal, the German military timetable started operating. This information, which until now could not be documented, is contained in the hitherto unknown "War Diary" preserved in the files of the General Staff of the Army. The War Diary gave a detailed hour-by-hour description of the entire "Operation Southeast" from the military point of view.[50]

The diary began on March 10. At about 2:30 p.m. an oral order came from Major Heusinger of Section I of the General Staff, saying that the marching orders for the SS Bodyguard Adolf Hitler should be prepared. The SS unit was to be set in motion first, because its task was the occupation of the industrial Ostrava region several hours before that of the rest of Bohemia and Moravia. This maneuver was to prevent the possible seizure of Ostrava by Poland. The orders to other army units were wired at 4:57 p.m. At the same time, the General Staff specified the meaning of A day and Y day. On A day, March 12, the troops were to start moving toward Czech frontiers. Y day, when the frontiers were to be crossed, was set for March 15.

Whereas there is no doubt about the preciseness of the military timetable, the question is open as to how far this timetable was coordinated with political actions. Seen *ex post facto,* it seemed almost certain that after March 10 the moves of the Slovak separatists were carried out in accordance with Nazi needs. Yet the records show that improvisation rather than coordination was the rule.

After the dismissal of the Slovak autonomous government, the Prague authorities sent troops to Slovakia and proclaimed martial law there. Although martial law was hardly enforced and the armed units of the separatist party were not hindered in their activities, the Slovaks did not proclaim an independent state immediately.

On March 11 State Secretary Keppler was sent to Vienna, where Gauleiter Bürckel had been unsuccessfully trying to coordinate political action with the Slovak leaders. On the next day Keppler re-

[49] Václav Král, *Pravda o okupaci* (The Truth about the Occupation) (Prague, Naše vojsko, 1962), pp. 128–29.

[50] "Kriegstagebuch, 5. Abt. (Ic) GenStdH, anlässlich der Besetzung Böhmens/Mährens," *Records of Headquarters of the German Army High Command,* microcopy T–78, film 301, frames 6252043–217.

ported to Altenburg in Berlin that the situation was "a mess" and that the Germans had been apparently fooled by the Slovaks. In particular, the "proclamation planned by Ďurčanský" did not come.[51]

Berlin had therefore to be prepared for the possibility that the invasion would take place without Slovakia's proclamation of independence. The German press and radio opened a propaganda campaign about the oppression of Germans in Bohemia and Moravia. Berlin unsuccessfully hoped that the Czechs could be provoked to open violence against the German minority.[52]

Foreign Minister Ribbentrop had a telegram ready to be sent to the Czechoslovak Government. The telegram, which was actually never dispatched, has been preserved in the East German Central Archives in Potsdam and only recently was made public by Czechoslovak historians. Its text began:

The events of the last days give a final proof that the government in Prague neither wants nor can create conditions . . . which would assure a permanent peaceful situation.

Unspecified "chaotic conditions" in Czechoslovakia were given as the reason for the Reich Government's decision

. . . to take immediately necessary measures. The action decided upon aims at bringing the peoples of Czechoslovakia rest and peace, and at making possible their prosperous coexistence. This objective makes it necessary to extend the said measures to the living area of the Czech people.

In gross exaggeration the telegram stated that "from all parts of the Czech country ethnic Germans, terrorized and persecuted in an inhuman manner, cry for help." In conclusion, the German Foreign Minister asked that Prague should send to Berlin a negotiator equipped with full powers.[53]

[51] Altenburg's memorandum, March 12, 1939 (NG–3045), *U.S. v. Weizsäcker, Prosecution Document Book No. 3B* (in English), p. 315. As far as approaching the Slovaks is concerned, there seems to have been strong rivalry between Bürckel and Seyss-Inquart on the one hand, and Keppler and Veesenmayer on the other.
[52] "The representatives of the [German] ethnic group deplore everywhere the entirely legal and even cooperative attitude of the Czechs," Toussaint and Hencke to Foreign Office, March 11, 1939, *Records of the German Foreign Office,* microcopy T–120, film 12, frame 17626.
"The behavior of all official organs and of the population towards the Germans is decidedly tolerant. Provocations are possibly avoided." Hencke to Foreign Office, March 13, 1939, *ibid.,* frame 17609.
[53] Král, *Die Deutschen in der Tschechoslowakei,* p. 380.

The Armed Forces High Command prepared military provisions which were probably to be added to Ribbentrop's telegram. German demands called for the abstention from any resistance to the advancing forces. Uninterrupted operation of public life and economy, especially transportation, was to be safeguarded.[54]

In German military files another document has been preserved, dated March 13. A general proclamation, which also was never used, indicated the dismissal of the Slovak Government as the first reason for the intervention. The document continued to repeat invented stories that

. . . hundreds of Slovak leaders were arrested and jailed, numerous Slovaks, Germans and Ukrainians killed. . . . Everywhere Slovaks and Germans are waging stubborn and desperate defense under the pledge of their blood and property against Prague's centralization efforts.[55]

The proclamation called for the peaceful acceptance of the German troops, who were not coming as enemies but as guarantors of peace and prosperity.

It is possible that in case the Slovaks would not have ultimately proclaimed their independence, the German invasion would have coincided with a Hungarian attack against Slovakia. There is evidence, although scarce and inconclusive, of an agreement between Berlin and Budapest to that effect. The Hungarian regent, Horthy, wrote to Hitler on March 13:

Heartfelt thanks! I cannot express how happy I am, for this headwater region is, in fact, for Hungary—I dislike using big words—a vital question. . . . On Thursday the 16th of this month a frontier incident will take place, to be followed on Saturday by the big thrust.[56]

The prospects for the Nazi plans changed again, when on March 13 Keppler phoned from Vienna that "there is a possibility that Tiso may come to Berlin." [57] Tiso's trip to Berlin was prepared by Kep-

[54] Keitel to Foreign Office, March 11, 1939, *Documents on German Foreign Policy*, IV, 313–14.

[55] "An Alle," March 13, 1939, *Records of Headquarters, German Armed Forces High Command*, microcopy T–77, film 820, frames 5555376–377. The proclamation was never used.

[56] Horthy to Hitler, March 13, 1939, *Documents on German Foreign Policy*, IV, 241. Feierabend, "The Pattern of a Satellite State," p. 129, expressed the opinion that Horthy's letter had referred to Carpathian Ukraine.

[57] Heinburg's memorandum, March 13, 1939, *Documents on German Foreign Policy*, IV, 239.
Interrogation of Veesenmayer, Sept. 1945, p. 6, *DeWitt C. Poole Collection*, RG–59.

pler's colleague, Veesenmayer. In a private letter four months later Keppler wrote about the situation on March 13: "Due to particularly good luck, it was possible to bring Prime Minister Tiso in time to a conference with the Führer in Berlin." [58]

On March 13, at 6:40 p.m., Hitler received Tiso and Ďurčanský in the presence of the highest Nazi dignitaries. He informed the Slovaks about the impending action against the Czechs, and pressed Tiso for the proclamation of Slovak independence. "If she [Slovakia] hesitated or refused to be separated from Prague, he would leave the fate of Slovakia to events for which he was no longer responsible." [59] This statement implied that the Slovaks would be left at the mercy of Hungary.

The proclamation of Slovak independence by the provincial diet in Bratislava followed on the next day, March 14. This event provided the Nazis with a badly needed excuse for the forthcoming invasion of Bohemia and Moravia.

In conformity with this new development, the draft of Ribbentrop's telegram to Prague was revised. Its modified text, preserved on microfilm in the National Archives in Washington and until now unknown, contained significant differences from the Potsdam draft mentioned above. The separation of Slovakia was given a prominent place among the grievances against Prague, whereas the stories about the terror against Germans were moderated in tone. Since time was running short, the paragraph asking for a negotiator to be sent to Berlin was left out. The demands for nonresistance and maintenance of public order were included. [60]

Yet not even this telegram was sent to Prague. On the eve of the invasion a new initiative from the Czechoslovak capital brought an unexpected element into the complicated situation.

Faced with the increasing German-Czechoslovak tension and with the upsurge of Slovak separatism, the Czechoslovak cabinet decided that President Hácha should make an attempt to save the situation by personal contact with Hitler. [61]

---

[58] Keppler to Himmler, July 11, 1939 (NG–2936), *U.S. v. Weizsäcker,* Prosecution Document Book No. 2 (in English), p. 88.

[59] Minutes of Hitler-Tiso conversation, March 13, 1939, *Documents on German Foreign Policy,* IV, 245.

[60] "Mitteilung an die Regierung in Prag," March 14, 1939, *Records of the German Foreign Office,* microcopy T–120, film 1077, frames 435188–190.

[61] Král, *Pravda o okupaci,* pp. 132–33.

In the night of March 13, a few hours after Tiso's visit to Berlin, Foreign Minister Chvalkovský phoned German chargé d'affaires Hencke and invited him to meet with the President at 9 p.m. In conformity with Ribbentrop's instruction of the preceding day, Hencke declined the invitation and stated that any communication must be sent to the legation in writing.

Chvalkovský's letter asking Hitler to grant an interview to Hácha was transmitted to Hencke on March 14 at 11:25 a.m.[62] The interview was granted and Hácha left for Berlin in the night of March 14. At that time the SS Bodyguard Adolf Hitler was starting to occupy the Ostrava region.

Hácha was a former Austro-Hungarian civil servant who held the position of Chief Justice of the Supreme Administrative Court during Czechoslovak independence. At the age of sixty-six, in November 1938, he was elected President of rump-Czechoslovakia. Until that time he had not been active in politics. His policy after the election emphasized friendly relations with Germany as the only alternative left to Czechoslovakia.

There is no clarity about the objectives Hácha hoped to achieve by meeting Hitler. On March 14, at 11:25 p.m., the Czechoslovak Government radio station quoted Hácha's words before his departure for Berlin:

He will see the goal of his mission in the recognition of the fact of the historical and geographical incorporation of the Czech state into the sphere of power of the German Reich.[63]

Two days later, after the incorporation had already become a fact, Hácha chose the theme of his own disbelief in Czech independence for the opening paragraph of his crucial address to the Czech people, who had just been crushed by German occupation:

When twenty years ago all Czech hearts were filled with joy [at the proclamation of national independence], I stood apart from those historic events. Over my joy for our unbelievable success was cast a gloom of anxiety, as to whether all external and internal guarantees had been given to assure the permanence of our success. Now, after twenty years, I can see with grief that my anxieties of that time were not without foundation. It has

[62] Hencke to Foreign Office, March 13, 1939, *Documents on German Foreign Policy,* IV, 248.

Original of the Chvalkovský letter, March 14, 1939, *Records of the German Foreign Office,* microcopy T–120, film 1077, frame 435232.

[63] Karl Megerle, "Deutschland und das Ende der Tschecho-Slowakei," *Monatshefte für auswärtige Politik,* VI, No. 8 (Aug. 1939), 770.

been proved, that what we held for a solution which would last for ages was merely a short episode in our national history. . . . By our union with [Germany] the former unity of the Reich has been restored.[64]

It is impossible to decide whether Hácha had doubts about Czech independence—as he said—since 1918, or whether—as seems more likely—he came to such a conclusion only under the impact of its actual decline in 1938 and 1939. The striking fact is, nevertheless, that the Czechoslovak President who arrived in Berlin on March 14, 1939 for critical conversations with Hitler was no ardent advocate of the independence of his own country.

The meeting in the Reich Chancellery soon after midnight on March 15 will probably remain a mystery in many of its interesting details, despite descriptions by almost every one of the numerous participants. The minutes of the meeting, written by Walter Hewel of the German Foreign Office, contained several obvious inaccuracies. Other descriptions, by the accused war criminals at Nuremberg, by Hácha himself, or by persons with second-hand knowledge of the event, were necessarily biased and often conflicting. The most objective account was probably given by interpreter Paul Schmidt in his interrogation by United States Army officers and in his memoirs.[65]

The Hácha-Hitler meeting opened with a submissive and self-derogatory speech by Hácha, possibly including a statement about his doubts as to whether independence had been fortunate for his country. Hácha did not advance any specific proposals. Then Hitler expressed his grievances against Czechoslovakia at some length and informed Hácha about the imminent occupation of Bohemia and Moravia. He asked Hácha to arrange that there be no resistance against the ad-

[64] Ulrich Thürauf, ed., *Schulthess' Europäischer Geschichts-kalender* (Munich, Beck, 1940), Vol. LXXX (1939), p. 62.

[65] Hewel minutes of Hitler-Hácha conversation, *Documents on German Foreign Policy*, IV, 263–69.

Examinations of Meissner and Keppler, *U.S. v. Weizsäcker*, Proceedings (in English), microfilm frames 4541–542, and 12916.

Hácha's report, March 20, 1939, *Mnichov v dokumentech* (Munich in Documents) (Prague, Státní nakladatelství politické literatúry, 1958), Vol. II, pp. 392–95.

French Ambassador Coulondre's report, based on fourth-hand knowledge, *The French Yellow Book: Diplomatic Documents (1938–1939)* (New York, Reynal and Hitchcock, 1940), pp. 96–97.

Cf. Věra Szathmáryová-Vlčková, *Putování za svobodou, 1938–1945* (Pilgrimage for Freedom, 1938–1945) (Prague, Československý kompas, 1946), p. 23.

vancing German forces, and gave promises about future Czech autonomy.

Although Schmidt and others report that the conversation was conducted in a formally correct manner and no pressure was used against Hácha, it is almost certain that serious threats were made in some form. At one moment Hácha held a conversation with Göring which Schmidt admittedly did not hear. Subsequently Hácha collapsed and had to be given an injection by Hitler's physician. Hácha himself later indicated that Göring had threatened him with the wholesale destruction of Prague from the air in the event the Czechoslovak Army offered resistance. If such arguments, however, were used to obtain Hácha's compliance, they were most probably only empty threats. The invasion armies were already in full motion, and although their orders called for the swift crushing of any resistance, no sizable resistance was in fact expected, and therefore the orders repeatedly stressed that the whole operation must appear as a mere police action causing as little damage as possible.[66]

Not only did Hácha phone to Prague and give orders that no resistance should be waged, but he also consented to sign a declaration, presented to him by the Germans and including the following words:

The Czechoslovak President declared that, in order . . . to achieve ultimate pacification, he confidently placed the fate of the Czech people and country in the hands of the Führer of the German Reich. The Führer accepted this declaration and expressed his intention of taking the Czech people under the protection of the German Reich and of guaranteeing them an autonomous development of their ethnic life as suited to their character.[67]

The declaration had been probably drafted in the Foreign Office on March 14 before the Hitler-Hácha talks started. Such advance preparation suggested that the Nazi leaders had expected Hácha to submit to Hitler's demands and eventually sign the agreement.

[66] "Sonderbestimmungen zu den Anordnungen für die Versorgung der Heeresgruppe 5," *Records of Headquarters, German Armed Forces High Command,* microcopy T–77, film 733, frames 1959726–734.

"Besondere Anordnungen Nr. 2" by the command of the Army Group 3, March 14, 1939, *ibid.,* microcopy T–77, film 732, frames 1958376–379.

"Anlage 2" to the order to the Army Group 3, March 13, 1939, *Records of German Army Areas,* microcopy T–79, film 131, frames 502–3.

[67] *Documents on German Foreign Policy,* IV, 27.

The exploitation of Hácha's visit for the purpose of the peaceful execution of the invasion was a brilliant last-minute improvisation on the part of the Nazis. Although this improvisation did not change anything about the fact that German armies were entering Bohemia and Moravia, it nevertheless significantly affected the manner in which the occupation was achieved.

In particular, Hácha's visit provided the Nazis with an excuse for the occupation which originally they had not even considered in their plan: a declaration that the intervention was taking place with the voluntary consent of the Czechoslovak President.

The first public word about the impending invasion came on March 15, at 4:30 a.m., from Radio Prague. From that time on the radio repeatedly broadcast that the German invasion would start at 6 a.m. and that no resistance must be offered.[68]

At 5 a.m. Propaganda Minister Goebbels read over the German radio Hitler's "Proclamation to the German People" announcing the operation against Czechoslovakia. As reasons for the military action, the proclamation repeated such themes as the separation of Slovakia and excesses against Germans. A historical argument was added saying that "for over a thousand years [Bohemia and Moravia] did in fact belong to the German Reich." [69] On the other hand, Hácha's compliance with the action was not mentioned. The omission might have been deliberate, although it is more likely that the text of the document had been prepared before Hácha's agreement with Hitler.

The Hitler-Hácha declaration was made public by the Germans at 6:10 a.m., ten minutes after the invasion had begun. With regard to its wording, stressing the quasi-voluntary character of the occupation, it was desirable that the political status of Bohemia and Moravia and their relation to the Reich should be clarified as quickly as possible. In that respect, however, the Nazis did not have any blueprint ready. This fact, which so far has not received any attention in historical literature, is supported by evidence both from German archives and the Nuremberg trial examinations.

Prior to March 15 the Army High Command had prepared an elaborate instruction concerning the establishment of a military administration in the occupied territory.[70] The basis of that instruction

[68] Keesing's Contemporary Archives (Weekly diary of world events. News supplied by the news agencies of many nations; translated from 26 languages. London, Keesing's Limited), 1939, p. 3485.

[69] Baynes, p. 1585.

[70] "Sonderbestimmungen zu den Anordnungen für die Versorgung der

was the routine directives for military rule in case of war, prepared and repeatedly revised since 1934. They provided for the exercise of the executive power by military commanders, assisted by chiefs of civil administration. In the case of Bohemia and Moravia, Czech local administration was to continue its functions, while the so-called *Landräte,* composed of German civil servants, were conceived as supervisory bodies. This kind of administration was actually set up immediately after the invasion.[71]

At the same time, on March 15, the Foreign Office prepared a confidential memorandum in which the establishment of two "protectorates," one in Bohemia and one in Moravia, was recommended on the following grounds:

It is opportune that possibly in an early state of the operation a proclamation by the Führer should announce main points concerning the future constitutional status of the Czechoslovak territory. This would cut off any attempt to make its organization an object of an international conference. At the same time, however, the fiction should be possibly preserved in the interest of legal continuity, that the new regime is in its main features based upon an agreement with the hitherto existing Czechoslovak central government, and not upon arbitrary decision of the occupying power.[72]

The author of the memorandum, possibly Dr. Gaus of the Foreign Office, proposed that in each of the two protectorates the Reich would be represented by an official called General Resident, Reich Commissioner, Governor, or Land Marshal. The protectorates were to elect their own governments, approved by the General Resident, and receive a constitution which would guarantee their autonomous national development. Their dependence upon the Reich in foreign policy, military, and economic matters was to be defined.

As to the origins of the subsequent Decree Concerning the Establishment of the Protectorate, promulgated by Hitler in Prague on March 16, 1939, many details are still, and probably will remain, obscure. The defendants and witnesses in the Nuremberg "Wilhelm-

---

Heeresgruppe 5," *Records of Headquarters, German Armed Forces High Command,* microcopy T–77, film 733, frames 1959726–736.

Instructions about military administration, 1934–1939, *ibid.,* microcopy T–77, films 168 and 170, *passim.*

Orders to the 10th Division, March 11, 1939, *Records of German Army Areas,* microcopy T–79, film 174, frames 677–85.

[71] It remained in force until April 16, 1939, when the military authorities surrendered their power to the Reich Protector.

[72] Undated Foreign Office memorandum (March 15, 1939), *Records of the German Foreign Office,* microcopy T–120, film 1094, frames 447271–273.

strasse" trial gave descriptions of the confusion which prevailed in the Prague Castle during the night of March 15 to March 16, soon after Hitler and his entourage had arrived there.[73]

The decree was drafted in Prague by several men, following Hitler's general instructions. The principal author was Wilhelm Stuckart, State Secretary in the Ministry of the Interior and since the *Anschluss* of Austria the leading Nazi expert in questions of territorial incorporation. He subsequently became the head of a special administrative body called the Central Office for the Implementation of the Führer's Decree. The possible participation of Dr. Gaus explains many similarities between the draft and the Foreign Office memorandum of March 15. The "Proclamation to the German People" of the same date, whose author was most likely Hitler himself, probably served as a model for the preamble to the decree. There may have been other persons taking part in the drafting, especially Foreign Minister Ribbentrop, Minister of the Interior Frick, and Chief of the Reich Chancellery Lammers.

Bohemia and Moravia became part of the Reich as an autonomous Protectorate. The Germans living in Bohemia and Moravia became German citizens, whereas other inhabitants of that area became citizens of the Protectorate.

The autonomy of the Protectorate was described in a very obscure way as the exercise of "sovereign rights conceded to it within the framework of the Protectorate, in conformity with the political, military and economic requirements of the Reich." [74] The autonomous administration, headed by the President and the cabinet, must enjoy the confidence of the Führer.

The Reich Protector, appointed by Hitler, held practically unlimited control powers over the autonomous organs. He could dismiss the members of the Protectorate cabinet, suppress the legislation and administrative measures of the autonomous organs, issue orders with the force of law, and nullify court decisions. On the other hand, the

---

[73] Examination of Stuckart and Lammers, *U.S. v. Weizsäcker,* Proceedings (in English), microfilm frames 24542–545, 22379, and 20831–832.

Affidavit by Gaus (NG–1635), *ibid.,* Prosecution Document Book No. 15B (in English), pp. 65–66.

Examination of Karl Hermann Frank, *Zpověď K. H. Franka: Podle vlastních výpovědí v době vazby u krajského soudu trestního na Pankráci* (The Confession of K. H. Frank: His Own Deposition during the Detention in the Circuit Criminal Court at Pankrác) (Prague, A. S. tiskařské a nakladatelské podniky, 1946), p. 106.

[74] *Documents on German Foreign Policy,* IV, 284.

Protector's authority in relation to the agencies of the Reich was ill-defined, thus opening the way to future direct interference of those agencies in the Protectorate.

Although Dr. Stuckart liked to point out with pride that the Protectorate had been a great achievement of the Nazi theory of government and constitutional law, this was not true.[75] As a legal instrument, the decree was full of ambiguities, partly intentional, partly probably due to its hurried preparation. Subsequent violations by the Germans themselves were to prove that the decree was not even suited to fulfil its main function, which was to provide a framework for the Nazi domination of Bohemia and Moravia.

Less than six months after the occupation of Bohemia and Moravia, the Second World War broke out. The Czechoslovak drama assumed a special position in the sequence of events leading to the war. The origins of the Second World War cannot be understood without an analysis of the nature of Nazi policy in the crisis over Czechoslovakia.

To label this policy as *either* design or improvisation would be meaningless, since it obviously contained both elements. We should rather attempt to define the characteristics of the Nazi design *and* improvisation in 1938–39.

The German leaders possessed a general, long-term goal believed to be in Germany's national interest: the domination of Czechoslovakia and her subordination to German needs. This goal was not originally elaborated into a formal plan. The Nazis worked toward the achievement of their specific objectives in Czechoslovakia on the basis of short-term planning. Such planning was in conformity with the long-term goal, but was also influenced by expediency, international situation, and available resources. This short-term policy was subject to changes. After Munich it took the Nazis at least ten weeks to decide upon the definitive plan for the occupation of Bohemia and Moravia which was subsequently materialized within three months.

If we choose to call this kind of policy planning design, we must keep in mind that its principal characteristic was the brevity of the time span between its formulation and fulfilment. The fact that the Nazis did not plan their actions against Czechoslovakia far in advance

[75] Wilhelm Stuckart, "Das Protektorat im Grossdeutschen Reich" (NG–2496), *U.S. v. Weizsäcker,* Prosecution Document Book No. 15B (in English), pp. 68–83.
  Wilhelm Stuckart, *Neues Staatsrecht,* 13th ed. (Leipzig, Kohlhammer, 1939), p. 186.

should not be surprising. They were experienced enough politicians to realize that international development was full of unknown factors. Any long-term planning beyond a mere notion of general goals would be likely to become later a burden rather than a help to the policy makers.

The short-term plan was not to be understood in the sense that the occupation of Bohemia and Moravia must be carried out at a certain time under any circumstances. The German leaders took the risks into account, and weighed potential gains and losses. The execution of the plan was contingent upon the existence of favorable circumstances. Although the entire German policy was conducted in such a way as to precipitate the coming of favorable circumstances in the form of the Slovak crisis, the creation of such circumstances depended on outside events and decisions of Czech and Slovak statesmen which could not be precisely foreseen. The extent of their unpredictability determined German readiness to improvise.

No matter how skillful the Nazis proved to be in the pursuit of this policy, they nevertheless cannot be credited with its invention. Such instruments as secret preparation of military invasion, encouragement of internal dissension in a neighboring state, or intimidation of foreign statesmen, had been widely used in power politics long before the Nazis came to power, and remained in use by the world's statesmen after the Third Reich went down in ruins. We may therefore be tempted to conclude with Taylor that Hitler was indeed only a conventional and "rational, though no doubt a wicked, statesman." [76] Yet the monstrous results of his policy make the historian rather reluctant to believe that what the Nazis did was but another version of the usual scheming and perfidy common to all statesmen.

The difference between the uses of power politics by other nations at other times and by Nazi Germany in the Czechoslovak crisis stemmed from the twentieth-century phenomenon of the totalitarian state. The ease with which the Nazis achieved their initial international success can be further accounted for by the novelty of totalitarianism and the ignorance of the outside world about its real nature. The effective central control over administration, resources, and public opinion, the ability to keep secrecy, and the disciplined cooperation of the rank and file of the German people, partly explained the astoundingly successful and efficient performance in March 1939. Another part of the success was the psychological impact of totali-

[76] Taylor, p. 193.

tarianism, which temporarily immobilized other nations and their leaders in the belief that the Nazis were stronger and more sure of themselves than was actually the case. Because of this attitude, Czechoslovakia's helplessness in 1939 was still greater than it need have been, and resulted in the fact that her leaders even contributed to making the occupation an easier and more complete success.

In the long run, however, the occupation served as a warning of danger and helped to mobilize European nations against German aggression. This was a consequence of March 15, 1939 which the Nazis failed to foresee in their planning.

T. G. Masaryk and the Slovaks
1882-1914

THOMAS D. MARZIK

In the year 1882 Dr. Tomáš G. Masaryk arrived in Prague to become professor of philosophy at the newly created Czech division of Charles University. The entry into Prague of the thirty-two year old Masaryk, Moravian born son of a Slovak coachman and a Czech cook, marked the beginning of his active and decisive participation in the national movement of the Czechs—and later of the Slovaks—which was to culminate in the unification of both those West Slav peoples in a single independent state in 1918.

Much has been written about Masaryk's role in the Czech national movement; however, the relationship of Masaryk with the Slovaks of Upper Hungary from 1882 until the outbreak of World War I has not been as thoroughly investigated. To this writer's knowledge there is no major work in any of the West European languages covering Masaryk's role among the Slovaks, nor has any specific study of the subject been made in Czech or Slovak since the time of Masaryk's death.

Due to the Czech-Slovak struggles which developed after the establishment of the Republic, all evaluations of Masaryk's role among the Slovaks at that time suffer from the bias of political motivation, and therefore must be read with caution. Slovak nationalist authors who consider Masaryk as an archfoe of Slovak national autonomy during the first Czechoslovak Republic either ignore, belittle, or denigrate the relations of Masaryk with the Slovaks prior to 1914. Modern Czechoslovak Marxist historians, in stressing the economic factor, see "liberal bourgeois" Masaryk's interest in the Slovaks as an attempt to find outlets for Czech capitalists. This writer's main sources consist of the works of Czechophile Slovaks who came into contact with Masaryk during that period. Those sources, written of course with the aim of supporting a Czechophile orientation, are extremely laudatory of Masaryk and exaggerate Masaryk's and their own importance in the Slovak national movement. Despite this obvious defect, however, they contain the most information on the topic and indicate most accurately the influence which Masaryk exerted upon that group of Slovaks before 1914.

At the time Masaryk was beginning his professorial career in Prague, the Slovak national movement was at a dangerously low ebb. The period between 1848 and the *Ausgleich* of 1867 was too brief a span for the creation of a broad base of national consciousness among the people before they were abandoned once again to complete Magyar domination. As an "unhistorical" people among the nationalities of Hungary, the majority of the two million Slovaks, deprived of a nationally conscious gentry, fell easy prey to the policy of forcible Magyarization which began in the 1870s.

As a result of the pressures of Magyarization, several members of the Slovak intelligentsia retired to Turčiansky Svätý Martin, a small, isolated town in Central Slovakia where the few national institutions —most important of which was the Slovak press—were allowed to exist. The undisputed leader of that Slovak national party was to become Svetozár Hurban-Vajanský, the most prominent Slovak poet, journalist, and novelist of the period. It was Vajanský who was largely responsible for the ideological content of the Slovak national movement until the end of the 19th century.[1]

Convinced that the Slovaks were too weak to combat the powerful Magyar opposition, the Slovak leadership adopted an attitude of fatalism. Practically, this policy of despair meant complete political passivity; ideologically, it took the form of messianism, which placed all hope for the Slovak nation in a major European conflagration out of which Russia would emerge as the liberator of the Slovaks. The mission of the national leaders was to keep alive the Slovak literary language and national consciousness until the time of deliverance. To this end Vajanský created a cult of romantic Slovak nationalism centered on himself at Turčiansky Svätý Martin. Conservative, aristocratic, chauvinistic, authoritarian, and exclusively intellectual, Vajanský's movement was extremely limited in its appeal among the Slovak

---

[1] Descriptions of the Slovak national movement under Vajanský's leadership can be found in Vavro Šrobár, "T. G. Masaryk a Slováci," in Jozef Rudinský, ed., *Slovensko Masarykovi* (Prague, 1930), pp. 87–90, and in Anton Štefánek, "Masaryk a Slovensko," in Miloš Weingart, ed., *Sborník přednášek o T. G. Masarykovi* (Prague, 1931), pp. 226–27.

masses. Nor did Vajanský seek the support of the Slovaks' natural ally in the Austrian half of the Empire, the Czechs; on the contrary, Czech culture and the Czech language were considered by Vajanský to be inferior to Magyar aristocratic manners and the more pure Slavic language of the Slovaks. In view of these attitudes on the part of the Slovak national leaders, it is not surprising that the Slovak cause, isolated from Hungarian political life, from Slavic life within the Empire, and from the masses of the Slovak people themselves, stagnated in its despair and passivity.

The Czech attitude toward the Slovaks during this period ranged from animosity to apathy. Many Czechs had been offended by the Slovaks' adoption of *štúrovčina,* a separate Slovak literary medium which had replaced Czech in the 1840s. Furthermore, the Old Czech Party's narrow program based on historical rights precluded concern for the Slovaks in the political sphere. During the 1880s, however, as Slovak students began to migrate to Bohemian and Moravian schools, interest in the Slovaks was gradually awakened, chiefly on the part of Moravian writers, who were close to the Slovaks of Hungary in spirit, origin, language, and geography.[2]

It was this state of affairs which existed in Bohemia when the young Professor Masaryk entered on the Czech scene in 1882. In recalling his early years in Prague, Masaryk told his famous friend, Karel Čapek: "We had a certain number of Slovakophiles who were conscious of natural unity, of brotherhood, but it was more a matter of literature than politics; they did not dare to carry it to its political conclusion." [3] But even at such an early period Masaryk was not content with a mere cultural interest in the Slovaks. In taking up from the beginning the struggle for natural as well as historical right, Masaryk made possible the later inclusion of the Slovaks in the political program of the Czech national movement. Masaryk described his conflict with the Old Czech Party on this point to Čapek as follows:

After I was in Prague I went to a meeting of University professors at the Hotel de Saxe; during our discussion I raised the point that we Czechs should work for political union with the Slovaks. A number of my colleagues opposed me and quoted the authority of Rieger, who had said that the Slovak question was *causa finita;* they considered it a matter of historical State rights: the Bohemian State was in law only Bohemia, Moravia,

[2] Štefánek, p. 218.

[3] *President Masaryk Tells His Story,* recounted by Karel Čapek, translated from the Czech (New York, Putnam's, 1935), pp. 191–92. (All quotations used by permission of Putnam's and Coward-McCann.)

and Silesia—they renounced Slovakia. But I was against their exclusively historical theory, because what, after all, is a historical right in reality? Is right independent of time and of whether or no a claim was realized in practice? Is not a right simply a right, no matter when it was or was not valid? . . . I have never refused to accept so-called historical right, but I combine it with natural right.[4]

This early concern for the Slovaks on the basis of natural right was a major step in the development of a Czech-Slovak union; in taking it Masaryk became the only Czech leader to show a real political interest in the Slovaks at that time.[5]

Masaryk's first actual contact with the Slovaks did not come until the summer of 1887, when he vacationed at a small village in Central Slovakia. During his stay he visited Turčiansky Svätý Martin, where he met the leaders of the Slovak national party. That first visit was so successful that Masaryk made a habit of returning to Slovakia every summer. He explained to Čapek the reason for those trips: "As early as the end of the 'eighties I had founded a regular summer school at Bystrička near Turčiansky Svätý Martin, with the deliberate object of getting to know the Slovaks at close quarters, and even influencing them. For more than ten years I went and stayed there at intervals." [6]

To a certain extent Masaryk achieved his twofold purpose. The "Martin" Slovaks at first received him enthusiastically, particularly when they learned about his interest in Dostoevsky and his disagreements with the Old Czechs on the question of historical right. According to an inhabitant of Bystrička whom Masaryk often visited, Dr. Ladislav Thomka-Markovický, Masaryk

. . . was eager to acquire first-hand knowledge of our country and of our leading men, in literature and art as well as in political and practical life. . . . He straightway . . . realised our situation better than we ourselves did, and was consequently soon able to warn us against the danger threatening us because of our sentimental attitude towards Russia, whom we regarded as the sole possible source of deliverance for the Slovak nation.[7]

This knowledge of the Slovak condition was essential to Masaryk's understanding of Slovakia's problems, and later enabled him to formulate a positive policy for the Slovaks.

[4] *Ibid.*, pp. 190–91.

[5] Jozef Jablonický, "Príspevok k česko-slovenským vzťahom od konca 19. stor. do roku 1914," *Historické štúdie*, IV (1958), 22.

[6] Čapek, *President Masaryk Tells His Story*, p. 192.

[7] Ladislav Thomka-Markovický, "T. G. Masaryk na Bystričke," in Rudinský, ed., *Slovensko Masarykovi*, p. 253; as translated in Paul Selver, *Masaryk: A Biography* (London, Michael Joseph, 1940), p. 169. (All quotations from Selver used by permission of A. M. Heath Ltd. and Paul Selver.)

In Prague, Masaryk's contacts with the Slovak students at the university began two or three years after his first summer visit to Slovakia. As early as 1882 the young Prague Slovaks—mostly students of medicine—had organized the *Detvan*,[8] a literary society, whose first president was Dr. Jaroslav Vlček, a Czech literary historian. This group was entirely under the influence of the Slovak national party in Turčiansky Svätý Martin; its members considered the Martin policies to be the only possible ones for Slovakia, and admired the Slovak leaders as great intellectuals. Masaryk probably became aware of this society through Dr. Vlček, who was well known in Prague. One day in either 1889 or 1890 Masaryk invited four members of the *Detvan*—Matej Bencúr, Ladislav Nádaši, Ján Smetanay, and Vavro Šrobár—to his apartment for tea.[9]

For hours Masaryk discussed with the students the conditions existing in Slovakia, and also their attitudes toward the Martin policies in the national struggle. During the conversation Masaryk suggested that the Slovaks in Prague found a journal independent of Turčiansky Svätý Martin which would throw needed light on the social, economic, and political problems in Slovakia and at the same time would criticize the Martin leadership for its failure to arrest the national decline of the Slovaks. He even promised to find financial support and a responsible Slovak editor for the proposed journal.

Masaryk's initiatives fell on unfertile ground. Not only was there no enthusiastic response to the journal among his Slovak listeners, but Masaryk was even disappointed in their lack of knowledge concerning Slovak affairs. After a few weeks Masaryk notified the students that he was abandoning the idea of the journal since he had been unable to find either funds or a willing editor. Masaryk decided to wait for a more propitious time to promote a new Slovak journal, but he kept the project in the back of his mind.

The four Prague Slovaks were, as Šrobár later admitted, "not yet ripe for Masaryk's programme and his ideas—we did not understand him."[10] Nevertheless, the meeting with the Czech professor who

---

[8] *Detvan* was the title of an historical tale idealizing Slovak peasant youth in the past. It was written by the Slovak romantic poet Andrej Braxatoris (pseud. Sládkovič) in 1847.

[9] Bencúr (pseud. Martin Kukučín) and Nádaši (pseud. Jégé) became important Slovak men of letters; Šrobár was appointed Minister Plenipotentiary for Slovakia at the beginning of the Republic. It is quite possible that this was not the first meeting of the Slovak students with Masaryk in Prague. Cf. Štefánek, pp. 219–20 and Vavro Šrobár, *Z môjho života* (Prague, 1946), pp. 159–61.

[10] Vavro Šrobár, "T. G. Masaryk a Slováci," in Rudinský, ed., *Slovensko*

showed interest in Slovak problems was not without effect. Šrobár began to read *Čas* (Time), the unofficial organ of Masaryk's Realist group,[11] and he also listened to Masaryk's lectures from time to time.[12] Smetanay took more direct action. In 1891—the year Masaryk entered politics and was elected to the Austrian Parliament as a member of the new Realist wing of the Young Czech Party—Smetanay published in Prague a pamphlet entitled *Slovensko* (Slovakia). Taking Masaryk's advice that the Prague students should criticize the Slovak leadership, Smetanay diagnosed the Slovak situation pejoratively and requested a revision of Vajanský's outmoded program.

Although this pamphlet had no effect on Slovak national party policy, since it was issued in Prague by an individual who lacked the blessing of the Martin editors, nevertheless it did evoke divided reaction from the Slovaks living in Prague, some of whom agreed with Smetanay's criticisms. In this respect Smetanay's pamphlet might be considered the earliest sign of a public split between the Slovak youth in Prague and the old national party in Slovakia.[13]

The Slovak students in Prague had no direct contact with Masaryk during his term in the Austrian Parliament from 1891 to 1893. In the summer of 1893, however, Masaryk returned to Bystrička and renewed his ties with Slovakia. During the early part of August he visited the town of Mošovce to commemorate the centennial of the birth of Jan Kollár, the famous Pan-Slavist and Czech literary figure who was a Slovak native of the town. When Masaryk attempted to pay homage to Kollár in the presence of the Slovak inhabitants of the town, Hungarian gendarmes prevented him from doing so. After reprimanding the policemen for their hostile actions, Masaryk retired to an inn with a group of Slovaks who had come from Turčiansky Svätý Martin for the occasion. There he described his reaction to the incident:

I came here with my children in order to show them the birthplace of Kollár. And what happened? No sooner had we stopped at the vacant site [where Kollár's homestead had stood] when they dispersed us with bayonets. I have been in political struggles, but only in Hungary, that

---

Masarykovi, p. 91, as translated by Selver in *Masaryk: A Biography*, pp. 170–71.

[11] Masaryk's Realist group was not primarily a political organization. It consisted of a small number of young Prague professors who sought to replace Czech romantic patriotism with a realistic nationalism based on critical and scientific thought.

[12] Šrobár, *Z môjho života*, pp. 160–61.   [13] Štefánek, p. 221.

country which is said to be the home of freedom, did I see a bayonet aimed at myself. . . . What would have happened, if all the Slovak people of this district had assembled here? I am truly sad that here in my native country, the cradle of my father, I was taught by means of the bayonet that we are not permitted to be the followers of Kollár. What did Kollár want? What was Kollár's idea? Be a human being! That in a few words was the idea of Kollár upon which he built the ideal of Slav reciprocity. In Hungary should we not be allowed to be human beings? A weak state, a weak society, in which the ideas of Kollár are considered a crime.[14]

At the end of his remarks Masaryk urged the young Slovaks to strive for the attainment of Kollár's ideals and exhorted them to "begin to think and to work, and then there will be no power which could suppress us." [15] The Viennese and Czech press carried the report of Magyar violence against a member of the Austrian Parliament, but the Magyar and Slovak newspapers apparently ignored the incident lest the Czech politician's sympathy for the Slovaks and his defiance of misused Hungarian authority be publicized. Nevertheless, the Slovak youth who witnessed the Mošovce affair and listened to Masaryk's words were much impressed and encouraged by what they saw and heard that day on Slovak soil.[16]

In late 1893 Masaryk resigned his seat in the Austrian Parliament as a result of factional struggles within the Young Czech Party. From that date until the turn of the century Masaryk devoted himself to an intensive study of Czech national problems. Relations with the Slovaks were maintained through his summer vacations in Slovakia, but inasmuch as the Slovak national party leaders opposed Masaryk's pro-Western and anti-Russophile orientation, Masaryk focused his attention mainly upon the Slovak students in Prague, most of whom belonged to the *Detvan*. Masaryk's influence on the society and on its individual members was more indirect than direct, but it was decisive.[17]

Detvan members were first attracted to Masaryk through his lectures at the university. As a teacher Masaryk was impressive both for his methods and for the content of his courses. He spoke in clear,

[14] As cited by Jan Herben, *T. G. Masaryk. Život a dílo presidenta osvoboditele,* 5th ed. (Prague, 1946), p. 82.

[15] As cited by Jaromír Doležal, *Masaryk osmdesátiletý* (Prague, 1931), p. 209.

[16] Milan Ivanka, "Po stopách Masarykových" in Rudinský, ed., *Slovensko Masarykovi,* p. 243.

[17] Masaryk's influence on the *Detvan* members is described in Šrobár's autobiography (*Z môjho života, passim*) and in his various articles. Also, cf. Štefánek, pp. 216–25.

simple, and concrete terms, and demanded from his audience critical analysis rather than unquestioned acceptance of what he said. Masaryk was a pragmatist, always insisting that theory be applied to the needs of society. As an example of his own teaching, Masaryk's activities in Czech political and national life were known far and wide.

Masaryk's personal contacts with the Prague Slovaks were few and limited, but Dr. Šrobár, who became Masaryk's most devoted disciple among the Slovak students, was a frequent visitor to the Masaryk home; and Masaryk himself occasionally invited other members of the *Detvan* for tea or dropped in on their meetings. Whenever Masaryk talked with the Slovaks he attempted to make them more conscious of and concerned about Slovak conditions, especially in regard to social and economic matters. He urged them to become well trained in their professions and then to use their talents and skills to improve Slovak national life.

Ideologically, the *Detvan* was slow to abandon its pro-Russian orientation. The Smetanay pamphlet of 1891 was somewhat of an aberration, for the society quickly returned to solid dependence on the Martin leadership. Masaryk obtained for the *Detvan* a collection of Russian philosophical and political writings which were avidly read and discussed at the society meetings. Thus, Danilevsky's *Russia and Europe* strengthened their Slavic national consciousness and their commitment to political Russophilism; and later the moral and religious teachings of Tolstoy impressed them greatly. Gradually, however, the society's intense Russophilism began to wane. This shift was in large part due to Masaryk himself, for as Dr. Šrobár later observed, "Masaryk was perhaps the first person to point out the erroneous Russophile— or, better termed, Tsarophile—direction of our Slovak politics and to demand a remedy." [18]

The greatest impact of Masaryk on the Slovaks in Prague was made through his extensive publications on national questions. *Naše doba* (Our Era)—a journal launched under Masaryk's editorship in 1893 —published the results of Masaryk's careful analyses of Czech national problems, and beginning in 1895 the most important of his articles were expanded into a series of larger studies on Czech nationalism. One of those works, *Česká otázka* (The Czech Question), was particularly significant for the Slovaks. Masaryk wanted the Realists to determine the place of the Czech nation among the other nations of Europe and also within the development of mankind. Convinced

[18] Šrobár, *Z môjho života,* p. 160.

that the answer to this central question lay in the traditions and spiritual thought of the Czech past, Masaryk in *Česká otázka* made a rigorous sociological analysis of modern Czech history. For Masaryk, the outstanding achievement and heritage of Czech culture was the Hussite spirit of reform, the essence of which was the "ideal of humanity." Masaryk insisted that this ideal had to be rekindled through the improvement of the cultural, moral, religious, and political foundations of Czech society if the Czech national movement was to succeed.[19]

Česká otázka had an important effect upon the young Slovak students in Prague. In treating Kollár as one of the greatest Czech humanitarians, Masaryk specifically called attention to the fact that Kollár was of Slovak origin and that his idea of Slav reciprocity could be explained by Kollár's Slovak background: "Kollár escaped the smallness of his race through reciprocity—without uniting with the rest of the Slavs, as he said to Kampelík, 'nothing would come' either of the Slovaks or of the Czechs." [20] He also praised Kollár's opinion that the Slovaks possessed the best qualities of the Slavs. Masaryk's statement that "in general, for us [Czechs] the Slovak question has the greatest importance" [21] was perhaps more impressive to the Slovak than to the Czech readers of *Česká otázka*.

The book also had definite relevance to Slovak national problems. Dr. Šrobár recalled that when he stated to Masaryk that the book was applicable to the Slovak situation as well as to the Czech, Masaryk replied that it pertained all the more so to Slovakia because of the much worse conditions there.[22] It was not long before *Česká otázka* became a topic of serious discussion at the *Detvan*. Masaryk's analysis of Czech life invited the Slovak students to perform the same task for the Slovaks—to make a penetrating criticism of the foundations of Slovak national life. It was a call to forsake the fatalism, passivity, and messianic Russophilism of the Martin leadership and to rebuild Slovak society in the manner of the Czech Realists through enlightenment and small-scale constructive work.

Thus, despite Masaryk's relative lack of direct, personal contact

---

[19] A concise summary of Masaryk's conception of Czech history as expressed in *Česká otázka* can be found in S. Harrison Thomson, "T. G. Masaryk and Czech Historiography," *Journal of Central European Affairs*, X (April 1950), 43–47.

[20] Tomáš G. Masaryk, *Česká otázka. Snahy a tužby národního obrození*, 2d ed. (Prague, 1908), p. 53.

[21] *Ibid.*   [22] Šrobár, *Z môjho života*, p. 310.

with the Slovaks in Prague from 1893 to 1897, the power of his written word—especially his studies of Czech national life and the critical
review, *Naše doba*—exerted a decisive influence on the development
of their political thinking in the years to come.[23]

In the summer of 1897 both Masaryk and the Prague Slovaks vacationed in Slovakia. On August 4 most of the Slovak intelligentsia
gathered at Turčiansky Svätý Martin for a national meeting. When
Šrobár challenged the leadership's policies by requesting space in the
Slovak press to present new ideas of the younger generation, he was
accused of sowing discord among the Slovaks. Rebuffed by the in-
transigence of the Martin group, Šrobár led a small delegation of
young Slovaks to nearby Bystrička in order to ask Masaryk to advise
them how to organize an independent Slovak journal and to suggest
ideas for the proposed undertaking.[24] Masaryk received the young
rebels enthusiastically, for the Slovak students were finally willing and
able to take up the venture which he himself had suggested seven
years earlier. As the delegation from Turčiansky Svätý Martin sat in
the garden of his summer home, Masaryk discussed Slovakia's problems with its members.

The program which resulted from the discussion covered all aspects of Slovak life and embodied the application of Masaryk's Realism to the Slovak situation.[25] It was based on the assumption that the
fatalistic passivity of the old generation had to be replaced by progressive thought and action directed toward the welfare of the Slovak
masses. Before anything could be done, however, it was necessary to
examine the reasons for the present national decline, which reasons
were to be sought in the Hungarian system of government and also in
the Slovak national party leadership. Following this critical analysis,
practical suggestions were offered to construct a new Slovak national
life on strong social, economic, and moral foundations.

A brief summary of the major points of that program will indicate
in general Masaryk's attitude toward the Slovaks at that time. An
important part of the program was a criticism of the Hungarian

[23] Šrobár, "T. G. Masaryk a Slováci," p. 92.

[24] Detailed descriptions of the meetings at Turčiansky Svätý Martin and at
Bystrička can be found in Šrobár's autobiography (*Z môjho života,* pp. 351–
56) and also in Vavro Šrobár, "Vliv prof. Masaryka na Slovákov," in Edvard
Beneš *et al,* eds., *T. G. Masarykovi k šedesátým narozeninám* (Prague, 1910),
pp. 186–94.

[25] Šrobár recorded the minutes of the meeting and published the program
derived from the discussion in outline form in Šrobár, "Vliv prof. Masaryka
na Slovákov," pp. 190–93.

state itself. Hungary was characterized as a feudal state in which bureaucracy was idolized and in which the Government represented only the interests of the gentry minority. Forcible Magyarization was considered as a sign of barbarism by Masaryk; it was a cultural and moral evil for the Slovaks, since it denied them cultural freedom and set Magyarized sons against their Slovak fathers. The Hungarian economy, however, was the most disastrous aspect of Hungarian life. Its feudal distribution of lands and privileges among the few, the exorbitant taxes, duties, and high prices forced upon the peasants, and the exclusive possession of capital by Jews and foreigners reduced the Slovak masses to a state of economic serfdom. In the light of these unfavorable circumstances, Masaryk's advice to the Slovaks was twofold: to study the statistics to find out how the operation of the Hungarian economy harmed the Slovak people and to learn everything possible about Hungarian culture and political life by reading Magyar publications. Equipped with accurate knowledge of their adversary, the Slovaks would then be able to devise the most effective means of overcoming the obstacles which the decadent Hungarian state had created for them.

Masaryk also turned his critical eye on the Turčiansky Svätý Martin leadership. He labeled the 1848 revolt of the Slovak intelligentsia as a ridiculous farce. Slovak political demands of 1848 and 1861, unreasonable even at those dates, had to be adjusted to the realities of 1897. Messianic Russophilism, which had acted as a shield for Vajanský's despair and had weakened the desire among the Slovak people to help themselves, also had to be abandoned. He condemned Slovak national isolationism and recommended in its place the Slav reciprocity of Kollár and Šafařík—a thorough knowledge of the cultures of all Slav nations. Slovaks were to look to their closest and strongest ally in the Empire, the Czechs, rather than to distant Russia, which was not in the least interested in the Slovak national cause.

Masaryk felt it necessary to define the content of Slovak nationalism carefully so that the Martin group could not interpret the Czechophile orientation of the young Slovaks as "Pan-Czechism." For this reason Masaryk made a special point of playing down the important language question as much as possible:

Language is not the goal of the highest efforts in a nation. Language is the beloved and precious instrument in the family, in literature—it is the means of communication. For the present circumstances and in the distant future scientific work in Slovak is out of the question.——Kollár and

Šafárik definitely and clearly determined the relation and degree: language, humanity, and religion. Adhere to them as your own predecessors. . . . The Czecho-Slovak language question is not the chief one. A skilled Czech or Slovak type-setter can convert the one language into the other. Language is not an obstacle to Czecho-Slovak reciprocity, even though there are differences everywhere.[26]

Thus, while advocating that the Slovaks continue to use Czech as a scientific language, Masaryk did not rule out the retention of a separate Slovak literary and vernacular tongue. It is interesting to note in this connection that Masaryk—unlike the other Slovakophile Czechs of that period—did not attach much weight to formal linguistic unity between the Czechs and Slovaks as a condition for cultural union.[27] Czechophile Slovaks would not be required to abandon the Slovak language for Czech.

Masaryk also anticipated and forewarned the young Slovaks that the charge of weakening the Slovak national cause through factionalism would be leveled at them by the conservative Martin group. He defended the use of polemics in Slovakia as he had in Bohemia. Masaryk, the Realist, placed the highest value on truth. In order to help themselves and to gain respect as a nation, the Slovaks above all had to learn the truth about their own culture, their national leadership, and their position in the Hungarian state.

Masaryk made several practical suggestions for the construction of a new national life for the Slovaks. He discussed the role of religion and the churches. Masaryk recognized that the churches were the natural allies of the Slovaks in the national struggle against the decadent liberalism of the Hungarian state, but in acknowledging the aid of religion, he did not wish to allow the clergy to use this as an opportunity to gain more power over the masses. The duty of the clergy was to become supporters of the Slovak national cause and to concern themselves with the economic and social problems of the people. Furthermore, Masaryk urged both Catholics and Lutherans to "positive morality" as opposed to "religious indifferentism" in the national regeneration. Although Masaryk, who had converted from Catholicism to Protestantism, did not believe in formalized religion, he always considered religion to be the central question in every man's life. Moral rebirth, in the Hussite reform spirit, was an essential part of Masaryk's national program.[28]

[26] From points 1 and 11 of the program, *ibid.,* pp. 190 and 192.

[27] Štefánek, p. 211.

[28] "The point of departure both of my philosophy and policy is the Czech Reformation, because, for me, it was above all a moral and religious movement,

At first sight Masaryk's suggestion that "anti-Semitism" was permissible in Slovakia seems wholly inconsistent with his philosophy of life.[29] Masaryk's motivation, however, was in this case not racial, but rather economic, moral, and cultural. He reasoned that the Jews in Slovakia as a group were detrimental to the national cause. The Jews had become Magyarized and were used by the Government as political and cultural tools in the assimilation campaigns among the Slovaks. The worst evils of the Jews as a social group, he maintained, were evident in the economic and moral spheres: as capitalists they dominated much of the Hungarian economy; as usurers they kept the Slovak peasants in degrading poverty; and as innkeepers with state liquor monopolies they were largely responsible for the acute problems of alcoholism which plagued every Slovak village. Masaryk's advocacy of "anti-Semitism" for Slovakia meant the elimination of the abuses allegedly arising out of the Hungarian Jews' privileged and powerful status in the land of the Slovaks.

The work of nation-building from the bottom up was the keynote of Masaryk's practical suggestions to Šrobár and the others. The Slovak people had to be awakened to national consciousness through education, and the entire moral, economic, and social level of the masses had to be lifted. In this task all Slovaks who had received professional training had an important obligation. Masaryk outlined the special functions which Slovak doctors, priests, teachers, and lawyers were to perform among the people, and he emphasized the dignity of this practical work in the process of improving national life.

Another point of the program was Masaryk's insistence that the Slovaks liberate themselves from the bonds of isolationism. He suggested that Slovak students learn foreign languages and study in foreign capitals to find out what was going on in the world, and at the same time to supply information to the outside world on the conditions existing in Slovakia. It was necessary for the Slovaks to make the Slovak question a European problem, just as Masaryk had attempted to do for the Czechs.

The program for the new journal ended with a plan for political

---

not a theological one. The starting-point of Hus . . . was the reformation of morals." Čapek, p. 210.

[29] In 1899 Masaryk publicly defended a Jew named Hilsner, who had been convicted of murdering two girls to obtain blood for Jewish religious ceremonies. Masaryk took up the Hilsner case in the face of explosive anti-Semitic emotions because he believed that Hilsner was innocent and because he wanted to debunk the widespread superstition of ritual murder. As a result of that *cause célèbre* Masaryk earned the reputation of being pro-Semitic.

action. Masaryk advocated the return of the Slovaks to political life, but suggested that they adopt a realistic program suited to the immediate needs of the people. Above all, it was necessary to avoid direct conflicts with the Magyars. For this reason Masaryk demanded the removal of as many obstacles as possible to the recognition of Slovak aspirations by the Magyars. Accordingly, he advised them to accept dualism, to commit themselves to a unified Hungarian state, and to use Magyar as the official state language. Pan-Slavism was to be apolitical; likewise, Czech-Slovak reciprocity was to appear to be economically and culturally—not politically—motivated.

On the basis of the advice given to the Šrobár delegation by Masaryk on August 4, 1897 in Bystrička, the independent Slovak monthly journal *Hlas* (The Voice) was founded. A Slovak follower of Masaryk, Dr. Pavol Blaho, agreed to edit the journal. The first issue of *Hlas* did not appear until July 1, 1898, almost one year after Masaryk had met with the Šrobár group. The publication of *Hlas* marked the definite public break with the Turčiansky Svätý Martin leadership on the part of the young, Prague-orientated Slovaks, who rallied around the new journal and became known as "Hlasists." Although the Hlasists were not bound by any dogmatic platform, they were in general committed to the political ideas of Masaryk's Realists and to Czechophilism. Their emphasis as a group was on the need for exacting criticism of every aspect of Slovak national life, for constructive work among the masses, and for the moral regeneration of the individual.[30]

The launching of an independent Slovak journal which he himself had initiated, and the infusion of his spirit into the Slovak political movement which originated with the establishment of *Hlas,* mark the point of greatest influence which Masaryk exerted on Slovak national life until 1914. Masaryk's contacts with the Slovaks were then to become more and more indirect, especially when he discontinued his summer vacations in Slovakia in 1902. Masaryk busied himself with the Czech national movement from 1900 to 1907, years which were filled with lecturing, writing, traveling, and political activities on behalf of the Czech cause. In 1907 he was again elected to the Austrian Parliament, where he devoted himself to the problems of the Empire until the outbreak of World War I.

To say that Masaryk played no role whatsoever for the Slovaks from 1897 to 1914, however, would be inaccurate; for although

[30] A summary of Hlasist views can be found in Štefánek, pp. 233–34.

Masaryk had little contact with Slovakia during that period, he did not forget the Slovaks or their national problems. In order to assist the Hlasists in publicizing Slovak news in the press, Masaryk used his influence to have Dr. Jan Herben, editor of *Čas,* publish special "Monday" supplements on Slovak politics. Also, in 1901 Masaryk, as editor of *Naše doba,* was instrumental in initiating a monthly column entitled "O věcech slovenských" (Concerning Slovak Affairs), which supported the Hlasist movement and discredited the Martin leadership for its lack of a program, neglect of the common people, and paucity of sound, scientific scholarship.[31]

Furthermore, Masaryk did not forget the Slovaks when the Czech Realists were formed into a separate political party on April 1, 1900. The party platform officially recognized the linguistic, national, social, and cultural oppression of the Slovaks under Magyar domination. Since Masaryk's insistence on natural right—dealt with by him in a pamphlet in 1900—favored the Slovaks in Hungary, the Realist Party included the Slovaks within its scope at least economically and culturally; it could not at that time advocate openly the possibility of political union between the Czechs and Slovaks.[32]

Another indication of Masaryk's interest in the Slovaks during that period was his sponsorship of a Czech pamphlet on the Magyarization of the Slovaks written by Karel Kálal. In 1903 Masaryk had the pamphlet translated into German under the title *Die Unterdrückung der Slovaken durch die Magyaren.*[33] In that form the contents of Kálal's report on the fate of the Slovaks were made known to the German-speaking world, especially in Austrian political circles.

Slovakia was continually kept before Czech political eyes through Masaryk's Realist Party. Again in 1906 the party passed an official resolution which protested the cruelty of the Magyars toward the Slovaks and expressed sympathy for the Slovak national and political leaders. That publicity was heightened immediately following the so-called Černova Massacre of October 27, 1907, in which Hungarian gendarmes fired into a crowd of Slovak peasants. When news of that incident reached Vienna, a great debate concerning the *Ausgleich* of 1867 was touched off in the Austrian Parliament by the Czech deputies. Masaryk, newly reelected to the Parliament, used the occasion to call attention to the plight of the Slovaks in these words:

[31] Examples of those criticisms can be found in *ibid.,* pp. 238–42.
[32] Selver, pp. 192–93.
[33] Karel Kálal, "Masarykovo učenie o práve prirodzenom," in Rudinský, ed., *Slovensko Masarykovi,* p. 75.

In Hungary we have two million Slovaks who belong to our nationality. A people of eight millions will not, without further ado, leave two million of its co-nationals to the tender mercies of Magyar jingoism. It is our duty, here and on every possible occasion, to inform this House, Austria and the whole of the general public, that the Magyars are treating our Slovaks in a manner which is utterly inhuman.[34]

This reference to the Slovaks as fellow countrymen of the Czechs is another indication of Masaryk's tendency to identify the Slovaks with the Czechs on the basis of natural right. This identification justified the interest of Masaryk's Realist Party in Slovak problems and provided an important precedent for Masaryk's later dealings with the Slovaks.

Masaryk's last major personal contact with the Slovaks took place in 1911, when he and other Czech members of Parliament visited the editors of the Slovak newspapers in Budapest. During his stay Masaryk delivered a lecture to several Slovak students and intellectuals on the problems of small, poor nations with special reference to the Slovak situation.[35] Masaryk stressed again the main points of his 1897 Slovak program. In addition, he recommended that the Slovaks find a more suitable national capital than Turčiansky Svätý Martin, for unless the national movement was centered in a large, cosmopolitan city, he predicted that it would suffocate from isolation. He also touched upon the delicate language question. While emphasizing that language should not be a barrier to Czech-Slovak reciprocity, he observed that since Slovak was still not sufficiently developed as a scientific language, the Slovaks would do well to continue to use Czech in that field. Those last direct words of Masaryk to the Slovaks before 1914 provided much material for discussion among the Slovak intellectuals who heard them in Budapest.

In considering Masaryk's relations with the Slovaks prior to the outbreak of World War I, an evaluation of the nature and degree of the influence which Masaryk exerted upon the Slovak national movement during that period must be made. Certainly the best gauge for measuring Masaryk's influence at that time is the Hlasist movement, for Masaryk was, as Dr. Šrobár rightly maintained, the "father" of that movement.[36]

The first important point which should be made concerning the

[34] As translated in Selver, p. 210.
[35] An outline of that lecture can be found in Štefánek, pp. 246–49.
[36] Vavro Šrobár, "Československá otázka a 'hlasisti' II," *Prúdy*, XI (May 1927), 274.

Hlasist movement is that it was extremely limited, not only in the number of its adherents, but also in its actual effect upon Slovak national life. Those active in producing the journal never exceeded thirty individuals; [37] and that rather exclusive group was for the most part restricted to lawyers, doctors, and students of philosophy, who had been educated in Bohemia or Moravia. As a minority of young Turks, the Hlasists remained a mere fragment of the small Slovak intelligentsia which existed prior to 1914. The majority of the Slovak intellectual leaders maintained their loyalty to the Slovak national party at Turčiansky Svätý Martin. And many of the young Slovaks who did turn away from the Martin group did not join the Hlasists, but rather looked to different ideological alternatives for national leadership.

The Hlasist adaptation of Czech Realism to Slovak national life did not find an enthusiastic response among the Slovak people. Hlasist Realism was ineffective in Slovakia, for the Slovaks, lacking the education, wealth, and historical right tradition of Bohemia, were in a much weaker position to perform the same type of self-criticism and constructive national work which Masaryk was demanding of the Czechs.[38]

As a result of the strong opposition of the non-Hlasist political majority and due to the lack of both financial and moral support, the literary organ of the movement, *Hlas,* ceased publication in 1904, only six short years after its founding. Hlasist ideas were represented partially through the *Slovenský týždenník* (The Slovak Weekly)—a newspaper established by Milan Hodža in 1903—but a more truly Hlasist-oriented journal did not appear until 1909 with the publication of *Prúdy* (Currents) by a few young Czechophile Slovaks.[39]

Despite the over-all weakness and limited influence of the Hlasist movement in Slovak national life prior to 1914, the Hlasists and through them Masaryk, as their spiritual father, do occupy an important place in modern Slovak history. As a result of their Czechophile

[37] Štefánek, p. 234.

[38] František Bokes, *Dejiny Slovákov a Slovenska. Od najstarších čias až po prítomnosť* (Bratislava, 1946), p. 301.

[39] It should be pointed out that the Hlasists and Masaryk were not the only advocates of Czech-Slovak reciprocity at that time. Milan Hodža, a Slovak member of the Hungarian Parliament, leaned toward the Czech Agrarians in his Czechophile orientation, and from the Czech side, the *Československá jednota* (Czechoslav Union) actively supported economic and cultural cooperation between Czechs and Slovaks. Other individuals and groups, both Czech and Slovak, also encouraged reciprocity.

orientation and of their assistance to Masaryk during the War years, several of the Hlasists were destined to become leading Government officials in Slovakia when Masaryk became President of the first Czechoslovak Republic.

In addition, it is to the Hlasists and in particular to Masaryk that a large share of the credit belongs for the awakening of the Slovak youth to the defects of the Martin leadership and for the revitalization of the Slovak national movement. It was perhaps as a negative re-action to the criticism of the old generation by the Hlasists that the Slovak national party eventually abandoned its outmoded passivity and that other movements—such as the Slovak People's Party (1905) and the Slovak Social Democratic Party (1905)—which, like the Hlasists, concentrated their efforts on action among the masses, but rejected either the Czechophile, bourgeois, or anticlerical orientation of the Hlasists, were founded. Masaryk's insistence on the need for polemics in 1897 was indeed vindicated; political splits did awaken the nation from its decaying slumber.

One more aspect of Masaryk's effect on Slovak national life during the prewar period should be mentioned, namely the issue of "Czecho-phobia," which was to become an important factor in the subsequent relations between the Czechs and Slovaks. Masaryk's activities among and influence upon the Slovaks were probably responsible, however unintentionally, for the intensification of Czechophobia among certain political groups in Slovakia. The causes of this phenomenon were both psychological and ideological.

The friendship between Masaryk and Vajanský gradually changed to a bitter animosity, which lasted practically until Vajanský's death in 1916. Vajanský's ardor for the Prague professor cooled when he became aware of Masaryk's disdain for political Russophilism and when he saw the Slovak students in Prague coming under Masaryk's influence. Masaryk suddenly appeared to Vajanský as a challenger to his position as sole leader of the Slovak national movement. When Šrobár and the Hlasists finally rejected him in favor of Masaryk's Realism, Vajanský vented his wrath on the Czech rival through the Slovak press,[40] severed all of his Czech connections, and attempted to save his position by intensifying the cult of Slovak nationalism.

[40] Sharp attacks upon Masaryk, the Hlasists, and the Czechs appeared in *Národnie noviny* (The National News) and *Slovenské pohľady* (Slovak Views) —publications of the Slovak national party—and in Vajanský's novel, *Kotlín* (1901). For the reasons and content of Vajanský's Czechophobia cf. Herben, p. 83 and Štefánek, pp. 242–44.

Masaryk, the "poisoner" of young Slovaks in Prague, became identified in Vajanský's mind with all the Czechs; and Vajanský's hostility to Masaryk-the-Czech was shared by many of Vajanský's followers—the rank and file of the Slovak national party, which represented the majority of the Slovak political leadership. Thus, Masaryk and the Czechs unjustly reaped much of the abuse which the over-zealous Slovak reformers elicited from the orthodox national leaders whom they had antagonized through their often tactless and devastating criticisms.[41]

The fact that most of the Hlasists were either Protestants or freethinkers—and for the most part anticlerical—and that Masaryk, a notorious apostate from Catholicism, was their spiritual mentor, alienated the overwhelming (more than 80 percent) Catholic sentiment of the Slovaks. The Slovak opponents of the Hlasists were to buttress their Czechophobia in future years due to this early identification of the Czechs with anticlericalism and anti-Catholicism. As the leader of the Slovak clerical party, the Reverend Andrej Hlinka, explained:

Between Dr. T. G. Masaryk and us there were insurmountable obstacles. We had been brought up in the Catholic faith and for us, the Church was great and holy; whereas Dr. Masaryk led the Realist, anti-Catholic party. This offended us very deeply, and Magyar policy certainly did not attempt to break up and disperse those black clouds. On the contrary, they painted the Czechs for us everywhere as the greatest and most stubborn enemies of Christianity.[42]

Finally, the fear of absorption into Czech nationality ("Pan-Czechism" or "Czechization") on the part of the Slovak national leadership —a fear which dated back to the revolutions of 1848—was constantly brought to the fore by the ultra-Czechophile Hlasists, who stressed Czech-Slovak union actively and vociferously. Masaryk himself, in his 1907 Parliament speech, had spoken of the Slovaks as belonging to Czech nationality. And those Slovak leaders, who had sacrificed much under the pressures of Magyarization to maintain their Slovak national consciousness and to save the Slovak literary language from extinction, were understandably quite suspicious of Masaryk's playing down of the language issue and of his constant advocacy of Czech as the most

[41] The views of the Hlasists were not identical with those of Masaryk and the Czech Realists; cf. Štefan Krčméry, "Masaryk a Turčiansky Svätý Martin" in *Slovensko Masarykovi*, pp. 111–12.

[42] As cited by Vladimír Sís, *Dr. Karel Kramář. Život—Dílo—Práce vůdce národa* II (Prague, 1937), p. 132, as cited by Jablonický, p. 33.

suitable scientific language for the Slovaks. Perhaps the latent fear of Czechization could help explain Vajanský's unshakable adherence to political Russophilism, and Slovak interest in the theory of Samo Czambel (a Magyarized Slovak philologist) that Slovak is a South rather than a West Slav language. In any event, the fact that many Slovaks looked upon Masaryk as a symbol of the Czechs' first and foremost political contact with the Slovaks in the prewar period was to become an impediment to Czech-Slovak cooperation in the years ahead.

Concerning his relations with the Slovaks before World War I, Masaryk later told Čapek: "It was a good thing, and one that stood me in good stead during the war, that I had been born half Slovak, that I had lived among Slovaks, and worked with them; I was able to talk to them, speak on their behalf like one of themselves." [43] Masaryk's Slovak activities from 1882 to 1914 testify to the truth in this statement, but perhaps Masaryk implied too much in that conversation with Čapek. During those years Masaryk did indeed have contacts with Slovaks, both at Bystrička in Slovakia and in Prague, where he did get to know the old as well as a segment of the young Slovak national leadership. And Masaryk had indeed worked with and for the Slovaks—as the Czech leader who brought the Slovaks into the scope of Czech politics on the basis of natural right; as the founder of the Czechophile Hlasist movement among the Slovak youth; and as an outspoken representative of Slovak national interests in Bohemia and Austria. But at the same time it is also true that Masaryk—perhaps as a result of his activities among the Slovaks—was able to talk to and on behalf of only a fractional minority of a small Slovak intelligentsia.

The fact remains, nevertheless, that Masaryk had a definite connection with Slovak national life prior to World War I and that this connection, despite it nature and limited degree, was to play an important role in the events after 1914 which led to the creation of the first Czechoslovak Republic under Masaryk's leadership.

[43] Čapek, p. 220.

China's Relations with Burma
1949-1964

B. LYNN PASCOE

For broad generalizations on Chinese foreign policy to have meaning, they must be based on data gleaned from case studies of China's relations with a variety of individual countries, and before we can speak of a line on the neutralist countries, the West, or the other Communist states, several of these case studies must be used. It is with a view toward this broader perspective that this paper attempts to review and analyze Chinese Communist policy toward Burma.

Burma, since independence, has pursued a careful policy of non-alignment in relations with both the Sino-Soviet and the Western blocs, from ideological and strategic motivations. The Burmese leadership group developed a strong sense of nationalism under British rule which has made them feel that ties to either bloc might impinge on their newly won independence, and they equally dislike and distrust the capitalist system of the West—equated as it is with imperialism—and the Stalinist police state enforced in both China and the Soviet Union. The other argument for Burmese neutrality is put forward on strategic grounds and was stated quite pithily by Prime Minister U Nu in September 1950:

Take a glance at our geographical position—Thailand in the east, China in the north, India in the west, and stretching southward, Malaya, Singapore, and so on. We are hemmed in like a tender gourd among the cactus. We cannot move an inch. If we act irresponsibly like some half-baked politicians who have picked up their world politics from one or two books and thrust the Union of Burma into the arms of one bloc, the other will not be content to look on with folded arms. Oh no! [1]

The Burmese are also quite aware that their twenty million population places them at a disadvantage with the neighboring giants of

[1] *Burma Weekly Bulletin,* Sept. 9, 1950, p. 133.

China, India, Pakistan, and even Thailand. Their pursuit of avoiding conflict has been so diligent that many authors have noted that it might be more accurate to describe their foreign policy as one of nonprovocation rather than of neutrality or nonalignment, and even though this overstates the case somewhat, it does, at least, emphasize the overriding consideration of any Burmese Government to avoid inviting annihilation by its neighbors.

A Review of Sino-Burmese Relations, 1949–1964

As the civil war developed in China, the AFPFL[2] and the Burmese Government led by U Nu were inclined to view the Communists in a generally favorable light. Not only had the Burmese leadership group been strongly influenced by Marxism in their student days—U Nu himself having proposed a Communist-sounding Leftist Unity Program in May 1948 to attempt to induce the Communists back into the ruling coalition—but they also had had considerable friction with the Nationalist Government of China over delineation of the Sino-Burmese border and Chinese troops on indisputably Burmese territory. It was therefore not unusual that they quickly recognized the Chinese People's Republic in late 1949—the first non-Communist state to do so.

The overtures of the Burmese nationalist leaders were not well received by the Chinese Communists, who upon coming to power eagerly looked forward to other successful Asian "national liberation movements." On November 16, 1949, at the Trade Union Conference of Asian and Australasian Countries in Peking, Liu Shao-ch'i noted that "the wars of national liberation in Burma and Indonesia are now developing" and also that "the fighters of the national liberation wars of Viet Nam, Burma, Indonesia, Malaya, and the Philippines have acted entirely correctly. They have merely applied the methods employed by the imperialists in conquering the colonies on the imperialists themselves." [3] As if to make it perfectly clear they were not referring to the nationalist leaders, the Burmese delegate to the Congress spelled it out.

[2] The Anti-Fascist People's Freedom League was a coalition of various parties formed in 1944 to oppose Japan and to secure the independence of Burma from Britain. It remained the ruling party of Burma until its split in 1958.
[3] New China News Agency (hereafter referred to as NCNA), Nov. 23, 1949.

Thakin Nu was selected as Prime Minister by the imperialists and a puppet government of anti-working class reactionaries was set up to carry out the secret negotiations, in accordance with the new strategy of British imperialism for reestablishing imperialist domination.[4]

The Burmese recognition was rather curtly received, and "People's China" crowed, "the victory of the Chinese people has been so overwhelming and decisive that they are left with no alternative." Although there was to be no "genuine friendship" with the government, the article noted that the establishment of relations would "enable the Chinese people to draw still closer to the peace-loving people of these countries." [5]

Although this militant line appeared out of place at the time in many of the Asian countries, in Burma there would seem to have been every justification for this line from the Chinese viewpoint. Burma had itself gained independence from Britain only twenty-two months before, and during 1949 eight separate groups were waging a civil war against the government. In addition to the two Communist groups (the White Flag Communists and the Red Flag Communists), there were in revolt several hundred thousand militiamen (the majority of Aung San's People's Volunteer Organization), several thousand army defectors, and tens of thousands of Karen, Arakan Moslem, Mon, and Kachin minority peoples. In truth, the U Nu Government was very near collapse in late 1949, and the outlook for a "liberated" Burma looked good indeed.[6]

Following this Chinese rebuff to closer relations, the Burmese leaders began in early 1950 to shift their foreign policy perceptibly toward a pro-Western stance. The Korean War greatly accelerated this movement as the Burmese began to fear their country might be the next to experience Communist invasion, and the Burmese Government strongly supported the Security Council resolution on Korea in the hope that the United Nations would also come to their aid in case of attack. In September a technical aid agreement was signed with the United States, and an American military mission made plans to visit Burma.

[4] *Ibid.*   [5] *People's China,* I, No. 2 (Jan. 16, 1950), p. 3.
[6] For firsthand reports on the conditions in Burma at the time, see: J. S. Furnivall, "Burma: Independence and After," *Pacific Affairs,* XXII (1949), 193–97; and the reports by Woodrow Wyatt in *New Statesman and Nation,* XXXVII (1949), 147, 196, 247.

This turn of events was certainly detrimental to Chinese interests, and coupled with the loss of the initiative of the insurgents in the spring of 1950, the outcome looked little short of disastrous. Two weeks prior to the outbreak of the Korean War, Radio Peking had threatened that China "would not tolerate the construction of airfields by Anglo-American capital in Burma, threatening the People's Republic," [7] but some American aid did go for airfield improvements and there appeared little hope that either the establishment of Sino-Burmese diplomatic relations on June 8, 1950, or U Nu's verbal reassurances of friendly relations, could stem the tide.

Friction continued into 1951, but the Burmese Government followed a determined policy of attempting to improve relations. They refused to vote for condemnation of China in the United Nations as an aggressor in Korea, actively campaigned for the admission of the People's Republic to that body, and generally championed—along with India—the Chinese cause in international bodies. They also played down all reports of clashes with Chinese Communist troops in the border regions, and did not protest the open Communist courting of the overseas Chinese community in Burma, visits to Peking of pro-Communist Burmese sympathizers, or propaganda broadcasts for the "liberation of Burma" originating in China.[8]

Subtle changes in China's Burma policy began in the last half of 1951. The visit of an official cultural mission to India and Burma headed by Ting Hsi-lin added an element of flexibility to Chinese policy which it had previously lacked. The visit was repaid in April 1952 by the Burmese Minister of Culture U Tun Pe on his return from the Moscow Economic Conference, and a Burmese land reform delegation followed in September and remained for two months.[9] Simultaneously with this increasing flexibility of the Chinese line, the U Nu Government became much more interested in the establishment of close relations due to a variety of factors causing disillusionment with the West. The first, and by far most serious, of these involved the Kuomintang guerrilla forces operating in Burma and the hesitation of the United States to secure their removal from Burmese national soil. Secondly, internal Burmese politics had again taken a more leftward and anti-imperialist course—the 1951 elections having securely

[7] *New York Times,* June 6, 1950.

[8] The best general information on Burmese history, government, and, to some degree, foreign policy, is John F. Cady, *A History of Modern Burma* (Ithaca, Cornell University Press, 1960).

[9] NCNA, Sept. 21, 1951; April 26, 1952; and Sept. 2, 1952.

placed the Socialists in a dominant position in the ruling AFPFL—with the consequent elevation of the position of the Asian Chinese vis-à-vis the Western Americans. Finally, genuine dissatisfaction had set in over the administration of the American aid program and its meager results. This trend was encouraged by an active Chinese campaign to prove United States' support for and equipping of the Kuomintang troops in Burma, and when the Burmese Government reached similar conclusions it dramatically announced in May 1953 that American aid would no longer be welcome.[10] Thus, a factor over which Peking had no control made Burma ripe for the extension of the more flexible approach.

The signing of the three-year Sino-Burmese trade agreement in April 1954 served as a harbinger for the active Chinese courting of the good-will of the nationalist Burmese Government through their strategy of peaceful coexistence. This new tactic of Chinese foreign policy reflected both the failure of the earlier militant policy, and the very real danger of a United States-sponsored military pact's being concluded among states on China's periphery if the ruling groups were not convinced of China's peaceful intentions. After discussions with Prime Minister Nehru of India in a recess of the Geneva Conference of April and May 1954, Chou En-lai signed the Five Principles of Peaceful Coexistence, as the pattern of relations to be pursued by China toward her neighbors. These now famous principles were: 1) Mutual respect for each other's territorial integrity and sovereignty, 2) Nonaggression, 3) Noninterference in each other's internal affairs, 4) Equality and mutual benefit, and 5) Peaceful coexistence. Chou then visited Burma for two days and issued a joint communiqué with U Nu reiterating the Five Principles and specifically noting that "revolution cannot be exported." [11] These new promises struck a highly responsive chord among Burma's leaders and were almost gratefully received.

The following August, U Nu made it clear that his Government had no intention of signing the Manila Treaty, and in December he was warmly received in Peking on an official state visit. His reception was one of the most notable diplomatic successes the Chinese leaders had accomplished. Emphasis was placed on the long tradition of economic and cultural ties between the two countries, their common need to

[10] *New York Times,* March 17, 1953. The development of this dispute was extensively reported in the *Times* in 1952 and 1953.
[11] NCNA, June 30, 1954.

develop their economies, and their opposition to imperialism,[12] and it was often noted that "there is no Sino-Burmese question which cannot be solved by negotiation in the spirit of the Five Principles of Peaceful Coexistence." [13] These conciliatory foreign policy statements, as well as the obvious discipline and progress of the People's Republic, greatly impressed Prime Minister Nu, and he left "firmly convinced Sino-Burmese friendship was possible." [14] During their talks they decided to exchange consulates-general and to open air, highway, and post and telegraph service between the two countries. Furthermore, China pledged to buy 150,000 to 200,000 tons of Burmese rice annually from 1955 through 1957, and to negotiate a settlement of the boundary and dual nationality of overseas Chinese problems.[15] In return, and as a final gesture of good-will, U Nu recognized the Chinese fear of a close Burmese-American relationship, and he pledged that "the AFPFL leaders would under no circumstances, be the stooges of any power." [16]

The exchange of visits in 1954 envisioned the inauguration of a new era in Sino-Burmese relations, and during the next few years a number of economic, military, and cultural exchanges took place between the two countries. Diplomatically, a similarity of interests produced close cooperation at the April 1955 Bandung Conference, and the Burmese continued and strengthened their advocacy of a place for Communist China on world organs and its recognition as the Government of China by other states. For China, Burma served as a "model of peaceful coexistence" [17] which could be held up to other Asian states to help induce them into close relations with Peking, and although India obviously was a more valuable prize to woo, the Chinese certainly did not fail to grasp the impact magnanimous treatment of its small and vulnerable neighbor would have on other potentially friendly Asian countries.

The honeymoon in their relations, however, proved shortlived. Military clashes along the 1,200-mile Sino-Burmese border and the Russian suppression of the Hungarian revolt did much to tarnish the favorable image so assiduously cultivated by the Communist states during 1955 and early 1956. The former resurrected all of the old

---

[12] See Chou En-lai's speech, NCNA, Dec. 2, 1954.
[13] *Jen Min Jih Pao,* Editorial, NCNA, Dec. 2, 1954.
[14] NCNA, Dec. 10, 1954.   [15] NCNA, Dec. 12, 1954.
[16] NCNA, Dec. 10, 1954.
[17] Chou En-lai, "The Present International Situation and China's Foreign Policy," *People's China,* June 16, 1955.

fears among the Burmese of the 600 million Chinese and Chinese intentions, and the latter was promptly denounced by the then Prime Minister U Ba Swe as "the most despicable form of colonialism." [18] Negotiations on the border issue proved difficult and slow, and although the exchange of delegations continued apace, a definite cooling of diplomatic contacts became discernible. Symptomatic of the increased friction was the decision of the Burmese Government (with U Nu once again as Prime Minister) to accept again a $25 million development loan from the United States; and although relations between the two neighbors remained quite correct and the Chinese embassy quite obviously became the most important mission in Rangoon, Peking had forfeited much good-will over the boundary dispute.[19]

The army take-over in Burma on September 26, 1958 under General Ne Win certainly did not please the Chinese, but their prompt congratulations to him implied that they nonetheless expected to maintain relatively friendly relations. The new Government continued the previous neutralist policy, but exchanges were brought to a virtual standstill, and the internal stability effected by the regime offered little hope for an early collapse of the Burmese Government. Chinese suppression of the Tibetan outbreak in April 1959, however, evoked an outcry in Buddhist Burma against the persecution of religion in Tibet, and appeared to create even more resentment among the Burmese than had the border incidents of 1956. A group of 1,000 Buddhist monks openly called for the repudiation of peaceful coexistence and support for the Chinese People's Republic in the United Nations,[20] the Ne Win Government quickly requested $31 million in economic aid from the United States,[21] and border clashes were again reported.[22] It is quite clear from selections from the Burmese press published by the Chinese that they had a very real fear that the Tibetan episode might drive the Burmese Government into a pro-Western position or even into an alliance with the United States.[23] When seen in the perspective of increasing friction with India over border areas, and with Indonesia on the overseas Chinese prob-

[18] Quoted in John Seabury Thompson, "Burma: A Neutral in China's Shadow," *Review of Politics,* XIX (1957), 330–50.
[19] See Aleksandr Kaznacheev, *Inside A Soviet Embassy* (New York, Lippincott, 1961), for the dominance of the Chinese embassy in Rangoon.
[20] *New York Times,* April 28, 1959; for the Chinese reaction, see NCNA, April 27, 1959.
[21] *New York Times,* July 7, 1959.   [22] *Ibid.,* June 1, 1959.
[23] NCNA, April 22, 27, 30, 1959.

lem, this development threatened completely to wreck the policy of peaceful coexistence and the good-will carefully developed since 1954.

To reverse the steady worsening of relations with their Asian neighbors, the Chinese Communists worked for quick resolution of the outstanding border issues with Burma and Nepal, and then held those settlements up as evidence that peaceful coexistence had not been abandoned. For its part, the Burmese Government certainly desired to settle this issue as soon as possible, and in January 1960 Ne Win visited China to sign an Agreement on the Question of the Sino-Burmese Boundary and a Treaty of Friendship and Mutual Nonaggression.[24] Chou En-lai hailed the Burmese policy of "peace, neutrality, and nonalignment," and at the April National People's Conference he noted that the Agreement and Treaty were "eloquent proof" that reasonable solutions could be found to complex questions left over from history, and that these agreements were "new examples of the friendly solidarity of Asian countries and important victories for the Five Principles of Peaceful Coexistence." [25]

The period of thirteen months from January 1960 through January 1961 marks the high point of friendliness in Sino-Burmese relations. China actively pursued a policy of conciliation toward Burma which now became the focus of the new peaceful coexistence effort, and unlike the 1954–55 era, when relations with Burma had been secondary to those with India, now Burma was to become the showcase of China's peaceful intentions. Every Chinese speech contained sentiments similar to those expressed by Ch'en Yi in August:

Some Western countries recently alleged with ulterior motives that China had given up the policy of peaceful coexistence between countries having different social systems. The development of friendly relations between China and Burma have given the lie to such allegations.[26]

When U Nu returned to power in April 1960, the pace of the new reapprochement was quickened. Cultural exchanges again became common, and the specifics of the boundary settlement found such quick solution that in October 1960 U Nu and Chou En-lai signed the boundary treaty amid a display of friendliness seldom equaled in international relations. Chou's triumphal visit to Rangoon in January 1961 on Burma's Independence Day, to exchange ratifications of the treaty, provided the fitting climax to the period proclaimed by the Chinese Premier as "Sino-Burmese Friendship Year," and the $84

[24] Text in *Current Background,* p. 612.   [25] NCNA, April 10, 1960.
[26] NCNA, Aug. 13, 1960.

million aid proffered to Burma led many observers to feel that the country might be destined soon to become a satellite of China.

However, as in the earlier period of closeness, even though interchanges continued and the speeches voiced mutual praise, a discernible cooling again began to enter Sino-Burmese relations. A rather strong hint that perhaps more than neutrality and nonalignment was desired by the Chinese occurred at a banquet for Ne Win in China in October 1961, when Lo Jui-ching, in the presence of Chou, Ch'en, and others, delivered a rather blistering attack on the United States, with whom Burma was maintaining relatively friendly relations.[27] Chou also berated the United States, though in more muted terms, and the entire visit appeared to have been much more perfunctory and less cordial than either the January 1960 Ne Win visit or the October 1960 U Nu-Ne Win mission. The Burmese, of course, had long since developed a wariness toward Chinese actions, and their reaction to the increased pressures was predictably restrained.

A second military take-over in Burma in March 1962 further complicated relations, as did the Sino-Indian War of the following autumn. Ne Win's second government again saw its primary task as imposing discipline and uniting the country, and to do this it jailed opposition groups on both the left and the right; it both expelled the Ford Foundation teams and sharply curtailed Sino-Burmese visits; it sought to halt the propaganda war being carried on through foreign embassies by enforcing strict rules equally on the British, American, Russian, and Chinese embassies, and by adopting a strict neutrality between China and the United States and later between the Soviet Union and China. Strict neutrality was also the policy followed on the Sino-Indian War, and although various Western observers attacked the policy as insufficiently pro-Indian, it is nevertheless true that the Burmese actively attempted to persuade the Chinese Government to accept the Colombo Conference proposals.[28] It was true that there were no American troops in Burma, and that the Ne Win Government continued to plead for Chinese Communist admission to world bodies —but Burma still received some American aid, the caliber of the weapons of its army was that of NATO, the Ne Win Government had made noticeable efforts to improve relations with the Soviet Union, and it had also not supported the extensive Chinese effort to convene a second major Afro-Asian Conference.[29]

[27] NCNA, Oct. 9, 1961.   [28] *New York Times,* Feb. 19, 1964.
[29] See Ne Win's speech, NCNA, Feb. 14, 1964.

As perhaps the harbinger of a harder line, the Chinese press broke its silence of over a decade on the Communist insurgents in Burma, to publish 1964 National Day greetings from the Communist Party of Burma (White Flag) calling for "the establishment of a new Burma of real independence." [30] The Burmese press was indignant, and the Burmese representative to the Cairo Conference (Foreign Minister U Thi Han) vented the obvious anger of his Government in a subtle but nonetheless important manner. While China's close supporters called for condemnation of the United States, and its enemy India pleaded for concerted opposition to the forthcoming Chinese atomic explosion, U Thi Han quite pointedly said:

I believe it is our duty not, indeed, to condemn this or that nation, but to appeal again to all nations to subscribe to those various measures, such as the Nuclear Test Ban Treaty of Moscow, which are intended to lead the way to general and complete disarmament.[31]

It appeared that Sino-Burmese relations were entering another period of strain.

The Kuomintang Troops in Burma

The two most serious diplomatic issues between China and Burma —the several thousand Kuomintang guerrillas in Burma, and the boundary dispute—deserve separate discussions not only because of their intrinsic importance but also for their demonstration of the flexibility of the Chinese Communist approach toward Burma. In both cases, Peking's first "big nation chauvinistic" reaction underwent substantial modification in the interest of amicable relations with Burma; in the end both issues were handled with skill, and Peking's attitude greatly aided its avowed policy of making relations with Burma a model of peaceful coexistence.

In 1949 and early 1950, remnants of the Eighth and Twenty-sixth Nationalist Chinese Armies crossed the Yunnan border into Burma under pressure from advancing Communist forces, and joined parts of the old Ninety-third Division left from the Second World War in roving sparsely populated northern Burma, pillaging for food and making preparations for raids on Yunnan Province.[32] Soon those forces were organized under General Li Mi into an effective fighting

[30] NCNA, Oct. 2, 1964.   [31] *Forward* (Rangoon), Oct. 15, 1964.
[32] *New York Times,* March 13, 1950 and July 28, 1951.

organization supplied with American weapons by airdrop from Taiwan. The troops not only insulted Burmese sovereignty and pillaged her villages, but also were an obvious irritation to the Communist Chinese, and there existed a deep fear that the Communists would advance into Burma against the marauders to eliminate the nuisance, or even worse to use their presence as a pretext for attacking Burma. The Burmese Army was engaged in suppressing the large number of serious internal revolts, and could not militarily oust the Kuomintang guerrillas much less hope to fend off a full-scale attack by Communist China.

In early 1952, Peking began a steady propaganda campaign aimed to link the United States with the guerrillas, and an article in *Ta Kung Pao* (February 3, 1952) both implied that the Burmese were not taking sufficient action to eliminate them and issued a serious warning:

The activities of the American imperialists in the Burma-Thailand border region have seriously jeopardized the security of Burma and will certainly bring catastrophe to the Burmese people.[33]

Later in the year a number of Chinese Communist troops crossed the border in pursuit of some Kuomintang units, and remained in Burmese territory until 1956.[34] The Burmese Government did not protest those incursions, because of its attempt to promote better relations with Peking, but it did step up its efforts to bring about the removal of the troops by increasing pressure on the United States to intercede with Taiwan. The sluggishness of American efforts to dissuade the Nationalists implied United States involvement—as indeed increasing evidence supported—and the Burmese Government, in March 1953, charged the Nationalists with aggression in the United Nations. With this, a partial withdrawal was effected by United States pressure on Taiwan, but both the Burmese and the Chinese Communist Governments considered the repatriation of only 2,000 of the reported 10,000 Kuomintang troops in Burma woefully inadequate, and denounced the effort as a sham. By the end of 1953, the relative restraint of the Chinese Communists on the question and the suspicion aroused in the Burmese Government over American motives had laid the groundwork for the policy of close friendship pursued in 1954 and 1955.

[33] Translated in *Survey of China Mainland Press* (hereafter referred to as *SCMP*), No. 266, p. 7.
[34] Chou En-lai, "Report to the National People's Congress on the Sino-Burmese Border Question," NCNA, July 9, 1957.

Throughout the rest of the 1950s the troops remained troublesome,
but constant Burmese military pressure, and Communist propaganda
attempts to bring about defections into Yunnan, reduced their importance as a major problem for either government. However, with the
economic disasters following the failure of the Great Leap in China,
and the Nationalists' preparations for an invasion of the mainland in
1961, Li Mi's bands once again became a serious threat to the Chinese
Communist Government, and the whole sequence—Chinese protests,
arousing Burmese fears of an invasion, and the consequent anger at the
United States for not forcing Taiwan to withdraw its troops—began
once again.[35] In an April 1961 Ch'en Yi-U Nu joint communiqué, it
was agreed to coordinate their actions and cooperate in eliminating
the Kuomintang forces from Burma.[36] This crisis passed with the
improvement of conditions on the mainland and the failure of a
Nationalist invasion to materialize; but the problem will probably
remain for a considerable period of time—especially since the Burmese insurgents have renewed their activity—and it could again
become serious whenever the guerrillas appear as an actual threat
to the Chinese People's Republic.

The Sino-Burmese Boundary Dispute

The frictions over the 1,200-mile Sino-Burmese boundary and its
exact location have been similar to those between other states emerging for the first time into the modern nation-state system. Traditionally, the area between the Chinese empire and the Burmese kingdom
has been inhabited neither by Han Chinese nor by Burmese, but by
minority peoples organized in small principalities and paying tribute
to either the Chinese or the Burmese states (whichever had won the
most recent victory in the area) or, not infrequently, to both. The
British signed agreements with Chinese representatives in 1894 and
1897, which demarcated all of the boundary except two hundred
miles of extremely wild land in the Wa States area, and began payment of annual rent on a small area of leased territory known as
the Namwan Tract. The Chinese Nationalist Government was never
satisfied with this arrangement, but after a League of Nations survey
it signed a boundary agreement in 1941 delineating the Wa States—

[35] Nationalist Government disavowal of the guerrillas in Burma made no
impression on the Burmese Government. It was certain that they still received
aid by periodic airdrops.
[36] NCNA, April 17, 1961.

Yunnan line. Independent Burma fell heir to those agreements and considered their retention a matter of national pride, but as early as 1948 the Chinese Nationalists had refused receipt of the Namwan Tract rent and had renewed its demands on a rather large area of legally Burmese territory.[37]

When the Chinese Communists came to power, they made known their view that the 1941 agreement had been forced on China by an imperialist power and therefore was not binding on their Government. This naturally made the Burmese leaders quite uneasy, but when they requested talks on the boundary they were assured that the new Chinese leaders desired a fair settlement but it would have to await the solution of more pressing matters. U Nu and his Government consistently played down the minor Chinese incursions occurring during the first few years of relations between the two states, and in 1954 he won agreement from Chou En-lai to begin negotiations for a final settlement of the boundary.[38]

While negotiations were in progress at a secondary level, violent clashes broke out in November 1955 between the Chinese troops that had been on Burmese territory since 1952 and some Burmese patrols, and when news of the incident received sensational reportage by the Burmese English language *Nation* in late July and August of 1956, the events caused a furor in Burma.[39] *Jen Min Jih Pao* labeled the *Nation*'s reports "entirely groundless," but it did note that a recent Burmese Government report might have substance and said that the Wa States' territory was an "unsettled zone" and that "In these circumstances, there is fundamentally no such question as 'crossing into' the territory of Burma." It did, however, conclude with a call for a solution through peaceful negotiations.[40] Burmese public opinion was genuinely outraged—so much so that the Prime Minister considered it necessary to publicly call for "restraint," and noted that "it behooves a small country to lessen tension." [41] Even the pro-Communist Burma Workers' and Peasants' Party felt compelled to call for negotiations to avert Burma's being drawn into SEATO.[42]

U Nu (temporarily out of power) appealed to Nehru for assistance,

[37] The best single article on the boundary negotiations is David Wolfstone, "Fast Work on the Sino-Burmese Border," *Far Eastern Economic Review,* XXIX (1960), 368–74.

[38] NCNA, Dec. 12, 1964.

[39] *New York Times,* July 31 and Aug. 1, 1956.

[40] *Jen Min Jih Pao,* Observer, NCNA, Aug. 4, 1956.

[41] *Nation* (Rangoon), Sept. 5, 1956; quoted in John Seabury Thompson, "Burmese Neutralism," *Political Science Quarterly,* LXXII (1957), 261–83.

[42] NCNA, Aug. 16, 1956.

held discussions with the visiting Soong Ching-ling, and then himself went to Peking in late September to negotiate an agreement. The Chinese agreed to withdraw their troops to behind the 1941 line— without admitting the line's validity—if the Burmese troops would withdraw from the three border villages of Hpimaw, Gawlun, and Kangfang claimed by the Chinese.[43] At that time they seemed anxious to settle the dispute on terms generally favorable to the Burmese position—with the three villages as a balm for Chinese nationalism— in order to avoid wrecking their carefully developed policy of peaceful coexistence with Burma, but the agreement could not be consummated because of resistance on the part of the leaders of the semiautonomous Kachin state to giving up any of their territory. Chinese priorities had begun to shift by the time the Burmese were willing to give up the three villages, so that when U Nu visited Kunming in March 1957 to make a final settlement Chou raised the price by including a demand for a tract occupied by the Panghung and Panlao tribes—in addition to the three villages—in return for clear Burmese title to the Namwan Tract. A letter sent by Chou in July again added conditions, and even placed the entire upper line in question.[44] The Chinese, obviously, did not consider the time ripe for a final settlement.

It might be useful to examine for a moment the Chinese decision to let a final settlement of the border question remain in suspension. The Chinese Communist leaders seem to have understood quite well that the settlement of the boundary was a diplomatic trump card which should not be wasted for a small amount of Burmese good will. In 1956 a settlement would have been desirable to preserve the policy of peaceful coexistence, but with the general hardening of Chinese policies in 1957 friendly relations with small and weak Burma and its tottering Government would have appeared much less urgent and hardly worth the loss of such an important means of applying pressure.

Three years later, however, the international situation greatly changed. In late 1959 China rapidly was becoming isolated from the rest of Asia, and an example of China's good will was desperately needed to repair the damage done to her image by the friction with India. It was now time to play the trump. Ne Win offered to settle with China by turning over part of the disputed Panghung area plus the three villages, in return for clear title to the Namwan Tract and

---

[43] *Jen Min Jih Pao*, Nov. 16, 1956; translated in *SCMP*, No. 1420, p. 32.
[44] See Note 37.

recognition of the rest of the British delineated line (including that of 1941). After he also agreed to a Treaty of Friendship and Mutual Nonaggression, the Chinese accepted immediately, and the two agreements were signed in January 1960. A specific Boundary Treaty followed in October, and relations between the two countries became indeed a "brilliant example of peaceful coexistence."

Trade and Foreign Aid

Sino-Burmese trade provides an excellent example of the use of trade by Communist China as a political weapon even where it profits her little in economic terms. Basically, the problem is that the rice and teak exported by Burma (a world leader in both) have a very low priority in the list of goods China desires to import for her industrialization, except when a severe rice shortage occurs as it did in the period 1960–62.[45] On the other hand, Burma has preferred whenever possible to purchase its industrial and luxury goods from Western countries (especially the United Kingdom), even though the Chinese have been increasing the variety and raising the quality of its goods for export; but fluctuations in the world market price for rice make Burma vulnerable to periods of foreign exchange shortages, and at such times barter with China becomes attractive.

Trade between the two states before 1954 was limited to small transactions, such as the sale of 1,500 tons of Burmese rubber to China near the end of the Korean War and the transfer of 300 tons of World War II stockpiled building materials left in Burma by the Nationalists.[46] Early in that year, however, the Chinese press began a strong campaign to develop trade with capitalist countries, and one of the earliest results of this effort was the signing of a three-year trade agreement with Burma on April 22, 1954, calling for barter trade between the two countries in a specified list of items.[47] For the Chinese this was assuredly part of the new strategy of peaceful co-

[45] See Yeh Chi-chuang's report on China's foreign trade during the First Five-Year Plan, *People's China*, Dec. 1, 1957.

[46] *New York Times*, March 28, 1953.

[47] China would export coal, silk and silk textiles, cotton textiles, agricultural implements, paper, light industrial products, handicraft products, enamelware, porcelain, canned goods, pharmaceutical and medical substances, tea, and cigarettes. Burma was willing to export rice and rice products, food beans and pulses, oil cakes, mineral ores, timber, rubber, and raw cotton. Text, NCNA, April 22, 1954.

existence; although their statements left little question that trade was meant to be promoted with Japan and Western Europe, the weakness of the world market price for rice made the agreement important to Burma. The Chinese agreed in November to buy 150,000 tons of Burmese rice on barter terms.[48] This offer found ready acceptance by the Burmese Government, which had been trying hard to get the United States to buy its rice. When the Soviet Union followed with a similar offer in 1955, it constituted a clear coup for the Communist camp. The value of Sino-Burmese trade for 1955 was thirty-one times that of 1954,[49] and the rice agreement most certainly contributed greatly to the close relations between the countries in the next year.

Of perhaps equal importance to China was the great amount of prestige it acquired in the eyes of the Burmese and other Asians, as a major exporter of industrial products such as steel and other metals, and construction materials. The Chinese trade fairs held in Rangoon in 1957 and 1961 drew large crowds which admired the advanced products of "New China," [50] and further prestige was gained by visits of Burmese buying missions to the Canton trade fairs and to industrial plants in China.

When the price of rice recovered in 1956 and the barter transactions did not live up to Burmese expectations, the Burmese were much less interested in continuing the system, and it lost much of its propaganda value for the Chinese. This resulted, in late 1957, in the inauguration of a Chinese foreign aid program to Burma, with a modest loan for the construction of a 40,000-spindle textile mill at 2½ percent interest.[51] China's second effort came in January 1961 with the Sino-Burmese Economic and Technical Agreement, providing the equivalent of $84 million in technical assistance and materials. It included complete sets of factory equipment, and building materials; Chinese technicians were to be sent to Burma, and some Burmese engineers were to study in China. The credit was to be used from October 1961 to October 1967, with repayment without interest to begin in 1970.[52]

Foreign aid, however, has proved for China to have many of the limitations which plague similar American and Soviet efforts, and in

[48] NCNA, Nov. 3, 1954.

[49] Yeh Chi-chuang, "China's Economic Relations with Asian-African Countries: Progress and Prospects," *People's China,* March 16, 1956.

[50] The 1957 exposition reportedly was visited by 430,000 persons. NCNA, *ca.* April 10, 1957.

[51] NCNA, Jan. 9, 1958.   [52] NCNA, Jan. 9, 1961.

Burma the distrust of Communist China has been so great that the leaders have been reluctant to use the proffered aid. The U Nu Government made no significant move toward spending the credit before its May 1962 ouster, and Ne Win has used it only sparingly.[53] Work on a sugar mill at Namtu and surveys for several bridges in the north have been carried out, but those projects represent only a fraction of the credit, and it appears probable that the Burmese will allow much of it to go unused. Actually, Burma has sufficient funds to carry out the slow pace of development desired because of its huge rice sales, Japanese reparations, and continuing American aid, and the Government is in a position to accept or reject Chinese aid at its leisure.

The lure of trade has provided the Chinese with very little leverage in their dealings with Burma except for the rice purchases in 1955; in the 1960–62 period it was Burma that held the upper hand. In 1961 China reportedly was to buy 350,000 tons of Burmese rice,[54] and the next year Chou En-lai thanked the Burmese quite profusely for selling the Chinese large amounts of rice in 1962 after a relatively poor harvest. Generally, however, the Chinese have purchased 100 to 150 thousand tons of Burmese rice annually, which amounts to well under 5 percent of Burma's exports. There seems little likelihood that this percentage will increase, unless China once again experiences an agricultural catastrophe, or a burgeoning population forces her to become a major rice importer. On balance it would appear that, except for the year 1955, the Chinese trade and aid offensive has not had great influence in Burma.

Sino-Burmese Cultural Exchanges

At certain periods in the past fifteen years there has been a great deal of contact between the two countries through the medium of cultural exchange, which the Chinese have promoted vigorously. A *Jen Min Jih Pao* commentator writing in 1956 noted that cultural contacts are "primarily aimed at increasing mutual understanding, eliminating differences and bridging the gap, thereby consolidating the peace and friendship between various countries," [55] and he listed

[53] *New York Times*, March 19, 1962 and Jan. 13, 1964.
[54] *New York Times*, Dec. 25, 1960.
[55] Chen Cheng-ching, "Further Develop China's Cultural Relations with Other Countries," *Jen Min Jih Pao*, April 15, 1956.

the range of activities China had attempted to encourage. They were: visits of performing troupes; international athletic competition; exchange of cultural workers, educationists, artists, scientists, doctors, journalists, and some students and professors; film exchanges; translations and publications; exhibitions abroad; exchange of cultural materials; and gifts of historical and cultural objects.[56] Several instances of each category have been exchanged with Burma. From the summary listing of these exchanges shown below, it can be seen that by far the greatest number of exchanges occurred in the periods 1955–58 and 1960–61, during the flowering of the peaceful coexistence line. Those were the periods when U Nu was Prime Minister of Burma; the Governments of Ne Win have adopted a strict policy of keeping such visits to a minimum. It seems unlikely, therefore, that extensive exchanges will be resumed in the near future.

It is difficult to evaluate the significance of these exchanges or their value to Chinese policy toward Burma. The Burmese have certainly been impressed by Chinese industriousness and by the country's disciplined route to revival as a great power, and although this makes them believe an accommodation with China is desirable and necessary, it also increases their fears of ultimate Chinese intentions. No number of Chinese opera performances can erase from the minds of Burma's leaders the memory of the rather tough attitude taken by China in 1957 on the boundary issue, and it is doubtful that such contacts will exorcise the specter of Chinese domination for most Burmese. In short, this modified form of people's diplomacy, maintained on a government-to-government basis, has serious limitations for the Chinese as an instrument of foreign policy in Burma.

A case in point is the campaign to convince the strongly religious Burmese that Buddhism enjoys great freedom in China. The Chinese loan of the revered tooth relic for the 2500th anniversary of Buddhism held in Burma in 1955 was certainly a novel act of good will. But actions of this kind were overshadowed by the suppression of the Tibetan revolt. Generally, it seems that the visits of cultural delegations were more the product of intergovernmental good will than the creator of close relations, and the diplomatic suavity of Chou En-lai was much more important than the exchange of propaganda films and cultural artists.

[56] *Ibid.*

Sino-Burmese Cultural Exchanges, 1951–1964 [57]

	From Burma	From China
1951		cultural delegation
1952	cultural delegation	
1953		
1954	trade union delegation	
1955	cultural delegation Buddhist delegation	cultural delegation trade union delegation Buddhist delegation
1956	film delegation women's delegation	Buddhist delegation football team culture and art delegation troupe of artists
1957	parliamentary delegation film delegation good will mission youth delegation health and medical delegation good will mission (U Kyaw Nein) good will mission (U Ba Swe)	women's delegation Yunnan song and dance ensemble basketball team
1958	journalists' delegation student delegation sports and physical culture delegation local government delegation educational workers' delegation	women's delegation cooperatives delegation
1959	art delegation cultural delegation	scholars' delegation
1960	journalists' delegation culture and art troupe culture and good will delegation trade union delegation journalists' delegation sports delegation	cultural and friendship delegation trade union delegation journalists' delegation Buddhist delegation cultural and art delegation film delegation sports delegation
1961	trade union delegation educationists' delegation parliamentary delegation	National People's Congress delegation
1962	trade union delegation	
1963	labor good will delegation	
1964		science delegation

[57] Source: NCNA releases, in *SCMP*. This list shows only missions sponsored by the Burmese and Chinese Governments. Visits obviously by Communist fronts in Burma are omitted.

The Minorities of China and Burma

Ethnic Burmans compose only perhaps two-thirds of the Burmese population, with the remainder of the country's twenty million distributed among Karens, Shans, Chinese, Kachins, and a variety of other less populous groups. The Karens, Shans, and Kachins have all at times spawned armed separatist groups, and the Karen rebellion beginning in 1948 almost caused the collapse of independent Burma.[58] Understandably, the Burmese ruling group has been extraordinarily sensitive to attempts of outside groups to collaborate with minority rebel leaders, and much of the vitriolic dislike of the Kuomintang units on Burmese soil derives from reports that Chinese Nationalist weapons are going to the Karen separatists.

Chinese Communist activity among the Kachin and Shan minorities has long vexed the Burmese Government, especially since the granting of asylum in Yunnan to Naw Seng, the leader of the Kachin revolt. The Chinese have reportedly made him a full colonel, equipping his 1,800 rebel troops and keeping them at the Yunnan-Kachin State border ready to return at any time.[59] Widespread immigration of "Chinese" Kachins (including a sizeable number of Communist cadres) has been reported in the Burmese press,[60] which attributes this movement to a determination on the part of the Chinese leaders to populate that frontier region and ultimately detach it from Burma. Perhaps it would be more accurate to say that most of the immigration is a result of pressures in Yunnan, but this explanation hardly makes the situation more palatable to the Burmese. There also has been genuine apprehension over the Thai Autonomous Chou with its championing of the Free Thai Movement, since it is suspected that the Shans—a Thai subgroup—might also be included in the movement's plans.[61] The *Nation* has reported that the leader of the Free Thai Movement visited the Chinese embassy at Rangoon several

[58] A great deal has been written in the West on the Karens. One outstanding article is W. S. Desai, "The Karens of Burma," *India Quarterly, VI* (1950), 276–82.

On the northern minorities, see Hugh Tinker, "Burma's Northeast Borderland Problems," *Pacific Affairs,* XXIX (1956), 324–26. See also Note 9.

[59] Aleksandr Kaznacheev, *Inside A Soviet Embassy* (New York, Lippincott, 1961), p. 214.

[60] Robert S. Elegant, *The Dragon's Seed* (New York, St. Martin's Press, 1959), pp. 257–58. See also Note 19.

[61] The Burmese Consul General in Kunming was very restrained after a visit to the Thai Autonomous Chou. His response is given in NCNA, Dec. 23, 1955.

times, purportedly on missions to coordinate actions among the Shans.[62] However, such activities are only relatively minor irritants to the Burmese Government because of their small scale, and they pale beside the much more vigorous and potentially dangerous actions by the Communists to win the allegiance of Burma's overseas Chinese community.

Traditionally, the Chinese in Burma have enjoyed friendly relations with the Burmese because of their small numbers, their partial assimilation, and their subordination to the more powerful one million Indian merchants settled throughout the country. Anti-Indian and anti-Chinese riots in the 1930s seem not to have weakened the friendly ties of the Burmese and their Chinese "next of kin," but the conduct of Nationalist troops in Burma in the Second World War and the evident rise in the number of Chinese in Burma have begun to introduce strains.[63]

Following the "liberation" of China, the Communists began an intensive campaign to capture the allegiance of the overseas Chinese in Burma. In the first months they had perforce to rely primarily on economic pressure through the Chinese Chamber of Commerce and the two banks it inherited from the Nationalists, but the establishment of close ties with the Chinese embassy later in the year facilitated this take-over, and by the end of 1951 90 percent of the overseas Chinese schools in Burma were under Communist control.[64] The economic approach, according to the *New York Times,* involved making loans readily available on the condition that the note would have two pro-Communist cosignatories, that the recipient would send his children to a pro-Communist school, that he was to fly the People's Republic flag on the Communist national holidays, and that the merchant could not hire any "known anti-Communists." [65] The fruits of this approach can be seen in the campaign conducted in November to gain overseas Chinese support for the "Resist America—Aid Korea" movement, and the sizeable delegations of overseas Chinese from Burma attending Peking's National Day and May Day celebrations.[66] The open fighting between opposing Nationalist-Communist strong-arm squads

[62] NCNA, Sept. 24, 1957.
[63] Victor W. W. S. Purcell, *The Chinese in Southeast Asia* (London, Oxford University Press, 1951), pp. 92–98.
[64] Elegant, p. 254.   [65] *New York Times,* Oct. 13, 1954.
[66] A delegation of 20 overseas Chinese from Burma attended the 1951 National Day celebrations. Thirty-three were in China for May Day 1952, and a 68-member delegation was there for 1953 National Day. NCNA, Sept. 25, 1951; *Nan Fang Jih Pao,* April 23, 1952; and NCNA, Sept. 29, 1953.

led to a Burmese Government warning to the entire Chinese Community in Rangoon. But the Burmese did not protest to Peking, and the increasing friction with the Kuomintang troops in northern Burma made the Government willing to see the Kuomintang organizations suspected of aiding the guerrillas destroyed.

As a part of their peaceful coexistence line adopted toward Burma in 1954, the Communist Chinese developed a very conciliatory stance on the problem of the overseas Chinese. It was first in a December 1954 joint communiqué with U Nu that Chou offered to negotiate the question of the dual nationality of overseas Chinese,[67] and during his 1956 visit to Burma he delivered a long speech at a Chinese meeting admonishing them to obey the laws and respect the customs, habits, and religion of Burma, to learn Burmese, to avoid making exorbitant profits, and (for those who do not become Burmese citizens) not to take part in politics. He ended by explicitly promising not to "recruit members of the Chinese Communist Party or other Chinese democratic parties or groups among the overseas Chinese." [68] The Burmese Government reciprocated the next year by proscribing Kuomintang celebrations of Double Ten, and in early 1958 all Kuomintang organizations were ordered dissolved and their flags, signboards, and emblems removed.[69]

To the Burmese leadership, Peking's control of the overseas Chinese in Burma was regrettable but unavoidable. The problem has gained in significance with the rapid growth of the number of Chinese in the country. Chinese immigration into Burma did not end with the establishment of independence, but on the contrary it has greatly increased. Official statistics from the 1941 census placed the number of Chinese in Burma at 193,549. By 1948 the number was estimated to have grown to 300,000. The *Nation* placed the figure at nearly one million in 1956, and today any estimate would have to be substantially above this figure.[70] Evidence that many of the newcomers have been transported across China from Fukien and Kwangtung provinces to enable them to blend in with the earlier immigrants strongly implies Chinese governmental support—and perhaps instigation—for the influx,[71] and it seems certain to continue unabated until the Burmese are able to police the long and rough border effectively. The fears this situation raises of eventual Burmese absorption by its much more

[67] NCNA, Dec. 12, 1954.   [68] *Guardian* (Rangoon), March 1957.
[69] NCNA, Oct. 12, 1957 and Jan. 9, 1958.
[70] See Note 18.   [71] See Note 59.

populous neighbor have not aided Sino-Burmese friendship, and if indeed the Chinese Government is aiding the migration its motives are difficult to understand. One million people per decade would hardly relieve the population pressure in China, and Burmese rice is obtainable through normal trade. Whether planned or not, the influx will undoubtedly be a growing source of friction between the two countries.

China and the Burmese Communist Insurgents

Communism took root relatively late in Burma. The first official Communist cell was formed in 1939, and the formation of the Communist Party of Burma followed in 1943. The Indian Communist Party served as the ideological guide of the founding members—some of whom had established contacts while students in India in the mid-thirties—and neither Yenan nor Moscow seemed to have been in touch with them. The principal leaders were Thakin Thein Pe Myint, the more fanatical Thakin Soe, and, by the end of the war, the able and moderate Thakin Than Tun. A controversy over continued Communist cooperation with the socialists and other nationalists in the coalition AFPFL led to the expulsion from the party of Thakin Soe and his followers in early 1946, and the group went underground in opposition to British and nationalist attempts to achieve independence peacefully. Because of the militant policies of Soe and his Red Flag Communists, the label of Trotskyite has occasionally been used to describe them, but Moscow did not appear to support one faction over the other, and it would be more nearly correct to view the matter as a personal dispute between the leaders than as connected to international Stalinist and Trotskyite groups. The Red Flag faction continues to exist, but its small size has always prevented its becoming a direct threat to the Government.

In October the majority White Flag faction of the Communist Party was also expelled from the AFPFL, but Thakin Than Tun was willing to remain in the open in the hope of wresting the nationalist leadership from Aung San, and in fact he cooperated with Aung San's AFPFL at the same time that Soviet propagandists were calling the nationalist leader a British agent. He also remained on friendly terms with Thakin Nu (U Nu) for several months following Aung San's assassination in July 1947.[72]

[72] See Note 8.

In February 1948, Thakin Than Tun and H. M. Goshal (a Burmese of Indian descent) attended the First Congress of Southeast Asia
Democratic Youth, in Calcutta, sponsored by the World Federation of
Trade Unions (WFTU), where the Yugoslav delegates expounded the
new Cominform hard line to the Asian radicals. It was alleged by
U Nu that the Burmese White Flag Communist leaders returned from
that conference with a booklet outlining tactics to be followed in a
Burmese uprising.[73] This allegation may be untrue, but nevertheless
the White Flags did openly revolt in March, and they have carried on
an active rebellion ever since. At the outbreak they could muster perhaps 25,000 partisans, but their activities became increasingly dangerous to the Government when they were joined in a loose alliance by the
majority of Aung San's still undisbanded militia—the People's Volunteers Organization—and when other groups such as the Karen and
Kachin bands also rebelled against the national authority.

The attempt of the White Flag Communists to establish a united
front against the Government in 1949 or 1950 [74] along Chinese
Communist lines implies the beginning of Chinese influence on the
Burmese Communists, and certainly this influence became strong after
the latter's delegate attended the November 1949 Trade Union Conference of Asian and Australasian Countries, where Liu Shao-ch'i
first put forward the essentials of success of the Chinese revolution.[75]
The reliance on Chinese tactics is even more noticeable in the program
drawn up after the united front of the White Flag Communists, the
Red Flag Communists, and the People's Volunteers Organization was
finally accomplished in the fall of 1952,[76] and the report that the
Burmese Communists came under complete Chinese direction in 1954
seems plausible in the light of the frequent known visits of the underground leaders to Peking since that time and earlier.[77] The *New York
Times* reported that thirty Burmese Communist leaders returned from
China in 1963 to participate in negotiations with the Government.[78]

[73] Virginia Thompson and Richard Adloff, *The Left Wing in Southeast Asia*
(New York, Sloane, 1950), p. 110.

[74] There seems to be some confusion on the exact date. John H. Badgley, in
"Burma's Radical Left: A Study in Failure," *Problems of Communism*, X
(1961), 51, gives it as March 1950; while Shen-yu Dai, in *Peking, Moscow,
and the Communist Parties of Colonial Asia* (Cambridge, Massachusetts Institute of Technology Press, 1964), p. 23, gives it as March 1949.

[75] See Note 3.

[76] This is Badgley's date. Dai gives July 1953 and lists the program on p. 27.
See Note 73.

[77] Kasnacheev, p. 214.   [78] *New York Times,* Dec. 30, 1963.

By the spring of 1950, however, the many rebellions in Burma had lost the initiative, and the likelihood of a Communist seizure of power by "revolutionary war" began to seem increasingly remote. The Russians reportedly gave up hope for the Than Tun group in 1954. In 1958 a Soviet embassy report stated, "the days of the Communist insurrection are numbered," and advocated evacuation of the remaining leaders in order to establish a government in exile.[79] This attitude was quite understandable following the widespread defections and factionalism plaguing the underground forces in the mid-1950s, and it has been suggested that by 1958 no more than a few thousand remained in rebellion.[80] Recently, however, the insurgents seem to have regained some strength, and they resisted a Government attempt in 1963 to negotiate a settlement.

Chinese aid to the Burmese "national liberation movement," as far as can be ascertained, has been limited to providing advice, money, and training of Communist cadres in China, but there can be no question that they have considered it in their interest to keep the movement alive and in reserve for the time when the benefits of peaceful coexistence seem insufficient. A suggestion that perhaps in their view Burma under Ne Win is becoming less acceptable was provided by the publication in Peking of greetings sent to China on the 1964 National Day by the underground White Flag Communists —a practice which Peking had discontinued after 1953—in which it was affirmed that "the Communist Party of Burma will continue to uphold the three banners of national independence, democracy and peace in the country, and will strive for the establishment of a new Burma of real independence, politically and economically, and of peace, democracy, unity and happiness." On that occasion the Burmese Communists strongly aligned themselves with Peking in the Sino-Soviet dispute.[81] Coming at a time of renewed insurrections in Burma, this action boded little good for the Burmese Government. If the Chinese should decide it is in their interest to supply large quantities of arms to the insurgents, such action would certainly be viewed as serious by the Burmese and could cause a radical deterioration in relations.

[79] Kaznacheev, p. 215.   [80] Badgley, p. 51.   [81] NCNA, Oct. 2, 1964.

China and the Burmese Communist Fronts and Sympathizers

While the Red and White Flag Communist insurgents in the past twelve to thirteen years have been little more than a bad nuisance and a drain on the resources of the Burmese Government, above-ground Communist fronts and their sympathizers have been more influential in Burmese politics, and it has been on those groups that Peking has relied heavily for the promotion of its policy of peaceful coexistence. The leading political figures in independent Burma trace their common background to their student days in the mid-1930s at Rangoon University, or to groups organized by activists from that center. One such group took the title of Thakin (meaning master, and previously used to address the ruling British), and adopted a common ideology of nationalism and Marxian socialism. Included in it are such notables of the Burmese political scene as Aung San, Nu, Than Tun, Soe, and many others. Its strongly leftist orientation has led many members to split from the moderate socialist policies followed by the U Nu and Ne Win Governments, and they have often led avowedly antigovernment, pro-Communist organizations which consistently espouse the programs emanating from Moscow and Peking.[82] In return, they have received substantial backing from the Communist powers.

The most notable example of this process was the Burma Workers' and Peasants' Party. Its leader, Thakin Lwin, had been a prominent labor leader of the AFPFL and President of the Trade Union Congress of Burma TUC(B) until he was expelled from the League for opposition to the Government's condemnation of the Korean War and his demand to affiliate the TUC(B) with the Communist-sponsored WFTU.[83] After expulsion, he created his own Burma Trade Union Congress, affiliated it with the WFTU, and became a frequent visitor as head of trade union delegations to special occasions in China. He also set up the Burma Workers' and Peasants' Party to participate in parliamentary elections. This party led the coalition National United Front, which performed the outstanding feat of capturing one-third of the parliamentary seats in the 1956 elections—reportedly with strong financial backing from the Chinese and Soviet embassies in

[82] See Note 8.   [83] *Burma Weekly Bulletin*, Sept. 23, 1950.

Rangoon. The elected deputies could be expected to promote and vote for actions beneficial to Soviet and Chinese interests. It was partly the reaction to the power wielded by the National United Front in U Nu's coalition government in 1958 that led to the army take-over of power. (Internal administrative chaos was also important in the take-over.) Five years later, in November 1963, 200 members of this group were arrested for not supporting the Government in the peace negotiations between the Government and the underground White Flag Communists.[84]

A second prominent China lobby in Burmese politics has been the Burma-China Friendship Association, headed by a founder of the Burmese Communist Party, Thakin Thein Pe Myint. His official membership in the Communist Party ended when the White Flags went underground, but he has consistently supported the Communist position short of being placed in jail, and his People's Unity Party has also attempted to come to power through the National United Front. Although leading the Burma-China Friendship Association, Thein Pe Myint has a long record as a confirmed Russophile, which, combined with the Soviet strategy pursued by the National United Front, probably accounts for the reported pro-Russian orientation of the Front on the Sino-Soviet dispute.[85]

It is difficult to assess the impact of the Front and other groups or their propaganda in Burmese politics. They have more often than not dominated the principal student associations at major universities such as Rangoon and Mandalay, and have been able to rely on student strikes in support of various Communist programs, but the closing of the universities for an extended period after riots in 1963 and the arresting of prominent agitators among the students have seriously weakened their hold. The maximum parliamentary strength of the Front was reached with one-third of the seats in 1956, and the eclipse of that body by Ne Win's military government has rendered this bloc ineffectual. In general, the parliamentary or aboveground road to socialism appeared to be a feasible route until perhaps the fall of 1958, but with the first army take-over it became clear that the military would oppose the realization of such a strategy, and the Ne Win Government has effectively ended any lingering hopes by placing the leaders of the Front under arrest.

[84] *New York Times*, Dec. 30, 1963.   [85] *Ibid.*

Basic Aims and Achievements of
Chinese Foreign Policy toward Burma

The major long-term goal of Chinese Communist policy toward
Burma most certainly has been the establishment of a Communist
satellite government at Rangoon. In the early years of the People's
Republic, the "Chinese road" appeared to have considerable applica-
bility to the Burmese scene, and the Chinese were quite generous with
plans and suggestions to the Burmese "national liberation army."
When this strategy appeared to have failed, the Chinese followed the
Soviet "peaceful road" approach from 1954 to 1958, while nevertheless maintaining the insurgent forces in reserve. The available evidence
suggests liberal Chinese Communist contributions to the 1956 National United Front election campaign. After the Ne Win Governments frustrated this approach, the insurgent forces once again became
active, and the October 1964 incident could imply that the Chinese
Communists were considering overt aid to the forces they have
nourished for so long. This move, however, would meet with firm
action by Ne Win's experienced counterinsurgency forces, and a take-
over by an indigenous Communist force in Burma does not seem likely
in the immediate future.

A second and ultimate long-range aim has often been mentioned.
Many people suspect that the true intention of the alleged Chinese
Government sponsorship of the migration of large numbers of Chinese
to Burma is not only to aid in the establishment of a Communist Burmese state, but to incorporate the entire area later into a new Chinese
empire. Of course, any such specter of racial absorption deserves
careful study, and it seems likely that the Burmese Government will
be able to police its borders effectively before the number of incoming
Chinese reaches a critical stage, but the outcome of this policy can
certainly not be predicted.

However, all Chinese actions toward Burma in the past fifteen
years have not been determined by these goals, and in fact for much
of the period shorter-term aims seem to have been dominant. The two
most important of these have been to minimize or eliminate American
(and British) influence in Burma—in order to avoid the establishment of American military power in the region of China's borders—

and to use Burma as a showcase of peaceful coexistence for Asia. To accomplish the former, Peking's tactics have varied from threats of military attack to appeals to anti-imperialism and assurances of China's friendly and peaceful intentions toward Burma. In the early 1950s, Peking attempted to frighten the Burmese Government into reversing its drift toward a pro-Western position, and although those attempts undoubtedly helped to discourage the signing of a Burmese-American military pact, the major factor involved was the fortuitous implication of the United States in aiding the Kuomintang guerrillas. After 1954 the Chinese generally have followed a policy of trying to convince the Burmese of their peaceful intentions, and they have been successful to the extent that most Burmese now seem to believe China will leave them alone unless provoked. Although the success of using Burma as a showcase of peaceful coexistence has varied with fluctuations in the relationship of the two countries, the general example of a benevolent China has undoubtedly exerted a favorable influence on other Asian countries.

In sum, it could be said Communist China has been relatively successful in attaining its short-run goals toward Burma, but progress toward long-term aims has been slow, with perhaps less chance today than in the early 1950s that they too will be realized.[86]

[86] Readers interested in a further investigation of the subject of this paper may wish to consult the following works:

Barnett, A. Doak. *Communist China and Asia.* New York, Harper, 1960.
Hinton, Harold C. *China's Relations with Burma and Vietnam: A Brief Survey.* New York, Institute of Pacific Relations, 1958.
Kirkpatrick, Evron M., ed. *Target: The World; Communist Propaganda Activities 1955.* New York, Macmillan, 1956.
Avarin, V. "The Economic Plight and the Struggle for National Liberation in Southeast Asia," *Voprosy Ekonomiki,* VII (1952), in *Soviet Press Translations,* VII, No. 17.
Dai, Shen-yu, "Peking and Rangoon," *China Quarterly,* V (1961).
Griffiths, Sir Percival. "Burma on the Road to Chaos," *Nineteenth Century and After,* CXLVII (1950), 279–86.
Maung Maung. "The Burma-China Border," *India Quarterly,* XVI (1960), 358–64.
Rigby, T. A. "Soviet Comment on Southeast Asia," *Australian Outlook,* V (1951), 203–13.
Sacks, Milton. "The Strategy of Communism in Southeast Asia," *Pacific Affairs,* XXIII (1950), 227–47.
Trager, Frank N. "The New Temper of Burmese Politics," *Foreign Policy Bulletin,* XXXVII ((1958), 172–79.
Wyatt, Woodrow. *Reports in New Statesman and Nation,* XXXVII (1949), 147, 196, 247. [Footnote continued.]

Burma, Director of Information. *Burma.*
—— *Burma Weekly Bulletin.*
—— Forward.
Peking Review.
U.S. Central Intelligence Agency Joint Publications Research Service. *Daily Report.*
U.S. Consulate, Hong Kong. *Current Background.*
—— *Survey of China Mainland Press.*

Development of
Modern Science Policy
in Japan

THEODORE DIXON LONG

It has often been pointed out that a prominent feature of the Meiji Restoration, implicit in its name, was its conservatism. The substance of this conservatism lay in the reform and strengthening of the central apparatus of national control which the Shogunate had, in effect, abdicated. In terms of motivation, it meant the pursuit of modernization partly to preserve the power of the modernizing oligarchy. But in so doing the leadership undermined its sources of support, though it failed to recognize the process until it was too late to halt it. This weakening of the foundations of political control was in large measure the work of modern science and technology.[1]

It is ironic, in this view, that some of the key domestic policies of the Meiji oligarchy were science policies. The establishment of a national system of public education for the teaching of scientific and technical subjects, and government initiative in founding industries which provided the means of transformation as well as the means for security, are typical examples. Those issues, in slightly modified form, are precisely the issues of science policy in mid-twentieth-century industrial nations.

To a remarkable extent, foreign relations as well as domestic decisions were shaped by Meiji science policy.[2] The importation of

[1] Thomas C. Smith, "Old Values and New Techniques in the Modernization of Japan," *Far Eastern Quarterly*, XIV, No. 3 (1955), pp. 355 ff., makes this point. He argues that the Meiji oligarchs based their faith on the incorruptibility of the past, overlooking the differential rates of change invoked by technology in different sectors of the society and economy. In agriculture, where their political power was greatest, change was slowest.

[2] This point has not been examined in detail by Western scholars, though it

teachers, technicians, and techniques, the dispatch abroad of young men for training, the use of missions for investigation and selection of foreign science and technology, were among the chief methods employed for fruitful contact with the Western world. Those contacts, which were by nature and by a long Tokugawa tradition the prerogative of government, produced demands for foreign currencies, knowledge of foreign languages and institutions, and other practical requirements. Thus there was established an initial linkage between various scientific and technical needs and the official source of foreign policy decisions.

This characteristic governmental initiative in scientific and technical matters contrasts sharply with the experience of most Western nations, where the process was essentially the reverse. Without underestimating the growth of Dutch studies and the achievements of Japanese scholarship in the century and a half before 1868, there was still no substantial private scientific or technological ferment which could compare with the industrial transformation of Europe, or with the budding technological culture of the United States of America.

Of course, Japan had been closed to foreign intercourse since the early seventeenth century, and this fact in itself goes far toward explaining the second significant contrast—the ambivalent character of science and technology in the Japanese setting. Before the Restoration, Sakuma Shōzan, in the phrase "Western science and Eastern morals," [3] expressed an attitude which influenced the whole course of Japan's foreign scientific and technical relations. Science for the Japanese has had two identities: one, as a new systematic approach to natural phenomena; the other, as a practical expedient in resisting a foreign challenge. While policy has steered an ingenious course between the two, it has never been clear whether the design was to extract science from its indigenous social setting or to import it with its foreign matrix. Sometimes decision has been forced,[4] but in general this dichotomy has persisted in efforts to formulate science policy.

---

is considered generally in several sources. The most useful are: William W. Lockwood, *The Economic Development of Japan* (Princeton, Princeton University Press, 1954), esp. Chap. 10; Chitoshi Yanaga, *Japan Since Perry* (New York, McGraw-Hill, 1949), esp. Chap. 5; and Thomas C. Smith, *Political Change and Industrial Development in Japan* (Stanford, Stanford University Press, 1955).

[3] Sir George Samsom, *The Western World and Japan* (New York, Knopf, 1950), p. 259.

[4] Robert S. Schwantes, "Christianity versus Science: A Conflict of Ideas in Meiji Japan," *Far Eastern Quarterly,* XII (Feb. 1953), pp. 123–32.

Some working principles may be derived from these observations about the early relationship of Western science and Japanese political institutions. First, developments in public policy suggest that government leadership, sponsorship, or advice is the normal course of events on the formulation of science policy. Second, there is a constant concern with the stature of Japanese science which goes beyond Western conventions of scholarship, and which has had much to do with the conduct of foreign relations.

These themes, with considerable variation and elaboration, have been dominant in Japanese science policy since the birth of constitutional government. The priority of government in scientific and technical affairs and the special relationship of science to questions of national stature provide a pattern for the developments of three-quarters of a century. While government initiative appeared to flag with the relinquishment of enterprise to private ownership in the 1880s, that step was part of a transformation in which the oligarchy became more broadly based, more securely in command, and more specialized for the tasks of planning and regulating the national destiny. During that period the technical service agencies originated, and Japan began the process of relating herself to international organs and instruments of scientific and technical communication, standardization, and guarantee of interests.[5]

The great watershed in institutional development in Japan and in the West is the period of the First World War. Interest in a progressive policy for science and technology was implicit in the establishment of the Institute for Physical and Chemical Research (IPCR) in 1916. Significantly, the source of the idea was Takamine Jōkichi, an expatriate scientist who had made his fortune in America. Takamine expressed to influential acquaintances, among whom was Viscount Shibusawa, a plan for utilizing Japan's scientific resources more effectively by making research facilities available to promising young scientists.

What resulted was an organization neither wholly public nor private, with a government subsidy for ten years and an apparent mandate to engage in basic research. Research results were in fact published in an English language journal, but the main work of the Institute turned out to be the development of promising inventions, from which royalties supported further research. The ideas spawned

[5] F. A. Bather, "Natural Science in Japan," *Natural Science,* IV (1884), 98–111, 183–93, traces the establishment of early government services and discusses the founding of scientific societies.

by the IPCR were capitalized by the government as new manufacturing industries, and until the end of the Second World War the IPCR was an important source of new Japanese enterprise.

In June 1919—three years after the IPCR had been set up—the Imperial Academy submitted to the Minister of Education a memorial advising the establishment of a National Research Council.[6] The Academy was itself the product of David Murray's [7] suggestion, and had been organized in 1879 to advise the Minister on educational matters and to promote the arts and sciences.[8] Because of its evolution into an honorary body and its reorganization in 1906 confirming this character, the members were keenly aware of the lack of any operating agency to advise on policy or to perform basic research in areas related to public welfare.

Thus a National Research Council (NRC) was established in 1920 as an advisory organ to the Minister of Education.[9] Knowledgeable people, however, were convinced that there was still no broad platform of support for basic research. One hundred influential individuals met to discuss the problem in January 1931, and after a number of further meetings established the Japan Society for the Promotion of Science (JSPS) in 1933.[10] That none of those efforts was successful in terms of its basic objectives is probably due to the period of social and political turmoil which Japan had already entered.

In one sense, the establishment of the IPCR, the NRC, and later the JSPS marked an important stage in the transformation of Japan into a modern scientific-industrial state. But in another, it was the beginning of that coordination of all effort for national ends, which in the sciences was consummated in the Science Department of the Cabinet Planning Board in 1939 (later upgraded to Technology Board) and the All Japan Federation of Scientific and Technical Associations in 1940.[11] "New Structure" was the order of the day, reflected in the

[6] Harry C. Kelly, "A Survey of Japanese Science," *Scientific Monthly,* LXVIII (Jan. 1949), 43.

[7] David Murray was an American educator whose advice was instrumental in the initial patterning of the Japanese educational system along American lines.

[8] Kelly, "A Survey of Japanese Science," p. 43.   [9] *Ibid.,* p. 44.

[10] *Ibid.,* p. 45.

[11] Hideomi Tuge, *Historical Development of Science and Technology in Japan* (Tokyo, Kokusai Bunka Shinkokai, 1961), pp. 129–30. Other accounts are Kelly; and U. Hashimoto, "A Historical Synopsis of Education and Science in Japan from the Meiji Restoration to the Present Day," *Impact,* XIII, No. 1 (1963), 15. No two sources agree on the detailed history of events up to 1945, but they support the broad outline presented here.

creation of the omnibus Science Mobilization Association in the same year. It was to bring into one hierarchical body every individual with a scientific or technical capability. But by leveling the distinctions between industrial, economic, scientific, and other research organizations, it ultimately produced only chaos.

Implicit in those domestic developments was a change in the character of fundamental and applied research. This was partly a result of widespread importation of concepts and techniques, but it was not generally comparable to the diffusion, on the level of private scholarship and industry, that characterized the experience of Western nations. The deployment of much modern science and technology in Japan was consistently linked with the nature and structure of foreign relations, and as diplomatic contacts narrowed, so did the inflow of knowledge.

Even in those fields where need or interest was dominated by local conditions, limitations were often determined by foreign relations. In fishery technology, for example, there were increasing demands on international negotiation as Japanese discoveries and applications brought conflicts over territory, catch limits, and the preservation of species. Japanese science made original contributions to sericulture, but developments aimed at increased returns from exports were largely negated by the interwar collapse of the American market and the discovery of artificial fibers. Agricultural science especially was the forte of Japanese scientists, but much of their work was built upon availability abroad of raw materials for chemical fertilizers.

The gathering momentum of the 1930s toward national unity and purity of purpose, and for international dignity and equality, combined these threads of experience—some leading from the Meiji Restoration—into a pattern that for science and science policy was pyramidal. By the time war broke out between Japan and the United States, there no longer existed a coherent expression of policy, but only subjective pronouncements from the summit of the monolith. Long before it became a possibility or a danger in the West, the governmentalization of science in Japan was complete.[12] Viewed from the peak of the structure, or looking downward from any level, the arrangement rep-

[12] Edward Shils, "Editorial," *Minerva*, I, No. 1 (Autumn 1962), pp. 5–17, stresses the growth of government intervention and control of science and learning in Western nations, especially since the end of the Second World War. He points to the likelihood of an enhanced political role for the scientific community, greater organization, etc., a situation already familiar to Japanese scientists.

resented the perfect achievement of conservative ambition. Governmental initiative was preserved, and Western methods had been abstracted from their intellectual and social matrix. It was the triumph of "Eastern morals."

The Occupation and the New Policy Machinery

Military defeat, occupation, and reformation of the political system of Japan in the period from 1945 to 1952 represent a distinct break in the continuity of policy organs and policy principles. But the fact of that break should not obscure the complexity which it introduced into Japanese government and politics. Far from simplifying, it blended new themes with old, and caused the reemergence of tradition in unsuspected channels. It is fairly satisfactory to view modern science policy in the United States and Great Britain simply as the result of trends which were intensified and elaborated by war, but this approach does not explain the situation in Japan.

While the view from above may have been spiritually rewarding to the organizers of the Japanese wartime state, the view from below was profoundly different. The physical handicaps to production gradually became overwhelming, and even the blinkers of ideology could not conceal the fact that lack of science policy resulted in lack of progress. "Even in applied science fields that were vital to the conduct of the war, activity was limited severely by the lack of an administrative policy for research and by shortages of every kind of raw material." [13]

The combination of a chaotic system for making war, and defeat in the war, destroyed the substructure on which it had been hoped to build a highly organized and productive scientific community.[14] But neither the conduct of war nor the conduct of the Occupation tells a complete story of transition. The pursuit of democratization measures in the relative vacuum of popular political consensus, and the restoration of initiative to the Japanese bureaucracy, are vital connections between prewar science policy and that of an independent Japan.

[13] Seishi Kikuchi, "Scientific Research," in Hugh Borton, ed. *Japan* (Ithaca, Cornell University Press, 1951), p. 214.

[14] Probably the best account of the Japanese war machine is Jerome Cohen, *The Japanese War Economy: 1937–1945* (Minneapolis, Minnesota University Press, 1949), p. 48 and Chap. 2.

Occupation policy for Japanese science had two relatively straightforward objectives, one destructive and one constructive. That which had temporal priority was the eradication of armaments and capacity to wage war or forcibly to resist the Occupation. To the nation which had dropped the first atomic weapons, cyclotrons presented a potential danger. Those located at Osaka and Kyoto Universities, and two at the Scientific Research Institute (the former Institute of Physical and Chemical Research) in Tokyo were dismantled and destroyed.[15] Facilities for the study of atomic physics and for research and development in aircraft of any kind were closed down, and violations of this restriction were prosecuted vigorously. Scientific equipment was sequestered for purposes of reparations, but due to later changes in policy much of it was retained.[16]

On the other hand, through directives expressing general policy and the handling of particular cases, Occupation authorities exhibited a concern for the reestablishment of basic research. Political purges were restricted to a few of the top-ranking scientists who had advised the military, and Japanese nuclear physicists were permitted to cooperate in the study of Hiroshima and Nagasaki.[17] Steps were taken toward the creation of new scientific advisory machinery for the Government, but in this regard ignorance of the Japanese internal situation rendered Occupation efforts somewhat less effective than was then assumed.[18]

Release from the systematic and arbitrary organization of wartime scientific and technical activities left Japanese scientists deeply divided, and uncertain of their obligation to the Government in a democratic system. Initial efforts to organize them occurred in January 1946, when the left-wing Association of Democratic Scientists held its inaugural meeting. But the establishment of the Yoshida Government in May confirmed that conservative forces were in the saddle. Representatives of the old hierarchy had already created the Scientific Research Organization Committee toward the end of 1945, but their identification with prewar and wartime organizations resulted in their dissolution by the Occupation.[19]

Searching for an alternative, the Supreme Command, Allied Air

---

[15] Tuge, p. 145. [16] *Ibid.*, pp. 146–47. [17] *Ibid.*, pp. 147–48.
[18] MacArthur's disdain of academic specialists is well known. Kelly, one of the architects of the plan, was optimistic, but chiefly because the influence of the "old guard" was avoided.
[19] Tuge, pp. 150–52.

Forces in the Pacific (SCAP) encouraged a group of younger scholars to form a Science Liaison Society in June 1946.[20] Similar societies were formed to represent medicine, engineering, and agricultural science, based mainly on the long-standing professional societies. Those new groups chose from among their members a body known as the Scientific Research Organization Advisors, who assisted the Occupation in carrying out a national election. One hundred eight men, including seven each from fifteen fields and one each from the Imperial Academy, National Research Council, and the Japan Society for the Promotion of Science, were returned to form the Scientific Research Organization Renewal Committee in August 1947. This group, which was to produce a plan for the rehabilitation of the Japanese scientific and technical community, was considered by an Occupation advisor to represent "a genuine break with tradition," as only six of its members were from the Imperial Academy, about half from the National Research Council, and the average age was below fifty.[21]

Meanwhile, an Advisory Mission from the United States National Academy of Sciences visited Japan in July and August 1947 at the invitation of General MacArthur. A combination of the Renewal Committee's plan for reorganization, and the recommendations of the Advisory Mission regarding the contribution of science to its sound democratic reorganization and to national economic recovery, guided the establishment of the Science Council of Japan (SCJ), in July 1948. It was to be the representative organ of Japanese scientists and the principal instrument of government for the promotion of science and technology. The old Imperial Academy with its oligarchic overtones was abolished, and replaced by the Japan Academy, a purely honorary organization within the Science Council.[22]

Because the Occupation hoped to establish a clear distinction between the old order and the new Science Council, the creation of a policy-making and implementing agency was delayed until the SCJ was functioning. A second Advisory Mission, headed by Dr. Detlev Bronk, was dispatched by the United States Academy in November 1948 to assist the Occupation in dealing with this problem. In March 1949 the Diet promulgated a law setting up the Scientific and Technical Administrative Conference (STAC),[23] an internal organ of the Office of the Prime Minister, to be appointed by the Prime Minister,

[20] Kelly, p. 49.   [21] *Ibid.,* pp. 49–50.
[22] Information in this paragraph is summarized from Kelly, Tuge, and Hashimoto.
[23] Tuge, p. 152.

with the guidance of the SCJ regarding the selection of half its membership.

It immediately became apparent that the legal terminology expressing the relationship of the SCJ to the Executive branch, as well as the well-intentioned hopes of the Occupation, was somewhat fictional and somewhat ironic. The law stated that "all transactions of the SCJ with the Government shall be through the Prime Minister," and that "the Government may seek the opinion of the SCJ on the following matters . . . ," [24] including budget, promotion of science, and general policy. But the first few meetings of the SCJ demonstrated that it preferred an oppositional to an advisory role, toward both the Government and the Occupation. The STAC stood in the eye of this political maelstrom, and from the beginning was the focus of criticism from all sides.

The key problem was that the Occupation, in clearing the field through "purges" of antidemocratic elements, also cleared the way for leftist political expression. This action, while inadvertently creating the conditions for stalemate in the formulation or execution of science policy by STAC and SCJ, was not even partially rectified in the subsequent suppression of leftist political agitation. This was the period when, even in the United States, the political consciousness of scientists was held in extremely low estimation, and when divisions in the Japanese intellectual community were not well known.

Initiative thus was shifted from the Occupation to the Japanese Government, and within the Government from the bureaucracy to party channels. In 1951 a special Standing Committee for Promotion of Science and Technology was set up by the Democratic Party, and in February and March 1952 a draft bill was circulated within the Party and presented for Cabinet approval.[25] It proposed the establishment of a Science and Technology Agency for comprehensive policy planning, as well as for studying the scientific and technical activities of each Ministry and the budget of each with a view to the unification of research activities. However, the impending Peace Treaty and more pressing matters of governmental reorganization following full independence forced the proposal into the background.

[24] Kelly, p. 52.
[25] Japan, Office of the Prime Minister, Kanchō Benran To-Gokan, Sorifu V (Keizai Keikaku-cho—Kagaku Gijutsu-cho) (Government Handbook, Vol. V. Office of the Prime Minister, Economic Planning Agency—Science and Technology Agency). Tokyo, May 10, 1960, pp. 68–69. (Hereafter referred to as *Kanchō Benran*.)

Administration and Policy-making

These developments took place in a context that was called an "occupation," but which was in practice a shogunate in which General MacArthur stood at the apex of nominal power and General Whitney, head of the Government Section of scap, supervised the formulation and enunciation of policy. The parallel breaks down at the level of the Japanese bureaucracy, although the actual power they wielded through tactics of deliberate misunderstanding, equivocation, and quiet insubordination was probably not altogether unlike that of the feudal *daimyo*. In any event, the decision to work through the established administrative machinery contributed much to the survival and reinforcement of bureaucratic power in postwar Japan.[26]

Thus Japan never suffered wholesale intervention of foreign power in the affairs of government, or the utter collapse of internal order that was the horror of postwar Europe. While reform of the bureaucracy was a feature of democratization, it was destined to be put off, then meliorated, and finally satisfied by token measures. It became a political issue under the Katayama regime in 1947–48, but expired with his Cabinet and was quietly subordinated to the more immediate benefits of cooperation with the articulate and amenable Premier Yoshida.

Moreover, the failure of specific reforms was less significant in the general framework of democratization than reform of the Diet and the provision for responsible Cabinets. Those features of the new constitutional order were supported by changes in the atmosphere of political activity and in some basic elements of bureaucratic initiative.

A distinctive attribute of the postwar political climate in Japan is the rise of bureaucratically trained men to the positions of power formerly held by hereditary aristocrats, military officers, or political party chiefs legitimized by support from aristocrats and officers. Occupation reforms had a great deal to do with this emergence, and the practical successes of recent administrations, to the extent that they

[26] Paul M. Linebarger, Djang Chu, and Ardath Burks discuss this point in their *Far Eastern Government and Politics: China and Japan* (Princeton, Van Nostrand, 1954), pp. 459 ff. They identify two tendencies in the Office of the Prime Minister after 1947: centrifugal, in the acquisition of a complex machinery, and centripetal in the "pull of power toward the Prime Minister himself," p. 501.

rest on nonpolitical factors, are rooted in their use of bureaucratic talent and technique.

Modern science policy, like economic policy or military policy, depends on the recognition of new opportunities in complex but familiar patterns. It requires intimate knowledge of the gross phenomena of industrial production, educational curricula, royalty and marketing arrangements, research techniques, and so forth. It cannot be formulated by dilettantes like Konoye, nor is it likely to be mastered by architects of organization like Tōjō. In this respect, Japan's postwar government is better equipped with conservative bureaucrats than with traditional autocrats.

Japan, like the United Kingdom, the United States, and other nations, became aware during the early 1950s of the social and political implications of the geometric increase of scientific and technical knowledge. The Science and Technology Agency was established in 1956 to perform a number of housekeeping functions, but was almost immediately recognized as far short of what was needed. A White Paper in 1958 pointed up the contrast between domestic development and progress abroad, and cited the narrow and specialized impact of foreign technology.[27] In 1959, concurrently with a reorganization of the Agency, the Institute of Physical and Chemical Research was reconstituted, to aid in development by concentrating on research in industrial technology. It was put under the direction of a Development Board consisting of ten members appointed by the Prime Minister from among "scholars and experienced specialists."[28] The same year saw the establishment in the Office of the Prime Minister of the Science and Technology Council, a principal policy-making organ and top-level check on the recommendations of the SCJ. This completed the essential machinery of science policy.

Post-Treaty Foreign Relations

Since the formal independence of Japan was secured by the San Francisco Treaty in 1951 (effective in April 1952), Japanese foreign relations have expanded on almost all levels of private and public activity. There are now probably more contacts between individuals,

[27] Japanese Consulate, New York, "White Paper on Science and Technology," *Japan Report*, IV, No. 11 (June 1, 1958), pp. 6–7. Hereafter cited as *Japan Report*.
[28] *Japan Report*, V, No. 7 (April 1, 1959), p. 3.

between private corporations, between governmental representatives, and between special missions of various sorts than ever before. It is not necessary for present purposes to categorize these relations, but it would be useful to summarize the broad trends which have affected science policy.

Cooperation with the United States has dominated Japan's foreign relations. This relationship has not been equal, for American military strategy has greatly influenced nonmilitary questions, and Japanese security and economic requirements have limited their freedom to negotiate these questions. American aid to and procurement in Japan has been a large, though declining, source of foreign exchange and hence of economic stability. American bases on Japanese territory have been another prominent aspect of the security relationship, and a continuing source of minor frictions, though the attitude of the Japanese Government has exhibited more restraint than that of the press and other private groups.

The trade relations of the United States and Japan are a fact of major importance, in terms of both cooperation between the two nations and Japan's drive to reestablish her foreign trade. For several years the United States has been Japan's principal customer, and Japan has been second only to Canada as the principal customer of the United States.

The program of high-level diplomacy and astute domestic policy which resulted in a series of reparations agreements with the nations of Southeast Asia (formerly occupied by the Japanese Army) was an achievement of economic sophistication and organizational initiative. Concern for future markets and sources of raw materials led to an extremely progressive program for promotion of trade. The establishment of the Japan Export Trade Promotion Agency (JETRO) offices, for example, has recently invited imitation by the United States and Korean Governments.[29] The system of annual trade fairs in Tokyo, Yokohama, and Osaka, and the enormously successful floating fairs (a fourth was planned to cruise ports of Western Europe in 1964) elaborated a unique pattern of cooperation between government and private industry. Budding development aid programs for countries in Southeast and South Asia provide additional evidence that the capac-

[29] "JETRO Becomes an Example for Other Nations," *Dentsu, Japan Trade Monthly*, CCVI (May 1963), 6. The article reminds readers that the original model of trade promotion agencies was the British Export Trade Promotion Agency (BETRO), set up after the war but dissolved in the early 1950s.

ity for fruitful government–industry cooperation has been of central importance.

That Japan aims to press her development toward the achievement of enhanced power in world affairs can perhaps be qualified but not denied. In 1954 she became the first non-Western contributor to a multilateral aid program, the Colombo Plan. Since 1958 she became the only non-Western nation to participate in an international loan consortium for the support of India's Third Five-Year Plan. During 1960 a consortium to aid Pakistan's Second Five-Year Plan included Japan.[30] In no case was her participation merely token, but comparable in terms of per capita gross national product to that of any other participating nation except the United States.[31]

Further, a development assistance program which commenced in 1954 under the United States sponsored Joint Third Country Program has brought Japan increasingly into the limelight as an able transmitter of modern techniques, and she is planning a Peace Corps inspired technical assistance operation in Southeast Asia.[32] In 1961 Japan was fifth among the nations aiding the less developed areas, and the invitation to full status in the Organization for Economic Cooperation and Development, which was proffered in August 1963, leaves little doubt that in the minds of Western economists, bankers, industrialists, and Government administrators, Japan satisfies the requirements for membership in the industrial club.

In short, Japan has provided herself with all the attributes of major status but one—military capability. Her programs of nuclear research, rocketry, space exploration, and other scientific activities with military implications, leave little doubt that she is closing the gap in technical capacity faster than she is overcoming the political and statutory obstacles symbolized by Article 9 of the Constitution.[33] Behind these somewhat speculative matters, however, stands Japan's expressed intention to play a major role in Asia, and by this measure alone she will have increasing weight in world affairs.

[30] International Bank for Reconstruction and Development, *The World Bank and IDA in Asia* (Washington), Aug. 1963, pp. 24–26.

[31] *Ibid.*, p. 26. Japan has committed $100 million to the consortium for India, and $45 million to the consortium for Pakistan.

[32] *Japan Report*, IX, No. 9 (May 15, 1963), p. 7.

[33] Lawrence Olson, "Atomic Cross Currents in Japan," *AUFS Reports Service* (American Universities Field Staff, New York, L0–4–59), April 29, 1959, p. 9. Olson estimated that the Japanese would be producing the ingredients for atomic bombs in ten years or less (i.e., 1969).

Objectives in Science Policy

Aside from the vaguely ominous "military implications" of Japanese science policy, there are a number of tangible and somewhat novel developments in the statements and actions of the Japanese Government. Without probing too deeply the multiple levels and uncertainties of "basic policy," it seems fairly certain that science policy represents two sides of the same coin. On the one hand, there is a strong desire to reduce dependence upon, and an implicit inferiority to, foreign science. On the other, there is a strong desire to build the foundations of Japanese science on a commitment to basic research.

The report of the Prime Minister's Science and Technology Council, in laying out the basis for long-range planning in science and technology, observed that "international relations in science and technology have at the present time dual characteristics: competition and cooperation." [34] While the report stresses flexibility in dealing with this situation, it is possible to focus on four main areas in which objectives have been identified in terms of foreign relations.

SUPPORT FOR BASIC RESEARCH

The Science and Technology Council was asked in 1959 to produce a long-range report on this question, and the substance of its recommendations were in effect a draft policy. That policy received official sanction in the Government's White Paper on Science and Technology, issued in December 1962.

The priority attached to basic research in the document issued in October 1960 is unmistakable. Japan was criticized for excessive dependence on foreign research, and the report called for increased investment from a level of less than 1 percent of national income in 1960 to 2 percent in 1970.[35] While recognizing the high level of military research in the United States and British figures, it nevertheless compared the Japanese effort extremely unfavorably.

[34] U.S. National Science Foundation (translator), *Report of the Inquiry into the Promotion of Science and Technology for the Next Ten Years,* Prime Minister's Office (hereafter referred to as *PMO Report*). Tokyo, American Embassy, Oct. 4, 1960, p. 12.

[35] *PMO Report,* p. 2. A report in *Nihon Keizai Shimbun,* March 10, 1964, p. 3, stated that research investment reached 1.8 percent of national income in fiscal 1962, equal to that of Germany and .1 percent higher than that of France.

There were no specific proposals for decreasing dependence on foreign research, but a whole range of measures was suggested for utilizing more efficiently the results of foreign research and available technical knowledge. A science information program was in existence when the report of the Science and Technology Council was published, operated by the Japan Information Center for Science and Technology (JICST) (established in August 1957) under the administration of the Science and Technology Agency, but programmatically independent.[36] Originally provided with joint Government-industry capitalization, the JICST has continued with Government funds and a small industry donation. The latter ceased after 1959, but total Government appropriations nearly doubled in 1961, and increased income from sales and services pushed the annual budget from less than $150,000 in 1957 to over $800,000 in 1961.[37]

The Japanese sense of geographical and linguistic isolation is particularly evident in scientific and technical fields, where rapid change threatens to leave Japan far behind. In addition to the work of the JICST, the National Diet Library publishes in English (with the assistance of the United States National Science Foundation) its Natural Sciences Section of the *Japanese Periodicals Index* (*Zasshi Kiji Sakuin*). Also, a Government-sponsored group of educators, scientists, administrators, and representatives of industry has been formed —the Japan Documentation Society. This organization has arranged for publication in English of a study of the domestic situation and foreign relations in scientific and technical information. Finally, the Science Council of Japan concerns itself with matters of foreign scientific and technical documentation, though with limited effect in view of competing activities.

Scientists claim heavy reliance on the personal exchange that is made possible by frequent professional gatherings. However, Japanese participation has been limited by high costs and great distances, as well as by the small number of qualified people who can surmount the language difficulties (compounded by the likelihood that the best linguists are not necessarily the best scientists). Further, there are a great many international scientific conferences and congresses from

[36] U.S. National Science Foundation (translator), *The Organization and Mission of the Japan Information Center for Science and Technology, and the Operation Program of the Japan Information Center for Science and Technology, 1961.* Tokyo, American Embassy, May 19, 1961, p. 2.
[37] *Ibid.*, pp. 2–3.

which to choose, and it is becoming apparent that their tendency to employ panel discussion techniques makes attendance of only one or two participants futile.[38]

One solution was to sponsor more conferences in Japan, and to this end there has been a marked increase in scientific gatherings there over the past two or three years. Moreover, the Ministries of Education and Foreign Affairs have been more lenient with funds and permission for study or work abroad of Japanese scientists for periods of one or more years. There is considerable risk that highly trained people once settled in the United States or Europe will not want to return. The United States especially has been attractive both financially and professionally to Japanese scientists. However, efforts of the United States Government have increased the possibility of more frequent visits of Japanese, as well as exchange visits of American scientists, thus diminishing the fear that return will result in isolation.

The attitude of the Japanese Government toward interdisciplinary research or research in new fields has been conservative, holding that "Scientists should explore new areas, but it is the government's responsibility to provide balance between old and new fields." [39] In the White Paper of 1962, research frontiers were identified, and exhortations for greater progress were issued, but the implication is that the Government's role is to survey rather than to participate. This attitude raises the important question of where support will be found for the projects in pure research that cannot be justified either by educational or industrial research organizations. At the present time, there is no program of Government-supported basic research within a relatively nonrestrictive framework, such as exists in the United States and Great Britain.

ACCESS TO NEW TECHNOLOGY

This objective overlaps that discussed above, with the principal difference that support for basic research has required a new framework of laws and organizations, while access to technology has been secured through conventional channels. The 1960 report of the Science and Technology Council noted that the exchange of "know-how" could only be expected when accompanied by monetary compensation. Thus it appeared "desirable to establish an international market in which [technology] circulates as a salable commodity." Since foreign companies were apt to have policies which would place

[38] *PMO Report*, p. 42.   [39] *Ibid.*, p. 10.

undesirable limitations on the purchaser, "the introduction of technology should be promoted under a carefully monitored plan." [40]

This is essentially a confirmation of the policy followed by MITI since 1950, and in view of the success of that policy it is not likely that any substantial alteration will occur. The increase of foreign patent applications is one aspect of that success. A more direct measure is the inflow of technology purchased from foreign firms, which is closely monitored by the Ministry of International Trade and Industry (MITI). A report in June 1963 put the total of contracts involving acquisition of new technology at 1,891 (as of December 31, 1962). Almost half have occurred since 1960; more than 60 percent are with United States firms, and 90 percent are related to the heavy and chemical industries.[41]

MITI estimates that the output of products made possible by imported technology increased 72 percent from 1951 to 1962. In terms of exports alone, 17 percent of all exports in 1961 were produced with imported technology. Of course, the acquisition of technology through private industry has its drawbacks, in the threat of foreign control and limitations on use. But if concessions have been made to foreign investors regarding the repatriation of capital, there has been no softening of the rule that Japanese firms may not expatriate more than 49 percent of their controlling shares. This is not a statutory limitation, but nevertheless it is one which is rigorously observed. On the other hand, even the scrutiny of MITI officials has not prevented the completion of contracts which authorized royalties of up to 10 percent of sales, or those which limit the scope of export markets in 53 percent of all cases.[42]

The surprising fact about Japan's policy with regard to technology is that she has maintained favorable relations with the other advanced industrial nations while reserving the right to protect Japanese business interests. To some extent this is the result of intelligent policy, for the gradual freeing of trade and monetary restrictions has kept just a pace ahead of criticism. On the other hand, there is some good fortune involved too, for Japanese success has been paralleled by the search of United States business and investment capital for foreign opportunities, and by the search of reborn European industry for alternatives to trade with the United States.

[40] *PMO Report*, p. 12.
[41] "Foreign Capital Induction," *The Oriental Economist*, June 1963, p. 339.
[42] "Foreign Capital Induction," p. 339. Sixteen percent of contracts permit *no* exports.

COORDINATION OF NATIONAL POLICY

Science policy is concerned with the key issues of economic development and education. Japanese economic policy is best summarized in the plan announced in late 1960 for doubling national income within ten years. Goals in education have been established by the Science and Technology Council, which forecast shortages and called for increased output of college graduates to meet a ten-year shortage of 170,000.[43]

The relationship between these domestic issues and objectives in foreign policy is rather indirect. In industry it involves the establishment of organizations with Government encouragement and support to back trade and aid relations with Southeast Asia. This program is gradually shifting toward Government administration of a program substantially supplied by industry, currently exemplified by the Japan Chamber of Commerce and Industry's service of matching foreign requests for technicians with a list of technicians willing to spend time abroad.[44]

Educational objectives have a less specific relation to foreign policy objectives, yet their general relevance is accepted and written into documents on scientific and technical education. Partly at issue is Japan's ability to maintain the level of technical competition in trade with other industrial nations. But there is also a growing requirement for scientifically trained administrators, and concern about the place of scientific and technical subjects generally in the compulsory educational system. To this end the report of the Science and Technology Council recommended a general review of the system established under the Occupation.[45]

The development of nuclear research is a good example of the need for policy coordination. Japan began with a negative public attitude and the prohibitions of the Occupation against atomic research. With no domestic sources of uranium, she has remained at the mercy of the international market. Purchases from the United States or the International Atomic Energy Agency (most of whose nuclear material is supplied by the United States) have been compli-

[43] *PMO Report,* p. 18.
[44] "Japan to Send Mechanics for Southeast Asian Development," *Dentsu, Japan Trade Monthly,* CCIX (Aug. 1963), p. 5, also reports plans afoot for a Southeast Asian "peace corps."
[45] *PMO Report,* p. 14. The Ministry of Education has issued a White Paper on Education, *Japan's Growth and Education,* Tokyo, 1963.

cated by clauses governing the disposition of by-products and inspection of facilities, which are degrading in the Japanese view. Thus as interest grew in a broad and advanced program of nuclear research and development, a combination of local and external factors inhibited progress.

Different motives within the business, governmental, and scientific communities in Japan resulted in a veritable explosion of interest in 1956, followed by a barrage of criticism and reconsideration of the appropriateness of foreign research to Japanese requirements. The situation is complicated by the awareness of scientists that research abroad continues to move faster than in Japan, while the financing of such research may exceed even the joint capabilities of Western European nations.[46] Yet in spite of this somewhat morose catalogue, no other industrial nation is more strategically connected through its foreign relations to the sources of nuclear materials and techniques,[47] or more thoroughly involved in the whole range of applied nuclear technology.[48] The Government by 1963 chartered a semipublic corporation to construct an atomic-powered ship. Only the Soviet Union had one in operation, and four other countries were in the running (West Germany, Norway and Sweden jointly, and the United States).[49]

A partial explanation of this paradox is the belief of the Ministry of Foreign Affairs that for practical purposes "science" relations are "atomic" relations. Japan therefore negotiated and signed instruments of cooperation with every non-Communist nation possessing a nuclear technology or access to it, including Canada, West Germany, the United Kingdom, and the United States. The Government encouraged the establishment of the Japan Atomic Industrial Forum to insure communication with the organization of private industry in the United States. Significantly, the first license granted by the United States Atomic Energy Commission for private sale of a research reactor was for shipment to Japan.

---

[46] "Nimrod: A Scientific Object Lesson," *The Economist,* Nov. 16, 1963, pp. 681–82, cites the attempt to build a new high-energy cyclotron for the International Atomic Research Center (CERN).

[47] Joint Publications Research Service (translator), *Science and Diplomacy* (New York, JPRS, L–1962–D), Dec. 1, 1959, p. 23.

[48] Olson, pp. 1–3.

[49] "The Yards Get Busy on Nuclear Ships," *The Economist,* Oct. 26, 1963, p. 402.

PARTICIPATION IN INTERNATIONAL SCIENCE

In this regard, it is difficult to avoid the conclusion that Japanese scientists and Government officials concerned with science policy are primarily concerned with stature, and only secondarily impressed with the rewards of new knowledge. This criticism is not, of course, uniformly applicable. While Japan has no claim in the Antarctic and only a minuscule research program, the scientific integrity of that project has excited the admiration of at least one observer.[50]

However, the pace Japan tries to maintain is little short of frantic. Only a few nations support membership in all the organizations of the International Council of Scientific Unions; Japan is among them. Japan's role on the scientific organs of the United Nations is prominent, and she is the only nation other than the United States and Great Britain to maintain science attachés in her diplomatic establishment. She is usually one of the large contributors of personnel and funds to international undertakings such as the International Geophysical Year, the Indian Ocean Survey, and the International Years of the Quiet Sun. Indeed, the level of Japanese participation is such that there is a real question whether she is stealing scarce resources from domestic pursuits to support international activities.

The fact remains that the international aspect of science policy, perhaps more than any other, is restricted in the whole range of Japanese foreign relations, from fiscal to cultural. Japanese scientists are hemmed by enormous continental and oceanic distances, by a written language which is incomprehensible to all but a few of their colleagues abroad, and by severe limitations on the resources that can be allotted to their work. In this situation, it is perhaps understandable that publicity accrues to those who make international headlines, as did the first Japanese Nobel Prize winner, Yukawa Hideki.

By the same token, the fields of activity that appear to promise stature and influence among the advanced nations have been the principal targets for organized efforts. The atomic energy program discussed above is exemplary, as is Japan's commitment to acquisition of a leading position in space science and rocketry, and the investigation and exploitation of the oceans.

The significance of these areas of activity is twofold. First, they are

[50] John Hanessian, Jr., *Japan and the Antarctic.* New York, *AUFS Reports Service,* III (April 1963), 5–7.

characterized by high initial research costs and by the existence of large gaps in available scientific knowledge. Second, they are peculiarly adapted by their geographical extent and their environmental character to cooperative investigation and pooling of information. Their importance in Japanese policy-making is indicated by the existence of cabinet level advisory organs for oceanic and space research.

The handicaps implicit in Japan's nonparticipation in regional research programs (except the Pacific Science Council, which supports little joint research) constituted the main impetus to Premier Ikeda's request in 1961 for closer scientific ties with the United States. Foreign Ministry statements had already confirmed that Japanese policy-makers viewed the United States as the primary foreign source of scientific and technical advice and information.

The Occupation planted seeds for friendly relations between scientists of both nations, and a key Occupation official later became a top administrator in the United States National Science Foundation. The program which developed was officially described as one of mutual exchange and reward, but there is little doubt that it is regarded by Japanese policy-makers as an aspect of the acquisitive program which in the long run will foster Japanese independence in multilateral relations. For the present, the United States–Japan Committee for Scientific Cooperation provides a relationship similar in its effect to OECD's Directorate of Scientific Affairs, or NATO's Division of Scientific Affairs.

The Evolution of
a Socialist Ideology in Algeria,
November 1954-April 1965

PATRICIA BERKO WILD

It has been suggested by Manfred Halpern [1] that a close connection exists between nationalism and social change. In his view, nationalism arose in the Middle East and North Africa as a response to the psychological insecurity experienced by Muslims who were caught between the conflicting claims of traditional Islamic society and Western modernity.[2] Halpern has further suggested that nationalism is a necessity, for it permits the concerted efforts of individuals freely associated in the task of modernization.[3] Most important to this study is his assertion that

. . . nationalism is the principal political manifestation of social change in the Middle East. Nationalists exist because there is social change, and hence *the basic problem confronting nationalists is not nationalism but social change.*[4]

The Algerian War of National Liberation:
Sentimental Nationalism

In their War of National Liberation, Algerian nationalist spokesmen neglected the problem of social change in favor of a sentimental nationalism. There was no mention of a program for social action in the "Proclamation to the Algerian People and to Militants of the National Cause," issued by the Secretariat of the Algerian Front of

[1] Manfred Halpern, *The Politics of Social Change in the Middle East and North Africa* (Princeton, Princeton University Press, 1963), p. 197.
[2] *Ibid.*, p. 200.   [3] *Ibid.*, p. 201.   [4] *Ibid.*, p. 197. (Italics added.)

National Liberation (FLN) on November 1, 1954.[5] The proclamation stated that a group of young militants had decided to rescue the Algerian nationalist movement from the lethargy into which it had fallen, and that their action ". . . is directed solely against colonialism." [6] The external objective was defined as "national independence . . . by . . . the restoration of the sovereign, democratic and social Algerian State in the framework of Islamic principles." [7] The domestic objectives of the national movement were limited to the eradication of reformism and corruption in order to set the national movement on the correct path, and to the mobilization of the Algerian people for the independence struggle.[8] Anticolonialism, rather than social reform, was the motto.

Nor do we find a blueprint for a postindependence Algerian society in the "platform to ensure the triumph of the Algerian revolution in the struggle for national independence," adopted by the FLN at the Soummam Congress on August 20, 1956.[9] The platform was concerned first with demonstrating the victory of the FLN over other national elements,[10] and second with outlining the organization and political objectives of the independence struggle.[11]

The platform did touch on a number of points which were relevant to the future evolution of a socialist ideology in Algeria. First, the platform took a most negative view of the political activities of the French and Algerian Communist Parties and the French Section of the Workers' International (SFIO).[12] The Algerian Communist Party was rebuked for its ties with the French Communist Party (PCF), which had caused it to "misunderstand the revolutionary situation," and to deny "the revolutionary nature of the Algerian peasantry." The platform asserts that the Algerian Communists were committed to evolutionary tactics which resembled those of the "neo-colonialist SFIO." The Algerian Communist Party and the General Confederation of Workers (CGT) were accused of defending "the Algerian working class against the problematical danger of falling under the direct domination of the "Arab bourgeoisie," and an appeal was made for the

---

[5] In *El Moudjahid* (*Organe central du F.L.N.*)—*Numéro Spécial* (Editions Résistance Algérienne, *ca.* Nov. 1956), pp. 7–8.
[6] *Ibid.*, p. 7. [7] *Ibid.* [8] *Ibid.*, p. 8.
[9] *Ibid.*, pp. 12–31. [10] *Ibid.*, pp. 14–16. [11] *Ibid.*, pp. 18–31.
[12] The following paragraph is based on the platform, *ibid.*, p. 16. The *El Moudjahid—Numéro Spécial* contains the FLN Proclamation of Nov. 1, 1954, and the Soummam platform of Aug. 1956.

formation of a purely Algerian labor union, the General Union of Algerian Workers (UGTA), which would provide the nationalist workers with a revolutionary organization.

The second point of interest is the recognition of the revolutionary role of the peasantry and the subordination of the economic demands of the Algerian workers to the political struggle. The platform asserted that the Algerian workers, now on the correct nationalist path, had been confined "within the narrow framework of economic and social demands, isolated from the general perspective." [13] The FLN was to make a concerted effort to rescue the workers from the nefarious influence of the French Communist Party and the SFIO.[14] National interests, rather than working-class objectives, were of paramount importance to the FLN leadership in 1956. The revolution was neither a proletarian vehicle nor a class struggle, but a truly national movement.

The final point of interest is the platform's concern with the problem of *"Transforming the popular torrent into creative energy."* [15] The platform noted that the French Government had recommended a program of agrarian reform, and that it had reformed the *khammessat* in an effort to detach the Algerian peasantry from the FLN. The platform asserted that the FLN must commit itself to a program of agrarian reform as a means of winning the peasants' loyalty.[16] We thus find a commitment to agrarian reform—a commitment which was left undefined and which appears to have been made for propaganda purposes only.

The Soummam platform was thus notable for its indictment of the French (and Algerian) Communist and Socialist Parties, for its stress on the revolutionary nature of the peasantry, for its insistence on the supremacy of national over working-class objectives, and for its grudging commitment to a still undefined program of agrarian reform.

FLN propoganda during the remaining years of the independence struggle did little more to formulate a program for postindependence social action. For example, with regard to agrarian reform, a truly revolutionary program was promised which would unite the peasants in collective and cooperative activities. A national industry would be created, and Algeria's natural resources would be exploited.[17] The

[13] *Ibid.,* p. 24.   [14] *Ibid.,* p. 23.   [15] *Ibid.,* p. 22. (Italics in original.)
[16] *Ibid.,* p. 23.
[17] *L'Ouvrier Algérien,* N.S. No. 1 (Jan. 11, 1958), in André Mandouze, ed., *La Révolution Algérienne par les textes* (Paris, François Maspero, 1961), p. 113.

Algerian Revolution came to be characterized as "political, economic, and social," with little definition of terms.[18]

It remained to be seen, first, how the populism implicit in the nationalist appeal would be taken into account by Algerian political leaders after independence had been attained, and second, how the negative content of Algerian nationalism (anticolonialism) would be converted into a doctrine or program for positive, constructive action after independence.

The Tripoli Program of June 1962: Commitment to Socialism [19]

The Tripoli Program was to provide at least a temporary answer to the above questions. It represented the first formal commitment of the FLN to the construction of a socialist state in Algeria. It was later to be enshrined in the preamble to the Algerian constitution, which states that the new state is "Faithful to the program adopted by the National Council of the Algerian Revolution at Tripoli" [20] and that it "orients its activities in the path of the construction of the country in conformity with the principles of socialism." [21] Moreover, the Tripoli Program was to provide the theoretical framework for Government action until the adoption of a new program by the FLN in April 1964.[22]

In striking contrast to previous FLN statements, the Program noted that:

The participation of the Algerian masses has not only brought about the destruction of colonialism and feudalism. It has also been the factor determining the birth of a collective awareness of the tasks demanded by the regroupment and construction of society on new foundations . . . [this participation] . . . has opened perspectives for a *radical transformation of society*.[23]

---

[18] "Intervention de l'U.G.T.A. à la deuxième conférence des peuples algériens à Tunis, janvier 1960," in Mandouze, p. 115.

[19] The following is based on an English translation of *The Tripoli Programme* in *African Revolution* (Algiers), July–Aug. 1963, pp. 29–66.

[20] Algerian Ministry of National Orientation, *La Constitution* (Annaba, n.d.), p. 5.

[21] *Ibid.*, p. 6.

[22] "Texte intégral du discours prononcé par le Président Ben Bella, le 16 avril 1964, au Congrès du Parti" in *Révolution Africaine,* April 18, 1964, p. 15.

[23] *The Tripoli Programme,* p. 32. (Italics added.)

The FLN leadership was strongly criticized for its neglect of "the profound revolutionary potentialities of the people of the countryside," [24] and for its failure to formulate an ideology which would have rendered effective the break with the older nationalist parties and with feudalism.[25] It was castigated for "paternalism" (authoritarianism within the Party structure), for "formalism" (lack of ideological creativity), and for the exhibition of a "petty-bourgeois mentality." [26]

Most important was the Program's insistence on the importance of ideology. It stated that "The only *raison d'être* for a party is its ideology. Once that is lacking, the party ceases to exist." [27] The revolution had not been completed, the Program stated, and "Ideological combat should succeed the armed struggle; the struggle for national independence will be succeeded by the democratic, popular revolution." [28]

The major task of the revolution was the construction of a socialist society, in order to satisfy the economic needs of the masses by means of collectivization of the means of production and a program for national planning.[29] This program could not be carried out by one social class, and "national unity is not unity around the bourgeois class." [30] This program was to be based on scientific methods and theory, in contrast to "subjectivity" and "intellectual laziness." [31]

The Program went on to outline an ambitious economic policy: (1) The end of "foreign domination and economic liberalism," so that the local bourgeoisie would not replace the foreigner. (2) A planning policy which would provide for the "participation of the workers in economic power." Planning was necessary in order to accumulate the capital necessary for industrialization in a short period.[32] (3) The revolution was primarily an agrarian revolution, which would provide for "collective forms of employing and sharing the land without parcelling it up." An attempt would be made to secure "the voluntary adherence of the peasants so as to avoid the disastrous consequences of imposed precepts regarding the use of the land." Property would be limited; excess property would be expropriated and redistributed to needy peasants; the peasants would be organized in production cooperatives; state farms would be created on portions of the expropriated land, and the peasants would benefit from government financial and material assistance.[33] (4) Credit, foreign trade, and mineral and energy resources would be nationalized. (5) Industrialization would

[24] *Ibid.*, p. 39.　　[25] *Ibid.*, p. 41.　　[26] *Ibid.*, pp. 40–41.
[27] *Ibid.*, p. 43.　　[28] *Ibid.*, p. 49.　　[29] *Ibid.*　　[30] *Ibid.*, p. 50.
[31] *Ibid.*, p. 51.　　[32] *Ibid.*, p. 57.　　[33] *Ibid.*, p. 58.

be promoted under government supervision, but with the retention of a private sector. The first concern in the promotion of industrialization was to provide a base for the expansion of agriculture.[34] Finally, this program was to be pursued with "the preservation of the popular cultural heritage." [35]

The FLN thus responded to the populism inherent in the nationalist appeal. The revolution was to be primarily agrarian, a scientific socialism was to be promoted with the democratic participation of the workers, and the popular heritage was to be preserved. Nationalism had been converted into a program to deal with social change.

Political Leadership and Scientific Socialism

It is interesting to note that the Tripoli Program stressed scientific socialism and largely ignored the Islamic heritage of the Algerian people. It is my contention that, within two years of Algeria's accession to independence, Algerian political leaders were forced to temper the proposals of Marxist advisers and to recognize the force of Islam in Algerian society.

Before proceeding to an examination of Algerian socialist ideology after independence, we must note that until recently socialism was condemned by most Algerians as an alien materialism.[36] There has been a real fear among ordinary Algerians, as well as among religious scholars, of de-Islamicization. During the year following Algerian independence, the Algerian press published a steady barrage of pro-Communist propaganda. The result was widespread popular disaffection. Unfortunately, the Ulema does not appear to be capable of offering a modern Islamic alternative to scientific socialism, and reformist Islam has never penetrated the Algerian masses, who are still dominated by superstition and maraboutism.[37] This religious problem was bound to become apparent to Algerian political leaders.

The changes in the composition of the governing elite shortly after Algeria's accession to independence resulted in the ascendancy of politicians who were more radical than those who had supervised the liberation struggle.[38] Ahmed Ben Bella and Colonel Haouari Boumedienne of the ALN General Staff emerged as the primary holders of

---

[34] *Ibid.*, pp. 61–62.   [35] *Ibid.*, p. 62.

[36] Raymond Valin, "Socialisme musulman en Algérie," *L'Afrique et l'Asie,* No. 66 (Paris, 1964), p. 38.

[37] *Ibid.*, pp. 39–40.

[38] I. William Zartman, *Government and Politics in Northern Africa* (New York, Frederick A. Praeger, 1963), p. 47.

power.[39] During the fall and winter of 1962–1963, a loose coalition of veteran nationalist politicians worked with President Ben Bella. This coalition had collapsed by the spring of 1963. Mohammed Khider resigned his post as Secretary General of the FLN Political Bureau in April 1963. Rabah Bitat resigned his party post in May 1963. Ferhat Abbas resigned his post as President of the National Assembly in August 1963, and was expelled from the FLN as a spokesman for the bourgeoisie.[40] By April 1963, diplomatic observers noticed that President Ben Bella's "brain trust" was composed of foreigners and Algerians who were radical leftists: Mr. Soleiman Loutfallah, an Egyptian who had been imprisoned by Nasser for leftist agitation; Mr. Pablo Raptis, a Greek who had been Secretary General of the Fourth International; and Mr. Tahiri, a Moroccan who was a former member of the Istiqlal. Those foreign advisers were said to work closely with Mohammed Harbi, former Secretary General of the Foreign Ministry of the Provisional Government (GPRA), and with Mr. Maachou, former cabinet head of Ben Khedda and then director of *biens vacants*.[41]

Against these Marxist influences must be measured the impact of Colonel Boumedienne and the Army. Boumedienne is also a leftist, but he has stressed the importance of creating a "non-Communist people's democracy," a fusion of populism with military government.[42]

The initial swing to the left has been tempered by the interaction of foreign Marxist and native Islamic influences. In September 1964, Mohammed Harbi, whose Marxist tendencies had offended Colonel Boumedienne, was removed as editor of *Révolution Africaine*.[43] At that time President Ben Bella was subject to increasing pressure by the more radical Marxists, and had adopted a more militant socialism as a means of satisfying them. Most opposition was henceforth driven to the right—a few ex-members of the GPRA, a vocal bourgeoisie, roving maquis in the poverty-stricken mountains, some religious leaders, Algerian students from Paris—while President Ben Bella's relationship with Colonel Boumedienne was complicated by the clash between the latter's Islamic attitudes and the former's Marxist advisers.[44] President Ben Bella's attempts to navigate between the Islamicists and the Marxists are reflected in official Algerian documents published during 1962–1965.

[39] *Ibid.*, p. 49.   [40] *Ibid.*
[41] *Jeune Afrique* (Tunis), April 28, 1963, p. 8.
[42] Zartman, p. 53.   [43] *The Economist* (London), Sept. 5, 1964, p. 896.
[44] *The Economist* (London), Aug. 22, 1964, p. 715.

A Purely Algerian Socialism

SELF-MANAGEMENT

Shortly after Algeria's accession to independence, President Ben Bella began to stress the unique quality of Algerian socialism.[45] By the winter of 1962–1963, this purely Algerian socialism was represented by the experiment with self-management committees.

The Algerian Government declared that the "revolution has confidence in the capacity of the people to take over the management of the economy." [46] Self-management committees, which had not been explicitly foreseen in the Tripoli Program, were instituted after Algerian peasants and workers had spontaneously expropriated land and commercial and industrial enterprises abandoned by Europeans.[47] These were the *biens vacants,* which were regulated by decrees of October 22 and November 23, 1962 creating self-management committees. In March 1963 it became necessary to define more rigorously the organization of the self-managed sector.[48] A decree of March 18, 1963 regulated the determination of property which might be treated as *biens vacants.*[49] A decree of March 22, 1963 regulated the organization and management of industrial, mining, artisan, and vacant agricultural enterprises. This decree described the self-management committee. Each enterprise in the self-managed sector was to have a general assembly of workers, which in turn would select a workers' council. The council would elect and control the self-management committee. The committee would supervise the formulation of development plans, production, and marketing programs, purchases of equipment and other supplies, and the distribution of tasks. The director of the enterprise was to be appointed by the Government, but could be removed by the committee for proper cause. Above the director was the communal "Animation Organism for Self-Management," composed of presidents of the self-management committees, and representatives of the FLN, UGTA, Army, and communal administration. The task of the organism was to coordinate the activities of

[45] Algerian Ministry of Information, "Déclaration Ministérielle à l'Assemblée Nationale Consitiuante le 28 septembre 1962," *Les Discours du Président Ben Bella du 28 septembre 1962 au 12 décembre 1962* (Algiers, 1963), p. 10.

[46] Algerian Ministry of Information, *Documents sur l'autogestion* (Bône, Aug. 1963), p. 27.

[47] *Ibid.,* pp. 25–26.   [48] *Ibid.,* pp. 28–29.   [49] *Ibid.,* Annex, pp. 54–56.

self-management committees in the commune, and to accept or refuse the nomination of the state appointed directors.[50]

The distribution of the revenues accruing to the self-managed enterprises was regulated by a decree of March 28, 1963.[51] The workers' remuneration was to consist of three parts: a basic minimum wage; social services, housing, education; the remainder of the profits after provision is made for the maintenance of initial capital and for future investment. Eventually, the workers would share freely in the profits, as greater production would make it possible to pay them more than subsistence wages.[52]

The self-management committee was promoted by the Algerian Government as a means of acquainting workers and peasants with democracy and socialism. Its democratic function was stressed.[53]

ISLAM

An evolution toward greater emphasis on the alleged Islamic content of Algerian socialism was apparent as early as May 1963, when President Ben Bella found it necessary to assert:

We are not Communists. . . . We are Muslims and Arabs. We want to apply socialism as did our first caliphs.[54]

In September 1963, President Ben Bella explained that it was not impossible to mix socialism with Islam. He stated that during the war for independence "The fellahs fought essentially because they realized that the colonialists wanted to destroy what they held most dear: the Arab-Islamic reality . . . Islam . . . has helped us to implement our revolution." [55]

In December 1963, the Algerian Minister of National Economy presented a review of the Government's economic policy to the Algerian National Assembly.[56] The Minister stressed the humanism inherent in Algerian socialism, which, he said, is based on selected Islamic values, as well as on non-Islamic experience. This humanistic socialism freely borrows from the French, Cuban, Chinese, and other

[50] *Ibid.,* Annex, pp. 59–62.   [51] *Ibid.,* Annex, pp. 64–66.
[52] *Ibid.,* p. 33.   [53] *Ibid.*
[54] Speech of Ben Bella, May 1, 1963. Algerian Ministry of National Orientation, *Les Discours du Président Ben Bella: Année 1963. 1ᵉʳ trimestre 1964* (Annaba, April 1964), p. 73.
[55] Speech of Ben Bella at the Third World Meeting of Journalists, Sept. 23, 1963. *Ibid.,* p. 149.
[56] Algerian Ministry of National Orientation, *Politique économique du Gouvernement* (n.d.).

revolutionary experiences, while retaining its base in traditional Algerian values.[57]

Socialism and Islam in the Charter of Algiers, April 1964 [58]

The Charter of Algiers, adopted by the FLN at its first postindependence congress in April 1964,[59] presented a number of striking departures from the Tripoli Program. Although the goals of the revolution remained those enunciated in the Tripoli Program, the Charter is noteworthy for its concern with the growth of a new privileged class (the bureaucracy),[60] as well as for its treatment of Islam. The latter is most germane to this study.

The Charter reconstructed the history of Algeria, which was characterized as an "Arab-Muslim country." [61] Special praise was accorded to the nationalist activities of Sheikh Ben Badis and the Association of Ulemas during the 1930s.[62] Moreover, the Algerian nationalist movement was said to have been receptive to the doctrine of Islamic renewal taught by Al-Afghani and Abduh, and to the Pan-Arab ideas of Chekib Arslan, as well as to socialist theory.[63]

The Algerian masses were said to be devout Muslims "who have struggled . . . in order to rid Islam of all . . . superstitions which have smothered or altered it." [64] This last assertion must be considered as an expression of hope rather than of fact, since the Charter went on to declare that "The Algerian revolution must restore to Islam its true essence, that of progress," [65] and that it was necessary "to *create* a political and social theory grounded in our own values, nourished by *scientific* principles, and armed against erroneous attitudes," which required in turn "a *new conception of our culture,*" [66] a culture which was to be "national, revolutionary, and scientific." [67]

While it is not surprising that an atheistic brand of socialism has been diluted by the addition of an Islamic component, it is difficult to escape the conclusion that the task of Islamic renewal and the marriage of socialism and Islam have yet to be accomplished in Algeria.

[57] *Ibid.*, pp. 14–15.
[58] Algerian FLN, *La Charte d'Alger.* (Ensemble des textes adoptés par le premier Congrès du Parti du F.L.N. du 16 au 21 avril 1964.) (Algiers, n.d.)
[59] *Ibid.*   [60] *Ibid.*, p. 39.   [61] *Ibid.*, pp. 9, 35.   [62] *Ibid.*, p. 15.
[63] *Ibid.*, p. 18.   [64] *Ibid.*, p. 35.   [65] *Ibid.*
[66] *Ibid.*, p. 43. (Italics added.)   [67] *Ibid.*, p. 44.

If the masses had already abandoned superstition, there would have been no need to assert an intent to create the revolutionary, scientific culture which the FLN considers necessary to the success of socialism. It appears that the Marxist and Islamic influences have not yet been merged. This may be due to their apparent incompatibility, as well as to the tenacity of folk Islam among the Algerian masses.

The Nature of Algerian Socialism Today

In April 1965, President Ben Bella presented to the Algerian National Assembly a review of socialist development in postindependence Algeria.[68] In spite of acknowledged setbacks in the self-managed sector, President Ben Bella declared that Algeria would continue to build socialism, but with greater state direction and financial control of the self-managed enterprises.[69] He declared that the decision to promote socialism was "irreversible," "sacred," and necessary to the true independence of the country.[70]

President Ben Bella's remarks indicated a temporary retreat to official sanction of a form of state capitalism. Of course, Algerian spokesmen have never pretended that a socialist society has already been attained in Algeria, and it is not possible to predict the future organization of Algerian society. It is interesting, however, to note the characteristics of Algerian socialist ideology.

First, Algerian socialism is eclectic. It would be misleading to equate Algerian socialism with "Arab socialism." By the admission of Algerian ideologues, Algeria has benefited from the revolutionary experiences of non-Islamic countries. More specifically, the self-management experiment recalls the workers' councils of Yugoslavia,[71] whose combination of one-party rule with planning and a non-Soviet brand of socialism has appealed to leaders of other underdeveloped countries. It is known that Tito had established close relations with the FLN during the War of National Liberation,[72] and one may speculate that the Yugoslav workers' councils directly inspired the Algerian experiment.

[68] "Pour le développement socialiste: planification et gestion équilibrée, discours prononcé par le Président Ben Bella devant l'Assemblée Nationale le 6 avril 1965," *Révolution Africaine* (Algiers), April 10, 1965, p. 13.

[69] *Ibid.,* p. 14.   [70] *Ibid.,* p. 13.

[71] William E. Griffith, "Yugoslavia," in Z. Brzezinski, ed., *Africa and the Communist World* (Stanford, Stanford University Press, 1963), p. 118.

[72] *Ibid.,* p. 119.

Second, Algerian socialism has an Islamic component. It appears that a scientific socialism in Algeria hits upon a bedrock of Islam, which is theoretically reformist but which is actually a variety of folk Islam.

The interplay of Islamic and Marxist influences has resulted in a purely Algerian socialism which resembles the Arab socialism of the Ba'thists in its humanism and theoretical rejection of an atheistic Communism. It differs from Ba'thist socialism in its failure explicitly to tie the success of socialism in Algeria with the spread of socialism to the Arab nations as a whole.[73] Nasser's version of Arab socialism —its insistence on the scientific adaptation of theory to local conditions, its provision for popular councils with control over production, its toleration of some private ownership, its combination of militarism and populism—[74] does resemble Algerian socialism in many respects. Of course, Ba'thist, Nasserist, and Algerian versions of socialism have in common their link to Arab culture, their concern for social justice, and, in practice, their implementation by military or quasi-military governments. However, in the adaptation of socialism to local conditions and in the attempt to reconcile Islam with the import of Marxist techniques, the socialism of contemporary Algeria is unique.[75]

[73] See. G. H. Torrey & John F. Devlin, "Arab Socialism," *Journal of International Affairs*, XIX, No. 1 (1965), 51–52.

[74] George Lenczowski, "The Objects and Methods of Nasserism," *The Journal of International Affairs, ibid.*, p. 70. President Ben Bella seemed to be concerned with the success of "revolution" in Africa and to be leaving the Arab world to Nasser's care.

[75] Readers interested in a further investigation of the subject of this paper may wish to consult the following works:

"Avant-projet du Programme du Parti F.L.N. établi par la Commission de préparation du Congrès," *Révolution Africaine* (Algiers), April 11, 1964, pp. 11–26.

Algerian Front of National Liberation. *Projet de Programme pour la réalisation de la révolution démocratique populaire* (adopté à l'unanimité par le C.N.R.A. à Tripoli en Juin 1962). Algiers, Imprimerie spéciale d' *Al-Chaab*, n.d.

Algerian Ministry of National Orientation. *Algérie An II: 1962–1964*. Annaba, n.d.

—— *Premier Congrès des Fellahs: 25–26–27 octobre 1963*, n.d.

The Attitudes of the African States toward the Katanga Secession July 1960 - January 1963

PETER H. JUDD

During the three-year crisis that saw a major United Nations involvement in the Congo, from July 1960 to January 1963, the Katanga secession remained at issue. A close examination of the attitude of the independent African states toward the secession may tell us something of their expectations, their views of any attempt to revise the old, artificial colonial boundaries, and their views concerning the form of internal government desirable for Africa. We shall also examine the divisions that grew up among the Africans as a result not only of attitudes toward the secession of Katanga, but of involvement in the Congo crisis as a whole. We shall as well gauge the degree of influence those states had in world affairs in imposing their will upon the policy of the world organization.

As a setting for our discussion it is well to recall the debate and the subsequent resolution on the issue of self-determination that took place close to the end of that spectacular Fifteenth General Assembly of the United Nations, in December 1960. The world organization was then in the coils of one of the worst phases of the Congo crisis; constitutional government in Leopoldville was suspended as Kasavubu and Lumumba engaged in mutual dismissals; several national contingents of the United Nations Operation in the Congo (ONUC) were ready to be withdrawn. A complete breakdown of law and order in the former Belgian colony threatened to involve the fate of the world organization in its chaos. It was, ironically enough, at this unhappy moment in the history of world decolonialization that the Assembly passed a resolution entitled *Declaration on the Granting of Independence to Colonial*

Countries.[1] It seemed scarcely the moment to urge more and faster granting of independence, yet it was passed by a nearly unanimous vote (89 states in favor, none against, and nine abstentions). The vote represented a great triumph for the Afro-Asian members of the Assembly; on the one hand, the substance of the resolutions was directed against several of the Western NATO powers; on the other, the Soviet Union had failed even of a simple majority, as its amendments setting up a rigorous timetable for independence were voted down one after the other.

The resolution must, however, be seen not only in the context of the chaotic situation in the Congo, but in reference to the secession of Katanga, the first major separatist movement in the decolonialization of Africa. Article 2 of the resolution read:

All peoples have the right to self-determination; by virtue of that right they freely determine their political status and freely determine their economic, social and cultural development.[2]

Thus far, Mr. Tshombe, the prime minister of the self-styled independent republic of Katanga, could have no quarrel with the resolution. As the debate on the resolution progressed, there were indications that the legal right provided for in Article 2 was to be hedged about with some political considerations. The only reference to Katanga in the debate came from the delegate from Morocco, Mr. Barietta, who used the provincial title to form a new word—and added an additional novelty that reflected Morocco's own interest in the matter of self-determination: "We refuse to accept 'Balkanization,' 'Katanganization,' and 'Mauritaniazation.' . . . Our task here today is to lead the attack against these tricks of division and disunity." [3] Mr. Quaison-Sackey of Ghana qualified his call for immediate independence for all colonies by—quoting his President—warning against "fake independence." [4] Although no one made the connection in so many words, one cannot avoid the impression that the Katanga secession prompted Article 6 of the resolution:

Any attempt aimed at the partial or total disruption of the national unity and territorial integrity of a country is incompatible with the purposes and principles of the Charter of the United Nations.[5]

Article 6, ingenuously enough, prepared the way for a political interpretation of the (in fact rather shaky) legal principle enshrined in Article 2.

[1] Resn. 1514 (XV).   [2] *Ibid.*
[3] GAOR (General Assembly Official Records) 945, Dec. 13, 1960, para. 48.
[4] GAOR 927, Nov. 29, 1960, para. 65.   [5] Resn. 1514 (XV).

Let us now turn to a chronological survey of the problem of the Katanga secession, its place in the whole of the United Nations involvement in the Congo, and the attitudes of the African states toward Katanga throughout the two and a half years under discussion.

It will be convenient to divide our discussion of these issues into five different phases.

July 11 through August 9, 1960

"In Hammarskjöld's mind the prerequisite for a successful United Nations operation in the Congo was the solid backing of the African states." [6] This prerequisite was to be denied the Secretary-General within a few days after the beginning of United Nations involvement on July 13, 1960, primarily as a result of the problem caused by Mr. Tshombe's separatist movement in Katanga.

Tshombe's announcement of the independent state of Katanga on July 11, 1960 was one element in the confusion that swamped the Congo in the second week of its independence. It was, however, the arrival of Belgian paratroopers into the independent state as a whole that triggered the launching of the United Nations operation. Ghana, Guinea, Morocco, Tunisia, and the United Arab Republic were quick in offering troops; [7] all united initially on the desirability of substituting a United Nations force for the occupying Belgians. Independence in other former colonies would be threatened by tolerating a precedent for reoccupation by the former imperial power. The only concession African nationalist opinion made at the outset was the removal of mention of Belgian aggression from the Security Council Resolution of July 14.[8]

By July 20 the major threat to nationalism everywhere in Africa represented by the reoccupation by the Belgians had abated; ONUC had been successfully organized and had replaced Belgian troops outside of Katanga. However, Tshombe denied ONUC entrance to that province, and the Belgians would not withdraw from their military base at Kamina. Mongi Slim, of Tunisia, a leader in African support for ONUC, pointed out the nature of this second threat on July 21; it was found in ". . . the attempt to dismember the young Congolese Republic by setting one group against another. One province, Katanga . . . [is showing] a tendency to dissociate itself from the rest of the

[6] King Gordon, *The United Nations in the Congo: A Quest for Peace.* New York, Carnegie Endowment, 1962, p. 21.
    [7] *Ibid.,* p. 22.   [8] S/4387.

Congo." [9] The specter of a more subtle form of colonialism than that represented by overt Belgian military intervention had raised its head. The Security Council resolution of July 22, therefore, by inference, referred to the Katanga situation:

Recognizing that the Security Council recommended the admission of the Republic of the Congo to membership in the United Nations as a unit.[10]

However, neither Tshombe nor the Belgians would budge, and ONUC was denied entrance to Katanga. The attitude of the Secretary-General was clear: ". . . ONUC cannot be a party to any internal conflict nor can ONUC intervene in a domestic conflict," yet at the same time he made it clear, without mentioning Katanga by name, that ONUC must be allowed to enter the secessionist province to ensure the success of the whole operation.[11]

This was not enough for Premier Lumumba of the Congo, who became more and more strident in his appeals to have ONUC carry out the will of the Central Government in forcing compliance. Support among the radical African states, Mali, Guinea, and Ghana, was soon forthcoming. The Katanga issue had prompted the first major crisis in the United Nations operation; it was clear that the most vocal of the African participants in ONUC wished to have it used as an arm of the Central Government and to enforce Katanga's compliance with the *loi fondamentale*. The Secretary-General was anxious to keep the United Nations force out of the domestic politics of the Congo. Whether or not this was an impossible ideal, the two conceptions met head on.

On August 1 Ghana's representative threatened "to ask the United Nations to declare Belgium an aggressor" because of its support of the secession.[12] On August 6 the representative of Guinea asked the Secretary-General "to make use of the Guinean ONUC contingent and threatened to place it directly under Central Government control." [13] Patrice Lumumba, during the first week of August, toured sympathetic capitals, Tunis, Rabat, Conakry, and Accra, to rally support for his contention that ONUC's mandate was to serve as an enforcement agent for the directives of the Central Government. In Accra President Nkrumah, whose Ghanaian troops had proved to be among the most effective of the ONUC contingents, joined him in a joint communiqué, which concluded with a major threat to the United Nations operation:

[9] SCOR (Security Council Official Records) 878, July 21, 1960, para. 32.
[10] S/4705.   [11] SCOR 877, July 20/21, 1960, para. 17.
[12] Gordon, p. 31.   [13] *Ibid.*, p. 32.

. . . in the event of the United Nations failing to effect a total and uncon-
ditional withdrawal of Belgian troops from the Congo as a whole they will
establish a High Command of military forces to bring about the speedy
withdrawal of these foreign troops from the Congo.[14]

This referred, of course, to Katanga, where Belgian troops alone
remained. The communiqué could not have made it clearer that Ghana
(later joined by Guinea and Morocco) supported the United Nations
operation only insofar as it fulfilled political purposes it considered
worthwhile.

The Secretary-General took note of this development (and by
inference the failure of the prerequisite for success, united African
support) during his intervention in the Security Council debate of
August 8:

. . . it does not help the UN effort if it has to live under a threat of any
one—or more—contributing governments taking matters in its, or their,
own hands, breaking away from ONUC and pursuing a unilateral policy.[15]

The Security Council resolution that followed [16] was the first that
dealt with Katanga specifically. It emphasized the importance of Belgian withdrawal and the requirement that Belgium conform with the
requests of the Security Council, yet it once again reiterated that ONUC
would not intervene in any internal conflict, and it did not provide for
the use of force to attain control over Katanga. Thus the resolution
represents something of a compromise with regard to the radical
African position; at least, however, the issue of Katanga was being
faced directly. What resulted was a temporary lull in the crisis in
ONUC.

This first phase is the most crucial of all, and attitudes formed at
the outset influenced the whole course of the United Nations Congo
operation; and, indeed, their presence is still felt in international affairs. It is well to pause to examine some of the elements in the situation.

1. The leaders of the newly independent sub-Saharan nations,
Ghana and Guinea, realized that the Congo crisis was the first great
international test of the African nations; it would measure their
influence and power to control the course of events on the Continent.
The legitimacy of their independence had been challenged by the
reintroduction of Belgian paratroopers into the Congo and continued

---

[14] *West Africa* (hereafter referred to as *WA*), No. 2254 (London, Aug. 13,
1960), p. 915.
[15] SCOR 884, Aug. 8, 1960, para. 15.   [16] S/4426.

to be affronted by the independent republic of Katanga. In addition, the clock was ticking away on the kind of radicalism, represented by Nkrumah and Touré, that emphasized highly centralized governmental control and the practice of an ideology of African nationalism; at the opening of the Fifteenth General Assembly in September, fourteen ex-French colonies, predominantly conservative in orientation, were scheduled to be admitted to the United Nations. On October 1 the Continent's most populous country, Nigeria, a federation—and thus disposed to a loose federal solution for the Congo—would become independent. This influx would drastically alter the character of the African bloc in the General Assembly; hence one explanation for the impatience of Ghana and Guinea.

2. The rich Congo would be a great prize for whatever brand of African nationalism triumphed. It would be safe to say that the kind of radicalism represented by Nkrumah and Touré would be strengthened internally by the triumph of a similar order under Nkrumah's disciple, Lumumba, in the Congo. The latter was the most passionate foe of Tshombe's secession.

3. One can also observe here a psychological problem. On the one hand there is the calling for an end to colonialism and all its works; on the other is the reality of the Congo, so ill-prepared for independence. More subtle is the tension between the denunciation of the partition of Africa, the "Balkanization" brought about by the imperialist's cynical "divide and rule" policy, and the equally passionate desire to uphold the colonial boundaries exactly as they were drawn by the hated imperialists.

4. There can be no doubt that the Secretary-General's policy of impartiality in domestic politics evoked no support—or possibly even recognition—from these activists.

To them the secession of Katanga was nothing but a Belgian ruse and Tshombe a counterrevolutionary and a stooge. Here is President Nkrumah, the self-appointed speaker for the vanguard of nationalism in Africa, writing to Tshombe on August 8:

Your name is now linked openly with foreign exploiters and oppressors of your own country. In fact you have assembled in your support the foremost advocates of imperialism and colonialism in Africa and the most determined opponents of African freedom. How can you, as an African, do this? I appeal to you in all sincerity to denounce those who are merely using you as a puppet, and who have no more respect for you than they have for African freedom and independence.[17]

[17] Kwame Nkrumah, *I Speak of Freedom* (Praeger, New York, 1961), p. 250.

August 10, 1960 through February 21, 1961

This second phase is characterized by increasing frustration among the early activists and by pronounced divisions among the more numerous African nations present as members during the Sixteenth General Assembly. Throughout much of the period the issue of the Katanga secession was pushed to the background by the Kasavubu-Lumumba controversy and by the breakdown of constitutional government in Leopoldville signified by the emergence of Colonel Mobutu. Yet the Katanga issue was only slightly below the surface, inasmuch as the controversy around Lumumba eventually had reference to a centralized solution to the Congo. Likewise, no one had more to fear from Lumumba than Tshombe, and the murder he condoned was entirely appropriate to his political ends.

The United Nations entered Katanga in the person of Dag Hammarskjöld on August 12. Significantly, he was accompanied by Irish and Swedish members of ONUC, not by any African contingents. He told Tshombe that he was there to establish a United Nations presence according to the Security Council resolution and not to enforce the *loi fondamentale* of the Central Government.[18] Lumumba took the opposite view and "interpreted the Security Council resolution as giving entree to his government." [19] Thus arose the split between the Secretary-General and the Congolese Premier, and the violent "hate" campaign that Lumumba launched against ONUC in Leopoldville.

To the African nationalists the United Nations presence in Katanga, insofar as it dealt with Tshombe at all, was anathema, despite the fact that Hammarskjöld had made it clear that he did not recognize Tshombe's Government as sovereign. It also, one may deduce, alarmed the radicals as setting a dangerous precedent for United Nations action in stabilizing—or insulating—a separatist regime. By the end of September Guinea and Mali announced withdrawal of their troops from ONUC in protest. The Soviet Union, waiting for a chance to court extremist opinion, had, following the split between Lumumba and Hammarskjöld, jumped ponderously on the Lumumbist bandwagon. This so threatened to bring the cold war to Africa that Ghana at the last moment canceled its threatened withdrawal of troops, and Nkrumah continued to support the organization as the best means of keeping the superpowers from a confrontation in the Congo.

[18] Gordon, p. 43.   [19] *Ibid.*, p. 42.

In New York in September a special emergency session of the General Assembly on the Congo was convened, the last before the influx of the French African states. The "17-power" resolution of September 20 [20] represented a new consensus of backing for the Secretary-General—in part surely because of the threat of Soviet intervention. Although it advocated maintaining the "territorial integrity of the Congo" and called upon member states to

. . . refrain from any action which might tend to impede the restoration of law and order and the exercise by the government of the Republic of the Congo of its authority . . .[21]

it did not enjoin the Secretary-General to use force to rejoin the pieces of the Congo. The resolution passed by a 70–0 vote; it represented a decisive defeat for the Soviet Union in its effort to influence Asian-African opinion, and showed the strength of that opinion when directed against a courting superpower. Nonetheless, the favored policy of the African radicals—enforcement action in Katanga—was not included.

There was surprisingly little mention of Katanga during the autumn session of the Fifteenth General Assembly, either during the debate on the Credentials Committee report recommending the seating of the representatives of the Kasavubu Government or in the plenary debates on the agenda item, "The Situation in the Congo." While none of the new French-speaking African members (except, perhaps, Congo-Brazzaville) was well disposed toward Mr. Tshombe, none advocated that ONUC force him to adhere to the writ of the Central Government. In fact, preceding events had made some of them (and other moderate African states such as Sudan) suspicious of the activists of the first stage. One of the very few comic moments of the entire Congo crisis occurred when Mr. Okala, delegate from Cameroon, spoke with a newcomer's candor from the rostrum to the representative of Ghana:

I observe that you would like to turn the Congo into a firm called "Zorin, Quaison-Sackey and Co., Head Office, Leopoldville." And I know who the manager will be. . . .[22]

(He was quickly called to order by Mr. Boland, President of the Assembly.)

Speaking for Nigeria, in a closely watched debut before the Gen-

[20] GA/RES/REV 1 (ES–IV).   [21] *Ibid.*
[22] GAOR 914, Nov. 9, 1960, para. 10.

eral Assembly, Prime Minister Tafewa Balewa did not mention Katanga in his speech but made it clear that it was his country's "policy to leave . . . [ex-colonial] boundaries as they are at present and to discourage any adjustment whatsoever." [23] This signaled the beginning of a kind of consensus of the African moderates: Tshombe's secession was not to be recognized, but it was not to be expunged by force either. A federal solution for the Congo, instead of being considered a weakening device of the imperialists, was supported.

However, there was no broader African or Afro-Asian consensus. An "8-power" draft resolution (African sponsors: Ghana, Morocco, and the United Arab Republic),[24] which would have entrusted ONUC with the responsibility for law and order in the Congo, failed of passage. Previously, on November 30, following Lumumba's arrest and imprisonment, ONUC itself was threatened with dissolution as Ceylon and Indonesia joined the United Arab Republic and Guinea in withdrawing their troops.

The controversy over the fate of the Congo was having its effects on African continental diplomacy as well. At Brazzaville in December the ex-French African states met to coordinate policy on the Congo. In a direct riposte to the activists, their communiqué said, ". . . a peaceful solution can only be found in a round-table conference." [25] Shortly after, in Conakry, the Presidents of Ghana, Guinea, and Mali announced their "merger" in conformity with their ideal of African unity.[26] Those three states met in January with representatives of the United Arab Republic, Libya, the Algerian Front of National Liberation, and Morocco, in Casablanca to form a policy on the Congo to counter that of the Brazzaville group. They focused their discussion on the problem of the composition of the Central Government; their anger at the United Nations for all its sins—most prominently the toleration of Mr. Tshombe—was great, but there was more to their discussion than Katanga. The United Arab Republic, Guinea, and Mali "favored the withdrawal of all troops and the recognition of the Stanleyville Lumumbist government." [27] Secession could, therefore, be tolerated, so long as one favored the seceder. The upshot of the

[23] GAOR 893, Oct. 7, 1960, para. 196.   [24] A/L 331 Rev. 1.
[25] *WA*, No. 2273 (Dec. 24, 1960), p. 1442.
[26] *WA*, No. 2274 (Dec. 31, 1960), p. 1486. In August Mali had split from its former partner, Senegal. The announced merger of the three nations on this date was never carried beyond the communiqué of the conference.
[27] Margaret Roberts, "Pan-Africa and the Congo," *WA*, No. 2276 (Jan. 14, 1961), p. 31.

conference was a compromise whereby Ghana and Morocco continued to adhere to the United Nations policy. The "Casablanca bloc"
was, however, angry, militant, and frustrated.

This second phase ended with the murder of Lumumba in early
February. The widespread revulsion caused by this act led to the
strongest Security Council resolution yet passed.[28] It called for the
departure of "all Belgian and other foreign military and para-military
personnel and political advisers"—a clear reference to Mr. Tshombe's
mercenaries.

What we have seen in this phase is a significant fracturing of African opinion regarding the means of dealing with the Katanga secession; although no nation recognized the Elisabethville Government,
it is clear that some governments' temperatures rose considerably
higher than those of others as they contemplated the secession. The
activists were deeply frustrated much of the time, but had their innings
—their last as it happened—in the February 21st resolution. Guinea,
Mali, and the United Arab Republic, and to a lesser extent Ghana,
had been so committed to the Lumumbist faction and the Lumumba
solution of the Katanga issue that they were never again to be as
influential in United Nations policy, even when ONUC was subduing
Tshombe by force. The brutality of the murder of Lumumba and the
sense of crisis it gave to the involvement of the world organization in
the Congo rallied other African states to advocate that the great
powers in the Security Council produce a strong resolution. Both the
United States and the Soviet Union found it in their interest to please
the Afro-Asian states; France and the United Kingdom, the powers
opposing the form the resolution took, did not feel free to use the
veto. Thus the stage was set for the operations of August and September 1961.

February 22 through September 13, 1961

The last three phases of the Katanga secession can be dealt with in
greater brevity. There are several reasons for this, the first of which
is a considerable diminution of documentary material. The General
Assembly did not, after the spring session of the Fifteenth General
Assembly, again debate in plenary session *the Situation in the Congo*.
The Security Council held debates on the Congo only in November
1961. The Advisory Committee on the Congo, appointed by the

[28] S/4722.

Secretary-General in August 1960, composed of representatives of nations contributing forces to ONUC, consulted infrequently by Hammarskjöld and used frequently and—apparently—importantly by U Thant, did not publish its proceedings. A second factor is that the resolution of February 21, 1961 represents a kind of agreed position for the African states vis-à-vis the Katanga secession; there was little further published debate on the issues involved or precedents established in Africa—although this was not the case in Britain, France, and the United States. In a sense we can say that this position during the next two years only awaited the decision of the United States to become its sponsor to become effective policy. It also required the accession of a new Secretary-General, not as scrupulous as Hammarskjöld in trying to keep ONUC from involvement in the internal affairs of the Congo, to bring this about.

As we have mentioned, the influence of the original activists declined during that period, one factor in which was surely the sheer inability of the states at their present stage of development to carry on a protracted diplomatic effort. However, if their belief in a highly centralized direction from the Central Government was lost, their principle—that the boundaries of the Congo must remain as they were and that a provincial authority had not the right to self-determination—became African policy. To that extent a compromise was reached.

During this third phase the diplomatic initiative regarding Katanga was taken by the French African States, who in March persuaded Tshombe to meet them in Tananarive. There they worked out with him and Colonel Mobutu a plan of reconciliation which would allow a certain degree of autonomy to Katanga. The agreement was short-lived, as Tshombe soon withdrew from it. In any event, according to Dr. O'Brien, the "confederation idea . . . was unacceptable to Afro-Asian opinion" (by which we presume he means radical opinion), and "also to the United States because it would condone Gizenga's Stanleyville regime." [29]

Meanwhile, in the reconvened General Assembly, President Nkrumah stated again the radical estimate of the situation: "Katanga province is being in practice detached from the rest of the State and converted into a new kind of Belgian colony." [30] He urged ONUC to

[29] Conor Cruise O'Brien, *To Katanga and Back* (London, Hutchinson, 1962), p. 98.
[30] GAOR 961, Nov. 1961, para. 30.

take active measures, to enforce law and order.[31] Yet his Government, along with Mali, Guinea, and the United Arab Republic, had recognized Gizenga's Government in Stanleyville. Mr. Thiom, delegate of Senegal, charged that this "constitutes in a sense, intervention in the domestic affairs of the Congo." [32] Yet, he also spoke of the United Nations' duty to "uphold the unity and territorial integrity of the Congo. During the past eight months Katanga has strengthened her position." [33] Once again a moderate position asserted itself.

This was further emphasized at the inter-African conference held at Monrovia in May, attended by the Brazzaville powers and all other independent African states except the Casablanca group (Guinea, Mali, Ghana, Morocco, and the United Arab Republic). There a federal plan for the Congo was proposed; Tshombe's Government was recognized by implication, but only within the framework of the old Congo territory.[34]

There could be no better illustration of the confusion of thought concerning this issue in African nationalist circles than the criticism uttered by Dr. Nkrumah in Accra following the release of the Monrovia communiqué:

In the new Africa we must be prepared to scrap outright the frontiers which were drawn to suit the convenience of the colonial powers without any regard whatsoever to ethnic or social groupings or the economic needs of the people.[35]

Does it all depend, then, on which political direction the revision of boundaries takes?

This phase ends with the debacle of *Rumpunch* and *Morthor,* the operations of August 28 and September 13 which were attempts, according to Dr. O'Brien, to carry out the resolution of February 21. O'Brien describes the point of view of Mohammed Khiari, the Tunisian United Nations official who was his superior: he did not hold to the theory of noninvolvement in internal affairs, but "saw his United Nations works as essentially a patriotic service, the collective defense of the small and vulnerable countries." [36] O'Brien himself felt that he was carrying out an operation in keeping with dominant Afro-Asian opinion.[37]

---

[31] *Ibid.,* para. 110.   [32] GAOR 967, March 9, 1961, para. 13.
[33] *Ibid.*   [34] *WA,* No. 2294 (May 20, 1961), p. 547.
[35] *Ibid.,* p. 555.   [36] O'Brien, p. 189.   [37] *Ibid.,* p. 220.

September 14 through December 31, 1961

Immediately following the outbreak of fighting in Katanga, the Brazzaville powers met in Tananarive, where they jointly denounced the use of force to end the secession of Katanga and commented unfavorably on the result of *Morthor*.[38]

However, U Thant, when he was appointed acting Secretary-General, was found willing to assume a more active role in Katanga for the United Nations. Indeed it could hardly have been otherwise, for whatever Thant's own sympathies with the Afro-Asian viewpoint, the prestige of ONUC and the world organization itself was at stake. The United Nations had a direct interest now in not being further shamed by Mr. Tshombe.

There was a further rallying of moderate opinion toward a hard line in Katanga, notably evidenced by the appeal by three conservative states, Ethiopia, Sudan, and Nigeria, to the Security Council in November to produce a resolution strong enough to empower ONUC to finally end the secession. Ethiopia and Liberia spoke for Africa before the Security Council. Absent were any representatives of the former activist group. Mr. Gebre-Egzy of Ethiopia spoke, presumably for others, when he said:

The secession of Katanga, in our opinion, was never the result of a genuine internal dispute, as it was clear from the beginning that the Katanga secession was engineered and maintained by foreign mercenaries and financial interests.[39]

The result of the Security Council deliberations was the strongly worded resolution of November 24, 1961, which authorized the Secretary-General to deport foreign mercenaries by force if necessary, and declared that "all secessionist activities against the Republic of the Congo are contrary to the *loi fondamentale* and Security Council decisions." [40] The pressure of the moderates had produced the strongest resolution of all in the Congo crisis.

During the "Battle of Katanga" in December, Thant received a statement expressing "wholehearted and unreserved support for the United Nations operation in Katanga" from the Afro-Asian group of the General Assembly.[41] The only African defector at this stage was

[38] *WA*, No. 2312 (Sept. 23, 1961), p. 1051.
[39] SCOR 973, Nov. 13, 1961, para. 41.   [40] S/5002.
[41] *United Nations Review*, April 1962, p. 43.

the Abbé Fulbert Youlou, premier of Congo-Brazzaville, who denied ONUC aircraft the right to fly over his territory.[42]

The fourth phase ended with apparent success for those who wanted to see Katanga reintegrated territorially into the Congo—and they were by this time the great majority of African nations.

January 1962 to January 1963

There were several factors of importance in this final phase. The first was the relative stability of the Adoula Government in Leopold-ville and the general acceptance of its legitimacy (after the collapse of Mr. Gizenga in Stanleyville) by other African nations. This Government also received increasing backing from the Belgian Government with a corresponding lessening of official interest in the Elisabethville Government. A second factor was that Tshombe, by squeezing out of one agreement after another, by allowing his foreign support such obvious prominence, managed to antagonize most African opinion. Indeed, it could be said that the whole of the attentive world began to tire of his cleverness. A third factor was the attitude of U Thant, who actively favored United Nations intervention to restore the *loi fonda-mentale*. This was a year of quiet diplomacy, the creation of a general consensus for ONUC action and Congolese national reconciliation that would carry the legal objections of France and the United Kingdom before it. The fourth factor was the growing impatience of the Kennedy Administration with the lack of resolution of the Congo problem.

It should be noted that during that year India, with 4,600 men, provided by far the largest contingent in ONUC. In a practical sense, the denouement in Katanga in December depended on this concern of Asia for the United Nations operation, not on the willingness (or ability) of African nations themselves to provide troops.

This practical weakness of the African states was revealed in August when a newspaper report from the United Nations said, "After days of discussion, the representatives of Britain, France, Belgium, and America are believed to have agreed to a tentative plan of action to 'force' the reunification of the Congo on Tshombe." [43] This report was not correct as to the agreement, but it did illustrate that an African policy was to be carried out by the major powers.

African diplomatic support for the U Thant "plan of national re-

[42] *Ibid.*   [43] *WA,* No. 2358 (Aug. 11, 1962), p. 879.

conciliation," announced in August, grew. In late August, a joint communiqué issued by the Foreign Ministers of Nigeria, Togo, and
Dahomey "agreed on the need for urgent and decisive action by African states on the Congo question." [44] The Brazzaville 12 (now the
Union Africaine and Malgache [UAM]) at Libreville in September
came around and "decided to give its 'total support' to the U Thant
plan." [45] In late October, as Ralph Bunche headed for the Congo, it
was "reported that the 19-nation Congo Advisory Committee [gave]
him 'full backing' in his proposal that sanctions should be applied
against Katanga if Mr. Tshombe refuses to accept the U Thant 'plan'
and the constitution worked out by the United Nations." [46]

The stage was set for the final operation, in which Indian soldiers
carried out United Nations policy, and the United States strongly
backed the operation and neutralized the resistance of its allies, France
and the United Kingdom. The other superpower, the Soviet Union,
dared not resist for fear of once again miscalculating and antagonizing
Afro-Asian opinion. The result was a decisive reestablishment of the
old frontiers of the Congo, an affirmation that secession was not to be
considered self-determination in the postcolonial era, and the by no
means inconsiderable feat of the expectation of the banishment of Mr.
Tshombe from the world scene.

Conclusion

We have seen the near-unanimity of all African states that the
Katanga secession was not to be considered an example of self-determination and so tolerated. We have seen how the moderate states
gradually came around to condoning the use of force by ONUC to end
the Katanga secession, once all efforts at conciliation by other means
had failed. We can conclude that in the postcolonial era all shades of
African nationalist opinion in governing circles reject any notion of
readjustment of colonial boundaries in the interests of self-determination; the legal doctrine is construed as having relevance only to relations with an imperial power. Secondly, we may conclude that the precedent of the United Nations interfering in the domestic affairs of a
member country appeared to most African countries as a legal consideration of no validity when applied to their political assessment of

[44] *WA*, No. 2361 (Sept. 1, 1962), p. 963.
[45] *WA*, No. 2364 (Sept. 22, 1964), p. 1047.
[46] *WA*, No. 2369 (Oct. 27, 1962), p. 1183.

Mr. Tshombe's regime. It was worthwhile to get rid of this particular challenge to African nationalism at any cost to the principle involved —and that principle does not appear to have been held clearly in view by any of the African states. Indeed, the precedent the activists, at least, feared most, was one in which a United Nations force would stabilize a secession movement.

Let us leave the last word to General Burns and Miss Heathcote:

Admittedly, one can hardly think of a cause less deserving of Hammarskjold's magisterial objectivity than Katangese independence . . . and everyone liked the outcome of January 1963. Yet the United Nations in the post-colonial situation has lost its reputation for impartial objectivity . . . no government would be wise to call in the United Nations without firm assurances that some great power such as the United States will work to keep the United Nations close to its mandate.[47] [48]

[47] Arthur Lee Burns and Nina Heathcote, *Peace-Keeping by U.N. Forces: From Suez to the Congo* (New York, Praeger, 1963), p. 208.

[48] Readers interested in a further investigation of the subject of this paper may wish to consult the following works:

Legum, Colin. *Congo Disaster.* Harmondsworth, Middlesex, Penguin Books, 1961.

Rivkin, Arnold. *Africa and the West: Elements of Free-World Policy.* New York, Praeger, 1962.

Goodrich, Leland M. "The Political Role of the Secretary-General," *International Organization,* XVI (1962), 720–35.

Hoffmann, Stanley. "In Search of a Thread: the United Nations in the Congo Labyrinth," in Norman J. Padelford and Rupert Emerson, *Africa and World Order.* New York, Praeger, 1963, pp. 63–93.

Lash, Joseph P. "Dag Hammarskjold's Conception of His Office," *International Organization,* XVI (1962), 542–66.

Legum, Colin. "What Kind of Radicalism for Africa?" *Foreign Affairs,* XLIII, No. 2 (Jan. 1965).

Africa Report, 1960–63. (Monthly published in Washington, D.C.)
United Nations Review, 1960–63.

The Causes of the
Herero Uprising of 1904-1906
in South-West Africa

MANFRED M. DECKERT

German colonial administration, and therefore German policy in Africa, can be divided into three periods. The first period lasted from 1884 until 1890 and was the era of acquisition and government by chartered companies. During that time colonial matters were handled in Germany by the Diplomatic Section of the Foreign Office. The attitude of the Germans in the colonies toward the indigenous people was, on the whole, rather one of caution, since German power in the colonial areas rested quite often only on treaties and depended on the willingness of the African chiefs to maintain those treaties.

The second period included the years 1890 to 1907. It was a time in which government control under the Empire was introduced and German claims were backed by military force. It was also a time in which serious mistakes were made and in which repeated abuses of Africans led to local uprisings. Colonial affairs were now being handled by the newly established Colonial Section of the Foreign Office.

The third period extended from 1907 to 1914. It was characterized by colonial reforms and economic development or, as the Germans referred to it, "scientific colonization." Colonial affairs were now under the Colonial Office, which had been established in 1907 as an independent agency of the Imperial Government.

The topic under consideration falls within the second period. The newly established Colonial Section and the new policy of direct control of the colonies by the German Government resulted from the failure of government by chartered companies. However, despite the fact that

Berlin inaugurated a new policy, most of the Europeans in the colonies maintained their old attitudes toward the colonies and the indigenous people. Brutal exploitation and cruelty continued. A number of colonists—even government officials—had to be convicted for cruelty, licentiousness, and lawlessness. The settlers resented the government's infringement of what they considered to be their business and administrative prerogatives. Feelings ran particularly deep because thus far the settlers had enjoyed almost limitless freedom of action.

In addition to the clash between government and private interests in the colonies, the position taken by political groups and parties in Germany added to the difficulties of the colonial administration. The new Chancellor, von Caprivi, had little or no interest in colonial matters. Many of the political parties which had supported Bismarck's colonial policy had now become opponents of any colonial policy. This was due primarily to economic failure in the colonies and to the constant threat of local uprisings. The Reichstag proved so anticolonial that it refused to vote the necessary credits for the colonies, and as a result the head of the Colonial Section, Dr. Kayser, was forced to follow the old policy and grant far-reaching concessions to private enterprises in order to maintain economic stability.

During Kayser's tenure, some laws were promulgated in Germany's East and West African colonies to protect the local people from exploitation. However, there was a lack of similar interest in South-West Africa. In 1896 Kayser was followed by von Richthoffen as director of the Colonial Section. The turnover in colonial directors was great, and from 1896 to 1905 four men held this position. The last three, von Buchka, Dr. Stuebel, and Prince Hohenlohe, were all officials of Prince Bülow, who had become Chancellor in 1900. They were therefore the direct servants of the bureaucratic-political system in Germany.

During Dr. Stuebel's tenure the Herero uprising occurred. The uprising itself was probably the greatest colonial fiasco Germany ever suffered. The rebellion was tragic not only because the losses in money and human life were greater than in any other uprising Germany experienced in her colonies, but also because it required two years and 20,000 European troops to quell it. Moreover, the uprising ended only when the Herero nation had been reduced from about 80,000 people to about 15,000.[1] This led to the accusation that Germany

---

[1] Government of the Union of South Africa, *South West Africa and the Union of South Africa*, p. 16.

had carried out an extermination policy against the indigenous people, an accusation which may have influenced the Paris Peace Conference to place the German colonies under the mandate of the League of Nations.

A rebellion of such magnitude and such consequence naturally demands an answer to the question: Why did it happen? To find this answer it is necessary to explore the antecedent conditions in Hereroland. First, there was the land question, involving the concession companies and the settlers, and their policies and actions, which led to clashes with the Hereros. There was also the question of trade, important since trade with the Hereros was the means by which most White settlers acquired a substantial part of their land and cattle. Third and finally, there was the problem arising from German administration, especially the question of judicial procedure, as it affected relationships between Europeans and Hereros.

Before we turn to an examination of the questions posed above, we shall briefly explore the conditions which prevailed in South-West Africa at the time of the first German penetration of that area.

First Encounter

The Herero nation is a branch of the great Bantu family. At the time of the annexation of South-West Africa by Germany, the Hereros occupied the heart of the colony. They controlled the area from Swakopmund in the west to the Kalahari Desert in the east, and from Outjo in the north to Windhoek and Gobabis in the south.

Early in 1884 a party of German scientists and prospectors visited Hereroland and Namaqualand, and inquired into mineral and agricultural possibilities. In the same year Prince Bismarck formally sanctioned the hoisting of the German flag at Angra Pequeña, and placed the acquisitions of the German merchant Lüderitz under the protection of the German Empire. Lüderitz had acquired, from the chief of the Topnaar Namas, who lived near Walvis Bay, rights to the territory extending from 26 degrees south to Cape Frio near the Kunene River in the north. The area of Walvis Bay itself, approximately fifteen miles in circumference, had been proclaimed British territory in 1878.

The hoisting of the German flag in Lüderitzbucht, as Angra Pequeña was called now, was followed by treaties with the Nama and Herero chiefs. The Hereros especially hoped that the "Protection Agreements" would safeguard them against the depredations and attacks of the Namas. In return for such protection the chiefs were required to give the Germans a most-favored-nation treatment, and they had also to agree not to grant facilities or rights to non-Germans without the express consent of the German Government.

At first, however, the German Government had neither the power nor the intention to stop the constant warfare between the Namas and the Hereros, and as a result both nations were soon disappointed about German protection, especially since each nation had been under the impression that the Germans had promised them help against their enemies.[2]

The first agreement between German representatives and the Hereros was made in 1885 with Maherero Katjimuaha, the chief of the Okahandja Herero tribe, whom the Germans, to suit their own purpose, were pleased to regard as the paramount chief of the Hereros. Not entirely satisfied with Maherero Katjimuaha's signature, the Germans went to Omaruru and convinced Manasse, the chief of the Omaruru Herero tribe, who was as powerful as Maherero, to sign a ratification. The other chiefs of the Hereros were ignored. Yet, as Dr. Meyer, at that time the foremost authority in Germany on the law of indigenous peoples, clearly points out, the chiefs Kambazembi, Muretti, Tjetjoo, Zacharias, and others in no way recognized Maherero Katjimuaha's pretensions to paramountcy and held that they were not bound by his agreement.[3] The Germans were, therefore, well aware of this fact, but ignored it on the plea that it was more convenient to deal with one authority than with many.

When Maherero died, his younger son, Samuel Maherero, was elevated to the chieftaincy and declared Paramount Chief of the Hereros by the German colonial administration. Dr. Felix Meyer had no doubts as to the legality of the German procedure. He stated:

Thereby the colonial administration not only created a new authority, which was probably in the interest of a simple and centralized system of government, but it also broke into the laws of succession and inheritance of the Hereros. . . . It can be easily understood how deeply this illegal interference with their laws must have aroused the feelings of the Hereros; more particularly when, at the same time, a hitherto nonexistent *de jure* ruler over the whole nation was forced upon them. One can appreciate how bitterly disillusioned Nikodemus and his supporters were, when not

[2] Heinrich Driessler, *Die Rheinische Mission in Südwestafrika* (Gütersloh, 1932), pp. 141–42.

[3] Felix Meyer, *Wirtschaft und Recht der Herero* (Berlin, 1905), *passim*.

Herero Areas at Time of German Annexation
of South-West Africa

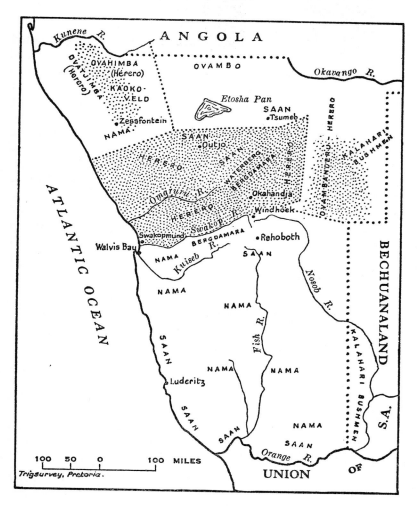

From *South West Africa and the Union of South Africa: The History of a Mandate* (New York, Union of South Africa Government Information Office, 1946), p. 93.

only the dignity to which he aspired, but also the Oruzo assets of his late uncle, were taken from him and bestowed on a younger and less worthy person.[4]

Maherero Katjimuaha's lawful heir was Nikodemus, chief of the Gobabis Herero tribe. Nikodemus was the eldest son of one of Maherero's predeceased brothers and therefore the recognized head of the Oruzo (the religious organization) to which Maherero's family belonged. Maherero had no sons by his principal wife.[5]

Nikodemus, in his anger, was at the bottom of an intrigue which resulted in the rebellion of his tribe, assisted by the Khauas Namas of Gobabis. Victory at Otyunda in 1896, however, enabled the Germans to nip this rebellion in the bud. After a trial before a military court, Nikodemus and his subchief, Kahimema, were shot as rebels at Okahandja in June 1896. They were the first victims of the clash between Germans and Hereros. After their execution the fire of rebellion was still alive, and it was fed by Asa Riasura, the half-brother of Nikodemus. An undying hatred inspired him and his party against the Germans, and this eventually led to the great rebellion of the whole Herero nation in January 1904. By that time even Samuel Maherero had turned on his protectors and was foremost in leading a now united nation against the colonial overlords.

The Land Companies and Hereroland

As soon as Germany had officially laid claim to South-West Africa, companies were formed with the intention of securing large land grants from the Government, and they were successful in obtaining them. Dr. Rohrbach, the economic expert of the Colonial Section of the Foreign Office, stated that the companies had been given land without being required to commit themselves to any reciprocal obligation, and that a situation of that kind was bound to lead to trouble, especially since the land was also claimed by the indigenous people who refused to give it up.[6]

In the area of Hereroland, a syndicate under the auspices of the

[4] Meyer, pp. 24, 38.

[5] See E. Schultz-Ewerth, *Das Eingeborenenrecht* (Stuttgart, 1930), pp. 235–47; and H. Vedder, "The Herero," in *The Native Tribes of South West Africa* (Cape Town, 1928), pp. 185–87.

[6] Paul Rohrbach, *Deutsche Kolonialwirtschaft* (Berlin, 1907), Vol. I, pp. 328–29.

German Colonial Company formally applied to the Government for a grant of 50,000 square kilometers (4,500,000 acres) east of Windhoek stretching toward Gobabis and Hoachanas. In reply, the Government informed the syndicate that the land was claimed by Rehoboths, Hereros, and Namas, and that as the German colonial forces were not strong enough to protect the area the request would have to be deferred until later. That was in 1892.

In April 1893, Von François, the commander of the German troops, noticed that the agents of the syndicate were giving out land to which they had no claim and were making promises which they were unable to fulfill. He wrote to Berlin suggesting that the syndicate's work should be suspended and that the Government should control all questions of immigration and land settlement.[7] The colonial director in Berlin, Dr. Kayser, refused to accept the recommendations of Von François and ordered the syndicate to continue its work, confining itself, for the present, to the neighborhood of Windhoek. Immigrants continued to arrive and were given or sold farms which existed only in the imagination of the managers of the syndicate.

The outlook of the land companies as well as that of the arriving settlers was best expressed by the *Koloniale Zeitschrift*. This paper suggested in its edition of July 24, 1902 that a colonial government (which only partially knows its business) in a land that has to be settled by a White population, should do its best to take away from the indigenous people part of their land in order to create White settlements, and should also deprive the indigenous people of their freedom to the extent needed to create a working force for the White farmers.[8]

In 1894 Governor Leutwein decided to solve the problem once and for all. He went to Okahandja, and in December of that year drew up an agreement for Samuel Maherero to sign, whereby the entire southern boundary of Hereroland from Swakopmund to Gobabis was defined. Leutwein had marked the boundaries in such a way as to secure for the land settlement syndicate the town and grazing lands of Gobabis and some of the finest land on the White Nosob River. Samuel Maherero was guaranteed an annual salary of 2,000 marks, provided the southern boundary line was respected by the Hereros and provided their cattle posts were withdrawn from the territory now falling under the control of the land syndicate.

This boundary line extended over 400 miles, and since Samuel

---

[7] C. von François, *Deutsch Südwestafrika* (Berlin, 1899), *passim.*
[8] Driessler, p. 146.

Maherero was not recognized by his fellow chiefs he had no right to make agreements concerning it. The southern boundary of his own district, Okahandja, was probably less than a sixth of the whole line. Yet, with a stroke of Samuel's pen, chiefs such as Zacharias, Tjetjoo, and Nikodemus were deprived of the rights which their ancestors had held for generations past.

Leutwein's action was strongly criticized in the Reichstag, and after the uprising had occurred he became a target for the attacks of the opposition, which saw in the Government's land manipulations one of the reasons for the rebellion. The Social Democrat, Bebel, condemned this contract with Samuel by pointing out that, according to Herero law, the chiefs had no right to sell tribal land and that such actions must inevitably lead to hate and unrest.[9] The reaction in responsible quarters to this accusation was denial. Prince Arenberg of the Center Party expressed the view of those who defended Government policy by declaring that a search for guilt in the uprising was interesting but that one should not get too involved in it. He also claimed that neither the administration nor the settlers could be held responsible for the uprising.[10] Dr. Stuebel, the colonial director, rejected outright Bebel's statement about the law of the indigenous people and declared:

I believe that deputy Bebel is not that well versed in Herero jurisprudence to make such a statement. As far as I know the Herero chiefs did have the right to dispose of land and other property of the tribe. But since there is no written law in Hereroland it is extremely difficult to go deeper into this subject.[11]

However, that the Government or at least the responsible people could or should have been aware that Herero law did not recognize the alienation of land, is made clear by the statement of Dr. Südekum, a Social Democratic deputy, in the Reichstag:

Concerning the land question, I am sorry that you could not hear the lecture of Dr. Felix Meyer given yesterday at the Society for Comparative Law. Dr. Meyer proved that, based on Herero law, the German colonial administration is responsible for the uprising, and if what he had to say about the common property law of the Bantu Negroes concerning land and soil, and about the psychological inability of the Bantu Negro to understand the alienation of land, is not enough, there is also Prof. Kohler,

[9] German Empire, *Reichstag*, 129 Sitzung (Montag den 30. Januar 1905), p. 4098.
[10] *Ibid.*, p. 4119.   [11] *Ibid.*, p. 4108.

Dean of Comparative Law at Berlin, who said: "The Bantu Negro cannot understand the alienation of land and one should demand that the colonial officials are instructed about this." As early as twelve years ago I emphasized that people who are sent to the colonies should be instructed in the elementary concepts of native law. It is against the nature of Herero and Bantu law that land can be transformed into private property and thus alienated.[12]

In 1895 Governor Leutwein made his next move. He entered into an agreement with Samuel Maherero whereby the German Government had the right to impound all Herero cattle found trespassing over the boundaries. The impounded cattle would be sold and the proceeds divided between the Government and the Paramount Chief. Leutwein justified his action by explaining that in consequence of this agreement the German Government had obtained the legitimate right to confiscate Herero cattle, whereas formerly such confiscation would undoubtedly have caused war.[13] The intention behind Leutwein's move was probably not so much to confiscate cattle as to make clear to the individual Herero that the German Government felt that he was bound by the agreement of Samuel Maherero concerning the new boundaries.

The Germans took advantage of this right in the beginning of 1896. A force under Major Müller confiscated several thousand cattle. Only then did the significance of the agreements become clear to the Hereros. Excitement and war fever grew throughout the colony. At the camp of Samuel Maherero tension lessened when the half share of the proceeds of the cattle sale was paid, according to the agreement, to the chief.

However, outside the residence of Samuel Maherero the desire for war increased, and Leutwein felt he had to act. In January 1896 Leutwein went to Okahandja and met with the Herero chiefs. He asked them what kind of boundaries they desired and what punishment they felt should be imposed on trespassers. At the same time he made it clear that if he should find their requests too impudent the result would be war, and that such a war could result only in the defeat of the Herero nation. After several days of deliberation the Hereros who supported Samuel Maherero demanded that the Seeis River, the water of which was indispensable for their herds, should fall within the limits of Herero territory, and that the Paramount Chief and the Governor should jointly decide on the punishment for trespass. Leut-

[12] *Ibid.*, 130 Sitzung (Dienstag den 31. Januar 1905), pp. 4137–38.
[13] T. Leutwein, *Elf Jahre Gouverneur in Deutsch Südwestafrika* (Berlin, 1907), pp. 92–93.

wein accepted this request, since it offered him an opportunity to divide the Hereros. Leutwein frankly stated his motives:

This first demand meant a shift forward of the boundaries some eight kilometers. As the advantage of this change of boundary would have been only of benefit to the Western Hereros, i.e., those of Okahandja, Nikodemus, on behalf of the Eastern Hereros, immediately came forward and on behalf of his people asked for the return of the Gobabis area to them. This gave me the most beautiful opportunity to put into force my *divide et impera* policy. Therefore I granted the wish of the Okahandja Hereros and definitely refused the request of Nikodemus. As a result of this the latter went into rebellion three months later, while the Okahandja Hereros remained on our side.[14]

Apart from losing their land through the arbitrary actions of the Government, the Hereros suffered from the depredations of individual settlers. In August 1901, the Herero chiefs of the tribes on the White Nosob River sent a petition to the Governor through a missionary:

Most honored Governor:

The undersigned Herero chiefs have just come to me and have requested me to convey the following to your honor: Kayata of Okatumba declares that in early 1900 a settler, Mr. Westphal, came to Okatumba, where he built a house of poles and operated a small store therein. Five weeks ago he started to build a house of limestone. Kayata and Muambo forbade him to do this, as he had no ownership; but Mr. Westphal took no notice of them. They cannot give Mr. Westphal a settlement at Okatumba, as the place will remain theirs and their children's. This treatment has caused them to call the other chiefs together to a council . . . last week Mr. Stopke came here, and he told us that he had purchased the place between the farm of Mr. Schmerenbeck in Ommandjereke and the farm of Mr. Conrad on Orumbo from the government at Windhoek, and he demanded therefore that Mbaratjo and his people who live there should leave the place. In Otjivero lives a Mr. Veldt. He has been there three years and has made every endeavor to buy the place. In Okamaraere, opposite Orumbo, lives a Mr. Wosillo; in Omitrara Mr. Gilers; and in Okahua Mr. von Falkenhausen has settled lately. . . . Otjipaue has been acquired by Mr. Schmerenbeck and Otjisaesu by Mr. Voigts.

But now, honored Governor, where are we to live when our entire river and all our land is taken away from us? We annex a sketch showing all werfts [Herero villages] in the area of Otjitsaesu up to Omitrara. These all water their cattle in the White Nosob, so we again ask, where are all these people to go? We see with dismay how one place after another is going into the hands of the white people and therefore, honored Governor,

[14] Leutwein, *Elf Jahre Gouverneur*, p. 96.

we pray you most respectfully not to sanction any further sales here in the area of the White Nosob.[15]

This letter, of which no notice was taken, is an example of how the land settlement syndicate managed its settlement work. Every one of the farms enumerated by the Hereros was situated in Herero territory on the White Nosob or near the river along the northern boundary of the concession territory belonging to the syndicate. The farmers wanted to stay as close as possible to the economic center of the colony, but because the companies asked too much for their land, a whole stretch of settlements was created on the land of the Hereros close to the concession areas of the companies. To understand the practice and attitude of the syndicate and its companies one has only to refer to the annual report of the Otavi Company for the year 1903, quoted in the Reichstag by deputy Lattman of the Economic Union. In its report the company announced that it had restricted the selling of land, since there was good reason to believe that it could receive far better prices in two or three years.[16]

Lattman, whose political affiliation was middle-of-the-road, quoted the annual report of the Otavi Company in order to denounce both the syndicate and the Government condoning its activities. The Social Democrats also took the point of view that the land policy of the colonial administration, especially in relation to the large companies, was decisive in causing the uprising. Their speaker in the Reichstag, Bebel, attacked this policy of the Government by referring to an article in the *Deutsche Tageszeitung* of January 15, 1904, in which a Dr. Förster reported that the Hereros had been pushed further and further into the eastern and northeastern parts of the colony, and that their existence was again threatened by the railroad construction of the Otavi Company. Bebel then continued, referring to a recent statement in the Reichstag by Dr. Stuebel:

This railroad construction will result, as we have heard from the colonial director, in large stretches of land on both sides of the railroad being taken over by white farmers and thereby lost to the Hereros. The Hereros have already been robbed of a large part of their land and have had to move further east. But if they now hear that new railroad construction is planned, which, according to their experience thus far, will result in further loss of their land and thereby threaten their existence, who can blame them if they do everything in their power to defend their property? [17]

[15] Rohrbach, pp. 330–31.
[16] *Reichstag,* 130 Sitzung (Dienstag den 31. Januar 1905), p. 4136.
[17] *Ibid.,* 14 Sitzung (Dienstag den 19. Januar 1904), p. 367.

Deputy Schrader of the Liberal Union deplored the fact that German rule in South-West Africa, in contrast to East Africa, had brought no advantages to the indigenous people. He pointed out that in East Africa Germany liberated the indigenous people from the tyranny of the Arabs, while in South-West Africa she acted only as a conqueror and affected deeply the existing conditions by restricting the indigenous people in their freedom of movement and by taking away large parts of their land.[18]

That the view of Social Democrats and left-liberal groups toward German colonial policy was not shared by all political parties in the Reichstag was made clear by a statement of deputy Stocker of the Economic Union:

But if one reads in certain Liberal papers that the government should confiscate all the land of the Hereros and make them propertyless and outlawed, I have to say that I consider this the greatest injustice. One is used to considering the lands of the indigenous people as free for the taking, but this is a presumption which should not exist.[19]

Stocker's reference to Liberal papers indicates that the National Liberals were in agreement with Government policy and advocated actions which would be of benefit only to the land companies and the settlers. This attitude of the National Liberals toward South-West Africa was made even more clear by Deputy Patzig, who declared that his party did not wish to criticize the military and civil administration at the very moment when they had to use all their energy to crush the uprising, and that it would be inadvisable to voice criticisms in public in any case. He objected to the accusations against settlers which he considered irresponsible from a "patriotic" and "cultural" point of view. He concluded his speech with an invitation to the parties of the middle to do everything in their power to prevent damage to German colonial prestige not only in the eyes of the Hereros but before the nations of the world.[20]

One of the most interested parties—most interested, that is, that the Government should confiscate the land of the Hereros—was the German Colonial Association. It voiced its opinion in the *Zeitschrift für Kolonialpolitik*. In 1904 an article was published in this journal which ran as follows:

Objections in past years have been directed against the land speculations of the companies, which were considered an obstacle to settlement, since

[18] *Ibid.*, 129 Sitzung (Montag den 30. Januar 1905), p. 4120.
[19] *Ibid.*, 60 Sitzung (Donnerstag den 17. März 1904), p. 1904.
[20] *Ibid.*, p. 1895.

the Government did not possess enough crown land for the establishment of farms and did not dare to dispossess the natives. A new attack against the concession companies has been planned, but I advise against such blunt action. What seemed a year ago the only possible step is today no longer valid. The Herero war has changed the situation completely. The war can almost be considered a good fortune insofar as the increasingly pressing land question is concerned. The necessity to use the companies' land for settlement does not exist any more, since there is no doubt that the whole Hereroland will become crown land.[21]

Another article in the same journal was even more outspoken in reference to the "good fortune" offered by the Herero rebellion. Here the author even admitted that the uprising was an attempt on the part of the indigenous people to defend their liberty and their homes. He then continued that it had to come to such a trial of strength in order to further the development of the colony. He concluded by saying that the country only gained through the uprising, because thousands had become acquainted with the area; business had found a field of activity and a stronger military force had been trained for colonial warfare.[22]

The opinion of the Government on the question was stated by Dr. Stuebel, who declared that if one looked at the reasons for the uprising one must take into consideration the fact that the indigenous people had not forgotten the time before the occupation when they enjoyed complete freedom. Dr. Stuebel admitted that increasing settlement restricted the indigenous people's freedom of movement more and more, and that their economic independence had been limited through their indebtedness to the traders. But, he concluded, the Hereros remained the enemies of public and social order, which had, therefore, to be forced on them.[23]

THE TRADERS AND THE CREDIT SYSTEM

The chief necessity, besides land, for the new settlers was an adequate supply of livestock. The difficulties in this direction increased in proportion to the growth of new farms. The White ranchers and farmers who had breeding stock were loath to part with them, and only sold them in cases of extreme necessity. For the recently arrived farmer no course remained but to trade with the Hereros and thereby acquire the necessary cattle.

In addition to breeding stock, the future farmer required transport oxen, since transporting goods between the coast and the interior was

[21] *Zeitschrift für Kolonialpolitik,* **VI** (1904), 520.
[22] *Ibid.,* **VIII** (1906), 857.
[23] *Reichstag,* 14 Sitzung (Dienstag den 19. Januar 1904), p. 363.

one way to make money, and the average farmer in South-West Africa was always in need of money because he usually started without any working capital.[24] The chief producers of the oxen were also the Hereros, and trade with them constituted the only method of acquiring the needed breeding stock. As a result, farming and trading were not separate and distinct occupations before the outbreak of the Herero rebellion. Dr. Rohrbach, an authority on the German colonial economy, describes this phenomenon:

One way to become an independent farmer was by trading, and one can say that with the exception of the farms around Windhoek and the Boers of Grootfontein, most farmers in the area of the Herero uprising became farmers this way. A few years of trading were sufficient to gain enough cattle from the natives through buying. The 10,000 hectares of grazing land necessary for a farm were acquired in a similar way.[25]

It is understandable that, due to the ignorance of the indigenous people, these trading deals were not always handled in a correct manner. The traders aimed at arousing the desire of the Hereros for trinkets and European luxuries, for which they then charged exorbitant prices.[26] How exorbitant the prices were is explained by Professor Karl Dove, the director of land settlement at Windhoek, who estimated that the Hereros never received more than twenty marks' worth of goods for an ox which was normally valued at forty marks.[27] This was because the traders were in a position to regulate prices and place their own valuation on the goods given by them in exchange for cattle. Not only did the traders ask exorbitant prices for their goods, they practically forced those goods on the Hereros. A trader would come to a Herero village, and when he could not sell his goods he would just leave them there. When he returned after a few days, and his goods had disappeared, he simply debited the Hereros with whatever amount he saw fit. In this way entire Herero villages became deeply indebted to the traders, who, once they considered the debt high enough to cover the cost of the land necessary for a farm, would simply confiscate the best grazing land of the village. It is obvious that this behavior on the part of the traders resulted in increased resentment among the Hereros. That this credit system was to a large extent responsible for the uprising was brought out in Reichstag debates, where Deputy Kopsch, of the Progressive Liberals, disclosed

---

[24] *Reichstag,* Aktenstück No. 540, p. 3212.   [25] Rohrbach, p. 320.
[26] *Reichstag,* 129 Sitzung (Montag den 30. Januar 1905), p. 4099.
[27] Karl Dove, *Deutsch Südwestafrika* (Berlin, 1913), p. 10.

that even a governmental memorandum admitted that the credit system of the traders accounted, in large measure, for the uprising.[28]

Even before the uprising the Government considered the credit system bad for the colony. In 1899 Governor Leutwein submitted a draft ordinance to Berlin, in which he proposed to create courts of law where claims against indigenous people by traders and others could be adjudicated. African chiefs were to be coassessors with Germans on the courts, and claims against Africans, based on credit, would after a certain period be considered null and void.

However, Leutwein, who wished to abolish in time the credit system altogether, had to face strong opposition from interested parties. The White settlers, especially, raised a cry of indignation. For five years the struggle continued between Leutwein on the one side, and the combined forces of the directors of the land and trading companies and the traders and settlers in South-West Africa on the other. Leutwein's policy in regard to the traders found the support of center and left parties in the Reichstag.[29] In 1903 he succeeded in obtaining definite decisions from Berlin, and the famous Credit Ordinance was promulgated in that year. This ordinance gave the traders one year in which to collect all outstanding debts. After the year had passed all debts still uncollected would be nullified.

The result of the ordinance was that the traders fell upon the Hereros in order to collect their debts before the deadline ran out. How the outstanding debts were collected is described by Deputy Erzberger of the Center Party in one of his addresses to the Reichstag:

The settler Erdmann [a member of the settler deputation to Berlin] has openly admitted that when an order for the collection of debts was not at once successful, the settlers simply took as much cattle from the Hereros as they thought necessary to cover their claims. It also happened that sometimes an additional number of cattle were taken to cover future claims.[30]

The National Liberals defended the actions of the settlers and traders. Their deputy, Patzig, explained that the collection of debts became difficult because the Administration had failed to support the farmers and traders, who, therefore, were forced to confiscate cattle from the Hereros in order to cover outstanding loans. Deputy Patzig also pointed out that all this happened shortly before the uprising, and

---

[28] *Reichstag*, 130 Sitzung (Dienstag den 31. Januar 1905), p. 4150.
[29] *Ibid.*, 60 Sitzung (Donnerstag den 17. März 1904), p. 1903.
[30] *Ibid.*, 130 Sitzung (Dienstag den 31. Januar 1905), p. 4148.

could therefore be considered irrevelant to the uprising itself. He took offense at Erzberger's statement that additional cattle had been taken to cover future claims, rejecting this as untrue and libelous.[31]

The Social Democrats, on the one hand, not only deplored the Credit Ordinance which had led to excesses toward the Hereros on the part of the settlers, but also blamed the inferior moral character of the settler element in South-West Africa for the frictions between indigenous people and Germans in the colony. Their speaker, Bebel, declared in the Reichstag:

I have here the *Kölnische Zeitung,* which has published an article from Outjo of January 25. In the article is mentioned, among other things: "Without going into detail of the set-up of the Credit Ordinance, it can be said that it is one of the direct causes for the dissatisfaction of the Hereros. The dubious past of the traders in Europe is quite often the reason for their being down here."

One can also say that the colony is considered, especially by our compatriots in the East, as a suitable place for troublesome and wayward sons. The traders are not very particular about the means by which they try to collect payments for goods, given on credit with excessive profit, before the deadline runs out.[32]

Bebel's statement about the personal qualities of the settlers in South-West Africa was not to the liking of the parties of the right and right center. On the contrary, the representatives of those parties felt obliged to defend the honor of the German colonists in Africa. Deputy Arendt informed the Reichstag of his personal acquaintance with men who had emigrated and for whose character he was ready to vouch. Arendt also aired the view that people who had emigrated to the colonies had done this, to a large extent, for idealistic motives, and should therefore not be considered the worst but rather the best representatives of the German nation.[33] Paasche, of the National Liberals, was a little bit more careful. He conceded that there had been a number of colonists who had the characteristics of the bully. But he pleaded that a tribe of haughty Negroes could not be ruled in the same way as civilized people, and that one could not always approach the Negro with politeness and kindness but had to show who was master.[34]

[31] *Ibid.,* p. 4136.
[32] *Ibid.,* 60 Sitzung (Donnerstag den 17. März 1904), p. 1890.
[33] *Ibid.,* 60 Sitzung (Donnerstag den 17. März 1904), p. 1890.
[34] *Ibid.,* 129 Sitzung (Montag den 30. Januar 1905), p. 4117.

German Justice and Treatment of the Hereros

Until July 1903 no provisions had been made with regard to the administration of civil law in South-West Africa. This neglect of an important arm of the administration was explained by Governor Leutwein on the basis of the fact that so long as the territory was inhabited by a small White population the introduction of a legal system was not necessary. The Africans relied on the mediation of the nearest official or officer if their case involved a White person. Should only Africans be involved in a legal action, then tribal usage was invoked and in most cases the chief acted as judge.

The German concept of judicial procedure in the colonies was best explained by Dr. Schnee, the last Governor of East Africa. Dr. Schnee described the system as patriarchal. The officials in charge were expected to use their knowledge of human nature and their familiarity with native customs and usages rather than, as Schnee put it, lose hold of themselves and bewilder the litigants with the technicalities of a Europeanized legal procedure. Schnee held the view that this method was effective even though a Court of Appeals was lacking in most of the colonies, and only the more important judgments were laid before the Governor for ratification.[35]

Such a system had its obvious flaws. A sound legal procedure demands equality before the law, but equality was the very thing the average White in Africa would not concede to the African. To gain a picture of the attitude of the Whites toward the Africans in the handing out of justice, one should look at a Colonial Association publication. The author of the article admitted that the Europeans had already violated the rights of the Negroes by taking possession of Africa, and he advocated that they should continue to do so in order to stay as masters of the Continent. He also rejected the idea of familiarizing Africans with Christianity, because Christianity was inseparable from the concept of equality, and the concept of equality, once accepted by the African, was incompatible with White rule in Africa.[36]

Major Kurt Schwabe, an officer who served with distinction in the German colonial forces in South-West Africa, and one of the officials to whom the Hereros had to turn if they were in need of legal protection and justice, wrote an article about the handling of justice in

[35] H. Schnee, *German Colonization Past and Future* (London, 1926), p. 123.
[36] *Zeitschrift für Kolonialpolitik*, VIII (1906), 227–37.

Africa. He recommended that White rule should not be cruel or exploitative but rather stern, just, and authoritative. Furthermore, it should be paternal and benevolent, but only insofar as the interests of the White race were not abridged. He attacked the suggestion that the judicial institutions of the Africans could form the basis for a colonial legal code, because, he explained, an expert and impartial judge of the Negro's concept of law, custom, religion, and government would always come to the conclusion that those concepts and the institutions based on them were virtually without exception hostile to "culture." [37]

The legal system, so greatly recommended by Dr. Schnee, combined with the attitude of the Europeans toward the indigenous people, as illustrated above, was bound to work to the disadvantage of the Africans in many cases. Stories of miscarriage of justice and mistreatment of indigenous people aroused public opinion in Germany, and finally, in July 1903, civil law was introduced in the colonies. But by that time it was too late to convince the Hereros of the honest intentions of the administration, and the Herero rebellion broke out half a year later. The Government was attacked in the Reichstag for its failure in the colonies in regard to justice. The colonial administration was accused of having hushed up cases involving criminal actions of colonial officials toward indigenous people. Bebel, addressing the Reichstag in 1905 on this matter, stated:

Another dark chapter is the story of ill treatment. The ill treatment which the African population have to suffer is immensely heavy and harsh. I wish only to recall the case of Prince Prosper Arenberg who murdered the African Kain in the cruelest and most barbarous way. There are similar cases.

I also have to report that it is very difficult for people in the colonies to send unpopular reports to Europe and Germany about the administration down there. If it becomes known that a person has sent unfavorable reports to Germany his whole existence is put into jeopardy. . . . For instance, the settler Groenvelde had brought to public attention the fact that Kossak, a noncommissioned officer, cruelly tortured to death an imprisoned Negro. . . . Groenvelde now aroused the hate and dislike of the district chief, Lieutenant von Stempel, who was able to influence the judges in the district. As result, Groenvelde was first indicted for smuggling of arms and received a fine of 1,000 marks. Groenvelde appealed, and since he had sold the guns with the permission of the district chief, who had levied on them a tax of 50 marks, the sentence was changed to a 450-

[37] *Zeitschrift für Kolonialpolitik,* XVI (1914), 208–10.

mark fine. Three months later he was called again before the judge, this time for trying to influence a third party to commit perjury, and was sentenced to three years at hard labor and loss of citizenship rights for five years. Groenvelde appealed and was acquitted. Three days later he was indicted and convicted for receiving stolen property. His sentence was two years at hard labor and loss of citizenship rights for five months. He again appealed, and the sentence was revised to two months in prison . . . the district chief now tried to ruin Groenvelde economically, and declared his store under boycott. Groenvelde complained to the colonial administration, and it took six orders from the Governor and the Colonial Section, during a one year and two months period, until the boycott was lifted.[38]

Kossak, who had caused the death of the unfortunate African, was dismissed from the colonial service; he was, however, never indicted or tried for his crime.[39] Not only does this episode show that the German judicial system worked to the disadvantage of Africans, but the constant revisions reveal a deficiency in judicial procedures and a lack of experience on the part of the judges. Finally, it brings out the fact that murders of Africans were treated lightly and where possible were kept secret. On the other hand, Africans who committed crimes were punished with the utmost severity. During the debates in the Reichstag about this problem, cases were mentioned which showed that children of the age of four to six years had been convicted and sentenced to prison. In one case a little girl of five had received a lengthy prison term for taking some milk from a goat. The conditions in many prisons were so bad that they resulted in a high mortality rate of the inmates.[40]

While these examples show how heavily the German judicial system bore down on the indigenous people, there were groups in Germany and in the colonies of the same mind as Dr. Hesse, one of the leading figures of the Colonial Association, who insisted that it was the duty of the state to punish with the utmost severity any recalcitrance on the part of the local people.[41] Those groups were behind the charges leveled against Governor Leutwein, after he had been relieved from his post, that he had precipitated the rebellion of 1904 because of his excessive leniency toward Africans. To show that leniency was hardly exercised in cases of Europeans murdered by Africans, Leutwein quoted the following details of murder trials: [42]

[38] *Reichstag,* 129 Sitzung (Montag den 30. Januar 1905), pp. 4100–1.
[39] *Ibid.,* p. 4180.   [40] *Ibid.,* p. 4102.
[41] *Zeitschrift für Kolonialpolitik,* VI (1904), 124.
[42] Leutwein, *Elf Jahre Gouverneur,* p. 431.

Europeans Murdered by Africans

	NAME	SENTENCE
1894	Christie (Englishman)	1 death, 1 penal servitude
1895	German soldier	6 death sentences
1895	Smith (Boer)	2 death sentences
1896	Feyton (Englishman)	1 death sentence
1899	Classen and Durr (Germans)	2 death sentences
1900	German policeman	3 death sentences

Africans Murdered by Europeans

	NAME	SENTENCE
1896	Namas Jantje and Kurieb	3 months' imprisonment
1901	Herero Leonard	1 year's imprisonment
1902	Herero Kamawu	2 years' imprisonment
1903	Daughter of Herero chief	3 years' imprisonment

It can be clearly seen that African murderers were invariably sentenced to death, whereas, in the four cases actually tried, the severest penalty imposed on a White man was three years' imprisonment. That kind of justice was bound to have repercussions. Concerning the last murder case, Leutwein wrote:

In the early part of 1903, an intoxicated white man shot a Herero woman, who was sleeping peacefully in a wagon, for the reason that he imagined he was being attacked by Hereros and fired blindly in all directions. The court rejected the entirely unfounded story of attack by Hereros, as alleged by the white man. The case turned entirely on the question of the hallucinations of a no longer sober person. Notwithstanding this, the judges in the first instance found the white man not guilty, because they accepted as a fact the defence that he had acted in good faith. This acquittal aroused extraordinary excitement in Hereroland, especially as the murdered person was the daughter of a chief. Everywhere the question was asked: "Have the white people the right to shoot the native women?" I thereupon traveled personally to Hereroland to pacify the people so far as I could, and also to make clear to them that I did not agree with the judgment of the court, but had no influence thereover. Luckily the prosecuter had correctly appealed. The accused was then brought before the Supreme Court at Windhoek and sentenced to three years' imprisonment. This event had, however, contributed its share toward the unrest among the Hereros which resulted half a year later in the outbreak of the rebellion.[43]

Even the staunchest defenders of German colonial policy in South-West Africa admitted the failure and inadequacy of the judicial pro-

[43] *Ibid.,* pp. 222–23.

cedures and the excesses committed by the White population. Von Staudy, a Conservative deputy, declared in the Reichstag that mistakes had been made by the colonial administration and crimes had been committed by Germans in the colony, but that the Germans, in general, were not a cruel or antagonistic people. The uprising itself he attributed to circumstances which could have happened under any colonial administration. Von Staudy also pointed out that other nations had had to face the same problems, but had found it easier than Germany to establish the necessary respect of the indigenous people toward their rule, perhaps because Germany was a late comer in the colonial field.[44] Dr. Stuebel, the colonial director, explained that it was not surprising that excesses had occurred in South-West Africa, since that colony was an establishment of recent origin, but he assured the Reichstag that those excesses had been deeply condemned by the administration, which had done and would do its best to prosecute violations of the rights of indigenous people with all the severity of the law.[45]

Conclusion

These examples reveal that there were people in Germany as well as in the colony who were of the opinion that arbitrary behavior against, and even murder of, Africans were actions which could be justified or excused. The belief that the life of the indigenous inhabitants of colonial areas was of minimal value seems to have been common among all European colonizing nations.

On the other hand, the strongest and most authoritative indictments of German policy in South-West Africa can be found in the writings and speeches of Germans. The bulk of the criticism in this paper has been extracted from the reports of the Reichstag debates and the works of German colonial experts. Based on this criticism, one can conclude with Bebel, one of the opposition leaders in the Reichstag, that there were several causes for the uprising. First, there was the completely unscrupulous greed of individuals and of land companies, especially their fraudulent selling and buying. Second, there were the rigorous demands for the liquidation of debts. Third, there was a lack of legal protection for the Hereros, even when, as often happened, they were in the right. And fourth, there were the

[44] *Reichstag*, 129 Sitzung (Montag den 30. Januar 1905), p. 4111.
[45] *Ibid.*, p. 4108.

actions of the White settlers, resulting in physical ill treatment and killing of individual Hereros, in cases where the settlers thought that the behavior of the Hereros demanded punishment.[46] To this may be added a statement of Dr. Stuebel, the director of the Colonial Section of the Foreign Office, who agreed that the general dislike of and hatred for the German occupation, followed by the manifold unjust actions of traders and farmers against the Hereros, were in large measure responsible for the outbreak of the rebellion in Hereroland.[47]

The Colonial Section itself had its share of responsibility for the uprising. As a result of its vacillation—best illustrated by Governor Leutwein's attempts to abolish the credit system—between concern for the settlers and concession companies on the one hand and the indigenous people on the other, it created an explosive and unhealthy atmosphere in the colony. In fairness it should be stated that these developments in the colony led to changes in the power and position of the colonial administration in Germany. In 1907 the Reichstag created the new Colonial Office, and Dr. Dernburg became the first colonial secretary. Not only did he possess the confidence of the Reichstag, but he also thoroughly prepared himself for his new duties by undertaking intensive study of colonial problems at home and abroad. Under Dernburg the "scientific era" of the German colonial period began, and German administration in Africa soon approached the level of British.[48,49]

[46] *Ibid.*, 87 Sitzung (Montag den 9. Mai 1904), p. 2748.
[47] *Ibid.*, p. 2789.
[48] W. O. Henderson, *Studies in German Colonial History*. London, 1962, p. 9.
[49] Readers interested in a further investigation of the subject of this paper may wish to consult the following works:

Amery, L. S. *The German Colonial Claim*. London, 1939.
Beiderbecke, H. *Among the Hereros in Africa*. Reutlingen, 1922.
Calvert, A. F. *The German African Empire*. London, 1916.
Clifford, Sir Hugh. *German Colonies*. London, 1918.
Cramer, Ada. *Weiss oder Schwartz*. Berlin, 1903.
Fabri, F. *Fünf Jahre Deutsche Kolonialpolitik*. Berlin, 1889.
Fischer, Adolph. *Menschen und Tiere in Deutsch Südwest*. Berlin, 1889.
Hamilton, L. *Colonial Education in Germany, in the United Empire*. London, 1911.
Henderson, W. O. *Studies in German Colonial History*. London, 1962.
Irle, Hedwig. *Wie Ich die Hereo lieben lernte*. Gütersloh, 1909.
Jacob, E. G. *Deutsche Kolonialpolitik*, n.d.
Kriegsgeschichtliche Abteilung des Grossen Generalstabes. *Die Kämpfe der Deutschen Truppen in Südwestafrika*. Berlin, 1906.
Langsdorff, W. von. *Deutsche Flagge über Sand und Palmen* (1936). [Footnote continued.]

Leutwein, T. von. *Kämpfe der Kaiserlichen Schutztruppen in Deutsch Südwestafrika*. Berlin, 1899.

Loth, Heinrich. *Die Christliche Mission in Südwestafrika*. Berlin, 1963.

Palgrave, W. C. *Report on his Mission to Damara and Great Namaqualand*. Cape Town, 1877.

St. Lys, Odette. *From a Vanished German Colony,* n.d.

Schoen, W. von. *Deutschlands Kolonialweg*. Berlin, n.d.

Townsend M. *Origins of Modern German Colonization*. New York, 1921.

The Role of the COPEI Party
in Venezuelan Politics

DONA BARON

Venezuela has become a cynosure of those who seek to vindicate the
feasibility of democratic revolution in Latin America. The success of
such a revolution would seem to be both contingent upon and indicated by the growth and development of modern and democratically
responsible political parties as essential organisms in the fundamental
processes of social integration. John D. Martz, a student of Venezuelan
politics, defines a modern political party as:

. . . a group of politically oriented individuals possessing a definite common ideology, permanent organizational structure, popular appeal on a
national basis, existence of at least a decade's duration, and an inner
justification based on participation in national government or at least a
reasonable prospect of achieving power in the foreseeable future.[1]

In the Venezuelan context, such a definition is suitable not only to
the once predominant Acción Democrática but also, perhaps as importantly, to the Partido Social Cristiano COPEI (Comité por Organización Politica y Electoral Independiente). It can be affirmed
that COPEI's loyal participation in Rómulo Betancourt's coalition
from 1959 to 1964 was crucial in the accomplishments of that Government. Furthermore, it can be argued that COPEI is the ascendant
political force in Venezuela today, and that both its activities and the
partisan reactions they precipitate are critical to the future of democracy in that nation.

The antecedents of Venezuela's party system are of recent origin.
Throughout the nineteenth century, Venezuela was the scene of an-
archy and tyranny. Autocratic *caudillos* functioned in the context of
a highly stratified social structure and a prevalent political ignorance

[1] John D. Martz, *Acción Democrática: The Evolution of a Modern Political
Party* (Unpublished doctoral dissertation, Chapel Hill, 1963), pp. 4–5.

of the masses. By the time of his death in 1935, the crafty and ruthless Juan Vicente Gómez had subdued local *caudillos* and established the authority of centralized government. Furthermore, the exploitation of petroleum, encouraged by the liberal oil law of 1920, had initiated irreversible economic and social changes.

A nascent liberal movement began with student demonstrations of the "Generation of '28." Those student leaders included such reformers as Rómulo Betancourt, Carlos D'Ascoli, and Rául Leoni, who continued their activities as anti-Government activists in the Organización Revolucionario Venezolana Electoral (ORVE), founded in 1936 and regrouped in the Partido Democrático Nacional (PDN). With the beginning of more liberal government under López Contreras, the rudimentary and previously clandestine petroleum unions were allowed legal activity. The extension of PDN organization into the union movement "represented the first effective attempt at 'grass roots' organization by a Venezuelan political party." [2]

After years of clandestine activity, the PDN gained legal status as Acción Democrática (AD) in 1941. AD opposed the Government principally because of its resistance to political and social reform, its restrictive labor control, and its shortsighted petroleum policy. Eager to institute its program of reform and realizing that incumbents did not lose elections in Venezuela, AD joined with a group of disgruntled young army officers in an alliance which overthrew the Medina Administration by force on October 18, 1945. Although interpretations vary as to which component of the insurgents initiated the coup, AD dominated the provisional governing junta and undertook a sweeping program of reform. In addition to the new atmosphere of political freedom, the most immediately significant political reforms were the introduction of universal suffrage for all Venezuelans over the age of eighteen and the direct election of the President.

It was at this juncture, on January 13, 1946, that the Comité por Organización Política y Electoral Independiente opened headquarters in Caracas and San Felipe. The antecedents of the electoral organization that was soon to be known as COPEI can also be traced back into the 1930s. Rafael Caldera represented Venezuela at the International Congress of Catholic Youth held in Rome in 1934. The theme of that conference was Christian Democratic Action, and the Latin Amer-

[2] Foreign Areas Studies Division, Special Operations Research Office, American University, *U.S. Army Area Handbook for Venezuela* (Washington, D.C., U.S. Government Printing Office, 1964), p. 235.

icans in attendance were encouraged to attempt the founding of such movements in their respective countries. Caldera was unable, however, to bring such an attempt to fruition in Venezuela in 1936.[3]

Caldera was a member of the Federación Estudiantil Venezolana (FEV) in 1936, when there was a split over the issue of the expulsion of Jesuits. Along with Pedro José Lara Peña, Lorenzo Fernández, Victor Giménez Landínez, and others, Caldera founded an opposition, firmly Catholic, student organization—the Unión Nacional Estudiantil (UNE). Besides differing with the FEV over religious issues, the UNE was more conservative in its political views, generally supporting López Contreras, from whom they hoped to see leadership toward political and social rectifications.[4]

After graduation, this group of Catholic youths founded Acción Nacional, another rather rudimentary political organism. In 1941 Caldera was elected Deputy to Congress from Yaracuy, and Pedro José Lara Peña also became a Deputy. Three other members were elected to the Caracas Municipal Council. After the coup of 1945, Caldera, who had been teaching sociology at Universidad Central, was named Solicitor General by the Provisional Government while the new political environment encouraged Caldera's colleagues to form the COPEI in opposition to AD.

Since its official origin in January 1946, COPEI's history has unfolded in four phases: 1) From 1946 to 1948, the inchoate organization waged an uneven political battle against AD. 2) From 1948 to 1958, it went through the period of repression under the Pérez Jiménez dictatorship. 3) From 1958 to 1964, COPEI participated in the Government coalition and truly established the requisites of a modern political party. 4) The period since 1964, unlike the previous phases of COPEI's evolution, does not represent basic organizational change as much as the adoption of a new political strategy—"autonomy of action" vis-à-vis the Government.

The First Phase

The period from 1945 to 1948 was one of intense and continuous political activity. Three separate elections were held: a National Constituent Assembly was chosen in October 1946; Presidential and

[3] Manuel Vicente Magallanes, *Partidos Políticos Venezolanos* (Caracas, 1959), p. 148.
[4] Martz, *Acción Democrática,* p. 113.

Congressional elections were held in December 1947; and municipal elections took place in May 1948. In all those elections AD won overwhelmingly, capturing from 70 to 78 percent of the votes, while COPEI was the second largest party, gaining from 13.2 to 22.4 percent in the various contests. The moderate reformist Unión Republican Democrática (URD) and the Partido Communista Venezolano (PCV) were the most significant of the remaining thirteen legal electoral organizations; however, "COPEI was AD's most bitter critic." [5]

In April 1946 Caldera resigned from the Government in order, in his words, "to make more resolute opposition to the revolutionary government." [6] While supporting the liberal ideals of the October revolution, COPEI attacked AD for its alleged attempts to establish an officialist party. The COPEI Manifesto of September 1946 emphasized political freedoms, and more pointedly criticized the use of labor unions as a partisan tool.[7] Although the Manifesto reads as a progressive document advocating a wide range of social welfare measures, agrarian reform, and state economic intervention, it also contains moderating statements which give the impression that the organization's program was rather a weak reflection of established AD doctrine. As COPEI's presidential candidate, Caldera continued to advocate democratic reform and social justice, but he was not totally master of his own house. As Caldera admits, the regional committees originally attracted extreme conservatives.[8] The party's strongest electoral support came from the Andean states of Táchira, Mérida, and Trujillo— traditionally the most Catholic and conservative in the land. At its national convention in 1948, retaining the name COPEI, the temporary aggregation of regional electoral committees officially became a permanent political party.

With Rómulo Gallegos as President and firmly in control of Congress, the AD Government apparently had a popular mandate to continue its program of reform. However, AD's political exclusivism and the haste and recklessness with which it proceeded increasingly alienated both conservative elites and the more moderate middle class. More critically, the Army came to suspect that AD intended to destroy its privileged status.[9] In mid-November, the young Army officers issued

[5] *Ibid.*, p. 112.   [6] Rafael Caldera, quoted in Magallanes, p. 153.

[7] Manifesto de COPEI, 1946, in *Documentos que Hicieron Historia* (Caracas, 1962), pp. 385–402.

[8] Caldera, quoted in *De Ce* (Santiago de Chile,) Febrero–Marzo 1965, p. 4.

[9] Edwin Lieuwen, *Venezuela* (New York, Oxford University Press, 1961), p. 88.

an ultimatum demanding Betancourt's exile and greater participation of both the military and COPEI in a new Government coalition. Gallegos refused, and Venezuela's first popular government was quickly superseded by a military junta. AD was dissolved and its leaders exiled.

The Second Phase

The Junta Militar, which ruled until 1952, ostensibly maintained the legality of COPEI, URD, and the "Black Communist" Partido Revolucionario Proletario. Immediately after the coup, Caldera communicated that COPEI, despite its acrimonious relations with AD, had had no part in the *golpe* and would not claim participation in its Government. Nonetheless, two Copeyanos, José Ramón Barros Mora and Hilarion López, accepted state governorships. The Junta headed by Delgado Chalbaud continued some of the programs begun by the AD regime, and until the Chalbaud assassination in 1950 COPEI more or less collaborated with the regime. Even during this period, however, the party suffered harassment. Its organ, *El Gráfico,* was closed several times and in 1949 its editor was imprisoned.[10]

After the demise of Chalbaud, the regime's repressive nature became more apparent and COPEI issued public protests against its transgressions. When the regime called for election of a constituent assembly in 1952, both COPEI and URD after much hesitation decided to participate. In September COPEI declared that although it was skeptical about the outcome of the elections, it felt "morally compelled to seek delegates in order to condemn anticipated abuses of democracy by government forces." [11] Despite the restrictions imposed during the campaign, both COPEI and URD continued to criticize Government manipulation of electoral procedures, infringements of political guarantees, and other instances of violence and repression.

Because of the obviousness of the electoral fraud which had given victory to the Government's Frente Electoral Independiente (FEI), both parties officially declined to participate in the assembly. In order to obtain the appearance of legitimacy, the Government persuaded some opposition elements to participate. The eight Copeyanos who did so had been lower alternates on the party slates, were immediately

[10] Magallanes, p. 156.
[11] Leo B. Lott, "The 1952 Venezuelan Elections," *Western Political Quarterly,* X, No. 3 (Sept. 1957), p. 545.

expelled from COPEI, and, moreover, their efforts to effect any changes at the assembly were completely unsuccessful.[12]

Under Pérez Jiménez, all overt political opposition was subjected to systematic efforts aimed at its eradication. Thus, like AD and URD, COPEI organized an underground resistance movement and continued its activities in clandestinity. Caldera himself was imprisoned at times and ordered to exile as the Pérez Jiménez regime was crumbling in January 1958. By 1956, AD had adopted the policy of full and active cooperation with all other parties. Both in exile and underground there was implemented a unified movement which disavowed partisan differences in the interest of securing the unity required for overthrow of repressive dictatorial rule. Representatives of AD, COPEI, URD, and the Communists united in the *Junta Patriótica,* which was instrumental in the revolution of January 1958.

The Third Phase Begins

Referring to a group of Latin American dictators that included Pérez Jiménez, Tad Szulc speculates:

They may even have rendered a profound service to their nations: because they negated freedom and democracy they stimulated it in the long run, and they taught their people what may be an unforgettable lesson—that democratic unity, though it calls for a selflessness and reasonableness that still are shockingly new to Latin American politicians, is infinitely preferable to dictatorial oppression.[13]

Venezuela's turbulent political history subsequent to the fall of Pérez Jiménez can be viewed as a manifestation of the tensions inherent in thoroughgoing social revolution and in the simultaneously held objectives of 1) maintaining political unity seen as requisite to secure a jeopardized nascent democracy, and 2) partisan differentiation seen as necessary for political gain. Immediately upon the fall of Pérez Jiménez, all political leaders voiced the primacy of the former goal. Perhaps of all Venezuelan political parties, COPEI has most consistently been sensitive to the risks of excessive partisanship, and perhaps because of self-imposed restraints that party will in the long run gain the greater partisan rewards. At any rate, its spirit of generally conscientious cooperation during the third phase of its growth not only benefited COPEI as a political organization, but also contributed,

[12] Lott, p. 555.
[13] Tad Szulc, *Twilight of the Tyrants* (New York, Holt, 1959), p. 22.

in a manner the importance of which cannot be overstated, to the establishing of a democratic regime in Venezuela.

The most important task of the provisional Junta which succeeded Pérez Jiménez was to prepare for and conduct the elections that were to found a democratic regime. The Junta was headed by Admiral Wolfgang Larrazábal, and composed of representatives of the military and politically independent civilians. The parties had agreed among themselves not to participate, in order to avoid partisan conflicts over the distribution of offices.

The period prior to the elections held in December 1958 was one of intense party activity, both in terms of interactions of elites of the several parties and at the level of intraparty organizational growth. Poignantly aware that lack of civilian political unity in the face of opportunist elements in the armed forces was a primary cause of the coup of 1948, and aware that a break in their recently established collaboration could provide the opportunity for a military coup on the pretext of preventing partisan strife, leaders of AD, COPEI, and URD anxiously sought for means to maintain some sort of political truce. A few days after the January revolution, exiled leaders of the three parties formed the Venezuelan Civilian Front, pledged to inter-party cooperation. By common consent, the Communists had been dropped from these discussions. Despite the underlying desire for cooperation, there was great difficulty in translating the spirit of national unity into a viable concrete form. As Robert J. Alexander comments, "the stumbling block was finding a suitable person to be joint candidate of all the parties, since it was early agreed that each party would run its own lists of candidates for other posts." [14] Negotiations continued for months. In April the consensus was that if a coalition candidate were selected and if such a candidate were a party man, that candidate would be Caldera.[15]

The need to reach an accord was made more salient by the two serious attempts to overthrow the provisional regime. Of the mobilizations against the Government which occurred in July and September in garrisons in and around Caracas, Alexander observes:

These attempted coups d'état came within an ace of success. Probably the decisive factor in preventing their success was the solidarity of the civilian population behind the government.[16]

[14] Robert J. Alexander, *The Venezuelan Democratic Revolution* (New Brunswick, Rutgers University Press, 1964), p. 40.
[15] *Hispanic American Report*, XI (April 1958, Stanford University Press).
[16] Alexander, p. 52.

While civilian support could be interpreted to mean that party elites had sufficient latitude to indulge in playing politics, that such practice could be hazardous should also have been indicated by the proposal of dockworkers to call a general strike by the end of September if political bickering continued.[17] Finally, with only seven days left for presidential candidates to register, representatives of AD, COPEI, and URD signed the Pact of Punto Fijo on October 31.

The expressed purpose of the Pact of Punto Fijo was "to guarantee the political truce without prejudice to the organizational autonomy and ideological character" of each party. Its basic principles were: defense of constitutionality and formation of a government in accord with electoral results, formation of a government of national unity to be headed by the successful candidate of an individual party but with an administration including representatives of all three parties. The pact included exhortations to a positive campaign avoiding divisive interparty strife, and went on to provide for formation of a *Comisión Inter-partidista de Unidad,* with representatives of all three parties to assure fulfillment of the principles of the accord.[18]

The official campaign lasted only one month. Betancourt was AD's nominee, while Larrazábal, the candidate of URD, was also endorsed by the Communists. COPEI named Caldera, who also received the support of two small parties—the Partido Socialista de Trabajadores and the Integración Republicana. While Larrazábal confined his campaign mostly to the central part of the country, Betancourt and Caldera toured throughout the land.

Betancourt won easily with 49.2 percent of the vote, while Larrazábal, his strong personal appeal especially manifest in the Caracas area, gained 34.6 percent. Caldera came in a poor third with 16.2 percent. COPEI was also third in congressional strength, with 6 of 51 senators and 19 of 133 deputies.[19] Betancourt's victory in spite of Larrazábal's personal popularity tends to justify the theory, adhered to both by AD and COPEI, that permanent party organization and support at the grass roots level are the keys to electoral strength. Yet Copeyanos explain Caldera's weak showing by describing the '58 contest as a "negative election," i.e., voters voted against Betancourt by voting for Larrazábal and vice versa, thus Caldera is seen to have

---

[17] *Hispanic American Report,* XI (Sept. 1958).

[18] Pacto de "Punto Fijo," in *Documentos que Hicieron Historia,* pp. 443–49.

[19] Institute for the Comparative Study of Political Systems (ICOPS), *The Venezuelan Elections of December 1, 1963,* Part III (Washington, D.C., 1964), pp. 11, 17.

lost votes in the double negation.[20] This theory seems rather tenuous, since one could have hypothesized that Caldera, supported by Catholics and conservatives who would have opposed Larrazábal because of his acceptance of Communist support, would gain if liberal votes were detracted from Betancourt and given to Larrazábal. Such personalist theorizing notwithstanding, COPEI has acted in a manner that would suggest that organizational and ideological factors are the primary requisites of electoral success. COPEI behaves institutionally as if Betancourt's victory in 1958 would have to be attributed essentially to AD's organizational superiority and greater programmatic appeal at that time. At any rate, COPEI's record in the Congressional elections amply demonstrated that in 1958 it had not yet attained broad national electoral strength. COPEI's congressmen came from only seven of the twenty-three states and territories, while its vote-getting power was heavily centered in the Andes.

COPEI IDEOLOGY AND PROGRAMMATIC PRINCIPLES

In order to comprehend COPEI's governmental role since 1958, it is necessary to examine the ideological and programmatic bases of the party. The fundamental orientation of COPEI in these realms was clearly delineated in the period of reconstruction that began with the resumption of overt political activity in 1958.

In 1958 COPEI was renamed Partido Social Cristiano COPEI, and "Caldera found himself increasingly free to shape the party along the lines of Christian Democratic reformism." [21] As a Christian Democratic party, COPEI is free to formulate its program around specifically Venezuelan problems, while at the same time it is part of an international ideological movement which can provide cohesiveness in terms of basic objectives and approaches. In Latin America, the positive character of the Christian Democratic movement is emphasized. Christian Democrats are striving to achieve a new era, new social conditions based on Christian values and concepts of Christianity. Christian Democratic parties are nonconfessional; to belong to the movement it is sufficient to ascribe to its ideals. Christian Democracy asserts the dignity of man, and stresses self-fulfillment in freedom and liberty within justice in a pluralist society. In addition to such rather abstract tenets, Christian Democracy emphasizes the need to put economic resources and the powers of the state to the service of man.

[20] *Boletín Informativo Demócrata Cristiano* (New York), Nov. 1962, p. 6.
[21] ICOPS, *Venezuelan Elections,* Part I, p. 9. (Martz essay.)

Economic development is seen as a means of achieving liberty and spreading social welfare. At the same time, democratic methods are seen as the most appropriate means of attaining the necessary fundamental reforms, and the role of political parties is seen to be crucial for the adaptations of social change.

In translating the Christian Democratic theses into party doctrine, COPEI arrives at a reformist program quite similar to that of AD or URD. In 1958 as in 1963, three basic themes can be found in all areas of the programs of the three parties: the capital importance of freedom and democratic government, advocacy of state economic planning and intervention where necessary, and state responsibility for the amelioration of conditions for all segments of Venezuelan society. COPEI's principles as enunciated in 1958 could be distinguished from those of AD by their emphasis on solidarity and harmony of social groups as opposed to AD's vaguely Marxist orientation. If AD's doctrine is elaborated more in terms of class and material needs, COPEI more often invokes spiritual motivations and eulogizes the family as the primary element of society. However, such nuances of difference as can be found seem tangential when compared to the fundamental consensus in basic commitment to democratic social revolution.

In terms of party program, since 1958 the three major parties have advocated agrarian reform, economic nationalism—particularly with regard to the petroleum industry—the use of resources drawn from the oil industry to develop other sectors of the Venezuelan economy, and the channeling of the land's basic wealth so as to benefit the majority of its people. They have endorsed social security, progressive labor legislation, state obligation to improve health and education. And, of course, there has been agreement on the need for greater administrative efficiency and, in the sphere of international relations, concurrence on the need for peace, sovereignty, and solidarity with other peace-loving states.

There were naturally some discrepancies between the parties on aspects of policies and their implementation. COPEI perhaps more strenuously emphasized the role of private enterprise, for example. Concerning matters of religion, COPEI specifically demanded a bilateral arrangement between Church and state to replace the 1824 Law of Ecclesiastical Patronage which gave the state, in theory, powers of appointment of Church hierarchy. On the other hand, AD endorsed freedom of religion, and took cognizance of Venezuela's fundamentally Catholic population and the antiquated nature of the legal provisions for Church-state relations.

In sum, in 1958, although there were variations in ideological perspectives and nuances of policy, COPEI joined with the other major parties in a fundamental consensus concerning the nature of Venezuela's vital problems, and the essential measures necessary to resolve them.

ON COALITION GOVERNMENT IN THE
VENEZUELAN CONTEXT

In accordance with the principles of the Pact of Punto Fijo, on February 13, 1959 President Betancourt announced selection of a cabinet composed so that all three major parties were represented. Of the fourteen appointments, there were two ministers from AD, three each from COPEI and URD, and the remainder were political independents. The coalition thus included representatives of parties which had been supported by 94 percent of the Venezuelan electorate. Inasmuch as those parties had achieved a basic consensus concerning their objectives, the success of the coalition would depend upon control of partisan frictions more than upon compromise of political principles. However, the implications of partisan conflict were to be magnified, since, to use David Easton's terminology, the coalition of 1959 had in effect identified government and regime in order to promote the legitimacy of the latter.[22] Yet, such an identification could easily have had the opposite effect, since it became more difficult to discredit the government without discrediting or in fact impeding development of the regime.

Schematically, the problems confronting the nascent democratic regime in Venezuela can be viewed in the context of that too familiar pattern—a vicious circle. An objective of the revolution is to establish the legitimacy of democratic procedures as the format of a viable political regime. And, the legitimacy of democratic procedural norms is linked fundamentally to their ability to promote the economic and social restructuring necessary (if not sufficient) for development of an integrated political culture in which democratic institutions can function meaningfully. However, as new groups are initiated into the political processes, they tend to be more fundamentally concerned with the output functions of government in concrete socioeconomic terms than they are sensitive to the complexities and difficulties of formulating and implementing effective policies. Thus the democratic revolutionary government must initiate and administer programs which

[22] David Easton, "An Approach to the Analysis of Political Systems," *World Politics,* IX, No. 3 (April 1957), pp. 383–400.

accord with the proclaimed economic and social goals of the revolution—and the results of those programs must be evident before the confidence implied procedurally by an electoral mandate can evaporate. This is not to say that specific objectives can or must be realized within a certain limited period, but it is to say that accomplishments are necessary in order that the electorate may be convinced of both the government's commitment and the regime's efficacy.

If confidence in the government dissipates, the inherent appeal of alternative extremist approaches can increase—the legitimacy not only of the government but of the regime itself may be challenged. Moreover, extremist elements in the society, wishing to impugn the legitimacy of the democratic revolutionary government, aim at fomenting political instability so that the regime will appear increasingly inadequate and iniquitous. But in order to achieve ambitious programs of socioeconomic development, a government requires the political stability conducive to the implementation of coherent programs and necessary to provide confidence for economic investment. Thus, insofar as intentionally democratic partisanship impedes the formulation and execution of effective policies, it tends to vitiate promotion of the democratically stable environment within which such partisan competition could be enjoyed without detriment to the legitimacy of the democratic regime itself. While partisan differentiation and the opportunities to criticize and to present alternatives are the *sine qua non* of democracy, in the milieu of an immature democracy restraint is both crucial and difficult to maintain. Inadvertently, too zealous democratic partisanship can create the conditions in which extremism might thrive.

Threats to the democratic regime in Venezuela have emanated not only from overt attacks on the regime—initially from the right, then increasingly from the left—but also from the risks latent in partisan conflict. Such conflicts have jeopardized not only the Government in question but the perpetuation of the regime itself.

In 1958, representatives of the major parties had demonstrated awareness that manifest threats to the democratic regime implied the need for a democratic solidarity in Government. Since that time there have been varying degrees of sensitivity to the potential dangers of partisanship in a society in the throes of social revolution. While hardly immune to criticism, COPEI seems to have exercised the greatest amount of self-discipline in limiting its partisan activities in such a manner as not to imperil the legitimacy of the democratic regime. A continuation of Venezuela's social revolution in a political context in which government and regime can safely cease to be identified would represent further advancement of the democratic revolution.

COPEI's third phase of development includes participation in the governing coalition, and that participation must be viewed in the light of COPEI's perception of its role in the democratic revolution. According to the party ideology, COPEI's fundamental commitment is to the establishment of a progressive democratic regime. Dr. Valmore Acevedo, former COPEI governor of Táchira, states that when the party's primary concern becomes the mere winning of votes it will have lost its *raison d'être*. "COPEI's deepest concern is with the good of Venezuela." [23] Thus, especially during its third phase, COPEI was generally willing to risk the sacrifice of short-run partisan gains in the interest of the democratic revolution. Such a position is not, of course, totally altruistic in terms of the party's future, for COPEI sees itself as having a stake in the regime. If the regime can endure, COPEI's leaders feel that by their organizational efforts and programmatic appeal they can gain control of the Government in subsequent elections. Such would be the expected disposition of a political party in a modern competitive democracy, but the novelty of such a philosophy in Latin America suggests that it deserves to be underscored. It is in this philosophical context that COPEI's positive and negative contributions to the functioning of the coalition and the effects of Government participation on the party's growth can be examined.

THE FUNCTIONING OF THE BETANCOURT GOVERNMENT

The magnitude of the undertakings of the Betancourt Government was enormous. The coalition was confronted by economic, social, and political problems that had accumulated or had been aggravated during a century and a half of more or less irresponsible rule by military dictatorships. Although petroleum had given Venezuela a vital source of income, at the same time it had been allowed to distort the entire economy. An agrarian nation, Venezuela had become an importer of foodstuffs. There were also the "usual" problems of economic and social underdevelopment—inadequate educational facilities, inadequate housing and health facilities, urban unemployment, rural underemployment, etc., combined with an explosive population growth rate which had risen to over 3.9 percent a year in the decade from 1950 to 1961. In addition, the coalition was confronted with a short-term

[23] Dr. Valmore Acevedo, interview, March 27, 1965.

economic crisis which had resulted from Pérez Jiménez' mismanagement, curtailment of the oil industry due to international factors, a collapse of the construction industry, and flight of capital which came with the end of the dictatorship.

Betancourt's Government undertook extensive programs in agrarian reform, economic diversification, and industrialization. Programs were adopted to improve education, while other measures were aimed at exerting greater national control and domestic participation in the oil industry and gaining better return from the exploitation of oil in terms of the nation as a whole. In sum, the Betancourt Government was compelled to initiate development programs for practically all aspects of Venezuela's economic and social life. In addition, it had to devise strategies and general policies conducive to the formation of an apolitical military institution and to the establishment of the bases of political stability.

In the original Betancourt Government, Copeyanos held three key cabinet posts: Victor Giménez Landínez was Minister of Agriculture, Andres Aguilar was Minister of Justice, and Lorenzo Fernández was Minister of Development. While Caldera was President of the Chamber of Deputies from 1959 to 1962, other Copeyanos held important positions in the Administration at national and regional levels. The allocation of posts was a natural source of tension between members of the coalition. Despite private bickering over patronage, in public COPEI would only go about as far as to "suggest revision in the distribution of political posts," while at the same time stressing that it "steadfastly ratified its support of unity government." [24] The contrasting attitude of URD was apparent earlier than October 1959, when it was threatening to withdraw from the coalition if readjustments were not made. At that time the drive in favor of cooperative government was still greater than partisan dissatisfaction; however, questions of patronage and of partisan tactics were important in subsequent ruptures affecting the coalition.

Prior to its withdrawal from the coalition in November 1960, the URD provoked frequent cabinet crises, all of which, according to Alexander, were not brought to the public notice.[25] The departure of URD from the Government suggests differences in the ideological commitment and organizational cohesiveness of the three parties. A disposition toward opportunistic tactics and the strength of the extremist elements within URD led that party more and more to favor radical causes. When extreme provocation led to the suspension of certain constitutional guarantees, Betancourt, rather than radical agitators and terrorists, was the target of URD criticism. At the OAS conference of September 1960, Foreign Minister Arcaya, expressing a URD position contrary to that of the Government as a whole, refused to support a resolution censuring Cuba. Interparty negotiations led to Arcaya's resignation, and his replacement, Marcos Falcón Briceño, voiced the Government view at the conference. However, attempts to avert imminent rupture were of little avail. While Betancourt maintained that URD cooperation was still to be welcomed, URD's attacks became vehement and unrelenting. They found it difficult to play the role of a "loyal opposition."

In the cabinet reorganization subsequent to the URD separation, URD members were replaced by independents; nonetheless, the significance of COPEI's continued participation had evidently been increased.

As President of the unity Government, Betancourt had formally renounced his AD party obligations. The cooperation and support which COPEI lent to Betancourt was to become more vital as splits within the AD party itself weakened the backing Betancourt could expect from elements which had supported his election. A conflict of generations and a related divergence of attitudes on radicalism led to the first AD intraparty cleavage in 1960. Those who quit or were expelled from AD at that time formed the Movimiento de la Izquierda Revolucionaria (MIR), and as violent opponents of the Government adopted strategy that became indistinguishable from that of the Communists.

A later, more serious split within AD ranks is closely related to COPEI's role in the Government. According to most observers, the ARS faction of AD did not differ significantly with Betancourt and the AD "Old Guard" on matters of principle. While personal ambitions were involved, ARS criticized the "Old Guard" in terms of tactics; ostensibly they felt that the Government reform program was not progressing rapidly enough and "they blamed this in large part on the presence of the COPEI party in the coalition." [26] While Betancourt attempted to conciliate both factions, he ultimately supported the "Old Guard" as the true representatives of AD. The Grupo ARS went into opposition in 1962, taking four AD senators and 22 AD deputies. In the Senate, the Government still enjoyed a 29 to 22 majority; how-

[26] Alexander, p. 81. The anti-AD press gave the faction its name from Publicidad ARS, whose slogan was "Let us do your thinking for you."

ever, it did not retain a majority in the Chamber. In March 1962 Caldera was deposed, and Arsista Manuel Vicente Ledezma became President of the Chamber. Although the Arsista opposition also went to opportunistic extremes in its criticisms, Government loss of assured congressional support was mitigated by the fact that most of the basic reform legislation had been passed prior to 1962.[27]

Although attention had already turned to the elections of 1963, in mid-1962 Betancourt spoke of COPEI in this manner: "I wish to say, now that I am on the eve of leaving Miraflores, that the men of COPEI merit the respect of this country, because they are loyal to the pledged word and to their given commitment." [28]

In contrast to both AD and URD, COPEI was able generally to keep its party united behind its position of support for Betancourt's Government. There were minor crises from time to time, often at the state level, especially in the COPEI strongholds of Táchira and Mérida where disagreements largely concerned questions of patronage. There have also been elements within COPEI ranks who have viewed cooperation with AD with varying degrees of enthusiasm. Particularly at the outset, it was feared that association with a unity government would lead to COPEI's extinction as an independent political force. Since dissension concerning continued participation in the coalition never precipitated a major cleavage, COPEI leadership was able to secure and maintain generalized party support for Government policies.

As chief of state in a governmental structure disposed toward a strong executive power, Betancourt sought to initiate policies in terms of the AD party program and principles. Within the context of an AD–COPEI general consensus on basic issues, the parties were able to compromise divergences in the formulation of Government policies. Thus COPEI usually could make concessions without detriment to its fundamental principles. Furthermore, given a mutual perception of the acute need to undertake basic reform measures, disagreements over peripheral issues could be postponed, and in some cases were actually more or less irrelevant. For example, in view of the need for a massive education program, AD could not afford to spend energy opposing private education, while if COPEI supports the incorporation

[27] Martz, *Acción Democrática,* p. 173.
[28] Rómulo Betancourt, *Tres Años de Gobierno Democrático, 1959–1962* (Caracas, Imprenta Nacional, 1962), Vol. III, p. 195.

of religious instruction in all schools, the shortage of personnel would have made such discussion at that time purely academic.[29]

As a spokesman for COPEI, Caldera with apparent frankness indicates that the party was conscious of discrepancies between its criteria for specific policies and those of AD. A typical Caldera exposition would point out instances where AD and COPEI views had coincided and where COPEI had recognized the right of the President's views to prevail. In taking responsibility for Government policies, Copeyanos would also indicate that "on many occasions our criteria came to orient the Government." [30] For example, COPEI objections to the currency devaluation proposed by Finance Minister Mayobre led to his resignation in November 1960. When his successor, Carillo Batalla, proposed a policy of exchange controls, COPEI had to accept it, however reluctantly.

On occasion, COPEI attempted legislative initiative distinctly identified with the party itself. Because Christian Democratic doctrine stresses the role of the family as the basic unit of society and consequently relates many aspects of the problems of juvenile delinquency and youthful violence to weaknesses in the family situation, COPEI proposed a Family Subsidy Bill. According to the proposal, each mother would receive a monthly subsidy for each child under the age of fourteen who was in school. The bill was passed in the Chamber, but not approved in the Senate, for "fiscal reasons." [31]

Agrarian reform was the most important plank in Betancourt's platform of 1958, yet COPEI played a responsible role in the elaboration of the Agrarian Reform Bill. Although Copeyano Giménez Landínez was Minister of Agriculture, COPEI's views on certain aspects of the agrarian legislation did not prevail. COPEI would have desired greater emphasis on colonization of uncultivated lands and more protection for the owner of large *productive* farms.[32] Nevertheless, COPEI did not, because of objections to particular facets of the proposal, attempt to obstruct its passing into legislation. Before Congress and in public, Copeyanos defended the Government agrarian policy and as members of the Government accepted responsibility for it—reserving the right to criticize more pointedly what they perceived as shortcomings against which they had forewarned.

[29] Dr. Valmore Acevedo, interview, March 27, 1965.
[30] Caldera, "Frente a la Prensa," television speech in *COPEI,* May 17, 1963, p. 15.
[31] *Ibid.,* p. 11.   [32] *Ibid.,* p. 15.

COPEI's role in relation to the agrarian reform might be taken as typical: basic support of an objective of the chief executive, an attempt to modify policy in terms of COPEI criteria, ratification of a policy either found generally acceptable on its merits or because concession was seen as necessary to progress of the regime and to political stability, and support for the policy tempered with criticism aimed at its future amelioration and as evidence of COPEI party differentiation.

In cases of acts of presidential discretion or policies more directly identified with Betancourt, COPEI continued its basic support. COPEI strategy would imply more evident endorsement of actions with which it wished to identify, and restraint of criticism in other instances. For example, while seeing them as regrettable, COPEI supported, as inevitable, security measures restricting extremist activity, and accused the "so-called democratic opposition" of behaving opportunistically in "extending to extremist forces an unjustified political protection they would not otherwise have had." [33] Although COPEI policy vacillated on specific controversial Government actions relative to terrorist activities, civil liberties, and parliamentary immunities, it never sought to discredit the Government by unrestrained censure, and in fact supported Betancourt under most trying circumstances.

In sum, during its third phase, COPEI played the role of loyal supporter of the democratic regime and its agent, the Betancourt coalition, of which it became an integral part. Not only did the party make vital contributions to the stability and progress of the Government, but it gained experience in the requirements and practical limitations of Government responsibility. In addition, COPEI benefited from its participation in terms of patronage. Such patronage advantages came not only in the form of positions in Government administration, but also in terms of increased opportunities to participate, for example, in the Venezuelan labor movement.

COPEI'S ORGANIZATIONAL GROWTH

COPEI's organizational development since it entered its third phase in 1958 is indicative of the strategy it was to follow in the 1963 elections and the role it was to assume on the parliamentary level during its fourth or most recent period. The 1958 elections had shown that COPEI was not yet truly a national political force, since its electoral

[33] *Ibid.,* p. 10.

strength had been more or less confined to the Andean region. Since 1958, COPEI has been working intensely to build a national organization with broad-based appeal.

The construction of a strong party apparatus is seen as a key to electoral success. According to the party statutes of 1961, COPEI is structurally quite similar to AD and URD, i.e., a regionally decentralized mass membership organization, governed by principles of internal democracy. There are four principal national organs. In theory the National Convention is the sovereign body. Composed of representatives of regional and "functional" or auxiliary organizations, it meets annually, approves the party program, electoral platform, and candidates for national elections, selects the presidential candidate, and establishes the "general lines of the movement." It also elects the National Committee, which is the highest executive authority of the party, and in fact its most powerful organ. Composed of the party president, two vice presidents, the secretary general, and eleven voting members, it meets regularly and fundamentally coordinates and controls the movement. The National Directory includes the members of the National Committee as well as delegates from regional and functional organizations. It "meets as its ends require . . . to discharge functions delegated by the National Convention, analyze problems, and fix policy lines." The fourth national organ is the Disciplinary Tribunal. These four bodies are paralleled on the regional level by structures which are in turn linked to party base organs in municipalities and local functional groups—COPEI youth, labor, and women's groups.[34]

While this structure serves to increase COPEI's strength on a national basis, it does not adequately indicate COPEI's present tactical orientation. COPEI is increasingly stressing the role of the ideologically committed, organizationally instructed, middle level activist. According to Dr. Acevedo, while COPEI is of course vitally concerned with cultivating grass roots support, it does not see such support as necessarily commensurate with massive direct party affiliation.[35] Nevertheless it could be noted that in 1963 COPEI's estimated party membership was 500,000, while that of AD was 900,000, and these figures rather closely parallel the party presidential electoral totals of 588,372 and 957,699, respectively.[36] In any case, COPEI is currently reorganiz-

[34] COPEI, *Estatutos*, 1961.   [35] Dr. Acevedo, interviews.
[36] ICOPS, *Venezuelan Elections*, Part III, p. 8.

ing its structure in a manner which places greater emphasis on various forms of functional specialization at all levels.

COPEI adhesion to the international Christian Democratic movement has been beneficial to the party in terms of the training of middle level activists. Since October 1962, the Christian Democratic movement has established in Caracas the Institutio de Formación Democrática Cristiana (IFEDEC). The aims of IFEDEC are to qualify middle level party leaders, to create a sensitivity to the Latin American focus of Christian Democratic problems, and to give an awareness of the tasks of party organization.[37] IFEDEC gives series of courses which last about one month each and seem to be on a reasonably sophisticated level. For each series about thirty students are selected from diverse social categories and fields of action. IFEDEC could prove to be invaluable in terms of leadership recruitment and organizational integration, while its graduates could be most effective instruments of party recruitment and mass political socialization.

COPEI AND THE BASES OF VENEZUELAN POLITICAL DYNAMICS

Since both COPEI's ideological orientation and its organizational structure are intended to recruit broad-based support, to assess COPEI's strength as a political force these factors must be related to the party strategy and the dynamics of Venezuelan politics.

Martz divides the country into five politico-electoral regions. (See map.) The Metropolitan center is characterized by its susceptibility to extremist and personalist appeals, while the Llanos Guayana interior, with the lowest population density, is essentially rural and has traditionally been dominated by AD. The Maracaibo Basin, as the major petroleum center and stronghold of organized labor, has traditionally supported AD. The Andean states, the most conservative and Catholic region, is the original basis of COPEI support, while the Coastal Range includes both rural and industrial areas and can be termed politically heterogeneous.[38]

More than half of the voters are in larger cities and towns, and the demographic structure is tending toward greater urbanization. While the average per capita income is over $700 per year, it is distributed most unevenly, with over 75 percent of Venezuelan families existing on less than $400 a year.[39]

---

[37] *Boletín Informativo Demócrata Cristiano,* various issues.
[38] ICOPS, *Venezuelan Elections,* Part I, pp. 3–5. (Martz essay)
[39] Raúl Leoni, *II Mensaje Presidencial,* March 11, 1965, Caracas.

Population Distribution by Political-Electoral Region, December 1963

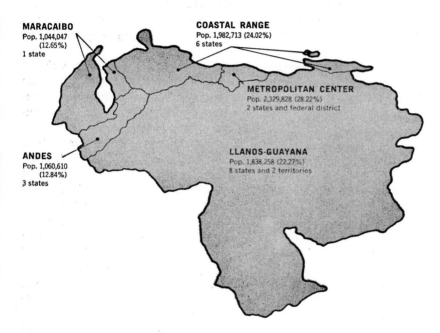

MARACAIBO
Pop. 1,044,047
(12.65%)
1 state

COASTAL RANGE
Pop. 1,982,713 (24.02%)
6 states

METROPOLITAN CENTER
Pop. 2,329,828 (28.22%)
2 states and federal district

ANDES
Pop. 1,060,610
(12.84%)
3 states

LLANOS-GUAYANA
Pop. 1,838,258 (22.27%)
8 states and 2 territories

From Institute for the Comparative Study of Political Systems, *The Venezuelan Elections of December 1, 1963* (Part III, Final Provisional Election Returns, Presidential and Legislative, Broken Down by Region and State, p. 6). Copyright © 1964. Reproduced by permission.

The most salient characteristic of Venezuela's rapidly increasing population is its youth. More than 70 percent of the population is under the age of 30.[40] In COPEI's attempt to capture the imagination of Venezuela's youthful population, Christian Democratic ideology could prove to be a decisive factor. Perhaps Christian Democratic ideology can supply that intangible—an inspirational impetus which evokes enthusiasm and dedication to a cause. Such "spiritual" factors can militate in favor of organizational unity within a party, and spontaneous appeal to the voter by contagion. Also, to the extent that the Christian Democratic movement is seen to be an ascendant force in Latin America, COPEI benefits from the enthusiasm engendered by successes attained elsewhere.

COPEI has been particularly active and increasingly successful in recruiting youthful adherents. The Juventad Revolucionario Cristiano (JRC) counted more than 60,000 university and secondary school students within its ranks as of March 1963.[41] The universities, particularly Central University in Caracas (FCU), have been the scenes of violent strikes and centers for radical activities, while the strength of the moderate parties at that level has diminished. In 1964 a left coalition of PCV, MIR, and others won 60 percent of the student votes at Central University, triumphing in 9 of the 12 faculties. Of the moderate parties, COPEI is decidedly the strongest. At FCU it holds two seats on the seven-man executive board. Copeyanos control the student governments at Carabobo and Zulia, where an AD–URD coalition gained 25 percent of the vote as compared to 42 percent for COPEI.[42]

The question of appeal to youth is also important in terms of party leadership recruitment and mobility. URD and AD leadership is still largely in the hands of the "Generation of '28." Villalba must struggle to keep the adherence of the URD's youthful left wing, while AD leaders recognize that the loss of their younger generation in the MIR and ARS splits makes invigoration imperative. COPEI's organization seems to exhibit greater vitality than that of the other moderate parties. Although Caldera at 48 is still head of COPEI, the party executive committee is manned largely by men in their twenties. While the party has not yet suffered an open split between generations, as could be expected, COPEI student organizations have sometimes expressed more radical views than those with which the party identifies.

[40] Alexander, p. 17. [41] *Boletín,* March 1963.
[42] U.S. Senate Committee on the Judiciary, *Communist Infiltration in Latin American Educational Systems* (Dec. 15, 1964, 88th Cong., 2d Sess.). (Washington, D.C., U.S. Government Printing Office, 1965)

By far the largest labor organization is the Confederacion de Traba-jadores Venezolanos (CTV), with 1.3 million members. Organized labor is still a bulwark of AD's electoral strength, yet COPEI has been making steady gains. COPEI benefited in the labor movement through its participation in government, and, as Martz observes, by 1962 COPEI labor strength was developing independently for the first time.[43] This progress has continued—for example, in 1965 COPEI won significant union victories among the iron workers in Bolívar.

COPEI is also active in the Peasant Unions, where it has certain regional strongholds in the Andean states. However, AD continues to retain the backing of the characteristically politically inert campesinos. Despite the trend toward urbanization, the campesinos still represent about 40 percent of the current electorate.

By 1963, about 10 percent of the population could be termed as the growing middle class.[44] COPEI has attempted both to build its middle class support and to mobilize middle class talents in its behalf. After months of preparation in 1962, it held the first Congreso Nacional de Profesionales y Técnicos de COPEI e Independientes Socialcristianos. The work of these experts contributed essentially to the formulation of the party's program.

In the 1963 campaign, Uslar Pietri attempted to stimulate middle class apprehension concerning COPEI's relation to the Church. As Copeyanos reiterate with emphasis, "the Church is one thing, the party is another"; and reputedly the Church in Venezuela is interested in protecting its accepted isolation from partisan conflicts.[45] Although about 90 percent of Venezuelans are baptized Catholics, reportedly only 25 percent are communicants.[46] Weak economically and in terms of personnel, the Church is not in a position directly to exercise temporal influence. Nonetheless, the hierarchy has demonstrated increasing social consciousness, expressed from a moral, social, and religious point of view. Although the two institutions might not be working at cross purposes, the electoral repercussions of their "spiritual" interrelation is highly problematical.

The Venezuelan upper class constitutes roughly 2 percent of the population, and is largely composed of industrialists who generally support the democratic revolution. Many, in fact, profess rather liberal ideals. In 1962, financiers and industrialists under the leadership of multimillionaire philanthropist Eugenio Mendoza formed the Asocia-

[43] Martz, *Acción Democrática*, p. 378.   [44] *Area Handbook*, p. 264.
[45] *Ibid.*, p. 198.   [46] *Ibid.*, p. 189.

cion Venezolana Independiente (AVI). AVI's stated aims include development of the national economy in order to raise the standard of living of the population, and achievement of more adequate income distribution.[47] Capable of acting as a pressure group, AVI attempted to persuade AD and COPEI to support a single unity candidate in 1963. Eventually Mendoza himself supported Uslar Pietri, while the AVI has developed no direct ties with any party.

While the party ties of labor and peasant leagues are manifest, Venezuela's commercial and industrial associational interest groups function more as nonpartisan pressure organizations. Many are linked in the Federación de Cámaras de Comercio e Industria (FEDECAMARAS), which takes an enlightened view of labor and social problems, and militates for domestic economic development in terms that stress the initiative of the private sector. Robert J. Alexander felt that after 1958 COPEI still had the sympathies of important elements of the industrial and commercial classes.[48]

The disposition of the Venezuelan military is crucial in discussion of COPEI's political strategy, as it is in that of any Venezuelan political party. The coalition Government, especially in its earlier states, was threatened by several military coup attempts. Betancourt seems to have cajoled the military into supporting the concept of civilian political rule. Inasmuch as it is essential for stability of the democratic regime, COPEI benefits from the development of an apolitical military institution, and conversely, to the degree that COPEI political strategy contributes to democratic progress and stability, the threat of military intervention should be dissipated.

In relating COPEI's strategy to the over-all dynamics of the Venezuelan political system, the problems of guerrilla terrorism and Communist subversion must be considered. While the threat of intervention from the military or overtly reactionary elements could be seen to have receded after 1960, the problem of left-inspired terrorism and guerrilla action has come to the fore. An extremely complex phenomenon, the threat from the extremist left, includes such elements as indigenous radical youths, Cuban commitment to export of the revolution, and Communist recognition of Venezuelan strategic importance, especially in terms of the political significance that would be inherent in a successful democratic revolution. The terrorist campaign conducted by the Castro-inspired Fuerzas Armadas de Liberación Nacional (FALN) aims to create an atmosphere of anxiety and turmoil,

[47] *Hispanic American Report*, XV (Nov. 1962).   [48] Alexander, p. 86.

to undermine the regime by demonstrating its inability to maintain public order. The objectives of such strategy are to discredit the Government by provoking it to excessively repressive measures, or to incite a military coup. Either eventuality is envisioned as leading to an inexorable triumph of the radical left. It is also hoped that acts of violence will debilitate the regime by creating conditions discouraging to investment and conducive to economic chaos. The extreme left also attempts to operate through legal channels such as political parties and the press. The Venezuelan democratic regime has been compelled to take protective measures against such activities, and consequently it has been assailed as repressive and antithetical to civil liberties. Yet, the elections of 1963 served as an apparent repudiation of Communist and leftist extremism and a demonstration of popular support of democratic procedures.

The problems of violence and Communist subversion have not, however, been eliminated. At a secret meeting of Latin American Communist parties in November 1964, Venezuela was pinpointed as a main target for guerrilla activities.[49] While COPEI today considers the continuation of guerrilla activities a primary political problem, the course COPEI pursued following the elections of 1963 would indicate a degree of confidence in the regime's increased ability to accommodate democratic competition and at the same time withstand the threats of extremism.

THE ELECTIONS OF 1963

By 1962 the campaign for the elections of December 1963 had in effect begun. The parties of the Government considered a continuation of the coalition for electoral purposes, since such a consolidation would seemingly be assured of victory. Possible approaches were an independent presidential candidate supported by both AD and COPEI, or a nominee identified with either party but supported by both. COPEI felt that Caldera was Betancourt's logical successor and could be accepted by AD, while COPEI might have supported AD's Gonzalo Barrios as a unity candidate.[50] In retrospect such proposals have an aura of unreality; party loyalties were too strong. Leoni began to gather increasing support for his candidacy, and he was both less

---

[49] U.S. House of Representatives Committee on Foreign Affairs, *Communism in Latin America* (April 14, 1965, 89th Cong., 1st Sess.). (Washington, D.C., U.S. Government Printing Office)

[50] ICOPS, *Venezuelan Elections,* Part I, p. 14. (Martz essay)

acceptable to COPEI and determined to see AD maintain its party identity by running its own nominee. In view of its organizational growth and increasing enthusiasm, COPEI also was strongly oriented toward preference of a distinctly COPEI nominee. After Leoni's nomination, Caldera's was a foregone conclusion. Even after the nominations, COPEI continued to cooperate at the governmental level. COPEI leaders remained in the Betancourt Administration until its termination.

As the campaign unrolled, both AD and COPEI were challenged primarily by URD's Villalba and the independent candidacies of Arturo Uslar Pietri and Wolfgang Larrazábal. There was a growing national consensus on such fundamental issues as agrarian reform, educational expansion, state planning of a mixed economy, and petroleum policy. The campaign revolved about the most effective means of formulating and implementing social and economic reforms, and the maintenance of democratic constitutionality in the context of increasing provocation by extremists. The opposition candidates assailed the Government's capabilities to formulate and execute effective reform measures, and impugned its sincerity with accusations of *ventajismo*—use of Government machinery and prerogatives to secure partisan advantage. The opposition candidates indicated that terrorism would continue under either an AD or COPEI administration, and deplored strictures on civil liberties and parliamentary immunities.

AD emphasized the primacy of continuing constitutional rule and "At all times AD placed its own victory second to the overriding goal of a free vote and selection of a new Government." [51] Leoni stood on the Government's record in reform and development, while AD's platform indicated objectives and plans of action whereby progress could be continued.

COPEI conducted an active campaign in which it continued the strategy of taking credit for the achievements of the Government, criticizing particular aspects of its policies, and dissociating itself from less popular measures—without necessarily condemning them. COPEI elaborated the specifics of a program of continued reform, placing particular stress on the housing problem. The COPEI slogan of *100,000 viviendas por año* was to project an appealing image of daring, calculation, and positive action in an area of basic need. While AD promised 75,000 units a year, Caldera marshaled figures to prove the feasibility of 100,000, and indicated further the additional benefits of such an undertaking in terms of stimulating the economy as a whole. Martz

[51] *Ibid.*, p. 30.

concludes that COPEI conducted a "truly outstanding campaign." [52]

The results of the 1963 elections served as a significant indicator of COPEI's past and future role in the Venezuelan political system. That 91.36 percent of the registered electorate of 3,369,986 took part in the electoral processes served as an affirmation of the democratic regime. The results also demonstrated the fruits of COPEI's organizational development as a party. Although Leoni won the presidential election with 32.8 percent of the vote, AD experienced a marked drop in electoral support: from 49.5 percent in 1958 to 33.2 percent on the basis of congressional returns. URD dropped from 26.8 percent to 17.6 percent, while COPEI advanced from 15.2 percent in 1958 to 21.2 percent. Not only did COPEI's congressional delegation more than double, but COPEI had elected representatives from 17 of the 23 electoral constituencies, as compared to 1958 when it had secured seats in only 7.[53]

In becoming a national party, COPEI was the only one of the three major parties to secure gains in all electoral regions. With some justification Copeyanos claim that their party is *the* ascendent political force in Venezuela, and tend to consider the 1968 elections as theirs. Perhaps Copeyano enthusiasm should be tempered by recognition of the strong showing of independent or antiparty candidates in the Metropolitan area, and realization that while they showed significant gains, a party securing support of 20 percent of an electorate can only with great difficulty be described as the dominant political force. Nonetheless, COPEI's positive orientation serves to give increased momentum to its organizational efforts and to guide its behavior at the congressional level. Furthermore, insofar as other political organizations perceive COPEI's increasing strength, they are persuaded to formulate strategies that would impede COPEI's progress.

The Fourth Phase Begins

Immediately upon his election, Leoni began what were to be protracted negotiations to aggregate a Government coalition. He had not been successful at the time of his inauguration in March 1964, when he was compelled to announce a cabinet composed solely of Adecos and independents. Initially, discussions were held between AD and COPEI. Within the AD party there was a strong current which felt that COPEI participation, while desirable, was not essential. Furthermore

---

[52] *Ibid.*, p. 31.   [53] ICOPS, *Venezuelan Elections*, Part III.

there were definite partisan reasons for which COPEI's participation could be considered disadvantageous to AD. In order to project an image of distinctiveness and vitality, AD could be seen to benefit in making some sort of a new start—in some way differentiating itself from the previous Government. Moreover, since COPEI hoped to challenge AD's electoral primacy, it could hardly find maximum partisan advantage in remaining linked with an AD government. From its strong bargaining position, COPEI demanded several key ministerial posts. While Leoni, in his inaugural address, urged the putting aside of partisan politics, discussion between AD and COPEI soon lapsed. Uslar Pietri, antiparty candidate and head of the new party, Frente Nacional Democrático (FND), proposed a broadly based government of national integration. After extended interparty discussion, in August a tripartite accord was reached between AD, URD, and FND, with the establishment of the Amplia Base Government. The Amplia Base represents roughly 68 percent of the 1963 electorate, and has the support of 34 of the 50 senators and 104 of the 133 deputies.[54]

There is no doubt that the Amplia Base Government is justified in terms of an interest in strengthening the democratic regime. In lieu of a workable Government coalition, the Leoni Administration could have easily been confronted with a disintegrating situation in which several partisan groups overtly competed for political advantage, to the possible detriment of the Government legislative program. The major enunciated objectives of the Amplia Base program are to halt the pro-Castro terrorists, to consolidate the democratic regime, and to develop the national economy.[55] On the other hand, the Amplia Base coalition is not without aspects of political opportunism. Since neither URD nor FND can reasonably expect to challenge AD in the next election, their leaders can enjoy the political power implied by Government participation and at the same time hope to insure their continuation in office by strengthening a force that would oppose COPEI's advance.

COPEI's response to the Amplia Base Government is a position termed "autonomy of action." As conceived by COPEI, autonomy of action does not strictly speaking imply opposition. Since it is no longer committed to support of Government programs, COPEI is "free to act without preestablished compromises . . . COPEI neither adheres to the Government nor to the opposition." [56] In terms of promoting de-

[54] *Ibid.* [55] *Hispanic American Report,* XVII (Nov. 1964).
[56] *El Nacional,* Caracas, Sept. 4, 1964.

velopment of the democratic regime, COPEI's role would be that of supplying a democratic alternative to the government in power. Had COPEI accepted the offer to join the Amplia Base Government, there would have been no such "loyal opposition." The only other choice for the electorate would have been the more radical and irresponsibly opportunistic splinter parties.

As COPEI entered its fourth phase, the Venezuelan democratic revolution reached a further stage in its development. The current situation will test whether the regime can endure without being strictly identified with the Government in power, and possibly whether the Government in power can be rejected without repudiation of the regime.

COPEI can be expected to play its role of loyal opposition with a certain amount of restraint. Aside from COPEI's basic commitment to the democratic system, it would hardly be advantageous in a partisan sense thoroughly to discredit or to attempt to undermine the Leoni Administration. From the COPEI standpoint, Leoni must function as a sort of trustee of the regime which Copeyanos are themselves confident of controlling in 1968.

Because it has become a modern political party in the terms of Martz's definition, COPEI has a real stake in Venezuela's nascent democracy. Whether that democracy will be able to establish its legitimacy, however, will depend not only upon COPEI's commitment. The regime must continue to demonstrate tangible success in attaining its social and economic objectives. The progress announced in President Leoni's Second Message to Congress in March 1965 would indicate that such a sanguine view is tenable. Venezuela's gross national product climbed 7 percent in 1964 and various other statistical indicators of economic growth were favorable, while such measures as agrarian reform continue to be pursued with some efficacy.

Further tests of the regime's endurance would be the Government's ability to cope with a strong opposition. Despite the asperities of the battle with the Capriles newspaper chain, and the more partisan aspects of the Amplia Base coalition, it does not seem that the present Government would resort to dubious or unconstitutional means in order to perpetuate itself in power. A decisive test of the regime will come in 1968 in AD's ability to pass over the reins of government to COPEI should COPEI secure sufficient electoral support, or in COPEI's ability to accept defeat if it does not achieve that electoral victory of which it is so confident. In terms of the histories of these parties, it seems safe to expect that they will meet this critical test. If Venezuela can continue to consolidate its democratic regime, COPEI will have played a positive role of a significance that cannot be exaggerated.[57]

D'Antonio, William, and Frederick B. Pike, eds. *Religion, Revolution, and Reform.* New York, Praeger, 1964.

Gilmore, Robert L. *Caudillism and Militarism in Venezuela, 1810–1910.* Athens, Ohio, Ohio University Press, 1964.

Lieuwen, Edwin. *Petroleum in Venezuela: A History.* Berkeley, University of California Press, 1954.

Wilgus, A. Curtis, ed. *The Caribbean: Venezuelan Development, a Case History.* Gainesville, University of Florida Press, 1963.

Alexander, Robert J. "Democratic Revolution in Venezuela," *The Annals,* CCCLVIII (March 1965), 150–58.

Beatty, W. Donald. "Venezuela: A New Era," *Current History,* XXXVIII, No. 223 (March 1950), pp. 144–49.

Betancourt, Rómulo. "The Venezuelan Miracle," *The Reporter,* XXXI, No. 3 (Aug. 13, 1964), 37–41.

Caldera, Rafael. "La Batalla que estamos librando," in Lino Rodrigues-Arias, ed., *La Democracia Cristiana y América Latina.* Lima, Editorial Universitaria, 1961, pp. 119–39.

—— "La Libertad Politica, Condicion Essencial del Desarrollo," *Cuadernos,* No. 92 (Paris, Jan. 1965), pp. 12–20.

Diezcanseco, Alfredo Parija, "Venezuela: Una Revolucion en Marcha (Declaraciones del Presidente Leoni)," *Cuadernos,* No. 86 (July 1964), pp. 28–36.

Harding, Timothy F., and Saul Landau, "Terrorism, Guerilla Warfare and the Venezuelan Left," *Studies on the Left,* IV, No. 4 (Fall 1964), 118–28.

Lott, Leo B. "Venezuela," in Martin C. Needler, ed., *Political Systems of Latin America.* Princeton, Van Nostrand, 1964, pp. 233–68.

Martz, John D. "The Growth and Democratization of the Venezuelan Labor Movement," *Inter-American Economic Affairs,* XVII, No. 2 (Autumn 1963), 3–18.

—— "Venezuela's Generation of '28: The Genesis of Political Democracy," *Journal of Inter-American Studies,* VI, No. 1 (Jan. 1964), 17–33.

Prieto, F. Luis B. "Immunidades Parlamentarias," *Política,* No. 16 (Caracas, June–July 1961), pp. 108–27.

Acta Final, I Congreso Nacional de Profesionales y Técnicos de COPEI e Independientes Socialcristianos, 15–18 de Agosto de 1963. Caracas, Secretaria Nacional de Organismos Profesionales del Partido Socialcristiano COPEI, 1963.

Caldera, Rafael. "El Crecimiento de la Democracia Cristiana y su Influencia Sobre la Realidad Social de America Latina." Mimeographed speech, Chicago, January 1965.

—— "El Impacto de las 100,000 Viviendas Por Año." Caracas, October 1963.

COPEI, *Programa Partido Socialcristiano.* Caracas, Secretaria Nacional de Propaganda, 1958.

FALN, "Our Errors," *Studies on the Left,* IV, No. 4 (Fall 1964), 129–31.

IFEDEC, *Coursos* (various).

A.D. (Acción Democrática party weekly newspaper).

Boletín de la Cámara de Comercio de Caracas, Caracas (monthly).

La Esfera, Caracas (daily).

[57] Readers interested in a further investigation of the subject of this paper may wish to consult the following works:

Bolívar's Program
for Elementary Education

JOHN L. YOUNG

In the *Selected Writings of Bolívar* there is one essay devoted entirely to the subject of popular, elementary education.[1] As it stands, this rough draft is rather opaque, for it has no footnotes to explain the allusions it contains and no introduction to suggest a context to which it might be referred. When Simón Bolívar penned this essay, was he developing his own original thoughts, or was he expressing ideas shared by others and already taking the form of action? In this paper we shall try to determine what kind of educational system Bolívar had in mind. Having found little that pertains to Ecuador, we shall confine our attention to Bolivia, Colombia, Peru, and Venezuela. We shall try to take the measure of the educational task to which he summoned the Governments of those new nations.

To begin with, can we estimate the relative importance of a concern for education in the life of the Liberator? It is possible to write a biography of Bolívar without discussing his educational ideas. Both Masur and Madariaga have done so by concentrating on what were undoubtedly the priorities in his career.[2] Those priorities were certainly three: the war of liberation, the establishment of constitutions for the nascent republics, and the promotion of Spanish American unity. It cannot be suggested that Bolívar gave as much time and thought to educational matters as to those tasks; but it can be seen that each of the tasks had in it the germ of an educational need. Liberation by war had left many colonial institutions and habits of

[1] Simón Bolívar, "Essay on Public Education," *Selected Writings of Bolívar,* compiled by Vicente Lecuna (New York, Colonial Press, 1951), Vol. II, pp. 555–60.

[2] Gerhard Masur, *Simón Bolívar* (Albuquerque, University of New Mexico Press, 1948).

Salvador de Madariaga, *Bolívar* (New York, Pellegrini and Cudahy, 1952).

mind virtually intact; so it remained for education to foment a cultural independence that war could not supply. Constitutions, to be more than scraps of paper, required that an educational program train citizens in democratic processes. Likewise, the peace and solidarity of Spanish America needed a general enlargement of horizons and a perception of the merits of international cooperation that it was hoped education might bestow.

Therefore, his public statements accorded a priority to education that Bolívar was not able to give it in his own career. He told the Congress of Angostura in 1819 that popular education should be its primary concern. Its great work, he said, was "to re-educate men who have been corrupted by erroneous illusions and false incentives." [3] By pausing in the midst of war to say this, he dramatized the urgency of the matter. He might have confined his remarks at that time to the conduct of the war, to immediate measures for dealing with the disorder and poverty that war was creating, and to narrow questions of constitutional amendment. Venezuela had suffered greatly by war. Half its livestock was carried off. Its population is estimated to have declined by one-eighth during the war.[4] Yet, at that moment he chose to direct the attention of legislators not alone to those topics but to repairing the neglect of popular education as well. It remained to be seen whether or not the priority that he called for would be accorded.

Was the educational concern of Bolívar drawn from a foreign source? Pierson writes that French ideas exerted a powerful influence on education in Latin America in the national period.[5] Some evidence of them can be seen in Bolívar. His tutor, Simón Rodríquez, was devoted to the writings of Rousseau, particularly the educational principles set down in *Émile;* and Bolívar stated that he had read Rousseau and other French authors.[6] We find a peculiar clue in the "Essay on Public Education," where Bolívar wrote that "the catechism of Fleurí [Fleury] and Father Astete can be used to advantage." [7] It does not appear that Claude Fleury (1640–1723) and Gaspar Astete, S.J. (1537–1601) collaborated on a single catechism, nor did Fleury edit

[3] Bolívar, Vol. I, pp. 177, 192.
[4] Charles C. Griffin, "Economic and social aspects of the era of Spanish American independence," *Hispanic American Historical Review,* XXIX (1949), p. 174.
[5] William Whatley Pierson, Jr., "Foreign influences on Venezuelan political thought, 1830–1930," *Hispanic American Historical Review,* XV (1935), p. 5.
[6] Clarence H. Haring, *The Spanish Empire in America* (New York, Harcourt, Brace, 1963), p. 226.
[7] Bolívar, Vol. II, p. 560.

any edition of Astete's work; so I think Bolívar cannot be taken to have meant that they were joint authors. However, Fleury *was* a French abbot, whose catechism had been translated into Spanish and published at Paris. The fact that Astete's catechism was also published at Paris in Spanish may have entered into Bolívar's choice if he did not wish schools in Latin America to be dependent on books printed at Madrid.[8] Fleury's reputation as an extreme Gallican gave Bolívar a more substantial reason to like him. His advocacy of the subordination of the Church to the state at the expense of papal control harmonized very well with the prevailing views of such statesmen as Bolívar. Before Bolívar wrote his "Essay on Public Education," Fleury's catechism was used in a primary school in Colombia.[9]

A single word in the "Essay on Public Education," however, warns us not to rest in the conclusion that the educational scheme Bolívar had in mind was patterned on a French model. Suitably enough, the monitory word is *monitor.* Bolívar directed that there should be placed "at the head of each class a child capable of directing it, who should be named the monitor (*celador*)." [10] Isn't this a peculiar idea, that the classes in a properly organized school are to be directed by capable children? Did he germinate this idea by himself or did he acquire it somewhere?

In 1810 Bolívar was in London with Andrés Bello on a diplomatic mission for the Junta of Caracas. In September of that year the two men were introduced to an English educator whose name was Joseph Lancaster. They heard him describe a remarkable system of education, then rising in England, which Lancaster had pioneered.[11] They learned that he had the patronage of King George III and the enthusiastic support of many eminent men; so Bolívar and Bello visited Lancaster's school at Borough Road. There they saw large classrooms

---

[8] These two catechisms were frequently reprinted in Latin America after 1830. The Paris editions of them are as follows:
Gaspar Astete, *Catecismo y doctrina Christiana con su breve declaración por preguntas y respuestas* (Paris, Rue du Temple, 1826).
Claude Fleury, *Catecismo histórico, o compendio de la historia sagrada y la doctrina christiana* (Paris, P. Witte, 1734).
The identification of these catechisms can be made in the following works: C. Somervogel, editor, *Bibliothèque de la Compagnie de Jésus* (Paris, Alphonse Picard, 1890), Vol, I, pp. 603–8; and *Catalogue Général de la Bibliothèque Nationale* (Paris, Imp. Nationale, 1913), Vol. LII, columns 670–723.
[9] An announcement in the *Gaceta de Colombia,* Feb. 13, 1825, cited in Armano Rojas, *Ideas educativas de Simón Bolívar,* 2d ed. (Caracas, Ediciones Edime, 1955), p. 80 n.
[10] Bolívar, Vol. II, p. 559.   [11] Rojas, pp. 68–69.

with a hundred or more children in each room seated at tables. Some of the tables were covered with sand to serve as blackboards. At each table there was an older child, a monitor, in charge of the younger ones. At 8:30 the monitors arrived for special instruction by the teacher; at 10:00 the children came to receive the day's lessons from their monitors. At intervals the teacher would blow his whistle, the children would march in an orderly fashion from one table to the next, and in that way would receive simple lessons on four or five subjects in the course of a school day. In the ninety-five schools he had established, Lancaster's staff was teaching about 30,000 children of the poor. The expense was small because one teacher could supervise up to one thousand pupils.[12]

Apart from its low cost, the system of mutual instruction, as it was called, had two outstanding merits. First, it was speedy. By it the poor in large numbers might quickly acquire a simple education. Bolívar perhaps overstated this feature when he described the system as one "by which a community can make extraordinary and brilliant progress in a short time"; but the statement betrays the importance he attached to quick results on a big scale. Second, it imparted discipline and social training. It was virtue and discipline, as much as academic knowledge, the Bolívar desired of popular education. He was quite willing to be specific: "the first habit to be inculcated in children is cleanliness." He also stressed the importance of learning good manners. He recommended that rewards and prizes be used to motivate pupils. He had seen that corporal punishment was not used in the Lancastrian system. This departure from the customs of that time in England may have reflected the Quaker principles of Lancaster. Bolívar concurred, writing that "the rod should only be used on beasts." In short, he wanted schools that would form citizens, men of principle, who would be "just, generous, humane, gentle, and modest." [13]

Bolívar named the principal subjects to be taught: reading, writing, the principles of religion, arithmetic, and geography.[14] Slender as it was, this curriculum was intended to qualify the pupil for citizenship. Reading and writing were the keys to public office. Bolívar, as he said when he addressed the Congress of Bolivia, did not favor property qualifications for electors; but he did recommend that an elector "be

[12] Webster E. Browning, "Joseph Lancaster, James Thomson, and the Lancastrian system of mutual instruction, with special reference to Hispanic America," *Hispanic American Historical Review,* IV (1921), pp. 54–58.
[13] Bolívar, Vol. II, pp. 555, 558–60.   [14] Bolívar, Vol. II, p. 559.

able to write out his ballots, sign his name, and read the laws." [15] Bare literacy was early envisaged as the proper goal of mutual instruction.

Andrés Bello, writing a friend in 1820, pointed out that the method of rote learning could never promote powers of observation and a critical attitude. By rote he thought children might learn to read, write, and count in one year. He did not think monitors ought to instruct beyond those rudiments.[16]

The Peruvian Constitution of 1828 seems to have anticipated that a degree of literacy would become general in about twelve years; for, while requiring literacy of all voters, it provided that this requirement should not go into force until 1840.[17] The free schools of Lima, Lancastrian schools as late as 1833, receded toward the minimum objective, as may be judged by a decree in that year which substituted "counting" for "arithmetic" in the primary curriculum.[18]

Bolívar loved the Spanish language. He wanted the schools to give training in its diction and grammar, so that people might appreciate its beauty and avoid barbarisms.[19] He cared little for Latin, preferring, as he said in the instructions he wrote down for the education of his nephew, that living languages be taught first.[20] This emphasis on Spanish has a special point with reference to the education of Indians, for most of whom Spanish was not the language spoken at home. It can be construed as an attempt to revive the earliest colonial policy, which regarded Spanish instruction as part of a program intended to integrate the Indian into Spanish culture. To determine the effectiveness of Bolívar's schools against countertrends that worked to perpetuate the Indian as an unassimilated element, we must inquire what progress was made in founding Lancastrian schools.

By the time Bolívar wrote his "Essay on Public Education," the monitorial system had already made big advances in South America. Like the armies of liberation, it moved simultaneously across the Continent from two directions.

In the south its apostle was a Scotsman, James Thomson, who arrived in Buenos Aires in 1818. Since his progress took him to the Bolivarian nations, it warrants a summary account. He was sent to South America by the British and Foreign Schools Society, the body

[15] *Ibid.*, p. 597. [16] Rojas, pp. 81–83 n.
[17] Jorge Basadre, *Historia de la República del Perú,* 5th ed. (Lima, Ediciones "Historia," 1961), Vol. II, p. 653.
[18] *Ibid.*, p. 654. [19] Bolívar, Vol. II, pp. 559–60.
[20] *Ibid.*, Vol. I, p. 309.

that ran the Lancastrian schools in England. Regarding himself as a kind of educational missionary, he brought a quantity of Spanish New Testaments with him. With some success he introduced them in the schools and used them for reading instruction, as was the practice in England. He also sold them from time to time when he needed cash. These vernacular New Testaments often aroused the clergy against him; but sometimes, as he reported it, even the priests bought them and read them eagerly because many had never seen a vernacular version before. In Buenos Aires he interested Bernardino Rivadavia, the friar Camilio Henríquez, and other influential persons in the Lancastrian system. They organized a school society and under Thomson's direction eight schools were set up. Next, at the invitation of O'Higgins he went to Chile and established three schools at Santiago. Then San Martín invited him to Peru. At Lima in 1822 he established a school in the Colegio de Santo Tomás, which San Martín put at his disposal, and there he taught elementary subjects and modern languages. San Martín gave him every possible assistance. Before withdrawing from Peru he decreed that all public schools not being conducted according to the new system of mutual instruction were to be closed after six months.[21]

Peru then came under the sway of Bolívar. Near the close of 1823 Thomson met the Liberator in a friendly interview and received assurances of his support. The war, however, was creating such a scarcity of food in Lima that Thomson decided to move to Colombia. He tells us that when the parents of his schoolchildren heard he was planning to leave, they begged him to stay and offered to pay his salary; so he stayed on three months more. When at last he made the overland journey to Colombia, he found four Lancastrian schools already established—one at Yahnará, two at Popayán, and one in Bogotá, which he found to have been started by a friar about 1822.[22]

Those schools represented an advance from the north that was entirely independent of Thomson. The pioneer in this region was Fray Sebastián de Mora. He is thought by Rojas to have studied the Lancastrian system (whether directly or in books, Rojas does not say) while he was an exile in Spain. In any case, when he returned to Venezuela some time before 1820, he settled in the remote village of Capacho and there founded a school on the Lancastrian plan. Hearing about de Mora, Santander brought him to Bogotá to establish and direct the school that Thomson mentioned. In 1822 de Mora was joined by a Frenchman, Pedro Commetant, who brought with him

[21] Browning, pp. 66–84.   [22] *Ibid.,* p. 91.

from abroad a quantity of teaching supplies such as chalk, blackboards, and pencils. First in Bogotá, then in other departments of Colombia—Magdalena, Panamá, and Zulia—Commetant busied himself setting up schools in which to train teachers in the new method. He was on the point of going to Caracas when a remarkable thing happened. Joseph Lancaster himself decided to come to Venezuela.[23]

The renowned educator had fallen out with the directors of the British and Foreign Schools Society over questions of money, as idealists often do when they collide with trustees, and had left England. From Baltimore in 1824 he wrote Bolívar that he would like to come to Venezuela, and in May of that year he was cordially welcomed in Caracas. In July he again wrote the Liberator, gratefully recalling "the stupendous reception" the city had given him and asking for three or four thousand pesos to propagate his schools.[24] Bolívar replied warmly from Lima, promising 20,000 duros out of funds which he expected to be sent shortly from Peru for deposit in London. The funds, however, were not dispatched to London.

What was worse, the Cabildo of Caracas within a year had grown cold toward Lancaster. Newly elected members, he complained to Bolívar, were systematically trying to undo all that their predecessors in 1824 had begun. They denied him teaching materials and kept back that part of his salary which they had undertaken to pay. Bolívar instructed the Cabildo in April 1826 to put 20,000 pesos at Lancaster's disposal from a loan then being raised in London, and he urged them to give Lancaster their fullest support and protection. Beyond this date there is no candid and unbiased account of the events that compelled Lancaster to leave Caracas in April 1827.[25] At the end Lancaster was bitterly estranged from Bolívar. Apparently the trouble had to do with whether purchases made by Lancaster belonged to him or to the Government. Wherever the fault may have lain, Lancaster declared that he and his wife "were glad to escape with their lives from that land of deceit, revolution, and blood."[26]

In Bogotá Fray de Mora met with better success. The vice president,

---

[23] Rojas, pp. 74–76.

[24] Daniel F. O'Leary, *Correspondencia de extranjeros notables con El Libertador* (Madrid, Editorial-America, 1920), Vol. I, pp. 14–18. Lancaster to Bolívar, July 9, 1824.

[25] Rojas, pp. 70–74. This author pictures Bolívar as Lancaster's faithful friend and patron. He is vague about the circumstances of Lancaster's departure, and his account does not square with that of Salmon's (*infra*, Note 26) in every respect.

[26] David Salmon, *Joseph Lancaster* (New York, Longman's, Green, 1904), p. 61.

Santander, attended examinations at the Lancastrian primary school in Las Nievas. It was an event announced in the press.[27] A textbook on the system of mutual instruction was published.[28] In a decree dated October 3, 1826, Santander called for the exclusive use of this method and offered to send textbooks and teaching materials wherever needed. Much as San Martín had done three years earlier, with the same kind of optimism made official by fiat, Santander prescribed a school of mutual instruction in every parish by the end of 1827.[29] This decree evidently had the approval of Bolívar, as may be judged from what he is reported to have said: "I have caused the Lancastrian system to be established throughout Colombia, and that alone will cause the next generation to be much superior to the present one." [30]

While Santander was active in Colombia, Bolívar was advancing what San Martín had started in Peru. By decree in January 1825, he ordered the Lancastrian system extended to all the departments of the Republic. In the capital of each department he ordered a normal school established, to which each province was to send six boys. Those lads, after completing the course, were to return home with what they had learned of the Lancastrian method. This, it will be noted, was a significant departure from the original system. Joseph Lancaster had put an experienced teacher in charge of each school, under whose eyes the monitors gave instruction. The procedure indicated by Bolívar's decree, however, was to train youths at centrally located normal schools and then to return them to their villages to set up classes more or less on their own. Ill educated, superficially acquainted with the method, and poorly supervised, the youths represented an effort to increase the number of schools at the expense of quality. Bolívar wisely did not rely on this measure alone, but in August of 1825 decreed that primary schools were to be set up in the convents. The regulars in charge of those schools were to be paid by the State. From convent schools also, according to the decree, pupils who distinguished themselves were to be sent into the provinces as teachers. Many convents opened such schools; but, it was reported to Congress, people generally neglected to send their children to them.[31]

In his "Essay on Public Education" Bolívar did not discuss educa-

---

[27] *Gaceta de Colombia*, Feb. 13, 1825, cited by Rojas, p. 80 n.

[28] *Manual del sistema de enseñanza mutua, aplicado a las escuelas primarias de los niños* (Bogotá, S. S. Fox, 1826).

[29] Rojas, p. 78.   [30] *Ibid.*, p. 79.

[31] Roberto McLean y Estenós, *Sociología educacional del Perú* (Lima, Gil, 1944), pp. 147–48.

tion for girls. However, like San Martín, he did attempt to introduce it. San Martín had provided that Thomson's school in the Convent of St. Thomas should receive girls as well as boys. There was a good deal of resistance to putting both sexes in the same classroom. Bolívar recognized this resistance by establishing a separate school for girls in Lima. This decree was issued in August 1825. In the primary section girls were taught reading, writing, catechism, and elementary arithmetic; to the secondary curriculum were added home economics, music, geography, and history. This school, in the Convent of the Conception, afterward took the name of *Escuela Central Lancasteriana para Mujeres.*[32]

After the victory of Ayacucho, when for the first time he could turn most of his attention to constructive matters, only six short years remained to Bolívar. The pace at which he drove himself, the number of letters he wrote and decrees he signed, give the impression of a man in a hurry. In particular he had very little time to exert influence in Upper Peru by his personal presence. He was there only once in peacetime when, from August 1825 through January 1826, he made a triumphal tour of the principal cities and towns. It was at this time that he wrote the "Essay on Public Education" and endeavored to provide for the financial autonomy of schools in that country. By decree he reserved to the schools the income of certain benefices and suppressed monasteries. To this he added the temporary right to collect a tax on each fanega of flour that entered the cities. He prefaced this practical, if unpopular, edict with a reminder that it was the first duty of government to educate the people and that this education should be uniform and general.[33]

On leaving Upper Peru he appointed his old tutor, the eccentric Simón Rodríguez, director of education. On two counts this was a disastrous appointment. The aging pedagogue, recently returned from Europe, was no brilliant administrator; but worse than that in the eyes of conservative people, he was deeply infected with the doctrines of Rousseau and Saint Simon. He was rumored to have boasted that in six years he would destroy the religion of Jesus Christ in Bolivia. Such a rumor must have alienated him from many Bolivians. Moreover, Rodríguez had no commitment to the system of mutual instruction. The model school that he established in La Paz under the name

---

[32] *Ibid.,* pp. 133, 147.
[33] Faustino Suárez Arnez, *Historia de la educación en Bolivia* (La Paz, Editorial Trabajo, 1963), pp. 47–48.

"Escuela de la Nación" was almost certainly not conducted by mutual instruction. It was not the school praised by Bolívar in his "Essay on Public Education," that one having been founded several months earlier. Rodríguez rejected a method that relied on rote learning, and called the monitorial school "the steam powered school" (*la escuela de vapor*). "Children," he said, "go to school to learn, not to teach or assist in teaching." [34] His appointment suggests that Bolívar's commitment to the Lancastrian idea yielded to his desire to befriend the mentor of his youth. Rodríguez was soon dismissed by Sucre, as much on account of his disregard for budgetary limits as for his irreligion. [35]

After the republic of Bolivia was created, the legislature passed the first statute of education, on January 9, 1827. It stipulated that there was to be a primary school in every city and town of more than two hundred souls, and a secondary school in the provincial capitals. Children of families that could afford it were to pay the teacher two reales a month for primary schooling, four for secondary. The salary of primary teachers was set at 180 pesos annually; that of secondary teachers, at 240 pesos. It can be seen that at this date the Lancastrian system was being abandoned. Reading and writing, according to this statute, were to be taught by mutual instruction; but the remainder of the curriculum—religion, morality, and agriculture—were to be taught by compendious catechisms. In the secondary schools where Spanish grammar, arithmetic, industrial arts, and animal husbandry were added, these subjects were to be taught by textbooks, not by mutual instruction. [36]

It should not be supposed that this statute was generally implemented. To be sure, Bolivia, if it was to function as a modern republic, needed to overcome its general illiteracy. Evidence of illiteracy can be seen in the year 1825, when the large *partidos* of Cordillera and Chiquitos were unable to send deputies to the Constituent Congress simply because they had not a single man who met the literacy qualifications. Those *partidos* were not even able to name electors, because of the universal illiteracy. Most of the deputies seated at that Congress held doctoral degrees from the University of St. Francis Xavier at Chuquisaca; but they had no enthusiasm for popular education. It is Arnade's opinion that they were a small clique of reactionaries without the slightest interest in the masses. In vain did Sucre urge them to

---

[34] Simón Rodríguez, *Consejos de Amigo* (Caracas, Imprenta Nacional, 1955), p. 164.

[35] Suárez Arnez, p. 55.   [36] *Ibid.,* pp. 50–51.

build schools. Apart from the indifference of the elite, there was an empty treasury to account for inaction on this problem. From the departure of Sucre from the presidency in 1828 until 1842, Bolivia was engaged in constant wars against Argentina and Peru to consolidate her independence, wars that left nothing in the treasury for school building.[37]

In Peru there was a similar gap between formal provisions and actual accomplishment. The Peruvian Minister of Government and External Relations took time off from his principal duties to report to Congress on the state of public education in 1829. He complained of the inertia of departmental juntas and the deficiency of national revenue for public instruction. He ended in the familiar way by inviting the attention of Congress "to what is the most sacred duty of society toward its members, and the most urgent necessity of civilized man." [38] In short, the guarantee of free primary instruction for all citizens contained in the Peruvian Constitution of 1828 was "forgotten in the turbulent times that followed," and no laws for public instruction were issued in Peru between that date and 1842.[39]

It is not easy to explain the causes of this inertia; for it amounts to trying to document something that did *not* happen. We can account for it more easily if we do not uncritically accept the assertion, so often repeated, that the countries had a great need for education at this time. It is true that, if they were to model themselves upon such an industrial power as England, they required popular education; but in the 1820s this was a remote and unrealistic prospect. Popular education came not only to England, but to France, Germany, and the United States, as those countries industrialized. Since it did not flourish in Latin America, perhaps the reason lay in the preindustrial condition. Did Indians working in the mines and fields need to know how to read and write?

Bolívar urged education as a means of making effective, loyal citizens. This is certainly a strong incentive if one is committed to universal suffrage; but few men in power at Bolívar's death were devoted to radical democracy. It may have appeared to the elite that the old order could be maintained well enough by ignorance, which would serve as a guarantee of the nonparticipation of the masses. The failure of popular education at that time seems to confirm that the Inde-

---

[37] Charles W. Arnade, *The emergence of the Republic of Bolivia* (Gainesville, University of Florida Press, 1957), pp. 185–89, 205.
[38] McLean y Estenós, p. 149.   [39] Basadre, Vol. II, pp. 653–54.

pendence movement was chiefly a war against an external oppressor, and not a struggle for social reconstruction.

In those circumstances educators also had to overcome a weight of apathy encumbering the imagination of the disinherited. It was hard for Indian parents, for instance, to see any cogent reason to take their children out of the field and send them to school. There was no law of compulsory school attendance. Free and universal education is not at all the same thing as compulsory attendance. Venezuela had a compulsory attendance law on the statute books from 1821 to 1830, but it was not enforced; and, so far as I can determine, the other countries had nothing of the kind.[40] The consequence was that some schools were poorly attended; but enforcement was not contemplated so long as it was felt that education for the lower orders might be undesirable. Not many years ago in Lima it was still possible to hear discussions of the positive dangers of educating the people in the high Andes.[41] Such an attitude is to be expected in the absence of a willingness to provide a degree of social reconstruction and upward mobility. What Horowitz says about Brazil is equally valid elsewhere: "to educate the [people] while leaving intact the basic social structure is simply to accelerate the patterns of alienation and discontent." [42]

As far as their own needs were concerned, the elite did not require public elementary schools. They could afford to send their own children to private schools, or have them tutored at home. In this they had Bolívar himself for a model. After his education was well begun by Andrés Bello and Simón Rodríguez, he completed it by European travel. He seems to have appreciated that this education gave him a very imperfect opportunity to cultivate the friendship of his peers; for he cited the advantage of friendships as one of those which public education affords.[43] He sent his own nephew to a private school in Germantown, Pennsylvania.[44] It labors the obvious to contrast the careful provision Bolívar made for his nephew's instruction in calculus, statistics, civil engineering, chemistry, botany, Roman law, etc., with the meager curriculum that was thought sufficient for the public

[40] Angel Grisanti, *La instrucción pública en Venezuela* (Barcelona, Casa Ed. Araluce, 1933), p. 132.

[41] Elizabeth J. Klemer, "Experiences with public education in Peru," *Education,* LXXVI (1956), 623.

[42] Irving Louis Horowitz, *Revolution in Brazil* (New York, E. P. Dutton, 1964), p. 394.

[43] Bolívar, Vol. II, p. 559.

[44] Rojas, p. 104. It was a nonsectarian school.

schools.[45] However, it seems fair to surmise that public schools, being schools for other people's children, exerted not quite the exigent claim on the elite that schools for their own children may have exerted.

The role of the Church at this time calls for an exposition that I am unable to supply. In the diocesan archives of Latin America there may be documentation; but I have not been able to find very much in printed sources. If some of the higher clergy resisted universal education because of the social changes it would have brought, some of the lower clergy, as we have seen, were enthusiastic supporters of mutual instruction. Camilo Henríquez and Sebastián de Mora were two of these. It is likely that James Thomson did great damage to the cause of mutual instruction by distributing New Testaments wherever he went and using them in his reading classes. Domingo Amunátegui Solar, who translated Thomson's letters into Spanish, took great offense at him on this account and considered him a Protestant missionary concealed as a schoolmaster.[46] Simón Rodríguez, without the motive of piety, was equally hostile. He charged that Lancaster had invented the monitorial system as a way of getting children to commit the Bible to memory.[47] He does not say that Lancaster was so rash as to use the Bible for teaching purposes at Caracas; but if this was what Lancaster tried to do, it would surely account for the resistance he met.

A second cause of trouble at this time was the conflict between Church and state over the control of education. This struggle threatened every scheme for primary instruction. The opening words of Bolívar's "Essay on Public Education" contain the germ of the controversy: "Government molds the character of a nation." [48] The essay then unfolds upon the significant deduction that it is the government that shall direct public education. There was some precedent for this idea in the colonial tradition of the *patronato;* but the colonial experience had been one of collaboration between Church and state, whereas the new policy, if the ideal of a separation of Church and state were to prevail, could easily result in a government monopoly of education to the exclusion of the Church. At this time most of the potential teachers in Latin America were clergy. Did the Church regard the monitorial system as an attempt to free the schools from dependence on clerical teachers? If the Church cooperated in staffing government schools, would the state appoint directors of education who could

---

[45] Bolívar, Vol. II, p. 559.   [46] Quoted by Browning, p. 64.
[47] Rodríguez, p. 163.   [48] Bolívar, Vol. II, p. 555.

command the confidence of the clergy? The appointment of Rodríguez in Upper Peru could scarcely have been designed to conciliate the clergy. If state and Church could not compose their differences, would two school systems emerge, one parochial and one public? In Peru by the 1840s this conflict was out in the open; but its development falls beyond the scope of this paper.[49] One thing is certain: Bolívar had no doubt at all about the position of the ecclesiastical authorities in the state. The state was supreme. "This," says Cleven, "was the one great principle from which he never deviated." [50]

When Bolívar wrote of government in education, one supposes he had the central government in mind. Yet the novelty of such an assumption is worth noticing; for neither in the United States nor in England at that time was primary education a concern of the central government. In England it was still organized entirely on voluntaristic lines. The education of the poor was the concern of philanthropic societies such as the British and Foreign Schools Society. The United States Constitution, being silent on the subject, left education entirely to the initiative of state and local authorities. That pattern asserted itself at the death of Bolívar, at which time schools began to come under the control of local authorities. In 1830, for instance, the constitution of Venezuela was amended to leave primary instruction entirely to the provinces. Grisanti writes that they did nothing.[51]

The first constitution of Bolivia, at the suggestion of the Liberator, gave a novel and celebrated form to the state's responsibility for instruction. It constituted the legislative branch of the Government in three parts—tribunes, senators, and censors. Censors, like the President, were to be chosen for life, and on that account had the promise of evolving into a very conservative body. It was they who had the general overseeing of the curriculum and teaching methods, as well as control of the press.[52] Suárez Arnez sees in this arrangement, however, an appreciation of the need for autonomy on the part of educators. Under this constitution they would not have been obliged to submit to the changes of party influence, but might have served the permanent ideals of the nation.[53] These provisions en-

[49] F. M. Stanger, "Church and State in Peru," *Hispanic American Historical Review,* VII (1927), 429.

[50] N. A. N. Cleven, *The political organization of Bolivia* (Pub. No. 510; Washington, D.C., Carnegie Institution, 1940), p. 192.

[51] Grisanti, p. 132.

[52] Vicente Lecuna, ed., *Documentos referentes a la creación de Bolivia* (Caracas, Litografia del Comercio, 1924), Vol. II, pp. 331–33.

[53] Suárez Arnez, p. 41.

dured but a short time. Sucre, the chief of state, was forced to resign in August 1828, and three years later the constitution itself was replaced.[54] Little as these events tell us of accomplishment, they do suggest that the arrangements Bolívar made for public instruction scarcely survived his death.

The year 1830 opened an era in which national school systems did not flourish. Exhausting conflicts between Centralists and Federalists, with the attendant bankruptcy of national treasuries, contributed to this result. However, the reputation of Bolívar as an educator survived. It is thought that no school in Latin America today perpetuates the name of Joseph Lancaster; but Bolívar is still esteemed the Teacher as well as the Liberator.[55] Key-Ayala calls him "the greatest we have had," adding that "he was such everywhere and at the most grave moments." [56] He merits this regard because he taught at every convenient occasion the ends and means of government. Among those ends he gave a high place to free and universal education, which he considered a responsibility of government. As a means to that end he endorsed a method that appeared to promise the rudiments of an education for a large number of people in a short time. He was not an original thinker on this subject. He had very little time to implement his plans, and the system of mutual instruction, despite the prestige of his authority, did not take hold; but his idea that education should impart civic virtues as well as technical knowledge, and that it should not be a monopoly of the religious authorities, have remained guiding principles in Latin America.

[54] Cleven, pp. 99, 101.   [55] Rojas, p. 181.
[56] Quoted by Virgilio Tosta, *Ideas educativas de Venezolanos eminentes* (Caracas, Dirección de Cultura y Bellas Artes, 1953), p. 50.

Biographical Sketches

GORDON M. ADAMS received his B.A. degree in June 1963 from Stanford University, graduating with Great Distinction; there he was on the Dean's list, received honors in Political Science, and was elected to Phi Beta Kappa. In 1963–1964, as a Fulbright Fellow, Mr. Adams attended the College of Europe at Bruges, Belgium, where he was awarded a Certificate; he also carried on firsthand research on the policies of the European Economic Community toward its associated members in Africa. As a candidate for the Certificate of the European Institute at Columbia, and a graduate student in the Department of Public Law and Government, Mr. Adams was appointed an International Fellow at Columbia for 1965–1966. During the summer of 1965 he served as an interne in the program of the Arms Control and Disarmament Agency.

DONA BARON received her B.A. degree in June 1964 from the University of California at Los Angeles. During her junior year she participated in the *Cours de Civilisation Française* at the Sorbonne, and was awarded the *Diplôme Annuel* in June 1963. Miss Baron wrote her article while a candidate for the M.A. in the Department of Public Law and Government at Columbia.

MANFRED M. DECKERT received a B.S. degree from Columbia University School of General Studies in October 1962, and an M.A. degree in the Department of History in June 1963. As a Ph.D. candidate at the time of publication of this article Mr. Deckert was doing research on his dissertation on the Army of the Federal Republic of Germany.

PETER FRIEDMAN received his B.A. degree with High Honors in the Division of Social Science at Swarthmore College in June 1958, and is a member of Phi Beta Kappa. He received his LL.B. from Harvard Law School in June 1961 and was awarded a Fulbright Fellowship, spending the following year in Berlin studying East German law. Mr. Friedman wrote this article during his candidacy for the Ph.D. in the Department of Public Law and Government at Columbia.

PETER H. JUDD received his B.A. degree, *cum laude,* in June 1954 from Harvard College. From 1956 to 1958 he was a Specialist 3d Class in the

United States Army, Office of the Chief of Staff at the Pentagon. Mr. Judd earned his Master of History at the Provincial Secondary School, Maiduguri, Northern Region, Nigeria, in 1959–1960. Admitted to Columbia University's Department of Public Law and Government in February 1964, Mr. Judd became a candidate for the Ph.D. He is the editor and compiler of *African Independence* (Dell Publications, 1963), and the author of several articles.

DAVID ALLEN KAY received his B.B.A. with Honors in 1962 from the University of Texas, and a Master's in International Affairs at Columbia University in June 1964. Mr. Kay spent the summer of 1964 in the Soviet Union and Western Europe under the auspices of an Honor Fellowship from the School of International Affairs. He wrote his article while a candidate for the Ph.D. degree in the Department of Public Law and Government at Columbia.

THEODORE DIXON LONG received his B.A. degree from Amherst College in 1955, and his M.A. from The Fletcher School of Law and Diplomacy, Tufts University, in 1958. After two years of Army service in Asia, from 1955 to 1957, Mr. Long taught for a short period at Doshisha University, Kyoto, Japan. Following his return to the United States he worked as an assistant to the Director of the American Universities Field Staff. Mr. Long received the Certificate of the East Asian Institute, Columbia University, in December 1964, and at this publication was a Ph.D. candidate in the Department of Public Law and Government. He is currently doing research in Japan on "Japan's Science Policy."

B. LYNN PASCOE received his B.A. degree with Honors in Political Science in June 1964 at the University of Kansas. He entered Columbia in September 1964 as candidate for the Certificate of the East Asian Institute, and the Master's degree in the Department of Public Law and Government.

THOMAS D. MARZIK received his B.A. degree, *magna cum laude,* in 1963 from the College of the Holy Cross. He is also the recipient of various fellowships and honors: Delta Epsilon Sigma National Honor Society, 1963; Honorary Woodrow Wilson Fellowship, 1963; Columbia Faculty Scholarship, 1963–1964; and National Defense Foreign Language Fellowships (Czech) in 1964–1965 and 1965–1966. At the time of this publication Mr. Marzik was a candidate for the Ph.D. in the Department of History, and for the Certificate of the Institute on East Central Europe, at Columbia University.

VOJTECH MASTNY is a graduate in history of the Faculty of Philosophy of Charles' University, in Prague, and a candidate for the Ph.D. in the Department of History, Columbia University. In 1964–1965 and 1965–1966 he held predoctoral fellowships in West European studies under the Foreign Area Fellowship Program.

FAY R. PAPA received her B.A. degree with High Honors in June 1963 from Mount Holyoke College. During the summer of 1962 she served as a Mount Holyoke Interne working in the Department of Legal Affairs and Public Relations at the Food and Agriculture Organization in Rome. At Columbia, as a candidate for the Ph.D. degree in the Department of Public Law and Government and for the Certificate of the European Institute, Miss Papa was awarded a Columbia University Fellowship for 1965–1966.

JAMES W. ROBINSON received his B.A. degree, *magna cum laude,* in December 1963 from the University of Washington at Seattle. A member of Phi Beta Kappa, he concentrated on East Asian studies in his undergraduate work, and he is fluent in Japanese. At Columbia Mr. Robinson was awarded a School of International Affairs Fellowship for the academic year 1964–1965, and wrote his article while completing the requirements for the Master of International Affairs and the Certificate of the East Asian Institute. Mr. Robinson is currently Far Eastern Analyst in the Legislative Reference Service at the Library of Congress.

PATRICIA BERKO WILD received her B.A. degree in June 1962 from Barnard College. During the year of 1960–1961 Mrs. Wild studied at the University of Geneva and the Graduate Institute of International Studies, under the Smith College program. From 1962 to 1964 she was employed by the Algerian Front of National Liberation in New York City, which later became the Permanent Mission of Algeria to the United Nations. During the summer of 1963 she spent some time in Algeria as a guest of the Algerian Government. At the time of publication of this paper, Mrs. Wild was an M.A. candidate in the Department of Public Law and Government at Columbia University.

JOHN L. YOUNG received his B.A. degree at the University of Texas in 1951, a B.D. at the University of Chicago in 1954, and his M.S. in the Department of History, Columbia University, in 1958. This article was written in the course of his work for his Ph.D. in the Department of History and for the Certificate in Latin American Studies at Columbia.